Studies in Church History

8

POPULAR BELIEF AND PRACTICE

POPULAR BELIEF AND PRACTICE

PAPERS READ AT
THE NINTH SUMMER MEETING AND
THE TENTH WINTER MEETING
OF THE
ECCLESIASTICAL HISTORY SOCIETY

EDITED BY

G. J. CUMING

AND

DEREK BAKER

CAMBRIDGE
AT THE UNIVERSITY PRESS
1972

Published by the Syndics of the Cambridge University Press
Bentley House, 200 Euston Road, London NW1 2DB
American Branch: 32 East 57th Street, New York, N.Y.10022

Library of Congress Catalogue Card Number: 77-155583

ISBN: 0 521 08220 X

Printed in Great Britain
at the University Printing House, Cambridge
(Brooke Crutchley, University Printer)

PREFACE

The present volume of *Studies in Church History* is the eighth to be produced by the Ecclesiastical History Society, and the third to be published by the Cambridge University Press, under an arrangement made for three years in the first instance. It is appropriate, therefore, to record the gratitude of the Society to the Syndics of the Cambridge University Press for the manner in which their undertaking has been fulfilled. The Society has never been so well served by its Publishers, as the success and wide circulation of recent volumes of *Studies in Church History* demonstrates. It is our hope that the basis of a long and fruitful collaboration has been established.

'Popular Belief and Practice' was the theme of the ninth summer meeting (held at Fitzwilliam College, Cambridge) and the tenth winter meeting of the Society. All the 26 papers included in this volume were read at one or other of these meetings, and are arranged in chronological order of subject matter. We were, unfortunately, deprived of the presence of Professor A. Latreille by illness, but his paper was read *in absentia* by Professor J. Rouschausse and is included here.

This volume is the last in this series to be edited by Canon G. J. Cuming. Since 1963, when he succeeded Professor Dugmore and Dr Duggan as editor, he has seen 7 volumes through the press, and worked with three publishers. It gives us great pleasure to register the Society's debt to him, and to record its gratitude. The series of *Studies* is his monument, and by his example and industry the future has been assured.

W. R. Ward
President

Derek Baker
Editor

CONTENTS

CONTENTS

CONTRIBUTORS

DEREK BAKER, Lecturer in Medieval History, University of Edinburgh

DENIS BETHELL, Lecturer in Medieval History, University College, Dublin

BRENDA BOLTON, Senior Lecturer in History, North London Polytechnic

MARJORIE CHIBNALL, Research Fellow of Clare Hall, Cambridge

CLAIRE CROSS, Senior Lecturer in History, University of York

W. H. C. FREND, Professor of Ecclesiastical History, University of Glasgow

SHERIDAN GILLEY, Research Student, Jesus College, Cambridge

ROY M. HAINES, Associate Professor of History, Dalhousie University

BASIL HALL, Professor of Ecclesiastical History, University of Manchester

MICHAEL HENNELL, Canon-residentiary, Manchester Cathedral

ROSALIND M. T. HILL, Reader in History, Westfield College, University of London

R. BUICK KNOX, Professor of Church History, Westminster College, Cambridge

A. LATREILLE, Professor of Modern History at the University of Lyons; Director of the Centre de recherches d'Histoire du Catholicisme

STUART MEWS, Lecturer in Sociology of Religion, University of Lancaster

ARNALDO MOMIGLIANO, Professor of Ancient History, University College London, University of London

COLIN MORRIS, Professor of Medieval History, University of Southampton

ALEXANDER MURRAY, Lecturer in Medieval History, University of Newcastle upon Tyne

CONTRIBUTORS

DOROTHY M. OWEN, Fellow of University College, Cambridge; Archivist to the Bishop and Dean and Chapter of Ely

MARJORIE E. REEVES, Fellow of St Anne's College, Oxford

GORDON RUPP, Dixie Professor of Ecclesiastical History, University of Cambridge

MARC L. SCHWARZ, Assistant Professor of History, University of New Hampshire

MARGARET SPUFFORD, Calouste Gulbenkian Research Fellow, Lucy Cavendish College, Cambridge

DAVID M. THOMPSON, Fellow of Fitzwilliam College, Cambridge

JOHN WALSH, Fellow of Jesus College, Oxford

W. R. WARD, Professor of Modern History, University of Durham

G. S. S. YULE, Professor of Church History, Ormond College, University of Melbourne

ABBREVIATIONS

ACO	*Acta Conciliorum Oecumenicorum*, ed E. Schwartz (Berlin/Leipzig 1914–40)
ACW	*Ancient Christian Writers*, ed J. Quasten and J. C. Plumpe (Westminster, Maryland/London 1946–)
An Bol	*Analecta Bollandiana* (Brussels 1882–)
ASOSB	*Acta Sanctorum Ordinis Sancti Benedicti*, ed L. D'Achery and J. Mabillon (Paris 1668–1701)
BIHR	*Bulletin of the Institute of Historical Research* (London 1923–)
CSCO	*Corpus Scriptorum Christianorum Orientalium* (Paris 1903–)
CSEL	*Corpus Scriptorum Ecclesiasticorum Latinorum* (Vienna 1866–)
CSHByz	*Corpus Scriptorum Historiae Byzantinae* (Bonn 1828–78)
GCS	*Die griechischen christlichen Schriftsteller der erste drei Jahrhunderte* (Leipzig 1897–)
JEH	*Journal of Ecclesiastical History* (London 1950–)
JMH	*Journal of Modern History* (Chicago 1929–)
JRS	*Journal of Roman Studies* (London 1910–)
JTS	*Journal of Theological Studies* (London 1899–)
LRS	*Lincoln Record Society*
Mansi	J. D. Mansi, *Sacrorum conciliorum nova et amplissima collectio*, 31 vols (Florence/Venice 1757–98); new impression and continuation, ed L. Petit and J. B. Martin, 60 vols (Paris 1899–1927)
MGH	*Monumenta Germaniae Historica inde ab a. C. 500 usque ad a. 1500*, ed G. H. Pertz, etc. (Berlin/Hanover 1826–)
SRM	*Scriptores Rerum Merovingicarum*
SS	*Scriptores*
ODCC	*Oxford Dictionary of the Christian Church*, ed F. L. Cross (Oxford 1957)
PG	*Patrologia Graeca*, ed J. P. Migne, 161 vols (Paris 1857–66)
PL	*Patrologia Latina*, ed J. P. Migne, 217 + 4 index vols (Paris 1878–90)

ABBREVIATIONS

PO	*Patrologia Orientalis*, ed J. Graffin and F. Nau (Paris 1903–)
PP	*Past and Present* (London 1952–)
PRO	Public Record Office, London
PW	*Paulys Realencyklopädie der klassischen Altertumswissenschaft*, new ed G. Wissowa and W. Kroll (Stuttgart 1893–)
RHE	*Revue d'Histoire Ecclésiastique* (Louvain 1900–)
RHEF	*Revue d'Histoire de l'Eglise de France* (Paris 1910–)
SA	*Studia Anselmiana* (Rome 1933–)
SCH	*Studies in Church History* (London 1964–)
Speculum	*Speculum. A Journal of Medieval Studies* (Cambridge, Mass. 1926–)
TRHS	*Transactions of the Royal Historical Society* (London 1871–)
WA	*D. Martin Luthers Werke*, ed J. C. F. Knaake, etc. *Weimare Ausgabe* (Weimar 1883–)

POPULAR RELIGIOUS BELIEFS AND THE LATE ROMAN HISTORIANS

by ARNALDO MOMIGLIANO

STUDENTS of historiography have become increasingly gloomy in their evaluation of the Greek founding fathers of historiography. All the limits, the shortcomings, and the failures of conventional history writing – the *histoire événementielle* of French terminology – have been laid at the door of Thucydides. Herodotus has escaped obloquy, either because he offered a promise of variety, curiosity, humour and sensitiveness which Thucydides spoiled, or because (as Professor Seth Benardete says in a very recent book) 'his foundations are not those of modern historiography'.[1] Thucydides has become the great villain of historiography in so far as he identified history with political and military events. Professor Moses Finley and I may in the past have said some unkind words about Thucydides – so did the late Professor Collingwood. But we are now made to look like mild apologists of Thucydides by Hermann Strasburger. This most penetrating interpreter of ancient historians has treated Thucydides's approach to history as the survival of a prehistoric mode of thinking, for which war was the most important event. According to Strasburger, Thucydides excluded *das Humanum* from history and therefore derived his scale of values from 'prescientific and ultimately precivilised, prehistoric strata of thought'.[2] Strasburger tries to show that some hellenistic historians, such as Agatharchides and Posidonius, showed more interest in the business of peaceful coexistence than Thucydides ever did, but he is under no illusion about their ultimate success. Thucydides's historical approach prevailed: deviationists were silenced. The Romans inherited from the Greeks a type of historical writing for which war was the central theme. What Thucydides did not know was not history.

Though we may reserve our gloom for nearer relatives in the historiographical family it must be recognised that classical historians did not cover all the field of history in which we are interested. They explored

---

[1] *Herodotean Inquiries* (The Hague 1969) p 2.
[2] *Die Wesensbestimmung der Geschichte durch die antike Geschichtsschreibung* (Wiesbaden 1966) p 71.

a limited field which corresponds to what we call military and political history, to the almost total exclusion of economic, social and religious phenomena. Furthermore, their interests were centred on contemporary history or on the history of the recent past; and their techniques of research implied a definite preference of direct observation for the study of the present and of oral tradition for the study of the past. When a classical historian ceased to be an independent enquirer about things seen or heard, he tended to become a compiler from previous historians. Research in archives was seldom, and unsystematically, practised by classical historians.

This limitation to political and military history was in itself an attitude towards religion. Religious (and moral) emotions were left out of history, unless they were regarded as having influenced specific military or political events. Even in such cases the historian was unlikely to emphasise direct intervention of the gods in history. Thucydides registered the profanation of the herms in 415 BC because it was directly relevant to the history of the Sicilian expedition. He did not mention the trial of Diagoras the atheist, which many of us would date, *pace* Felix Jacoby, in 415 and consider very significant for the religious situation of the time.

Xenophon states that the gods punished the Spartans for having treacherously seized the acropolis of Thebes,[1] but he does not extend his religious interpretation to the whole period of history with which he is dealing. He just hints at the wide implications of Socrates's dissent during the trial of the generals after the battle of the Arginusae.[2] He does not interpret the catastrophe of 404 BC as a divine punishment for the miscarriage of justice. If Theopompus relates the political decline of Cotys, king of Thrace, to a vulgar episode of impiety[3] or reports ominous signs about Sicilian tyrants,[4] we are not entitled to generalise his specific allusions to divine intervention in given situations. Timaeus was notoriously accused by Polybius of writing histories 'full of dreams, prodigies, incredible tales and, to put it shortly, craven superstition and womanish love of the marvellous'.[5] What we know of Timaeus, either directly from the fragments of his work or indirectly from the

---

[1] *Hellenica*, V, 4, 1.
[2] *Ibid*, I, 7, 15.
[3] Theopompus, *Die Fragmente der griechischen Historiker*, ed F. Jacoby (Berlin 1926–30) II, B, p 115, fr 31.
[4] *Ibid*, fr 331.
[5] Polybius, *Histories*, ed and trans W. R. Paton, 6 vols (London, Loeb Library, 1922–7) XII, 24, 5. Cf F. Taeger, *Charisma*, I (Stuttgart 1957) p. 381.

authors who used him as a source, shows that Timaeus attempted no more than an occasional and unsystematic correlation of divine and human affairs in the field of political and military history. Even Livy, in the most religious of his books (Book V on Camillus, Veii and the Gauls), does no more than relate Roman victories and defeats to proper observance of rituals.[1] What meaning Polybius attributed to fortune and Tacitus to fate is a favourite subject for academic disputes, but no one has yet made out a reasonable case for Polybius or Tacitus as religious interpreters of history.[2]

Interventions of gods, miracles and portents, together with other curiosities, were often confined by the historians to digressions and excursuses. Many Greek and Roman historians had some chapters or even books about extraordinary happenings. Theopompus created a model with his excursus on *thaumasia* in Book X of his *Philippic Histories*: in it he spoke about Zarathustra and about the Cretan Epimenides who woke up after fifty-seven years of sleep in a cavern. *Thaumasia* grew into a literary genre, as is shown by Pseudo-Aristotle's *Thaumasia*. Much information about religious beliefs and practices was also included by historians in their ethnographic chapters and books. Posidonius provided information in this manner about Celtic and Jewish religious practices. Roman historians, who imitated the Greek technique of excursus, added of their own the registration of *prodigia* which they inherited from the archaic annals of the pontiffs: though we must hasten to add that the relation between the *prodigia* of the pontifical records and the *prodigia* of Livy and his excerptors is by no means simple and clear.

Such isolation of religious phenomena in special compartments amounted to more than a declaration that the historian's real business was elsewhere. The historian with the mind either of a politician or of a general or of a learned man established a distance between himself and the religious practices or miraculous events he described. If he classified them as *thaumasia* he disclaimed responsibility for the truth of what he told: his excursus represented a parenthesis of amusement. If he included religion in a piece of ethnography he automatically placed it outside the world of the educated Greek or Roman: ethnography applied either to barbarians or to backwater Greeks or provincials, according to time and circumstance. Timaeus may have had a superstitious, and Posidonius a

---

[1] G. Stübler, *Die Religiosität des Livius* (Stuttgart 1941); W. Liebeschütz, *J[ournal of] R[oman] S[tudies]*, LVII (London 1967) pp 45–55.

[2] Much information in R. Häussler, *Tacitus und das historische Bewusstsein* (Heidelberg 1965).

I-2

religious, mind (a distinction to which we shall soon return), but neither of them presented what he wrote about the beliefs of foreign nations as the truth. The attitude of the historian towards religious beliefs underlined the inherent aristocratic character of history writing. This detachment is equally evident, though in a different form, in Livy's attitude towards the Roman *prodigia*. True enough, he deplored the negligence of those who no longer announced the *prodigia* or reported them in the Annals.[1] But he made it only too plain that in his concern with prodigies there was an element of literary pose: 'vetustas res scribenti, nescio quo pacto anticus fit animus'.

A partial exception is represented by writers of biography. The biographer has to register the beliefs and superstitions of his hero, whether they influenced his political and military activity or not. Many biographies dealt with non-political and non-military men. Furthermore, Roman biographical writing seems to have made a special feature of collecting portents about a man in order to bring his exceptional personality into prominence. To judge from what we know of Sulla's and Augustus's autobiographies it was indeed perfectly respectable for a Roman politician to emphasise his own *charisma* by mentioning divine signs and other miracles. It would not be very helpful here to observe that in the ancient theory biography was never quite a part of historiography. What is more important is that the main account of the life of a man was not seriously affected either by the report of his religious beliefs or by the encroachment of the religious beliefs of his biographer. To find in the pagan world the biography of a religious man as such, we must perhaps go to the life of Apollonius of Tyana by Philostratus in the third century after Christ. In any case biography was not likely to reflect popular beliefs except incidentally: the proper subject for biography was by definition a man above the crowd.

Broadly speaking, a historian's approval of a religious belief would be registered in Greek by putting it in the category of *theosebeia* or *eusebeia*, while disapproval would be expressed by the word *deisidaimonia*. The corresponding (though not semantically identical) expressions in Latin would of course be *religio* and *superstitio*. *Deisidaimonia* and *superstitio* applied both to foreign cults and to the religious beliefs and practices of the lower orders. *Deisidaimonia* is the word chosen by Polybius to indicate the religious feelings of the lower classes which the Roman upper class fostered and exploited. Livy applied *superstitio* to the penetration of foreign cults into early Rome[2] or to the excessive trust in

---

[1] Livy, XLIII, 13, 1. [2] *Ibid*, IV, 30, 9.

prodigia at the end of the second Punic war.[1] Tacitus speaks, *inter alia*, of Christianity as *exitiabilis superstitio*[2] and of the *superstitio vana* of the Druids.[3] Modern studies have done more to clarify the notion of *deisidaimonia* in Theophrastus and Plutarch or the earlier meanings of the difficult word *superstitito* than to interpret the actual usage of *deisidaimonia* and *superstitio* in historical texts. Livy, for instance, avoids the word *superstitio* and speaks of *simplices et religiosi homines* about the belief in *prodigia* in 214 BC, when we would expect the mention of *superstitio*. His prudent usage of *superstitio* in relating the scandal of the Bacchanalia – a *coniuratio* – should be noticed. It would be premature to say that we are at present well-informed about the distinction between *theosebeia* and *deisidaimonia* or between *religio* and *superstitio*. But we are perhaps justified in stating that, before Christianity complicated matters, *deisidaimonia* and *superstitio* were key-words in the evaluation of religious phenomena by Greek and Roman historians.[4]

2

Although historians of the hellenistic period, as Professor Strasburger has shown, were less exclusively interested in politics and war than their masters of the fifth and fourth centuries BC, a real change in the methods and contents of historical research did not take place until the late Roman empire. Ferdinand Christian Baur taught us 150 years ago that if Herodotus was the father of history, Eusebius was the father of a new history. The notion of ecclesiastical history implied a new importance being attributed to documentary evidence, a true universal scope both in time and in space, and finally a revolutionary change in contents. Religious beliefs and practices replaced military and political events as the central subject of historiography.

Some change of emphasis is, however, also noticeable in those pagan historians who in the fourth century AD intended to continue the pagan tradition of history writing. Ammianus Marcellinus continued the narrative of Tacitus; the *Historia Augusta* was modelled on Suetonius's *Twelve Caesars*. Eunapius as a historian continued Dexippus and as a biographer modelled himself on Philostratus's lives of the sophists. In each case greater emphasis was placed on religion and magic.

[1] *Ibid*, XXIX, 14, 2.   [2] *Annals*, XV, 44, 5.   [3] *Histories*, IV, 54.
[4] P. J. Koets, 'Deisidaimonia' (diss. Utrecht 1929); H. Fugier, *Recherches sur l'expression du sacré dans la langue latine* (Paris 1963) p 172. Cf also the general histories of Greek and Roman religion by M.P. Nilsson and K. Latte.

The *Scriptores Historiae Augustae* are aware of the new value attached to documents in contemporary writing, and where they have no documents they invent them. On the level of frivolity and even of obscenity they produce much information about religious beliefs. They mention *Iudaeorum libri*,[1] *doctissimi mathematicorum*,[2] a golden column inscribed with Egyptian letters.[3] Flavius Vopiscus, one of the alleged six biographers, claims to have received information from his own grandfather about the *omen imperii* of Diocletian.[4] There is nothing new in the fact that emperors should show interest in foreign cults and travel to remote sanctuaries, as the *Historia Augusta* tells us about Septimius Severus.[5] But Hadrian is made to say in a letter that in Egypt those who worship Serapis are Christians, while those who claim to be bishops of Christ are devotees of Serapis.[6] This passage must have been written before the destruction of the Serapeum of Alexandria in AD 391. No pagan author after that event could have joked about bishops of Christ being devotees of Serapis.[7] The *Historia Augusta* is certainly written from a pagan point of view under the shadow of christian victory. According to the *Historia Augusta*, Hadrian wanted to build a temple to Christ but was prevented by those who, having consulted the sacred books, discovered that if Hadrian had done so 'omnes Christianos futuros... et templa reliqua deserenda' – Christianity would have prevailed.[8] Christian hostility to *libri Sibyllini* is openly mentioned. But it was not yet absurd to consider placing Christ in a pagan pantheon. Jews are looked upon with a certain sympathy and knowledge, and even Samaritans are mentioned.[9] Trebellius Pollio quotes in the life of Claudius Gothicus[10] a legend about Moses who was said to complain about having to die young at the age of 125 – a legend which has some parallels in the Talmud.[11]

The attitude of the *Historia Augusta* towards Christianity would be

---

[1] S[criptores] H[istoriae] A[ugustae], ed D. Magie, 3 vols (London 1930–2), *Claudius*, II, 4.
[2] *Ibid.*
[3] *SHA, Tyranni triginta*, XXII, 13.
[4] *SHA, Caracalla*, XIV, I.
[5] *SHA, Severus*, XVII, 3.
[6] *SHA, Quadrigae tyrannorum*, VII, 4.
[7] For a different opinion see W. Schmid, *Historia Augusta Colloquium 1964–65* (Bonn 1965) pp 153–84.
[8] *SHA, Alexander Severus*, XLIII, 7.
[9] *SHA, Heliogabalus*, III, 5; XXVIII, 4. *Alexander Severus*, XXIX; XLV, 6; LI, 7. *Gordian*, XXXIV, 2. *Quadrigae tyrannorum*, VII–VIII.
[10] *SHA*, Trebellius Pollio, *Divus Claudius*, II, 4.
[11] J. Geffcken, 'Religionsgeschichtliches in der Historia Augusta', *Hermes* LV (Berlin 1920) p 294.

even more interesting if it were true that its author or authors knew and mocked christian writers such as St Jerome. As this point is of basic importance for the evaluation of the *Historia Augusta*, I may be allowed to show by a single example why in my opinion, and contrary to present orthodoxy, the matter is still *sub judice*. Professor André Chastagnol, in a brilliant chapter of his newly published *Recherches sur l'Histoire Auguste*,[1] has argued that the *Historia Augusta* knows and ridicules St Jerome's letter to Rufinus about their mutual friend Bonosus:[2] a letter which must have been written about 375. The *Historia Augusta* includes a life of the usurper Bonosus. The identity of name with the holy friend of Rufinus, according to Chastagnol, suggested a certain number of literary tricks to the humorous author of the *Historia Augusta*. One of these tricks would have been to transform Onesimus, the faithful follower of the holy Bonosus, into one of the many imaginary sources of the *Historia Augusta*. Now we happen to know from the *Suda* that a historian by the name of Onesimus lived under Constantine; and it is certain that the *Suda* does not depend on the *Historia Augusta* for this piece of information. It follows that the historian Onesimus was not invented by the *Historia Augusta*. We are in the fortunate and rare position of being able to say that the suggestion that the *Historia Augusta* found the name of Onesimus in St Jerome's letter (where Onesimus has nothing to do with history writing) is disproved by good evidence. Future researchers may find echoes of christian Fathers in the *Historia Augusta*, but up to the present, in my submission, the search has not been fruitful.

Even if we suspend judgement on the *Historia Augusta*'s alleged mockery of christian writers there is enough in this work to make it a first-class document of the reformed paganism of the fourth century. Not once does the word *superstitio* occur in it. Pagan practices of every class and country are registered with sympathy and benevolent irony – unless they happen to offend morality *and* to be supported by emperors hostile to the Senate (as in the case of Heliogabalus). *Sortes Vergilianae* are mentioned,[3] and there is in the life of Probus a strange messianic pacifism which seems to have been introduced to compete with christian millenarian dreams: 'brevi milites necessarios non futuros'.[4] The sympathy towards Jews and the desire to see Christianity dislodged

[1] Bonn 1970, pp 69–98.
[2] Ep 3.
[3] SHA, *Alexander Severus*, XIV, 5. Cf Y. de Kisch, *Mélanges de l'Ecole Française de Rome*, LXXXII (Rome 1970) pp 321–62.
[4] SHA, *Probus*, XX, 3; XXII, 4; XXIII, 1.

from its pre-eminence and turned into a syncretistic cult are, as I have said, hardly concealed. While the traditional aristocratic attitude of the Roman historian towards lower-class beliefs and foreign superstitions does not disappear altogether – as is obvious from the life of Heliogabalus – it is fundamentally affected by the new situation. The pagans cannot afford to be divided at a time when the Christians are all out to occupy the key positions in the Roman government. The weakness of the position of the *Historia Augusta* betrays itself in the utopian character of many of its serious statements – and in the triviality of much of the rest.

Ammianus Marcellinus, who is never trivial, does use the word *superstitio*. He uses it very prominently in the passage in which he accuses the emperor Constantius of having corrupted the simple religion of the Christians by encouraging theological disputes: 'Christianam religionem absolutam et simplicem anili superstitione confundens in qua scrutanda perplexius quam componenda gravius, excitavit discidia plurima'.[1] By the second half of the fourth century *superstitio* and *deisidaimonia* were current names for paganism in christian writers. To quote only the obvious, Lactantius says: 'nimirum religio veri cultus est, superstitio falsi...sed quia deorum cultores religiosos se putant, cum sint superstitiosi, nec religionem possunt a superstitione discernere nec significantiam nominum exprimere'.[2] The polemical intention of Ammianus is therefore patent: state protection introduced an element of superstition into the christian religion. Superstition is not the prerogative of the pagans.

No less significant is Ammianus's usage of *superstitio* in his excursus about the Huns. The Huns, according to him, have neither religion nor superstition: 'nullius religionis vel superstitionis reverentia aliquando districti'.[3] What puts the Huns outside the world of human beings is the absence of both religion and superstition. There is a difference between the Huns who have no superstition and the Alani who with barbaric rites worship the naked sword.[4] Ammianus is altogether no longer prepared to draw a sharp distinction between religion and superstition. Pagans and Christians have something of both. A vague monotheist and fatalist himself, he is above all a tolerant man who would like to be surrounded by tolerant men. With all his admiration for Julian, he disapproves of his persecution of the Christians. He even reproaches Julian with being 'superstitiosus magis quam sacrorum legitimus

---

[1] Amm[ianus] Marc[ellinus, *Res Gestae*], ed C. U. Clark (Berlin 1910–15) XXI, 16, 18.
[2] *Divinae Institutiones*, IV, 28, 11. For editions see *ODCC*.
[3] Amm Marc, XXXI, 2, 11. [4] *Ibid*, XXXI, 2, 23.

observator'. He praises Valentinian I because 'inter religionum diver-
sitates medius stetit nec quemquam inquietavit'.[1] He believes in magic,
astronomy, and divination, for the last of which he gives a scientific
explanation at some length.[2] He regrets that portents were no longer
expiated by public rites.[3] He appreciates the religion of the Egyptians –
the cradle of all religions – and the religion of the Persians, in which
astrology and divination were prominent.[4] In practice, therefore,
Ammianus is open to the amplest appreciation of different cults and
tenets, including the cult of the christian martyrs.[5] Whatever objection
he has to Christianity is confined to the intolerance, the feuds, and
above all the greed of certain christian emperors, high civil servants and
bishops: he does not generalise about them either. On a different level
of intellectual refinement and integrity, Ammianus is not very far from
the outlook of the *Historia Augusta*. The difference between religion and
superstition is kept alive for polemical purposes only. Within the
empire there is no significant distinction between the beliefs of the
upper classes and those of the lower classes. What we would normally
call superstition, such as readiness to believe in prodigies and magic
practices, is quietly incorporated in religion.

A few years later, at the beginning of the fifth century, Eunapius
was in a different mood. He belonged to the generation of pagan intellectuals for whom the official prohibition of pagan cults and the destruction of the Serapeum in AD 391 were the central experiences. He
accused the monks, 'the men clad in black raiments', of having opened
the gates of Greece to Alarich in 395.[6] But he, too, within the range of
pagan opinions, practically ignored any distinction between religion
and superstition. His philosophers and sophists, quite unlike the sophists
pictured by Philostratus, are deeply concerned with the knowledge of
the nature of the gods, and consequently with divination and magic.
Apollonius of Tyana, as we know, became a model for these men. It
was not now infrequent for such philosophers to combine theology,
rhetoric and medicine. Two kinds of divination were open to them. As
Eunapius explains, one type of divination was given to men for the
benefit of medicine, the other derived its dionysiac inspiration from
philosophy.[7] There were of course doubts and discussions about the

---

[1] *Ibid*, XXV, 4, 17; XXX, 9, 5.   [2] *Ibid*, XXI, 1, 7.
[3] *Ibid*, XIX, 12, 20.   [4] *Ibid*, XXII, 16, 2; XXIII, 6, 32.
[5] *Ibid*, XXVII, 7, 5–6.
[6] Eunapius, [*Vitae Sophistarum*], ed J. F. Boissonade (Paris, Didot edition, 1849) p 476.
Ed and trans W. Cave Wright (London, Loeb Library, 1922).
[7] Eunapius, p 499.

legitimate limits of magic and divination. Prudence had its part. One of these philosophers, Antoninus, 'displayed no tendency to theurgy... perhaps he kept a wary eye on the imperial views and policy which were opposed to these practices'.[1] Eusebius of Pergamum warned his pupil Julian, the future emperor, against the impostures of witchcraft. Julian managed to extract from Eusebius the information that he had alluded to Maximus of Ephesus. 'You have shown me the man I was in search of', exclaimed Julian, and went off to Ephesus to be taught by Maximus.[2] Eunapius himself was present when a hierophant of Eleusis foretold the overthrow of the temples and the ruin of the whole of Greece. He even foresaw that the cult of Eleusis would come to an end during the office of his own successor.[3] Christian sophists were not necessarily excluded from this circle. But when the famous christian rhetorician Prohaeresius showed his ability to foretell future events it was discreetly assumed that he had stolen his knowledge from the hierophant of Eleusis.

Zosimus must have derived from Eunapius the story that when Alarich approached Athens in AD 395 he saw Athena Promachos touring the walls and Achilles dressed as if he were marching against the Trojans to revenge the death of Patroclus.[4] The pagan Olympiodorus, who about 425 continued Eunapius's history, wrote that the removal of an old cult image at Rhegium was followed by a barbarian invasion of Sicily and by eruptions of Etna.[5] In the same way the removal of three silver statues in barbarian clothing from a pagan holy place in Thrace opened the gates of the region to Goths, Huns and Sarmathians.[6] In Zosimus the death of Serena, Stilicho's wife, is connected with a sacrilege she was alleged to have committed against Vesta:[7] this may be derived either from Eunapius or from Olympiodorus. But what Zosimus has to say about the revivals of pagan rituals in Rome during the siege of Alarich almost certainly comes from Olympiodorus. He must be the source of the information that the bishop of Rome, Innocentius, putting the preservation of the city before his religious opinions, consented to this revival.[8] Unfortunately, according to Zosimus, lack of popular support spoilt the experiment. The *Liber prodigiorum* by

---

[1] *Ibid*, p 471.   [2] *Ibid*, p 475.   [3] *Ibid*.

[4] Zosimus, [*History of the Roman Empire*], v, 6, 6. For editions see *ODCC*.

[5] Photius, *Bibliotheca*, Code LXXX, 57b, in *PG*, CIII (1860) col 261; ed and trans (French) R. Henry (Budé edition, Paris 1959).

[6] *Ibid*, LXXX, 60a, *PG*, CIII (1860) col 268.

[7] Zosimus, v, 38, 2.

[8] *Ibid*, v, 41, 2.

Popular religious beliefs and the late Roman historians

Iulius Obsequens may well belong, as has recently been suggested, to the same type of pagan apologetics based on verified prodigies.[1]

Pagan historians of the fourth and early fifth centuries give more space to religious events than their predecessors and models, not only because the situation makes this inevitable: they are themselves much more directly involved in the religious controversies. They no longer maintain the traditional distinction between religion and superstition. Pagans needed miracles to neutralise christian miracles. We have heard much about democratisation of culture in the late Roman empire since Santo Mazzarino's important paper at the Stockholm congress of 1960.[2] If there is one operation to which the term democratisation can perhaps be applied, it is the removal of the barriers between superstition and religion in the pagan field.

3

The Christians, as we have already mentioned, set up their palisade between religion and superstition to coincide with the frontier between Christianity and Paganism. Within Christendom the dividing line was heresy, not superstition. We need, however, to know much more about the various attitudes of the Christians of the late Roman empire towards miracles, magic, astrology, popular medicine, etc. Professor Grant's study on *Miracle and Natural Law in Graeco-Roman and Early Christian Thought* (1952) and the recent Cambridge symposium on miracles[3] are welcome contributions to the understanding of the notion of miracle among those whom Professor Lampe calls 'the more serious Christians'. For a sociology of beliefs in miracles we can expect important results from the research in progress in Paris under the leadership of Professor Michel Meslin. Professor Meslin intends to find out how the christian notion of miracle and the pagan notion of prodigy competed with and modified each other in a world which daily needed the reassurance of miracles.

It would indeed be impertinent of me to contribute to a debate in which any member of this Society is more competent to speak than I am.

---

[1] It will be enough to refer for these pagan writers to A. Demandt, *Zeitkritik und Geschichtsbild im Werke Ammians* (Bonn 1965); J. F. Matthews, 'Olympiodorus of Thebes and the History of the West', *JRS*, LX (1970); W. E. Kaegi, *Byzantium and the Decline of Rome* (Princeton 1968) pp 59–145. Cf my characterisation in *Rivista Storica Italiana*, LXXXI (Naples 1969) pp 286–303.

[2] *XIe Congrès International des Sciences Historiques, Rapports*, II, *Antiquité* (Uppsala 1960) pp 35–54.

[3] C. F. D. Moule (ed), *Miracles* (London 1965). Cf M. Meslin, *Le Christianisme dans l'empire romain* (Paris 1970) p 168.

But it may be useful briefly to turn our attention to one specific social group in a clearly circumscribed historical situation in order to see how the distinction between upper and lower-class beliefs became meaningless even in highly sophisticated christian circles. The court of Theodosius II – and especially the enigmatic figure of the Athenian Athenais, who on baptism was renamed Aelia Eudocia – has never ceased to attract attention since Ferdinand Gregorovius wrote his romantic book *Athenaïs, Geschichte einer byzantinischen Kaiserin* (Leipzig 1882). There is, however, no comprehensive scholarly research on what was one of the most impressive intellectual circles of the ancient world: the court of Constantinople during the long period between 408 and 450 in which Theodosius II reigned and, for the most part, his sister Pulcheria ruled.

To people who a hundred years later looked back on that society the reign of Theodosius II seemed to be the beginning of the decline of Latin as the language of administration and culture in the empire. There was much more than a little truth in this impression of John Lydus[1] because the court of Theodosius II consolidated the eastern part of the empire at the expense of the west. While Gaul, Spain and Africa were invaded by barbarians, and the emperors at Ravenna progressively lost control of the situation, Constantinople kept Persians and Huns at bay and could afford the luxury of being more concerned with religious dissent than with external attack. But it was never the intention of Theodosius II and his advisers to abandon the west to its fate. In the new university of Constantinople there was a place for instruction in Latin as well as in Greek.

For the first time the christian faith permeated the court in earnest. It was most characteristic of the age that women played a leading rôle in that society. While Pulcheria and her two sisters dictated the rules of behaviour at the court of Constantinople, Galla Placidia shared the government in Ravenna – and Hypatia was savagely murdered in Alexandria. A number of exceptionally cultivated and active christian women emerged who on the one hand were interested in theological problems and on the other hand kept in close contact with the devotion of the masses. Cyrillus of Alexandria could dedicate some of his theological writings to the queens, that is, to the wife of Theodosius II and to his sisters. But these women entertained, and were entertained by, monks who came from peasant stock and whose command of Greek was dubious. This alone – the predominance of women – represented a bridge between the faith of the intellectuals and the beliefs of ordinary

---

[1] Johannes Lydus, *De magistratibus*, II, 12; III, 42.

people. Eudocia herself, the daughter of a pagan Athenian philosopher, embraced the new faith in a mood of total acceptance. Very conscious of her Hellenic heritage, as her famous address to the citizens of Antioch showed,[1] she turned her poetic gifts to the metaphrasis of the prophecies of Zacharias and Daniel and to the exposition of the legend of St Cyprian of Antioch. Little did she suspect that by re-telling the legend of the magician who repented and became a Christian – a legend known to Gregory of Nazianzus – she was to become the second chapter of any respectable book on '*die deutsche Faustsage*'.

Eudocia shared with her friend and spiritual guide Melania the younger the taste for theological controversy and the cult of relics. She and Melania were very active in that hunt for relics which was an integral part of the craving for miracles and sanctity and cannot therefore be dismissed as a replacement of the earlier hunt for Greek works of art. Eudocia brought relics of St Stephen to Constantinople. According to a modern interpretation of a doubtful medieval tradition, the church of S. Pietro in Vincoli in Rome owes its name to the gift which Eudocia made to her daughter Eudoxia of one of St Peter's chains. Following the example of Melania, Eudocia chose Jerusalem as her permanent residence when she was compelled to leave the court of Constantinople. Her deviation in the direction of monophysism in those late years of anguish was halted by the intervention of no less a person than Simeon the stylite.

Eudocia's husband, Theodosius, was even less aware of the distinction between belief and superstition than his wife. Credulity may well be an element of the domestic tragedy which parted for ever two persons who seemed so obviously made to understand each other. The founder of the university of Constantinople, the organiser of the code of laws which takes his name, was known to Sozomenus as someone

---

[1] Evagrius, *Historia Ecclesiastica*, I, 20, 3–5. The main texts on Eudocia are collected and critically sifted by O. Seeck in *PW*, VI, 1, cols 906–10. Add *Vita Sanctae Melaniae*, ed D. Gorce, *Vie de Sainte Mélanie* (Paris 1962) ch 58–9, pp 240–6. For the question of the chains of S. Pietro in Vincoli see E. Caspar, *Geschichte des Papsttums*, I (Tübingen 1930) p 421; R. Krautheimer, 'S. Pietro in Vincoli', *Proceedings of the American Philosophical Society*, LXXXIV (Philadelphia 1941) pp 353–429; R. Valentini and G. Zucchetti, *Codice topografico della città di Roma*, III (Rome 1946) p 42. We have no critical account of Theodosius II. The best anecdotic evidence has been collected by F. Gregorovius, *Athenaïs* (Leipzig 1882) esp pp 95–102. Cf in particular Socrates, [*Historia Ecclesiastica*], VII, 22; Theodoretus, [*Historia Ecclesiastica*], V, 36; Iohannes Malalas, *Chronographia*, XIV; Nicephorus Callistus [(Xanthopoulos), *Historia Ecclesiastica*], XIV, 3 in *PG*, CXLVI (1865) col 1063. For editions of all these authors see *ODCC*. See also *Chronicon Paschale*, ed L. Dindorf, *CSHByz*, 2 vols (Bonn 1832) pp 575–90, reprinted in *PG*, XCII (1865) cols 9–1160.

who spent his nights reading by the light of a specially contrived self-refilling lamp. He read and patronised history, poetry, and theology. He copied books with his own hand. One branch of our manuscript tradition of Solinus goes back to the copy made by him.[1] In the fourteenth century a Bible was still shown at Constantinople which Theodosius had copied in lines forming a cross on each page. Our text of Cornelius Nepos probably derives from a copy made for him by Probus.[2] A copy of the Virgilian *cento* by Proba was presented to him.[3] His reputation as a calligrapher reached Mauretania, if we can trust De Rossi's convincing supplements of an African inscription.[4] The contemporary forger of the Apocalypse of Paul tried to exploit Theodosius's name by asserting that Theodosius declared the text as authentic and that he sent a copy of it to the library of Jerusalem.[5] Sozomenus, who knows about the alleged discovery of this Apocalypse and evidently doubts its authenticity, leaves the emperor out.[6] Theodosius acquired and wore the garments of a bishop who had died as a saint. When excluded from communion by an impatient and vulgar monk he refused to eat until the monk was persuaded to revoke the ban. He decided the choice of his own successor by submitting himself to the practice of incubation in the church of St John the evangelist at Ephesus.

Theodosius tried to the best of his ability to make up his mind about the theological controversies of his time. He had his own soul to think of. But he also had to think of the peace of the realm. He tried to put pressure on theologians, and at least once he used Simeon the stylite to make Theodoretus less intransigent. But we may suspect that the theologians and monks put at least as much pressure on him. He was not an invariably careful reader of what was submitted to him. We have the story that to teach him a lesson Pulcheria made him sign the sale of his own wife.[7]

---

[1] See, however, H. Walter, *Die 'Collectanea Rerum Memorabilium' des C. Iulius Solinus* (Wiesbaden 1969) p xi, n 6.

[2] Cf my paper in *RSI*, LXXXI (1969) pp 290–1.

[3] Cf the remark by [H.] Dessau, *I[nscriptiones] L[atinae] S[electae]* (repr Berlin 1954–5) no 809.

[4] Dessau, *ILS*, no 802.

[5] W. Speyer, *Bücherfunde in der Glaubenswerbung der Antike* (Göttingen 1970) pp 60–2.

[6] Sozomen, *Historia Ecclesiastica*, ed J. Bidez and G. C. Hansen, *GCS*, L (Berlin 1960) VII, 19.

[7] The famous story – Theophanes, *sub anno mundi* 5941; Georgius Monachus (Hamartolos), *Chronicon Syntomon*, ed C. de Boor, 2 vols (Leipzig, Teubner edition, 1904) p 611; Cedrenus, *Synopsis Historion*, para 600, *PG*, CXXI (1894) col 654; Iohannes Zonaras, *Epitome of History*, ed M. Pinder and R. Büttner-Wobst, 3 vols, *CSHByz* (1841–97)

In such an intellectual and political climate bishops, lawyers and mere radicals wrote about ecclesiastical history for the same reason which impelled English bishops, bankers and mere radicals to write about Greek history in the thirties and forties of the last century. It was a way of clarifying one's own ideas about the past and of expressing one's own views about the future. For the majority of these ecclesiastical writers of the fifth century it was also a clear attempt to influence the court and particularly the scholarly emperor. Socrates, Sozomenus, Theodoretus (and, we may add, though his work is lost, Philip of Side) were close enough to the centre of the theological spectrum to hope to be heard at court. Sozomenus unblushingly expected a gift from the emperor for his *Ecclesiastical History*. My heart therefore goes out to the Euno-mian Philostorgius who had no such hope – indeed no worldly hope. He wrote in an apocalyptic tone about his own time and made it abundantly clear that there was no natural cause for earthquakes. Earthquakes happen by the will of God for the purpose of bringing sinners to repentance: plenty of earthquakes had accompanied the coming of age of Theodosius II.[1] Photius who saved Philostorgius's history from total destruction accused him of attributing miracles to heretics.[2] He was less surprised that Philostorgius, a lover of geography, had such a precise knowledge of the topography of the earthly paradise.[3]

The more orthodox ecclesiastical historians propped up not only theology, but also politics, by miracles. If the manner of Arius's death was taken as proof that his theology was impious, the death of Valens at the battle of Adrianopolis was interpreted as retribution for his persecution of the orthodox. Two new Dioscuri appeared to Theodosius I before the battle of the Frigidus: one said that he was John the evangelist, the other that he was the apostle Philip. According to both Socrates[4] and Theodoretus,[5] God with thunderbolts and lightning burned down the Huns in AD 434: the prayers of Theodosius II had been heard.

There is only one step from the stories of miracles and ascetic feats which spice the ecclesiastical histories to the lives of saints which have nothing but miracles and ascetic feats. One of these books came straight to the circle of Theodosius II. Palladius wrote the *Historia*

XIII, 23, 44A; Nicephorus Callistus, XIV, 23, col 1130 – seems to be authentic, but wrongly dated. Its source seems to be Theodorus Lector. Cf G. Gentz, *Die Kirchengeschichte des Nicephorus Callistus* (Berlin 1966) p 129, n 2.
[1] Philostorgius, [*Historia Ecclesiastica*], ed J. Bidez, *GCS*, XXI (Berlin 1913) XII, 10.
[2] *Ibid*, IX, I.   [3] *Ibid*, III, 9ff.
[4] Socrates, VII, 43.   [5] Theodoretus, V, 373, 3.

Lausiaca for Lausus, the chamberlain of Theodosius, an admirer and a protector of Melania. Palladius was also interested in non-christian asceticism and dedicated his *De vita Bragmanorum* to another important man whose name we do not know. It is particularly fortunate that we have the *Religious History* of Theodoretus, because it teaches the vanity of any attempt at separating hagiography from ecclesiastical historiography. Cardinal Newman was naturally puzzled by 'the stupid credulity of so well-read, so intellectual an author'.[1] But Theodoretus lived in the world of the miracles he described. His mother's eyesight had been saved by Peter of Galatia. Peter's girdle functioned as a first-aid box for Theodoretus's family and neighbours. The birth of Theodoretus himself had been due to the prayers of the holy Macedonius. In his youth Theodoretus travelled to visit the Syrian saints whose feats he was later to register. The precise purpose of the *Religious History* cannot be ascertained exactly because we do not know when it was written: the date about AD 440 is only an intelligent guess. It is not impossible that Theodoretus was trying to curry favour with the monks who in the past had made his life and that of John of Antioch very difficult.[2] But the essential fact remains that Theodoretus makes no concession to popular tastes. One has to take him literally when he declares that those who believe in the miracles of Moses and Joshua, Elijah and Elisha must also believe in the miracles told by him. The comparison with biblical situations is a constant feature of Theodoretus's stories. Modern researchers are of course free to use these stories either to illustrate the diffusion of certain magical practices or to measure the popularity of the new asceticism. We are glad to know that the holy Macedonius compelled a devil to be a witness for the prosecution in a trial for black magic, or that artisans in Rome had little images of Simeon the stylite to protect their workshops.[3] To characterise Theodoretus, it is more important to remember that to him the existence of holy nuns was the proof that Christ did not separate virtue into male virtue and female virtue.[4]

[1] *Historical Sketches*, II (London 1876) p 315.
[2] Cf the discussion between P. Peeters, *An Bol*, LXI (1943) p 29, and M. Richard, *Mélanges de Science Religieuse*, III (Lille 1946) pp 147–56. See also H. Bacht, 'Die Rolle des orientalischen Mönchtums' in A. Grillmeier and H. Bacht, *Das Konzil von Chalkedon*, II (Würzburg 1953) pp 193–314; A.-J. Festugière, *Antioche Païenne et Chrétienne* (Paris 1959) pp 241–401. The identification of the author of the *Vita Bragmanorum* with the author of the *Historia Lausiaca* is made more probable by the important researches of L.Cracco Ruggini, *Athenaeum*, XLIII (Pavia 1965) pp 3–80. Cf Palladius, *De gentibus Indiae et Bragmanibus*, ed W. Berghoff (Meisenheim am Glan 1967).
[3] *PG*, LXXXII (1864) cols 1406, 1473.   [4] *Ibid*, col 1493.

Popular religious beliefs and the late Roman historians

As is evident from Theodoretus – and also from Eunapius – biographers of late antiquity included a large number of personal recollections in their work. This lent credibility to the many strange stories they told and at the same time reflected their direct involvement in the experiences they described. The life of Mani which has recently been discovered in a papyrus at Cologne shows that this biographical technique was adopted by the Manichaeans, too. We must now await the publication of the entire text, of which only fragments and a general summary have so far been published in the *Zeitschrift für Papyrologie und Epigraphik.*[1]

Christian intellectuals succeeded where pagan intellectuals had failed for centuries, both in transmitting their theories to the masses and in sharing the beliefs of the masses. Such a delicate balance between the learned and the popular could not be maintained without frequent crises. If some of the crises involved heresy, others represented a temptation by the pagan gods. Hellenism still had its attractions. Even at the court of Theodosius II some pagan literati, such as the poet and historian Olympiodorus, were acceptable. For very good reasons Philostorgius wrote against Porphyry, and Philip of Side against Julian the apostate. Cyrus of Panopolis, the poet who by a singular distinction combined the position of prefect of the city with that of prefect of the *praetorium* under Theodosius II, was removed from the court on being accused of paganism. It is characteristic of the time that he was relegated to a small town of Phrygia with the rank of a bishop.[2]

The christian abolition of the internal frontiers between the learned and the vulgar had clear implications. For cultured persons it meant the reception and acceptance of many uncritical, unsophisticated beliefs in miracles, relics, and apparitions. For the vulgar and uncultivated it meant appreciation, to the point of fanaticism, of the importance of theological controversies and consequent participation in these struggles. It is probably a modern legend that the factions of the circus, as such, had a share in the religious movements of the fifth and sixth centuries. But anyone who reads in Socrates and Sozomenus the story of

---

[1] v (Bonn 1970) 97–216.

[2] Cf Alan Cameron, *Claudian* (Oxford 1970) p 192. Cameron will have more to say on Cyrus in a forthcoming study. The statement by W. E. Kaegi that Cyrus was a pagan seems to be due to a misunderstanding; see W. E. Kaegi, 'The Fifth Century Twilight of Byzantine Paganism', *Classica et Mediaevalia*, XXVII (Copenhagen 1966) p. 265. Further bibliography for all the questions treated in this paper will be found in Jacques Le Goff, 'Culture cléricale et traditions folkloriques dans la civilisation mérovingienne', *Annales: Economies, Sociétés, Civilisations*, XXII (Paris 1967) pp 780–91.

the two banishments of John Chrysostom is left in no doubt about the weight and the consequences of mob theology.

My conclusion, as might be expected, is that there is no way of defining a clear separation between an upper-class culture and a lower-class culture in the second half of the fourth century and in the first half of the fifth century. While this applies also to the pagans, it is really a distinctive feature of christian culture. The pagans are compelled to accept in self-defence a reshaping of their own world. By the end of the fourth century even the most unperceptive pagan rhetorician and philosopher must have been acquainted with saints, miracles and relics.

However divided they were, the Christians were not divided culturally in the upper and lower strata. Their divisions cut across the social pyramid and were influenced by national, doctrinal and institutional factors. It would be very surprising if the christian historians reasoned differently from the other intellectuals. There is one chapter in Sozomenus which is worth special attention. It is chapter 19 of book VII, in which he reflects on the variety of customs within orthodox Christendom. With almost Herodotean wisdom Sozomenus observes that those who have been brought up in the observance of certain customs would consider it wrong to abandon them. The differences which interest him are due to local tradition. He ignores distinctions, if any, between educated and uneducated Christians. Indeed I do not know of any ecclesiastical historian who condemns a christian practice simply as being vulgar. Philostorgius condemns the cult of an image representing Constantine as a god:[1] what else could he have done?

Thus my inquest into popular religious beliefs in the late Roman historians ends in reporting that there were no such beliefs. In the fourth and fifth centuries there were of course plenty of beliefs which we historians of the twentieth century would gladly call popular, but the historians of the fourth and fifth centuries never treated any belief as characteristic of the masses and consequently discredited among the élite. Lectures on popular religious beliefs and the late Roman historians should be severely discouraged.

[1] Philostorgius, II, 17.

18

POPULAR RELIGION AND CHRISTO-
LOGICAL CONTROVERSY IN THE FIFTH
CENTURY

by W. H. C. FREND

HOW far does the great religious controversy of the fifth century centred on the mystery of the Incarnation reflect popular religious ideas of the east Roman world? It is well known that factors that had little to do with theological speculation, such as the rivalry for prestige and leadership between Constantinople and Alexandria, played a large part in bringing the controversy between rival concepts of christology to their climax in the twenty years that separate the councils of Ephesus and Chalcedon.[1] More discussion, perhaps, is needed concerning the contribution of articulate public opinion to the course of events, and in particular, to the persistence of the opposition to the Chalcedonian definition after 451.

In the fifth century there was no longer the same gap between the outlook of the theologians and that of more ordinary Christians, as there had been in the time of Origen. The great Alexandrian theologian had been conscious of his isolation, and had ruminated on the vast mass of the faithful who knew nothing but Jesus Christ and him crucified, who were separated from those who partook of the divine Logos as He was in the beginning with God.[2] To Athanasius belongs the credit of making the theology of Alexandria also the religion of the Coptic-speaking monk. His deep religious sensitivity had enabled him to demonstrate the *Homoousios* in a way that satisfied the needs of Trinitarian definition and those of the simple Christian, who wanted assurance that Him whom he worshipped needed no redemption Himself, and was indeed God. In the last part of the fourth century both halves of the Roman Empire witnessed religious debate developing as one of the predominant aspects of society, and in addition, the political and social problems

---

[1] See N. H. Baynes,'Alexandria and Constantinople: a study in Ecclesiastical Diplomacy', *Byzantine Studies and other Essays* (London 1955) pp 97–116.

[2] See H. J. Carpenter's article, 'Popular Christianity and the Theologians in the Early Centuries', *JTS*, new series XIV (1963) pp 294–310, especially p 309.

of the Roman Empire were often interpreted in religious terms. Even Arianism, whose arid progress through the reign of Constantius II seemed to be more the concern of the emperor and his bishops than their congregations, roused fervent discussion among the populace in the capital[1] as well as deep interest among the ever-increasing numbers of educated and highly placed laity.[2] In Africa the Circumcellions of Optatus of Milevis's and Augustine's day provided visible proof that the popular quest for the millennium and the rule of the saints and martyrs of the church, could also involve overturning existing social structures on earth.[3]

The christological controversy could be expected to arouse deeper concern among ordinary Christians, since questions of personal salvation were even more directly involved than in Arianism. How was the saving work of Christ to be understood in terms of His own being? As in the arian controversy Alexandria spoke for the majority. Athanasius's ability to interpret subtle theological concepts successfully to people of an entirely different religious and cultural outlook from himself was perfected by Cyril. The essence of the Alexandrian appeal to popular opinion was put by the latter in the spring of 429 in a superb lawyer's brief addressed to the Egyptian monks. Cyril aimed at convincing them that even though the term *Theotokos* (bearer of God) was nowhere to be found in Scripture it was nonetheless an essential element of belief from the point of view of salvation. If, he said, Christ was not by nature God, but equal to us and nothing more than an instrument of God, how could he overthrow death, and how could we be exhorted to worship a mere man? Nicaea had implied that what was born of the Virgin was 'of the same substance as God', and hence the title *Theotokos* was justified. Moreover, the great Athanasius had used the term. Could he err?[4] The medicine worked. The doubts of the monks were stilled, and at Ephesus I and II they were prepared to dare all to destroy 'the divider of Christ', Nestorius.

Even so, Cyril's argument ran into serious difficulties outside Egypt which his Antiochene opponents were quick to point out. In the con-

---

[1] For Gregory of Nyssa's well-known description of his experiences with Arian-minded tradesmen in Constantinople, see *De Filii Deitate*, PG, XLVI (1863) col 557.

[2] Such as Count Terentius, to whom Basil wrote one of his most interesting letters on the Trinity, Ep 214, ed R. J. de Ferrari (London, Loeb ed, 1930).

[3] For instance, see Optatus of Milevis, *De Schismate Donatistarum*, ed C. Ziwsa, *CSEL*, XXVI (1893) III, 4, p 81.

[4] Cyril, *Ep I Ad Monachos*, PG, LXXVII (1864) cols 3–40, and *ACO* (1914–40) I, l, i, p 5; dated by L. S. Lenain de Tillemont, *Mémoires pour servir à l'histoire ecclésiastique des six Premiers Siècles*, XIV (Paris 1690–1712) p 330 to 'a little after Easter 429'.

troversy that spanned nearly a quarter of a century between 428 and
451, the opposition had found a champion in the historian and philosopher Theodoret, bishop of Cyrrhus in northern Syria. At the time of
Ephesus Theodoret had already characterised Cyril's views as a compound of arian and apollinarian heresy.[1] Sixteen years later, in the course
of a Dialogue (*The Eranistes* or *Beggarman*) ostensibly between a
representative of Cyril's theology and an Antiochene, he demonstrated in popular form that Cyril's assertion of the essential (hypostatic)
union of Godhead and manhood in one incarnate nature of Christ led
to the complete separation of Christ from humanity and thus an in-
ability to save.[2] How could, he asked with others, He save what He did
not assume? Christ saved by His assumption of entire humanity and
destroyed sin and death through the complete harmony of His will
with that of God. Where to Cyril Christ was the Word made flesh of
John 1 : 14 manifesting the fullness of God to a worshipping humanity,
to the Antiochenes He was the great high priest and pioneer of the
Letter to Hebrews, who pointed the way to salvation by his own example and obedience to God.

Antioch and Alexandria represented two different ideas of salvation.
They continued to do so despite verbal concessions on each side which
found their expression in the Formula of Reunion in 433 that restored
communion between them after the council of Ephesus. The Alexand-
rine looked forward to the ultimate divinisation of humanity and its
reabsorption into God as the ultimate source of its being. Antioch, on
the other hand, was concerned to preserve the reality of man, each
individual moving by the right exercise of his will towards communion
with God, and receiving the merited rewards and punishments on the
way.

There is, however, no doubt that in the Roman east in the fifth and
sixth centuries Cyril's conception of salvation corresponded more to
popular religion than the Antiochene, despite the skill and dedication of
Theodoret. One hint of this may be gathered from the manner in which
writings either by Apollinarius himself or by his disciples were fathered
on figures as orthodox and respected as popes Felix and Julius, and
Athanasius himself, and were accepted as genuine by both the mass of
the people and by theologians. Cyril's Twelve Anathemas, for instance,
would hardly have been conceived without the authority of the

---

[1] Theodoret, Ep 153, *PG*, LXXXIII (1864) col 1444D.
[2] For an account of the debate see A. Grillmeier, *Christ in Christian Tradition*, Eng tr
J . S. Bowden (London 1961) pp 419ff.

apollinarian forgeries to support them![1] The part which these played in shaping the christology of Cyril and his adherents needs no emphasis. The ground had been well prepared for Cyril's triumph at Ephesus. At the council itself both Theodoret and Cyril have left graphic descriptions of the dramatic events of 22–7 June 431 when Nestorius was condemned by Cyril's council as 'the new Judas' and deposed on 22 June, while four days later John of Antioch declared Cyril and his ally Memnon of Ephesus deposed as heretics and disturbers of ecclesiastical order. The populace of Ephesus and to a lesser extent of Constantinople had a major say in the eventual decision favouring Cyril. The latter was very conscious of the need of carrying popular opinion with him and immediately wrote an account of the events to the clergy and people of Alexandria.[2] In this letter he describes how the populace of Ephesus demonstrated night and day in favour of his vindication of Mary as *Theotokos* (God-bearing). He was preceded, he said, from the church dedicated to the *Theotokos* where the council had met, by a torchlight procession, men and women rejoicing at Nestorius's downfall. The picture was not exaggerated. Theodoret's accounts written to the emperor and the court of Constantinople tells the same story from the opposite point of view.[3] The bishops of the oriental diocese (i.e. the patriarchate of Antioch) had arrived in Ephesus to find the city in turmoil. Cyril and Memnon had 'banded together and mustered a great mob of rustics' who had closed the churches of the city against them and prevented the celebration of Pentecost. In Constantinople also there were rejoicings at Nestorius's deposition. Whatever part was played by ecclesiastical rivalries and the ability of Cyril to bribe his way to success, popular devotion to Mary as *Theotokos* and the equally deeply held belief reflected in Cyril's teaching that the Word of God truly suffered in the flesh to redeem mankind, carried the day. Theodoret's charge that Cyril's ideas were simply a development of Apollinarianism fell on deaf ears.

When the crisis was renewed in 447 Alexandria continued to hold the trump cards, and had Cyril's successor Dioscorus been an abler diplomat and less vindictive a character, Alexandrian theology might well have become the standard of christian orthodoxy. That popular

---

[1] Grillmeier suggests the period 429/30 (i.e. during the interchanges with Nestorius) as that in which the apollinarian formulas find their way into Cyril's theological language: *Christ in Christian Tradition*, p 400.

[2] Ep 24, *PG*, LXXVII (1864) col 137 (*ACO*, I, l, i, pp 117–18).

[3] Ep 152, *PG*, LXXXIII (1864) col 1441, compare Epp 153, 154 and in 157 where Theodoret protests to Theodosius II that the Antiochene bishops were becoming 'a prey to tyranny'.

opinion continued to favour Alexandria, this time supported by the emperor himself, is evident from the events surrounding the summoning of the notorious second council of Ephesus in August 449. In the spring of that year a striking demonstration in favour of the one-nature christology took place at Edessa, the capital of the province and former client-kingdom of Osrohene.[1] Cyril's adherent Rabbula who had been metropolitan had died in 435, and his successor, Ibas, was an equally convinced Antiochene. For thirteen years, however, he presided over the see uneventfully, though there was an undercurrent of discontent, and certain unwise statements he had made were eagerly remembered by his enemies. In 448 the storm broke over him. Dioscorus was determined to root out all traces of Antiochene teaching and assert the primacy of Alexandria over Antioch and Constantinople. He had the full support of Theodosius II; and Ibas, the metropolitan of the see celebrated in history and legend as the 'city of the believing people of Mesopotamia',[2] was among his prime targets. Ibas was accused by Dioscorus's agents, the local monks and by some of his presbyters of blasphemy, nepotism and embezzlement of church property. He had been heard to say in the presence of presbyters, 'I do not envy Christ that he became God, for I have become that, as he is of my own nature.' He did not believe in hell, it was said, regarding it only as a threat, and had asserted that the Jews had only crucified a man. He had also sold church plate for his own benefit. Ibas was acquitted, however, by two ecclesiastical tribunals, the last of which was composed of bishops in no way favourable to his views. When he returned to his see in March 449 there were vast demonstrations against him. So hostile was the crowd that he had to withdraw, and on 12 April the provincial governor of Osrohene entered the city accompanied by his staff to conduct an inquiry; the verbatim report shows what transpired. Amid loyal shouts of 'Long live the Roman Empire', 'Many years to Theodosius', there were others more menacing: 'To the gallows with the Iscariot', 'Ibas has corrupted the true doctrine of Cyril', 'Long live arch-bishop Dioscorus', 'The Christ-hater to the arena', 'Down with the Judophile', 'The works of Nestorius were found with Ibas', 'Where has the church property gone?'.[3]

The cries show a strongly pro-imperial and anti-nestorian tendency,

---

[1] Recorded in detail in the *Acta* of the second council of Ephesus, ed [J.] Flemming, *Akten* [*der Ephesinischen synode vom Jahre 449*], in *Abhandlungen der Königlichen Gesellschaft der Wissenschaften zu Göttingen*, neue Folge xv (Göttingen 1914–17) Phil. Hist. Klasse, pp 15–55.   [2] See Rufinus, *Historia Ecclesiastica, PL,* xxi (1849) ii, 15, col 513.

[3] Flemming, *Akten*, p. 19.

and were supported by an abundance of sworn testimony by city magistrates, clergy, monks and artisans. Edessa had at one time been pro-Parthian in sentiment, yet there was now no doubt as to the loyalty of its people to the empire. This loyalty was associated in their minds with adherence to the christology of Cyril.

These instances of public feeling help one to understand the attitude of the 135 bishops who assembled at Ephesus in August 449 where, amidst lurid and violent scenes, they reinstated the Constantinopolitan archimandrite Eutyches, who held extreme Cyrilline views, deposed his judge, the patriarch of Constantinople and those who had been his accusers, and acclaimed Dioscorus the true champion of orthodoxy. 'Let him who preaches Two Natures himself be cut in two', so the assembly cried out.[1]

Despite the violence of their proceedings, Dioscorus and his colleagues spoke for the east, a fact which Theodosius II recognised when he told his distracted relatives at the western court at Ravenna that at Ephesus 'in full respect for the truth various disturbers of the peace had been removed from the office of the priesthood', and that 'nothing contrary to the rule of faith or of justice had been done there'.[2] The council had in fact been a large-scale disciplinary body whose membership had been restricted to ten bishops from each metropolitan area. Though the faith of Cyril had been vindicated, and in particular, his Twelve Anathemas declared canonical, it had not been intended as a general council such as was its successor at Chalcedon held by Theodosius's successor Marcian in October and November 451.

Here too, despite the combined influence of emperor, pope and episcopate, the popular verdict against the *Tome* of Leo and the definition of Christ as subsisting in two inseparable and unconfused natures was overwhelming. The bishops had not spoken for the people and the subsequent bitterness ending in the monophysite schism during the sixth century was a reflection of this fact. Half a century after the council the Monophysite, John Rufus, bishop of Maiuma near Gaza, collected and wrote down a part of the mass of floating tradition surrounding the reception of the definition in the various eastern provinces.[3] Strongly

---

[1] See L. Duchesne's summary in *The Early History of the Church*, III (Eng tr L. Jenkins, London 1924) pp 288–91.

[2] Theodosius II, Letter included in Pope Leo's correspondence, Ep 62 'Nihil igitur ab his (episcopis) contrarium regulae fidei aut justitiae factum esse cognovimus', *PL*, LIV (1846) cols 875–7. Compare Epp 63 and 64.

[3] Edited by F. Nau, in *PO*, VIII, (1912) pp 1–161.

prejudiced against Chalcedon though he was, these *Plerophoria (Revelations)* as they were called ranging from province to province are impressive in their unanimity. It was not only in Egypt, and in Palestine where the monks had a special grievance against the turncoat bishop Juvenal, that feeling was strong. In Isauria for instance, the monks found it impossible to understand how their bishops drawn from their own ranks could have restored Ibas and Theodoret to their sees after condemning them to deposition now and hell hereafter only two years before.[1] In Pamphylia, where there was to be a long history of anti-chalcedonian feeling, a layman openly rebuked the metropolitan for preaching heresy.[2]

Monks in the same province saw visions of Christ cursing Chalcedon as Chalcedon had denied him, or of Satan asking them why they did not follow the example of their bishops and worship him.[3] All over the east families were divided, no greetings exchanged in the streets between adherents and opponents of Chalcedon, and in particular the latter refused to receive communion at the hands of bishops who had signed the definition.[4] Only the Jews were reported to be pleased with the decision. They were said to have written to Marcian in the following terms:

To the merciful emperor Marcian: the people of the Hebrews: – For a long time we have been regarded as though our fathers had crucified a God and not a man. Since the synod of Chalcedon has assembled and demonstrated that he who was crucified was a man and not a God we request that we should be pardoned this fault and that our synagogues should be returned to us.[5]

All this was in addition to the riots and popular execration that greeted the return of Juvenal, bishop of Jerusalem,[6] who had betrayed both Dioscorus and his own strongly expressed convictions in order to safeguard the patriarchal status of his see, and the even worse disorders that greeted the promulgation of the definition by the new patriarch of Alexandria Proterius. The latter was popularly regarded as a 'wolf', and an 'anti-Christ'.[7]

Why was this the case? Why was any christology that deviated from Cyril's rejected by the populace? The clues are to be found in the utterances of contemporaries. Antipathy to anything that smacked of

---

[1] *Plerophoria*, xxiii, *PO*, VIII (1912) pp 54–7. Compare *ibid*, xxi, p 44 and lix, p 115.
[2] *Ibid*, lxiv, p 120. [3] *Ibid*, ix, p 22.
[4] *Ibid*, lxx and lxxii, lxxv, lxxvi, lxxviii, lxxiii, etc.
[5] Michael the Syrian, *Chronicle*, ed J. B. Chabot (Paris 1901) VIII, 12, p 91.
[6] *Plerophoria*, xvi–xx. [7] *Ibid*, lxvi and lxix.

Judaism was one reason, and Chalcedon was regarded by its opponents as acceptable to Judaism,[1] but behind this was a deeper theological ground. The one-nature christology implied confession in unequivocal terms that 'Christ is God', and associated the suffering and redemption of mankind with divine suffering and glorification, whereas 'two natures inseparably united' either seemed nonsense or implied the existence of 'two Christs' (pre- and post-Incarnation) one of which could not be God. At Chalcedon the distraught cries of the Egyptian bishops against the proposed two-nature christology make this clear. 'As he was begotten, so he suffered. Let no one divide the king of glory. Let no one divide the indivisible. Let no one call the one Lord two. Thus Nestorius believed.'[2] Nearly a century later, in 541, Silko king of the Nobatae explained why he accepted the monophysite christology preached by missionaries sent by the empress Theodora in preference to those from Justinian representing Chalcedon. The latter did not preach monotheism, he explained. If God was one, and Christ saved as God, then he must also be God.[3] There could not be two natures, one divine and one not. Similarly, twenty years before in 523, the monophysite christian confessors at Najran in Yemen explained why they preferred martyrdom to embracing Judaism (or Nestorianism). 'You must know', said the Christian Habsa, 'that not only will I not say that Christ was a man, but I worship and praise him because of all the benefits He has shown me. And I believe that He is God, maker of all creatures, and that I take refuge in His Cross.'[4] Cyrilline theology as interpreted by the opponents of Chalcedon touched the sources of popular Christianity in the east. Once again, the behaviour of the Egyptian bishops at Chalcedon itself is revealing. Pressed to sign the definition of faith that Christ subsisted 'in two natures' without separation that had been accepted by the remainder of the bishops they gave way to despair. 'We shall all be killed if we subscribe to Leo's epistle', 'Every district in Egypt will rise against us.'[5] The fate of the ambitious but luckless presbyter Proterius who accepted consecration in Dioscorus's stead, torn to pieces by the Alexandrian mob on Maundy Thursday 457, showed that they were speaking the truth.

If one probes deeper and asks why popular religion in the east in the

[1] *Ibid*, xiv.
[2] Schwartz, *ACO*, II, l, i, paras 171–5 = Mansi, VI, col 636.
[3] John of Ephesus, *Historia Ecclesiastica*, ed E. W. Brooks, *CSCO*, 3 series III (Paris 1935) IV, 7.
[4] See *The Book of the Himyarites*, ed A. Moberg (Lund 1924), Introduction p cxxiv.
[5] Schwartz, *ACO*, II, l, ii, pp 110–13 = Mansi, VII, cols 58–60.

fifth century preferred Cyril's ideas to those of Nestorius and Flavian of Constantinople, the answer is complex. Monasticism certainly accounts for much, and one can indicate a tendency for the mysticism of the monks to lead towards the glorification of Christ and the *Theotokos*. This is particularly the case in Palestine, where, in the sixth century, despite the loyalty of the great majority of monks to Chalcedon, owing perhaps to the fact that Jerusalem's standing as a patriarchate like that of Constantinople depended on a decision of that council, a very large proportion of churches built at that time are dedicated to the *Theotokos*,[1] and Cyril's theology was regarded as canon. It is not quite adequate as a complete explanation. A considerable minority of monks in Syria and in the capital sympathised with the two-nature christology, and monks in Syria are recorded as having used their influence on popular religious belief to prevent the spread of the extreme one-nature christology taught by Apollinarius.[2] Moreover, the dogmatic writings of the leaders of Egyptian monasticism, particularly Shenoudi of the White Monastery, show all the literalist milleniarism of a biblical fundamentalist with no concern at all for the Mary of the one-nature christology. Yet Shenoudi could imagine himself striking down Nestorius at Ephesus.

Perhaps at the back of these monks' minds and the popular religion which they expressed was the fear of the old gods dispossessed of their power by Christ, but ever-menacing in the form of demons. Only Christ as God and wholly God could avail against them. The demons, whether dwelling on the edge of the Egyptian desert or in the upper atmosphere, were a constant threat in the minds of all classes. They were responsible for all irrational aspects of life from the onset of plague or earthquake to the outbreak of civil disturbance. Both at Antioch in 387[3] and Edessa in 449[4] the presence of demons – at Edessa 'Nestorian' demons – proved a welcome alibi for the ill behaviour of the citizens. In the plague at Antioch early in the sixth century, one arch-demon was identified. It was Phoebus Apollo now associated with destruction of life and not with healing.[5] After death, as Severus

---

[1] See G. M. Armstrong, 'Fifth and Sixth Century Buildings in the Holy Land,' in *The Greek Orthodox Theological Review*, XIV (Brookline 1969) pp 17–30.

[2] Sozomen, [*Historia Ecclesiastica*] ed J. Bidez and G. C. L. Hansen, *GCS*, L (1960), VI, 27, 10, p 276.

[3] *Ibid*, VII, 23, 4, p 337.

[4] Flemming, *Akten*, p 33.

[5] John of Beith-Apthonia, *Life of Severus*, ed/trans M. A. Kugener, *PO*, II, 3 (1904) p 246. For the old gods as 'demons' who had been dispossessed of their temples and

the monophysite patriarch of Antioch pointed out, failure to receive the sacrament at the hands of a truly orthodox priest would entail the soul being captured by demons and frustrated in its efforts to move towards God.[1]

Such ideas lay at the back of popular religion in the fifth and sixth centuries in the east. The emphatic christology expressed in the formula 'out of two natures, One' guaranteed the believer against the victory of the irrational powers of chaos and evil in the universe which surrounded him. In the minds of many too, the unity and continuity of the imperial monarchy was also associated with a one-nature christology. As James of Sarug, the monophysite bishop of the east Syrian see of Batnan pointed out to the emperor Justin, the symbol of the cross which he wore on his diadem had no meaning unless Christ was one and was God.[2] The emperor Marcian was abused by the Monophysites precisely because he broke the unity of the empire and Christendom through the decisions of Chalcedon.[3] There was a clear tendency in the fifth and sixth centuries for the people to associate themselves with the imperial monarchy through their concept of Christ, for just as Christ was One, so the emperor His vice-regent was also one.

The emperors themselves were not blind to such ideas. Theodosius II shifted his support from Nestorius to Cyril in 431 once he saw that opinion favoured the latter, and from that time on his aid to the adherents of the one-nature christology was unstinted. In touch with public opinion throughout the eastern provinces through the monks who acted as standing channels of complaints from the provincials, the eastern emperors were far better able than their western counterparts to inform themselves of situations and remedy wrongs. In 387 Antioch survived the wrath of Theodosius I thanks to the intervention of Macedonius the Barley-Eater. Thessalonica in 390 had no monastic intercessor and suffered massacre. The existence of these relationships between emperor and provincials, together with acceptance of common religious ideas,

rendered powerless by the word of Christ, see the sixth-century inscription from Ezraa near Bostra in the province of Arabia, published by C. Mondésart, *Syria*, XXXVII (Paris 1956) pp 125–8. In the capital, Atlas, believed to be responsible for earthquakes, came readily to the lips of the people in moments of crisis. At the time of the Nika riot the spokesman of the Green fraction claimed he actually ordered baptism in the name of the 'One God'. See Theophanes *Chronicle, Sub anno mundi* 6024, ed J. Classen (Bonn 1839) p 280.

[1] *Select Letters*, ed E. W. Brooks (London 1902–4) III, 4, pp 246–7.
[2] Cited from A. Vasiliev, *Justin the First* (Dumbarton Oaks 1950) p 234.
[3] Michael the Syrian, *Chronicle*, VIII, 14, ed/trans J. B. Chabot, 4 vols (Paris 1899–1924) II, p 122. Compare pp 88–9.

contributed much to the maintenance of popular loyalty to the empire. The demonstrations at Edessa in 449 in favour of Cyril's doctrines were significant in this regard, and we are fortunate in having a full contemporary account of what took place. A study of popular religious sentiment in the fifth-century east Roman Empire may throw a good deal of light on why Byzantium survived while Rome fell.

THE MEROVINGIAN MONASTERY
OF ST EVROUL IN THE LIGHT OF
CONFLICTING TRADITIONS

by MARJORIE CHIBNALL

HISTORIANS of early monasticism in Frankish Gaul either
have little to say about the monastery founded by St Evroul
or, like Dom Laporte,[1] devote their attention to a discussion
of the probable date of his life. The disappearance of almost all early
documentary sources is one reason for this: there was certainly a break
in the occupation of the site for perhaps half the century between the
destruction of the monastery in the tenth century and its refoundation
in 1050, and only one charter, dated 900, was rescued and copied in the
eleventh century. The fact that there has been no systematic excavation
of the site, so that archaeological evidence of buildings before the
thirteenth-century church is lacking, is another. Early annals and reliable
lives of other saints have nothing at all to say on the subject. The first
historian to tackle it, Orderic Vitalis, writing in the early twelfth century, had to admit that he could discover nothing about the abbots for
the four hundred years after St Evroul;[2] and he had to draw on the
memories and tales of the old men he knew, both in the monastery and
in the villages round about. Needless to say he harvested a luxuriant
crop of legends and traditions of all kinds. The problem of the modern
historian is to winnow a few grains of historical truth out of the stories
that he garnered, and the hagiographical traditions, some of which he
did not know.

In the main, there are two streams of tradition. One is hagiographical,
developed from the eighth or ninth centuries, when the various *Vitae* of
the saint were written. The second is popular, and is made up of legends
from a common tradition locally applied, and the stories that gathered
around ruined buildings, healing springs and place-names, to explain
their origins. To some extent both were distorted by the more sophis-

---

[1] [Dom J.] Laporte, ['Les origines du monachisme dans la province de Rouen'], *R[evue]
M[abillon]*, XXXI (Ligugé 1941) pp 35–6

[2] Ord[erici] Vit[alis], *Hist[oriae] Eccl[esiasticae] Libri Tredecim]*, ed A. Le Prevost, 5 vols
(Paris 1839–55) III, pp 67–8.

ticated historical interests of the early Norman period, when well-intentioned annalists and historians, with limited and inaccurate sources, fitted them far too neatly into a chronological framework, or explained the events of the seventh and eighth centuries in the light of their own preoccupations with contemporary problems, such as the correct interpretation of the Benedictine Rule, or the relative merits of monks and canons.

The earliest written evidence comes from the hagiographical tradition. The *Vitae* of St Evroul have been severely criticised, but as the saint's day is 29 December they have not yet come under review by the Bollandists. Of the two versions in print the *B Vita* was published from eleventh- and twelfth-century manuscripts by Mabillon,[1] who believed it to date from the ninth century, though it may be later. This was the version copied and interpolated by Orderic. The *A Vita*[2] was not known to Orderic and not used by Mabillon. In 1855 Delisle drew attention to a thirteenth-century copy from the library of St Evroul,[3] and this was later published uncritically by Hommey.[4] Both Delisle and Baedorf, who made a critical examination of the printed *Vitae*, believed it to be the earlier of the two lives. But though Baedorf[5] listed the manuscripts in which it occurred he did not actually examine two almost identical versions that were in England. One, which has been dated by Dodwell as 1100–30,[6] is from St Augustine's, Canterbury,[7] and the other, which is slightly later, is from the library of Hereford Cathedral.[8] This version, which I will call the first *A Vita*, contains a text that is both more grammatical and more intelligible than the printed version, and is certainly the earliest and purest text that we have at present.

The variations in the three *Vitae* are of some importance. For though the *B Vita* was probably based in part on the first *A Vita*, and the second *A Vita* in its turn made use of *B*, all three versions vary in the details they record of the monastic customs, liturgical *cursus*, and sometimes too the government of the monastery. In fact both the *B* and the second

[1] *ASOSB*, I, pp 354–60; B[ibliotheca] H[agiographica] L[atina], ed Soc. Bolland., 2 vols and suppl (Brussels 1898–1911) no 2377.

[2] *BHL* no 2374

[3] 'Notice sur Orderic Vital' in Ord Vit, *Hist Eccl*, v, p lxxx, n 3.

[4] *Bulletin de la société historique et archéologique de l'Orne*, VI (Alençon 1887) pp 273–92.

[5] B. Baedorf, *Untersuchungen über Heiligenleben der westlichen Normandie* (Bonn 1913) pp 111–24.

[6] C. R. Dodwell, *The Canterbury School of Illumination 1066–1100* (Cambridge 1954) p 123.

[7] [Oxford, Bodleian MS] Fell 2, pp 432–9.

[8] Hereford Cathedral Library, MS P vii. 6 fols 223r–5v.

A *Vitae* were never intended as copies, but were freely composed lives, using a number of sources and either unintentionally misinterpreting them in the light of their own experience of normal monastic practices, or deliberately distorting them to prove a point. We must look to the first *A Vita* for the earliest traditions about the monastery founded by St Evroul, and since the account that emerges is in fact both coherent and possible we may find it necessary to treat this version of the saint's life with more respect than any of the published versions have – quite rightly – hitherto commanded.

The author of the first *A Vita* claims to have known the saint;[1] this may not be true, but it is less impossible than Baedorf believed, since all the anachronisms detected by him are in the interpolations. He has little to say of Evroul's early life, except that he came from Bayeux, was of noble birth, and was brought up in the court of an unnamed Frankish king; and that in time he renounced the world, placed his wife in a nunnery and received the tonsure. No details are given of the monastery which he entered; but since he and the three companions who accompanied him in his 'flight to the wilderness' in the forest of Ouche are said to have recited monastic hours from the first, the account presupposes monastic training somewhere. Whilst there is no indication of date, except that he died in the twelfth year of a king Childebert, the evidence of this *Vita* as a whole strengthens the conclusions reached by Laporte[2] and Musset[3] that he was born about 626 and died on 29 December 706, and that these events belong to the latter part of the seventh century.

The account becomes more detailed when Evroul and his three companions established the hermitage that was to grow into a great centre of monastic life in a spot which the author, accepting a convention from the common stock of hagiography, attributes to divine guidance. 'They fell on their knees', records the *Vita*, 'and rendering thanks praised God...After finishing their prayer they called on the name of the Lord with chapter and blessing as the monks' way of life requires. Then they set to work to make a small enclosure with the branches of trees, and began to live there in a small hut.'[4] In time

---

[1] Fell 2, p 437, 'Vir autem domini magno confectus senio, videlicet octogenarium excedens numerum sicut ab ipso didicimus....'.

[2] Above, p 31, n 1.

[3] L. Musset, 'St Evroul', in D[ictionnaire d']H[istoire et de] G[éographie] E[cclesiastiques] ed A. Baudrillart, A. de Meyer, and E.Van Cauwenbergh (Paris 1909–) XVI, pp 219–20.

[4] Fell 2, p 433, 'Ubi genua flectentes cum gratiarum actione Deo referunt laudes... Expleta autem oratione nomen Domini invocabant cum capitulo et benedictione sicut

recruits were attracted by their holy way of life, and as the saint's fame spread wealthy benefactors in various provinces persuaded him to found fifteen monasteries of men and women. After completing this work Evroul returned to his own monastery with a great company of monks, and spent the remainder of his life there. The account of the organisation given at this point in the first *A Vita* is particularly interesting because it is completely omitted in the *B Vita*, and so garbled that it sometimes makes nonsense in the second *A Vita*. 'His own dwelling was so wretched that it seemed like a shepherd's hut. The brethren dwelt round about, divided up into different cells, living within a distance of 1,500 *dextrae* on all sides. He himself frequently went round among their cells, riding on a mule or donkey.'[1] It seems in fact to have been a scattered, semi-eremitical community of the *laurae* type, akin to Lérins or Luxeuil in its early days, though perhaps more scattered, since the enclosure was about 1½ miles in diameter.[2] Towards the end of the saint's life a stone church dedicated for St Peter, a dedication very popular in the early eighth century, was completed as the basilica of the monastery.[3] The first *A Vita* adds some details of the internal observance of the monastery:

The holy man's custom was, after the brethren's collation, when he returned to his bed to rest, to summon his attendant silently and ask him to read to him ... He used to recite the monastic hours according to the Roman and Gallic customs of St Benedict, and the Irish custom of St Columbanus. Every day, with a priest, he offered the sacrifice of the Mass to God, and on Sunday the priests were accustomed to sing three Masses in his presence.... He shaved his head three times a year.[4]

monachorum exposcit ordo. De virgultis etiam frondium circumcingere claustra parvula sunt aggressi ubi in modico tugurio hospitari coeperunt.' For the 'chapter and blessing' see Dom Odilo Heiming, 'Zum monastischen Offizium von Kassianus bis Kolumbanus' in *Archiv für Liturgiewissenschaft*, VII, 1 (Regensburg 1961) pp 141–3.

[1] Fell 2, pp 434–5, 'Erat enim habitatio eius tam vilis ut videretur tugurium esse pastorum. Fratres vero in circuitu eius commanebant cellulis inter se divisis, habitantes per dextras mille quingentas in unaquaque parte. Ipse vero circumibat cellulas eorum frequenter sedens mulo vel asino.'

[2] See [Dom J. M.] Besse, [*Les moines de l'ancienne France*] Archives de la France Monastique (Paris 1906) p 322.

[3] Fell 2, p 439, 'Sicque venerabilis pater in basilica beati Petri principis apostolorum quam ipse ex lapidibus dudum aedificaverat in saxo marmoreo cum decore sepultus est.'

[4] *Ibid*, p 436. 'Consuetudo enim erat sancto viro ut post collectas fratrum, dum ad lectum suum revertebatur ad pausandum, ministrum suum ad se silenter vocans legere rogaret ...Et ut omnes cursus compleret, scilicet Romanum Gallicanum Sancti Benedicti, Scotticum seu Sancti Columbani, per diversa horarum spatia psallebat. Cotidie etiam cum sacerdote oblationes suas Domino studebat offerre, et dominico die sacerdotes ante eum tres missas canere solebant.'

Twice a year, in fulfilment of a vow, he gave 100 *solidi* to the poor, and at other times he gave what he could. The account of his death speaks of the brethren singing psalms and hymns round his body, including the psalm *In exitu Israel*, and waiting for three days for the arrival of the '*conventus servorum Dei*', by which may be meant the brethren from the nearer monasteries founded by him.

In all this, allowing for the fact that the more archaic, eremitical phase would have belonged to the seventh century, there is nothing that would have been impossible in a Frankish monastery of the eighth century. Many of the customs recorded are columbanian. In columbanian monasteries much of the night was devoted to psalmody.[1] The abbot might be attended by one of the younger brethren acting as a kind of secretary or *minister*.[2] The abbot did not necessarily take holy orders, and even if he did might prefer to leave the administration of the sacraments to a specially-designated priest.[3] By the end of the seventh century, daily Mass was becoming normal: it would have been somewhat unusual at an early date.[4] Whether or not the *Vita* can be taken as evidence for the influence of the benedictine *cursus* on the liturgy in Evroul's own lifetime is more doubtful: the author may have incorporated some details from the practice of his own day, and the exact date of this *Vita* is uncertain. But no one would deny benedictine influence in the abbeys of Gaul by the mid-eighth century at the latest.[5] There are in fact no real anachronisms in the monastic customs recorded in this *Vita*, and this supports its early date.[6] If it is a ninth-century forgery it is an unusually skilful one.

The author of the *B Vita*,[7] which is later, showed almost no interest in details of this kind. His work was designed to provide a series of readings in church, and the moral side is developed. He adds a short account of the movements of St Evroul before he came to the forest of Ouche, which has much in common with the Life of St Wandrille and could have been taken from other saints' lives. Of the monastery of Ouche he says merely that the first dwelling was a hut surrounded

---

[1] *Sancti Columbani Opera*, ed G. S. M. Walker (Dublin 1957) p xiii.

[2] *Ibid*, p xv.   [3] Besse, pp 457–8.

[4] [Terence P.] McLaughlin, [*Le très ancien droit monastique de l'occident*] Archives de la France Monastique (Paris 1935) p 77.

[5] This has been a subject of controversy. Dates suggested for the appearance of benedictine influence range from *c* 629 (McLaughlin, p 19) to the mid-eighth century (James O'Carroll, 'Monastic rules in Merovingian Gaul', *Studies*, XLII (Dublin 1953) pp 407–19).

[6] One phrase (*cursus suavorum*) which might be an anachronism is more likely a scribal error (*saevorum*, as in Alençon, [Bibliothèque municipale] MS 11, fol 143).

[7] *ASOSB*, I, pp 354–60.

by a small enclosure. He is more interested in the constitutional framework, describing the fifteen monasteries founded by the saint, and stating that he placed suitable persons at the head of each and himself presided over his own monastery. This is also the first account to add the detail that he died when Robert was bishop of Séez: an implied hint, perhaps, of episcopal control. All the liturgical details are omitted.

Since Orderic Vitalis appears not to have known the first *A Vita* it must have found its way to the abbey of St Evroul some time after about 1140, but before the beginning of the thirteenth century, the approximate date of the manuscript of the second *A Vita* surviving from the library of St Evroul.[1] This manuscript gives a free version of the first *A Vita*, making some use either of *B* or of Orderic's account based on *B*, and attempting to paraphrase rather than to copy. The result is that some of the practices described, which by this date were unfamiliar, were distorted and changed. The author was plainly baffled by the account of Evroul riding round the scattered huts of the brethren on his ass, and rendered it thus: 'The man of God showed great solicitude over the condition of those *pastores* whom he had established round about in the monasteries built by him, and to fulfil the obligations of his cure of them he often travelled 1,500 *dextrae* (which is 6 *stadia* and 20 *passus*) in one day's toil, riding on a donkey or an ass.'[2] To a twelfth-century monk a senior abbot visiting the spiritual superiors of a group of dependencies on the cluniac model would have been intelligible, whereas monastic *laurae* may have been unknown: but to twist the words into that sense, since the monasteries were in different provinces, he had to render the 1,500 *dextrae*, approximately three-quarters of a mile, not as the radius of a monastic enclosure, but as an arduous day's journey for a man on a donkey, which is absurd. The writer seems also to have misinterpreted the account of the daily *oblatio*, or offering of the Mass, that was made by Evroul with the aid of a priest.[3] His account is intelligible only if we take 'oblation' in the sense of offerings of the faithful which were blessed by the monk-priest – an interpretation that would have been quite natural at a time when the right of monks to receive the offerings of the altar was a

[1] Alençon, MS 11, fols 143–6.
[2] *Ibid.* 'Erat autem viro Domini maxima sollicitudo erga habitationem pastorum illorum quos subrogaverat circum circa monasteriis a se constructis ut pro oportuna necessitate cure illorum mille quingentas dextras itineris, conficientes stadia sex insuper et passus viginti, frequenter in unius diei labore, asini aut muli evectione sustentatus, circuiret.'
[3] *Ibid.* 'Oblationes etiam per singulos dies sacerdotibus sacrandas offerebat, et diebus dominicis omnibus tres jubebat se presente missas celebrari, in quibus solitas offerebat oblationes.'

burning question. Elsewhere the author slips in a word or two which show that he assumed an institutional framework quite unlike that of Evroul's own day: the bishop's rôle is enlarged, and in the account of the saint's funeral the author states that the monks waited three days for the coming of the bishop as well as a great community of the faithful.[1] This is less, I think, deliberate distortion than a failure to appreciate that the eighth century was unlike the twelfth.

Apart from the evidence of the earliest *Vita*, distorted in the later and better-known versions, there are two other sources for the early history of the monastery. One is the evidence collected by Orderic from the traditions of old men and the surviving remains of the earlier church; he was the first to write down these popular stories, and incorporate them in the legend. Orderic was a more thorough and conscious historian than the author of the second *A Vita*. He was misled as to date by the *Annals of St Evroul*,[2] which placed the death of Evroul in the time of king Childebert II, not Childebert III, and he filled in the chronological background so thoroughly on this assumption[3] that until nineteenth-century historians began to question the dating[4] the saint's life was invariably placed over a hundred years too soon. And the collection of legends and miracles that he added to the *B Vita* was of uneven value. But among them are some that deserve close examination.

Orderic contributes the suggestion that Evroul first learnt monastic discipline, before seeking a hermitage in the wilderness, in the abbey of Deux-Jumeaux;[5] and what he tells of the origin of this abbey has been confirmed by recent excavations.[6] Also he states that a nunnery was founded by the wife of king Childebert on the hill just across the valley from Evroul's church of St Peter, and that this became the church of Notre-Dame-du-Bois. Its cemetery became a burial ground for persons of rank as well as monks because the ground in the valley was too marshy for burials, and he noted that ancient tombs were there in his day.[7] Topography supports this; and, though there are now no visible sarchophagi, Orderic made a similar statement about the church of St Céneri-le-Gérei,[8] where carolingian sarcophagi can still be seen, built into the foundations of the church. Whilst an early columbanian monastery, where each altar was in a separate building, might have

---

[1] *Ibid*, fol 145 v.　　　　[2] Ord Vit, *Hist Eccl*, v, p 147.
[3] *Ibid*, III, pp 65–7, 81.
[4] The date was first questioned by Abbé J.-B.-N. Blin, *Vies des saints du diocèse de Séez* (Laigle 1873) pp 535–7.
[5] Ord Vit, *Hist Eccl*, III, pp 68–71.　　　[6] *DHGE*, XVI, p 219.
[7] Ord Vit, *Hist Eccl*, III, pp 68–71.　　　[8] *Ibid*, pp 298–9.

included two churches as far apart as St Peter's and Notre-Dame-du-Bois,[1] one has only to recall the double monasteries so numerous in seventh-century Gaul,[2] or the relationship between Jumièges and Pavilly[3] to recognise the plausibility of this tradition. Even one of the most improbable of the legends in Orderic's collection[4] seems to contain a grain of truth. It describes how, when the saint was living for three years in retreat with one attendant monk in a cave some distance from the rest of the community, a devil sowed discord among the brethren. This account of the setting of the legend is surely a plausible piece of further evidence for the eremitical mode of life favoured by Evroul, even though the further details of how the saint disposed of the devil by incinerating him in the oven (*four*) that was believed to have given its name to Echauffour deserved the summary dismissal accorded to it by Mabillon.

Since the *B Vita* contains few details of monastic customs and observance, Orderic was unable to describe this side of life in the early monastery. Elsewhere when he had occasion to look at early monasticism in Gaul, he certainly gave currency to the belief that the Benedictine Rule came to Gaul when Benedict's pupil, St Maur, founded the abbey of Glanfeuil before the middle of the sixth century.[5] He had at the same time a great respect for St Columbanus and his Rule, and in his treatise on the new monastic orders he commented on the varieties of observance in earlier centuries; but he believed that the combination of the Benedictine Rule with some columbanian practices came into being almost in the lifetime of Columbanus.[6] To him, therefore, the Benedictine Rule had a prominence in the Frankish kingdom at an earlier date than modern research would allow. His assumptions may explain his handling of the one piece of documentary evidence from the Frankish period.

This brings me to the last piece of evidence: the diploma of Charles the Simple of the year 900, addressed to the *canonici* of St Evroul.[7] It confirms property in the Hiémois and Maine, which is reserved for the use of these *canonici*; and forbids the abbot, who was almost certainly a lay abbot and probably Hugh count of the Hiémois, to appropriate

[1] Cf 'Vita Wandregisili abbatis Fontanellensis', *MGH SRM*, IV, pp 19–20.
[2] W. Levison, *England and the Continent in the Eighth Century* (Oxford 1946) pp 22–3.
[3] *Jumièges, Congrès Scientifique du XIIIe centenaire* (Rouen 1955) I, pp 33–8.
[4] Ord Vit, *Hist Eccl*, III, pp 71–3
[5] *Ibid*, III, p 438   [6] *Ibid*, III, pp 451–2.
[7] *Recueil des actes de Charles III le Simple, roi de France*, ed Philippe Lauer (Paris 1949) pp 74–6.

anything or give it away as a benefice. Whatever these *canonici* may have been at this date, they were certainly not benedictine monks; yet Orderic in his history of the monastery never speaks of anything but *monachi*. Le Prévost felt so strongly that Orderic was incapable of guile as to suggest that he never saw the diploma, and that his superiors had withheld it from him because of its content.[1] In fact this hypothesis is quite untenable, because the deed is copied into one of the volumes from the library of St Evroul in Orderic's own hand, with a note explaining that Robert of Grandmesnil, the second abbot, had found it at Orleans and had a copy made as a record of the great fame the saint had formerly enjoyed among the Franks.[2] The truth may perhaps be that this fame and no more is exactly what the document conveyed to the eleventh-century monks. The language of the diploma was unfamiliar, the names of the properties listed had changed so much that few can have known where they were since there was never any attempt to reconstitute the old patrimony. It might well be wrong to assume that the term *canonici* caused any embarrassment to Orderic. His preconception of a community of monks may have been so strong that the possible significance of the term simply never registered in his mind. It is not easy even now to be sure what the term *canonici* meant at this date. The subject is too complicated for discussion here; but recent research on the early communities at Mont-Saint-Michel suggests the possibility that it might sometimes have been applied to monks following a columbanian, or mixed rule.[3] Whilst the character of the community at St Evroul may have changed, monks giving way to secular canons, this is not the only possible explanation.

Indeed, putting together the evidence of the best text of the *A Vita*, of popular tradition, and of the more sophisticated historical tradition stemming from the time of Orderic, the picture that emerges is of a community in some ways like that envisaged by Dom Jacques Hourlier at Mont-Saint-Michel before the tenth century: at first a very subtle institutional framework, with a system of *laurae* of the type familiar in the east and certainly also existing in the west; later a tighter structure, but still a mixed rather than a purely benedictine form of observance; finally possibly, though not certainly, a community of secular canons. The associated nunnery is paralleled at Jumièges and elsewhere: how

[1] Ord Vit, *Hist Eccl*, III, p 102, n 1.
[2] Alençon, Bibliothèque municipale, MS 14, fols 38r-38v.
[3] Dom Jacques Hourlier, 'Le Mont-Saint-Michel avant 966', in *Millénaire Monastique du Mont-Saint-Michel*, I (Paris 1966) pp 19-28.

long it survived we do not know. Certainly the institution showed a toughness and adaptability that enabled a community of some kind to survive and prosper – as far as the evidence goes – from the late seventh until the mid-tenth century, when the monastery was destroyed during the civil wars. Its existence as a benedictine abbey probably began only with its refoundation in 1050.[1]

[1] Ord Vit, *Hist Eccl*, III, pp 96–7.

VIR DEI:
SECULAR SANCTITY IN THE
EARLY TENTH CENTURY

by DEREK BAKER

S recent anniversary studies have emphasised,[1] the *vir Dei*, the man of God, has been a christian type since the time of St Antony, and whatever pre-christian elements were embodied in the Athanasian picture the *Vita Antonii*[2] possessed a christian coherence and completeness which made of it the proto-type for a whole range of literature in late antiquity and the Middle Ages. In hagiography the Antonine sequence of early life, crisis and conversion, probation and temptation, privation and renunciation, miraculous power, knowledge and authority, is, in its essentials, repeated *ad nauseam*. Martin, Guthlac, Odo, Dunstan, Bernard are all, whatever their individual differences, forced into the same procrustean biographical mould: each is clearly qualified, and named, as *vir Dei*, and each exemplifies the same – and at times the pre-eminent – christian vocation. Yet if the insight provided by such literature into the mind of medieval man is instructive about his society and social organisation, and illuminating about his ideal aspirations, the literary convention itself is always limiting, and frequently misleading. As Professor Momigliano has said, 'biography was never quite a part of historiography',[3] and one might add that hagiography is not quite biography.

Martin, Guthlac, Odo, Dunstan, Bernard were all men who abandoned their position in secular society in order to adopt a 'regular' life. With each of them, as their biographies record, conversion was preceded by a personal crisis, but in no case is this crisis more than touched on, given more than superficial, conventional treatment: there is no personal immediacy in these accounts.[4] It may be that it is unreasonable

---

[1] *Antonius Magnus Eremita*, ed B. Steidle, *SA*, XXXVIII (1956) particularly pp 148–200, 229–47. See also Derek Baker, 'St Antony and Biblical Precedents for the Monastic Vocation', *Ampleforth Journal*, LXXVI, I (York 1971) pp 6–11.

[2] St Athanasius, *The Life of Saint Antony*, trans R. T. Meyer, *ACW*, X (1950).

[3] Above, p 4.

[4] The lack of information about the conversion of St Evroul in the best life of the saint

to expect more, that it is necessary to wait for that short-lived age of 'humanism' in the twelfth century[1] for the personal expression of feelings like those of Newman eight centuries later. It is probable that conventional platitudes, as in the case of Antony himself, were all that could be expected of biographers, educated to other purposes, through-out most of the medieval period.[2] Whatever the cause, however, the limitation is serious. If Odo, Dunstan, Bernard seem similar as saints, as *men* they were clearly very different, and yet we have no indication of their personal beliefs and observance, their individual attitudes towards their faith and its requirements, before their moments of crisis. What did they believe? How did they worship? What were the conventions of the faith they professed, and how did these impinge on their lives while they were still of the world? Such questions need to be asked, and answered, not only for a Dunstan or a Bernard, but for the classes from which they stemmed, and which they represent, and as so often in the medieval period answers are hard to come by. Saints' lives are concerned primarily with the period after conversion to the religious – and usually regular – life, and the apprentice saint, the pious layman, while cer-tainly existing, is very seldom chronicled before the thirteenth century,[3] and seldom then. Nor is there much alternative evidence. Mention of witchcraft in Anglo-Saxon law codes and charters;[4] condemnation of Roman New Year revelry in the letters of Boniface,[5] comments on

may be taken as representative of the whole class of literature. The biographer 'has little to say of Evroul's early life, except that he came from Bayeux, was of noble birth and was brought up in the court of an unnamed Frankish king; and that in time he renounced the world, placed his wife in a nunnery, and received the tonsure'. See above, p. 33.

[1] See D. Knowles, 'The Humanism of the Twelfth Century', repr in *The Historian and Character*, ed C. N. L. Brooke and G. Constable (Cambridge 1963) pp 16–30.

[2] The biographer 'had little concern with the portrayal of individual character, though sometimes indeed a small modification or omission in words borrowed from an earlier source will, as it were accidentally, throw light on a personal idiosyncrasy on which it was no part of the biographer's duty to insist', R. W. Southern, *St Anselm and His Biographer* (Cambridge 1963) p 320. For the development of medieval biographical writing see the whole of this section. See also A. Stacpoole's comments on Eadmer – 'the first man of letters in the Middle Ages to achieve what we would now judge to be a sufficient understanding of the inner motivation of his subject for us to call his study a biography' – in his review of *Memorials of Saint Anselm*, ed R. W. Southern and F. S. S. Schmitt (London 1969) in *Downside Review*, LXXXVIII, no 291 (April 1970) pp 160–80.   [3] For example, Joinville's *Life of St Louis*.

[4] See *The Laws of Alfred*, Intro 30; *The Laws of Athelstan issued at Grately* (II Athelstan) 6; *Anglo-Saxon Charters*, ed A. J. Robertson (Cambridge 1939) no 37.

[5] See *Die Briefe des heiligen Bonifatius und Lullus*, ed M. Tangl, MGH, *Epistolae Selectae*, I (Berlin 1916, 2 ed 1955) no 50. See also Derek Baker, 'Sowing the Seeds of Faith: Theory and Practice in the Mission Field', in *Miscellanae Historiae Ecclesiasticae*, III, ed Derek Baker (Louvain 1970) pp 92–106.

soothsayers in Adam of Bremen's history[1] may be of value in demon-
strating the survival of pagan attitudes and customs into a nominally
christian world,[2] but they are as of little use in delineating the attitudes
and assumptions of ordinary, popular belief as noble patronage of
monasteries and churches, so often a combination of family *pietas*,
worldly business sense and spiritual fire insurance. How christian was
William of Aquitaine when he founded Cluny? What did their religion
mean to the barons and lesser men who founded and endowed the
mushroom monasticism of Stephen's reign?

   These are questions which can never be fully answered without the
writings of the men themselves, or of their close associates. Even in the
thirteenth and fourteenth centuries the polemics of Langland, poems of
protest and social comment, the speculations of mystics do no more
than colour different areas of the overall picture.[3] There is no Jocelyn
for a secular Samson, no baron as articulate as an Ailred to speak for
himself. Frustrating as the problem is as a whole, however, it is not
entirely intractable. In his discussion of Guibert of Nogent's *On the
Relics of the Saints*[4] Professor Morris has illuminated one aspect of
popular piety, and in showing how all classes of medieval society, with
very few exceptions, participated in it has demonstrated the common
credulity and lack of critical sense which underlay the observance of
literate and illiterate alike. Nor is Guibert of Nogent the only author to
be of assistance here. From an earlier century there survives one saint's
life which is of considerable value and interest in this context – the *Life
of St Gerald of Aurillac* by Odo, second abbot of Cluny.[5]

   Gerald of Aurillac was born in *c* 855[6] and died in *c* 909.[7] Little is
known of his ancestry, but he was certainly nobly born,[8] and may have
been directly related to the carolingian house.[9] On his father's death he

1 Adam of Bremen, *History of the Archbishops of Hamburg–Bremen*, trans F. J. Tschan,
   Columbia Records of Civilization, LIII (New York 1959) III, 39, pp 146–7.
2 For a later period the instances quoted by D. M. Owen are relevant, below, pp 141–2.
3 See particularly W. A. Pantin, *The English Church in the Fourteenth Century* (Cambridge
   1955).   4 Below, pp 55–60.
5 Odo of Cluny, *Life of St Gerald of Aurillac, PL*, CXXXIII (1881) cols 639–710, trans
   [G.] Sitwell, in [*St Odo of Cluny*] (London 1958) pp 90–180. The Life survives in two
   versions, one much shorter than the other. For discussion of these two versions of the
   text see A. Poncelet, 'La plus ancienne Vie de S. Géraud', *An Bol*, XIV (1895) pp 89–103.
6 Sitwell, p 94, n 2.
7 Probably on Friday 13 October, see Sitwell, p 165, n 2.
8 Sitwell, I, 1, pp 94–5. Odo named Caesarius of Arles amongst his ancestors, and commented, 'He was so illustrious by the nobility of his birth that among the families of
   Gaul his lineage is outstanding both for its possessions and the excellence of its life',
   ibid, p 95.   9 Mabillon is the sole authority for this claim, see Sitwell, p 94, n 2.

succeeded to wide estates and numerous dependants,[1] and to large responsibilities: 'After the death of his parents, when he attained full power over his property...His power of ruling increased...He was compelled to be occupied in administering and watching over things which...came to him by hereditary right...his household and dependants demanded that he should break into his repose and give himself to the service of others.'[2] Throughout Odo's account he can be seen discharging the duties of a count, and, though it is not clear when he acquired it, he came to hold the title of count.[3] He was, in addition, a crown vassal, and it is possible that his comital title derived directly from this relationship, for when 'Duke William of Aquitaine...urged Gerald not by threats but by entreaties to leave the king's service and commend himself to him...Gerald would not agree since he had only recently assumed the title of Count.'[4] Whatever the truth about this, however, the incident demonstrates Gerald's local influence, and the value of his support both to the king and duke.[5]

Physically Gerald was athletic[6] and, though this is underplayed by his biographer, plainly a good soldier.[7] Temperamentally, however, he seems to have preferred letters to the lance, and here circumstances intervened to assist his inclination:

By the grace of divine providence he applied himself to the study of letters, but by the will of his parents only to the extent of going through his psalter; after that he was instructed in the worldly exercises customary for the sons of the nobility; to ride to hounds, become an archer, learn to fly falcons and hawks in the proper manner. But lest, given to useless pursuits, the time suitable for learning letters should pass without profit the divine will ordained that he should be a long time sick, though with such a sickness that he should be

---

[1] Sitwell, I, 1, p 94. [2] *Ibid*, I, 6, pp 98–9.

[3] The account of his succession to his lands and responsibilities (see above, n 1) makes no mention of the title of count, and later in the life it is remarked that Gerald 'had only recently assumed the title of Count': Sitwell, I, 32, p 122. The latin – 'favore comitis nuper usurpato' – could bear a stronger translation. As Sitwell points out there was no count of Aurillac before or after him. [4] Sitwell, I, 32, p 122.

[5] It is not absolutely clear which king was Gerald's lord. William of Aquitaine succeeded his father Bernard of Auvergne as duke in 888, and the early years of his rule were marked by considerable confusion in western Francia. In 887 the emperor Charles the Fat had died, and Odo, count of Paris, had been elected to succeed him as king in the west. The choice was not unanimous, however, and in 893 the young Charles the Simple was brought back from England by Odo's opponents. William of Aquitaine's opposition to Odo is well-known (see Sitwell, p 6, n 1), and in view of the continuing friendship between Gerald and William it is more likely that Gerald was the vassal of Charles the Simple than of Odo. See also Mabillon's view, *PL*, cxxxiii (1880) col 707.

[6] Sitwell, I, 5, p 97. [7] *Ibid*, I, 5, p 98, see also below.

withdrawn from worldly pursuits but not hindered in his application to learning. And for a long time he was covered with small pimples that it was not thought that he could be cured. For this reason his father and mother decided that he should be put more closely to the study of letters, so that if he should prove unsuited for worldly pursuits he might be fitted for the ecclesiastical state. So it came about that he not only learnt the chant, but also learnt something of grammar.[1]

Elsewhere we are told that 'he learnt almost the whole series of the Scriptures, and surpassed many clerical smatterers in his knowledge of it'.[2]

For all his scriptural expertise, and in spite of his own inclinations, Gerald did not, however, abandon his secular inheritance and responsibilities and enter the church. 'He could scarcely bear to leave the inner solitude of his heart, and he returned to it as soon as he could', but nonetheless he 'exerted himself to repress the insolence of the violent, taking care in the first place to promise peace and most easy reconciliation to his enemies'.[3] When, at a later stage in his life, he did decide to renounce the world, declaring that 'he was weary of the life he was leading,...desired to enter religion, to go to Rome, and to make over his property by will to the blessed Peter, Prince of the Apostles',[4] it was the church which prevented him. His friend Gausbert, bishop of Rodez,[5] whom he consulted, 'finally recommended that for the sake of the general welfare he should continue to wear secular dress, but that he should dedicate the property to the blessed Peter as he wished'.[6] Gerald complied, but as a layman he approached as nearly as he could to his ideal – and closer than many of his contemporaries who called themselves monks.[7] He was tonsured, but wore a cap and swore his chamberlains to secrecy so that none might know. 'He surrounded himself with the better type of men and with clerics of good name, with whom, whether at home or abroad, he performed the divine office either in common or privately.'[8] He recited the psalter daily; was assiduous in his attendance at mass, gave alms, and fed the poor. At his table 'the talk was of necessary or virtuous subjects, or indeed of religious ones' and 'there was always reading for some time to begin with, but for the sake of the seculars present he used to suspend the reading at intervals

[1] *Ibid*, I, 4, p 97. [2] *Ibid*, I, 5, p 98.
[3] *Ibid*, I, 6, p 98; I, 8, p 99. [4] *Ibid*, II, 2, p 134.
[5] Bishop *c* 900–9. [6] Sitwell, II, 2, p 134.
[7] For example, the *canonici* and abbot of St Evroul mentioned in Charles the Simple's diploma of 900, see above, pp 38–9. See Odo's comments, Sitwell, II, preface, p 152.
[8] Sitwell, I, 11, p 104.

and ask the clerics what had been said in it – those whom he knew to be able to reply'.[1]

Sober and austere himself, he demanded sobriety of his entourage, and maintained an exaggerated personal purity.[2] Nor was his zeal confined to his domestic life. He had a particular veneration for Rome, going on pilgrimage there every second year, and was renowned both as pilgrim and collector of relics, 'generous in the price he paid', all along the route. He established, after much difficulty, a monastery on his lands at Aurillac, though neither its spiritual nor its material foundations would seem to have been very secure.[3] Before his death miracles were associated with him.[4]

All in all he was a remarkable man, and, as Odo said of him, 'If... one considers his desire he was true to the monastic profession through his devotion to Christ. And it is indeed high praise for a man in secular dress to keep the rule of religious.'[5]

Here, it might seem, we have that rarity in the Middle Ages: a contemporary picture of the pious layman – 'the man of God, Gerald', who yet remained a man of the world, not of the church. Yet if the picture which Odo gives, and which it was his purpose to give, is looked at more closely it becomes curiously unsatisfactory, for what are we left with but the tonsured layman, the monk *manqué*? It is difficult to reconcile Odo's Gerald with the anarchic, feudal world in which he lived and, apparently, flourished, and it is clear, even from Odo, that there was much more to Gerald than the piety and sanctity which he set out to record. Not, indeed that we have any way of checking or supplementing Odo's account, for his brief life of Gerald is our only source for the saint's career.[6] We are, therefore, dependent for our knowledge of Gerald on a second-hand account produced by a man who never knew him[7] some thirty years after the saint's death.

Odo wrote at the request of his friends Aymo, abbot of St Martial at Limoges[8] and his brother Turpio, bishop of Limoges, who had ordained Odo priest, and received the dedication of Odo's *Collations*. The pre-

---

[1] *Ibid*, I, 15, p 109.
[2] See Sitwell, I, 9, pp 101–3; I, 34, pp 123–4.
[3] *Ibid*, II, 4–8, pp 136–40; III, 1, p 162; III, 3, pp 163–4. The difficulties encountered by Gerald in all aspects of his monastic foundation is one of the clearest extant indications of the state of contemporary society, ecclesiastical institutions and spiritual standards.
[4] See Sitwell, II, 10–13, pp 141–3.   [5] *Ibid*, II, 16, p 145.
[6] For Gerald's will, and an occasional reference to Gerald in a tenth-century chronicle of Aurillac, see the references given by Sitwell, p 136, nn 1, 2.
[7] See Odo's preface, Sitwell, pp 91–3.
[8] 936–42.

face to Odo's Life of Gerald plunges us at once into a world which, for another century, Guibert of Nogent has described so well – a world of false saints and discreditable cults where the loyalty of friends was sorely tried by the unscrupulous promoters of new, and profitable, centres of pilgrimage and veneration:[1]

Many doubt whether the things that are said about the blessed Gerald are true, and some think that they are not true, but fantastic. Others, as though seeking excuses for their own sins, extol him indiscreetly, saying that Gerald was powerful and rich and lived well, and is certainly a saint. They strive indeed to excuse their luxurious lives by his example. It seemed to me therefore that I ought to reply a little to these according to my ability. For I too, formerly, hearing the fame of his miracles, was nevertheless in doubt, and for this reason chiefly, that stories get about here and there, through I know not what channels, and are then gradually discredited as empty.[2]

Odo, however, while on a visit to Tulle, some fifty miles from Aurillac, took advantage of the occasion to visit Gerald's tomb; consult those who had known him, and investigate his miracles. He concluded, 'I could no longer doubt of his sanctity...as in the days of Noe, a man of God was found who lived according to the law.'[3] Odo's inquiry was searching and thorough: 'I investigated his behaviour and the quality of his life in detail. Now with the others, now alone, I carefully investigated what each one said and whether they agreed, silently pondering if his life was one in which miracles were fitting.'[4] From Odo's account it is clear, on the one hand, that miracles were regarded as a prerequisite to sanctity, and on the other that Gerald's were perhaps a little threadbare, rather common-place. At the beginning of Book II Odo declares that 'those who rashly dispute about Gerald's merits may satisfy themselves if they will consider the nature of his life', and though he continued 'let them therefore be satisfied by the testimony of the miracles which Christ deigned to work through him both in his lifetime and after his death', he returned once more to Gerald's actual life: Gerald was a confessor through resisting vice and doing good, and he could

all the more truly be called a confessor as he confessed God by more righteous deeds. What do those who, like the Jews, seek signs, do about John the Baptist, who is not reported to have worked any miracle after his nativity? With regard to this man, although miracles are by no means absent I say one thing,

---

[1] For Professor Morris's discussion of Guibert of Nogent's *On the relics of the saints* see below, pp 55–60, particularly p 57. See also the comments on false relics in D. Bethell, 'The making of a twelfth-century relic collection', below, pp 71–2.
[2] Sitwell, preface, p 91. [3] *Ibid*, pp 91–2. [4] *Ibid*, p 91.

that as he did not put his hope in money or riches, he performed, as it is written, wonderful things in his life.[1]

Again, at the end of Book II, Odo returned to the same theme:

Let this suffice for his miracles, and it may satisfy those who assess the glory of a saint not from the amount of his good works, but from the number of the signs which he performed. To such as these perhaps his sanctity would have seemed less, if they had heard nothing about the miracles which he did in his lifetime...But since both are to be found in him, namely a holy justice and the glorification of miracles, they know him with a more secure and lively devotion. If he had happened to have the spirit of prophecy no one, I think, would have denied that he was a saint. But he accomplished more than this, because he conquered avarice...Do not look for any great miracle in Gerald, therefore, because this is he who did not put his hope in money or in treasures...There is much evidence for the wonderful things which Gerald did. For it is well known that he preserved those things which were given him by his parents and by kings...that he increased his property without injuring anyone,... that he was exalted in power, but nevertheless remained poor in spirit.[2]

Odo had put his trust 'in the words of witnesses, who have recorded not many of the miracles, which ordinary men think of great moment, but rather a disciplined way of life, and not a few works of mercy pleasing to God'.[3] Here, then, is an obscure local cult,[4] like so many others, seeking recognition and respectability from an eminent apologist and, for once, gaining it. Without such recognition, without Odo's endorsement, Gerald himself would have been virtually unknown, his piety and excellence of life, clearly exceptional in a layman of that disturbed time, unacknowledged.

Gerald was not exceptional, however, simply in the spiritual qualities which he displayed: he was remarkable in combining them with high secular office, and maintaining them in spite of his wordly commitments. His position in the world is emphasised by Odo's repeated rebukes to 'those who find satisfaction in remarking that Gerald was both a man of great position and holy',[5] and it is worth stressing, in particular, how difficult it was to be both count and royal vassal in Aquitaine in the second half of the ninth century. William the Pious,

[1] *Ibid*, II, preface, pp 132–3.   [2] *Ibid*, II, 34, pp 159–60.   [3] *Ibid*, preface, p 93
[4] See the comments on the diffusion of Gerald's cult and reputation in Sitwell, IV, 12 p 180 and p 180, n 1. There is, however, no precise indication when the cult became established, or diffused, and it seems more likely that this occurred after Odo's endorsement of it than before.
[5] Sitwell, II, preface, p 132. See also Odo's preface, Sitwell, p 91.

duke of Aquitaine from 888 to 918, showed extreme hostility to Odo of
Paris, in 893 spitting a captured royal vassal on his spear, but whoever
the king, the erosion of his power was rapid, 'for, the state being in a
most disturbed condition, the marquises in their insolence had sub-
jected the royal vassals to themselves'.[1] Leaving aside the studied piety
of his later years, William of Aquitaine, in whose household Odo had
spent his adolescence, is a good example of the successful magnate of this
ruthless period. His father, Bernard of Auvergne, had established the
family's fortunes in Aquitaine, and William showed himself an able and
worthy successor. Yet when William sought Gerald as his own vassal
Gerald was able to refuse and still retain the duke's friendship,[2] being
found in close and influential association with him on campaign.[3]
Later in Odo's account there is a similar rejection by Gerald of count
Ademarus's attempt to secure his allegiance.[4] Clearly Gerald was a man
'of great position',[5] and great strength of character.

The impression of strength which emerges from these encounters is
confirmed by Odo's references elsewhere to Gerald's military exploits.
Reluctant though Odo is to admit that Gerald was more than a competent soldier, and assiduously as he ascribes Gerald's successes to
divine intervention, he cannot escape the fact that Gerald is always
successful in combat. It may be true that Gerald seldom waged war on
his own initiative, and that 'when the unavoidable necessity of fighting
lay on him he commanded his men with imperious tones to fight with
the backs of their swords, and with their spears reversed'. This, however,
as Odo rightly says,

would have seemed ridiculous to the enemy if Gerald, strengthened by divine
power, had not been invincible to them. And it would have seemed useless to
his own men, if they had not learnt by experience that Gerald...was always
invincible. When therefore they saw that he triumphed by a new kind of
fighting which was mingled with piety, they changed their scorn to admiration, and sure of victory they readily fulfilled his commands. For it was a
thing unheard of that he or the soldiers who fought under him were not
victorious.[6]

[1] *Ibid*, I, 32, p 121.
[2] Odo links this acceptance by William of Gerald's refusal with Bernard of Auvergne's
earlier commendation (*commendavit*) of the young William to Gerald. Quite what was
involved in the relationship between Gerald and William it is impossible to say without
precise knowledge of the social relationship between Bernard and Gerald, and between
the two families. Sitwell, I, 32, p 122.
[3] Sitwell, I, 33, p 122; I, 35, p 124.   [4] *Ibid*, I, 35–6, pp 124–6.
[5] *Ibid*, II, preface, p 132.   [6] *Ibid*, I, 8, p 100.

The fact of the matter is that, moralise as he might, Odo cannot entirely cloak his subject's warrior qualities: Odo is describing a highly successful feudal lord in a highly turbulent age.

To his secular lordship Gerald added the office of count. As count he was as much occupied with the administration of justice as with war, and here again he shows himself very much a man of his times. Odo may stress Gerald's concern for the protection of the weak and poor, and his insistence on justice for all in equal measure – and there is no reason why we should doubt these characteristics – but what emerges, unintentionally, from the narrative is the essentially personal nature of justice at this time, and just how arbitrary, how dependent on personal caprice, it could be. The stories of Gerald contriving the escape from prison of a man who had blinded a priest,[1] and allowing the escape of two criminals, presented to him 'accused of a great crime',[2] may have been edifying to Odo and his audience: to us they are likely to appear simply as unaccountable and arbitrary acts of will, against all justice. The character of Gerald's justice is, however, most clearly demonstrated in another incident recorded by Odo:

Robbers had taken possession of a certain wood, and plundered and murdered both passers-by and those who lived in the vicinity. Gerald, hearing of this, immediately gave orders for them to be captured. It happened, however, that a certain countryman had been driven by fear to join them. But the soldiers who captured them, fearing that Gerald would either release them, or blame them for showing him the prisoners unpunished, forthwith put the eyes out of all of them. And so it came about that this countryman was blinded.[3]

Odo is quick to emphasise Gerald's distress at this occurrence, and tells us that the unfortunate countryman ultimately received one hundred shillings from the count. The real interest of the passage, however, lies not in Gerald's edifying reaction, but in the attitude of Gerald's soldiers. They were not clear what Gerald wanted, were uncertain what his attitude would be to the prisoners, and to them, and were afraid and unsure of their own treatment at his hands. Against this background, and in this atmosphere of fear and uncertainty, they blinded their prisoners.

Gerald was plainly a man who inspired fear, and not simply in the processes of government or in his administration of justice. In discussing miracles performed during Gerald's lifetime Odo remarks that Gerald was reluctant to attempt healing, and disturbed that petitioners should

[1] *Ibid*, I, 19, pp 112–13.   [2] *Ibid*, I, 20, pp 113–14.   [3] *Ibid*, 18, p 112.

seek miraculous cures at his hands or through his possessions. When he discovered that the water in which he washed his hands was being used to effect cures

> he was moved to violent threats that no-one should do such a thing again, saying that if a serf did it he should be maimed, if a free man he should be reduced to servitude...his people could not make light of the mutilation which he threatened, knowing that he would not yield in the matter of punishment.[1]

Gerald had this reputation for unyielding tenacity in all aspects of life – 'whatever he said he would do he carried out unhesitatingly'[2] – and he had a sharp tongue – 'when he spoke rebukingly his words seemed like goads and were feared more than mere words'.[3] Clearly Gerald was a man of considerable presence. He was certainly loved and respected: equally certainly he was feared. When Odo, speaking of Gerald's practice of having passages of scripture read while he was at table, remarks that 'while he was listening to reading no-one easily presumed to break in on him for any reason, for according to the saying of Job he was terrible to those beneath him, and the light of his countenance fell not on the earth',[4] it is not difficult to evoke the atmosphere which Gerald created amongst his household and dependants.

Where then do we stand with this pious layman, this 'man of God' of the late carolingian age? That 'those who set themselves a higher standard than the ordinary looked to the monasteries for their examples', and that 'from their liturgical experiments and experiences there grew up a body of devotional practices which became part of the inheritance of every pious layman' is, as Professor Southern has emphasised,[5] axiomatic for the period. There can be little doubt, whatever the exaggeration and bias of Odo and his informants, and despite the fact that Gerald's death is almost coincident with Cluny's foundation,[6] that this was true for Gerald of Aurillac. It is, of course, this side of Gerald's life and character which is stressed by Odo in an account which is wholly of the mainstream of conventional medieval hagiography. Yet the consequences of writing in this way of a layman are revealing. Gerald may be a tenth-century Roger de Coverley – pious, formally religious, concerned for justice, considerate to his serfs and dependants beyond the

---

[1] *Ibid*, II, 11–12, pp 142–3; see also II, 13, p 143.
[2] *Ibid*, I, 12, p 106.   [3] *Ibid*, II, 14, p 144.
[4] *Ibid*.
[5] *The Making of the Middle Ages* (London 1953) p 158.
[6] Cluny was founded on 2 September 909; Gerald died on Friday 13 October 909.

level of his time – but he is above all, and of necessity, strong, able, successful in war, arbitrary, capable of inspiring fear as well as respect, and these were qualities which entered as much into his religious observance as into his secular life. In this he was no different in type, though far removed in quality, from his contemporaries. God's word was to be accepted by His vassals, like Gerald's by his men, without question: His precepts were known through custom, and learnt by rote, rather than intelligently understood; He demanded a ritual customary service and obedience, and disobedience was punished by divine retribution as bloody as that of any contemporary feudal judgement. God could be knelt to in symbolic serfdom – as by Gerald himself at the tombs of the apostles in Rome[1] – or his favour bought like that of any secular judge by what approximates to spiritual bribes – a Cluny for a lifetime of war and oppression. God was lord in a way which any of Gerald's feudal contemporaries could have understood.

Gerald's personal worship and observance is formal and ritualistic – and compulsory for those with him. When he decided, having missed mass at home in order to preside in court on Sunday, and found nowhere else to hear it, to recite the psalter 'lest we should seem to have spent the holy day quite in vain',[2] his attendants and soldiers had no option but to join him. For the layman, even a layman as exceptional as Gerald, observance was limited and primitive – as primitive, as C. H. Talbot emphasised in his unpublished lectures, as, in its way, the observance at Cluny under Odo – and it was underlaid, as a number of speakers have stressed,[3] by a credulity and superstition common to all classes in society. Above all, and for all Odo's references to the love which Gerald inspired, there is in Gerald's piety and austerity no real human warmth. For such qualities one must wait two centuries, for the sympathy and understanding of an Ailred, or the visions and counsel of the cistercian lay-brother Sinnulphus – *homo simplex et illiteratus* – moving a Yorkshire landowner, and future cistercian abbot, to tears as they talked familiarly together.[4]

Yet, however closely Gerald is related to the temper and conventions

---

[1] 'He made it a rule to go every second year to their tombs [St Peter and Paul] as a serf with ten shillings hung round his neck that he might pay them as a due to his lord', Sitwell, II, 17, pp 144–7.

[2] 'After saying this he went through the psalter from the beginning with them, singing no mortal song. And he made it now his custom to recite the psalter almost daily', Sitwell, I, 11, p 105.

[3] See, for example, the comments and conclusions of Momigliano and Morris.

[4] Hugh of Kirkstall, *Narratio de Fundatione Fontanis Monasterii*, ed J. R. Walbran, *The Memorials of Fountains Abbey*, I, Surtees Society, XLII (Newcastle 1862) pp 118–20.

of the limited and violent age in which he lived, he remains a remarkable figure in, and for, his period, and he is significant for the state of
secular piety in the early tenth century. Like every *vir Dei* he witnessed
a great example in the context of his times, but, as Odo repeatedly
stressed, it was not the extraordinary, the miraculous, which made him
remarkable, but the conduct and content of his everyday life:
'not many of the miracles which ordinary men think of great moment,
but, rather, a disciplined way of life, and not a few works of mercy
pleasing to God'.[1]

[1] Sitwell, preface, p 93.

A CRITIQUE OF POPULAR RELIGION: GUIBERT OF NOGENT ON *THE RELICS OF THE SAINTS*

by COLIN MORRIS

IN his fascinating paper,[1] Professor Momigliano drew to our attention the degree to which the aristocracy of the late Roman Empire accepted within its religious ethos beliefs and practices which we would be inclined to label as 'popular'. In doing so, he raised the recurrent problem of cultural diffusion. How far, in a given period, were intellectuals willing to accept as normative the piety of the simple faithful? Conversely, how far did the more critical attitudes of scholars influence popular devotion? These are permanent questions which we may ask of the history of the church, but perhaps the problem was never so acute as in the medieval church. Its intelligentsia (the humanists of the twelfth century, the philosophers of the thirteenth) had received a long and exacting formal education. The ordinary faithful, conversely, were illiterate, cut off, we might think, from the very sources of christian spirituality, for they could neither read the Scriptures nor follow the latin liturgy. Critics of the medieval church have been inclined to see two religions rather than one: a philosophical, indeed over-rational, religion of the intelligentsia, and a set of popular superstitions. A valuable piece of evidence in assessing the truth of this estimate is to be found in the first book of the treatise on *The Relics of the Saints*[2] written in about 1120 by Guibert abbot of Nogent. Its significance lies, not only in the useful information which it contains about popular practice, but in the fact that it was an attempt to assess it, made by one

[1] 'Popular religious beliefs and the late Roman historians', above, pp 1–18.
[2] *de Pignoribus sanctorum*, PL, CLVI, (1853) cols 607–80. The occasion for the treatise was the claim of Saint Médard to own one of Christ's teeth, and therefore much of it is concerned with the doctrine of the body of Christ, the first book alone providing a discussion of popular religion. It is surprising that Guibert has not been more used as a source for the spirituality of his time; he appears only once in the excellent study by J. Leclercq, F. Vandenbroucke and L. Bouyer, *La Spiritualité du Moyen Age* (Paris 1961). The work is discussed by B. Monod, *Le Moine Guibert et son temps* (Paris 1905) pp 282ff, where the author claims with considerable justice, that 'cet ouvrage n'a point de similaires dans toute la littérature théologique du moyen âge'.

of the more learned and attractive men of the time. Although Guibert made little direct impact on the history of the age, he was in close sympathy with many of the leaders of the twelfth-century Renaissance, and was a fine scholar in his own right.[1]

The relics of the saints had been venerated since the early days of the church, but in Guibert's lifetime a rapid extension of the cult was taking place, with the writing of the lives of many saints, solemn translations of relics, and an architecture designed to provide pilgrims with access to the church's relics and a covered space for solemn processions on holy days. Relics occupied a major place in the economic and political history of the time.[2] Guibert did not object in principle to their veneration, but he was profoundly uneasy about some of the features of the developing cult. For one thing, many of the alleged saints were not real ones. He gave a lively account of the way one such saint originated:

I have in fact seen, I regret to say, how a young man of low birth, the squire it was said of some knight or other, died on a Good Friday in a village near Beauvais...Because of the holy day on which he died, he began undeservedly to be revered as a saint. When the peasants, looking for something new, celebrated the fact, offerings and candles were suddenly carried to his grave from all the surrounding countryside. The next thing was that a tomb was erected, the place was covered over with a building, and bands of pilgrims came right from the ends of Brittany, but only peasants and not nobles. The most wise abbot and his monks saw these things and, won over by the gratifying frequency with which gifts were brought, they accepted that miracles, which had not really taken place, had been worked... What is a wise and modest man, who professes a resolution of sanctity, doing to encourage such things?[3]

Guibert contrasted the desire of the populace to revere such pseudo-saints with the reticence of the church in abstaining from making claims which could not be verified from reliable evidence.[4] He had himself

[1] He was taught for a time by Anselm of Bec, and knew personally Anselm of Laon. His ideas on interior religion are reminiscent of the new orders, among whom he particularly admired the Carthusians, while in other respects (such as his interest in autobiography and his concern with the doctrine of intention) he reminds one of his younger contemporary Abelard.

[2] For instance, the discovery of the Holy Lance encouraged the first Crusade at a critical moment in its fortunes (*Gesta Francorum*, ed R. Hill (London 1962) pp 59–60). The prosperity of northern France rested in part on the Lendit fair, a major commercial occasion which originated as a joint procession of the relics of Saint Denis and Notre Dame   [3] I, 2, col 621.
He instanced in particular the stringent tests which were applied before a martyr was recognised, and the Church's unwillingness to proclaim the bodily assumption of our Lady, in spite of its obvious appropriateness, because there was no solid evidence. This last hesitation was only overcome in our own century. I, 3, cols 623–4.

rejected several invitations to write the lives of saints in the distant past about whom no real information was available.[1]

Moreover, even if the saint is genuine, the relic might well not be. He has some hard words to say about the churches of Constantinople and Angéli, both of which claimed to have the head of John the Baptist, as if the saint had been two-headed.[2] One way in which such embarassing duplicates might arise is indicated by Guibert's story of Odo of Bayeux, who purchased the body of Saint Exupéry from Corbeil. The custodian of the relic supplied him instead with the body of a peasant of the same name together with a highly ambiguous guarantee, which satisfied bishop Odo while leaving Corbeil in possession of the genuine relic.[3]

Even granting that the veneration of relics was, as Guibert thought, of some secondary spiritual value, the cult had clearly become so corrupt that there was little to be said for it. Yet the established rulers of the church included men of good conscience and intelligence; why, then, did they allow or encourage the growth of these popular cults? The first reason given by Guibert is the discreditable one of desire for profit. All the features which he most disliked, the disentombing and breaking up of the bodies of the saints, the carrying them about and the use of settings of precious metals or ivory, were ultimately, he thought, designed to increase the flow of offerings.[4] Even men who were opposed to such practices were silenced by a sense of professional solidarity, as Guibert admits he himself was when a campaign manager once went too far in his presence:

A very famous church was organising a tour, in order to appeal through a speaker for funds to carry out repairs. When he had gone on at length about its relics, he produced a pyx and said (I was there myself at the time): 'I tell you', said he, 'that in this box is some bread which the Lord bit with his very own teeth. If you do not believe me, here is a champion (he meant me) whom you know is a thoroughly learned man, and who if necessary will be a witness to what I say'. I must admit I blushed to hear it, and had I not been afraid that, in the presence of his sponsors, it would have been taken as a rebuke to them rather than the speaker, I would have had to denounce him as a forger.[5]

---

[1] I, 3, col 624.   [2] *Ibid.*

[3] 'I swear to you that this is the body of Exupéry, but I will not swear to his sanctity, for many have that name who were in reality far from holiness.' I, 3, col 625.

[4] I, 4, col 627. Compare the views of Saint Bernard in his *Apologia ad Guillelmum* a few years later: 'Money is spent, that it may be multiplied. It is expended to increase it.' *PL*, CLXXXII (1854) col 915.

[5] I, 2, col 621.

Guibert, however, gives another reason for the tolerance of popular religion, besides greed and collusion. In the eyes of God, he believes, it is genuine faith which counts, and a prayer made through a false saint will still be of avail if the petitioner honestly believes in his sanctity. It is, Guibert thinks, as if an unlearned man misunderstands a latin prayer and asks for what he does not want. 'For God is not interested in grammar. The voice does not reach to him; he hears the heart.'[1] These are generous words, but one cannot help wondering what degree of error Guibert is willing to accept provided that the intention is honest.[2]

In assessing Guibert's comments on popular religion, we must remember that he was more clearly aware of its difference from catholic practice than were most of his contemporaries, for he was a man of critical, although in no way sceptical, temperament. Many bishops and abbots would not have been aware that there was a problem of authenticity, either of saints or relics, for their sense of evidence was poor. Odo of Bayeux, as we have seen, was prepared to pay good money for a body without even making sure that he had received the right one. It must also be recognised that popular religion contained some of the same themes, more crudely expressed, as those which had become prominent in the twelfth-century Renaissance. To our eyes, popular worship contained a great deal that was external and superstitious. We might instance the extreme veneration of relics and of the consecrated bread in the Eucharist, and the reverence extended to images of Christ. The Epiphany plays, for instance, culminated in the worship of the 'majesty', as the statue of the virgin and child was called.[3] But there was another aspect to these ceremonies of adoration. They showed a marked tendency towards the humanisation of religion, parallel to the same process in monastic and scholarly circles. Compassion for the sufferings of Christ, seen as a man, is a marked feature of the spirituality of Anselm of Canterbury, Abelard and Aelred of Rievaulx, and an increasingly affectionate warmth towards our Lady is a marked feature of this age. The peasants turned to the saints whose relics were available to them, and to images of Christ, to fulfil the same need. Guibert,

[1] I, 4, col 630.

[2] Guibert was perhaps even more interested in intention than Abelard was, but his introduction of it at this point seems to collide with other parts of his argument, notably his exclusion of Donatists and Manichees from the title of martyr, and his anxiety lest secure faith be undermined by appealing to dubious saints. If an honest intention was all that was needed, historical reliability was perhaps not so important.

[3] See I. H. Forsyth, 'Magi and Majesty. A study of Romanesque sculpture and liturgical drama', *Art Bulletin*, L (New York 1968) pp 215–22.

impressed by the corruption of popular religion, does not point out this
similarity, but the personal and human element of the cult of images is
shown in a pleasant story which he tells:

There was at Saint-Quentin a little boy, whom his parents had chosen to
become a clerk, and who had now, I believe, become an acolyte. He was
standing one festal day in front of the apse, that is between the altar and the
apse, to carry out his functions. He was bearing a paten with the host which was
to be offered. There was a plaster statue standing at the front of the chancel,
made in the likeness of the crucified Lord, and placed not far from the tomb of
the martyr Quentin. When he was beside this statue, and bearing the offering,
he said to it with childish simplicity: 'Would you like some of my bread,
Lord?' To this, He deigned to answer very clearly: 'In the next world, I will
give you some of *my* bread.'[1]

To many educated men, the cult of relics and images seemed natural,
and this story indicates that Guibert was not a disbeliever in them. On
the whole, however, he was more impressed by the corruptions than
the advantages of the existing reverence for relics. It was almost inevitable that he should take this critical view, not only because he had a
keen sense of evidence, but because his idea of religion was an interior
one, and the location of physical bodies was a matter of irrelevance.
Guibert's idea of the Ascension would probably have commended itself to the former bishop of Woolwich:

We may without doubt say that heaven (*coelum*), that is the upper part of the
three-decker universe (*triplicis machinae*), which because of its nobler character
is also called the throne of God, is nothing other than that spiritual inwardness
where God is seen to reign as if beyond this world...For he did not ascend to
heaven in the sight of his disciples so as to leave a lower place and enter a
higher one. Rather, he showed that he had received a better place and revealed
to those less able to understand that he was seated in the Father's presence, for
in that inward world nothing is either high or low or localised, for there is
there neither time nor place.[2]

The possession by a church of relics is naturally marginal to this spirituality, although Guibert readily agreed that they were given us 'for
reverence and honour, for the saints' example and protection'.[3] The
use of dubious relics of uncertain saints was especially destructive,

---

[1] I, 2, col 617. The anecdote reveals a liking for tall stories which casts doubt on Guibert's
critical qualities; in his autobiography, he shows himself even more credulous. But he
often cites his source, and the stories are not ones of the miraculous, but of visions and
other manifestations which are not susceptible of historical tests.

[2] IV, 8, cols 678–9.   [3] I, I, col 613.

because it undermined that secure faith which lies at the heart of religion. If one knows nothing reliable about a saint, it is not possible to ask for his intercession without doubt or hesitation.[1]

For a healthy religion, Guibert found two things more significant than the cult of relics. One was preaching. He wrote a useful and original exposition of the art of preaching, and stressed in particular the preacher's duty to hold up a mirror to his audience, so that they might see the truth of their inner selves.[2] The other method in which he felt confidence was the confessional, which during his lifetime was being widely adopted in the French church. It provides an interesting and direct example of the wide cultural diffusion of an idea, for it took into every village the ideals of self-examination and inner self-awareness professed by Guibert and many of his educated contemporaries. To Guibert, confession and faith were closely related, for the essence of the grace bestowed in the confession was a secure belief in forgiveness: 'See the value of faith in penitence. See the value of perseverence in the intention to correct oneself. To have faith in penitence it is necessary, after the grace of confession, on the strength of the amendment of life which has been undertaken, never to despair of pardon.'[3]

Here, then, is an assessment of popular religion by one of the writers of the twelfth-century Renaissance. Guibert may be said to have been typical of this movement in his stress upon inward spirituality, more exceptional (although by no means unique) in his sensitivity to historical evidence. These attitudes led him to a severe criticism of the cult of relics which was growing so rapidly. At its best, he saw it as somewhat marginal to the christian life; at its worst, it was a gross abuse and tended to undermine that secure faith which was at the heart of true religion. He did not, however, despair of popular religion, but turned to preaching and the confession of sins as the means to a true self-awareness. It was a programme which the medieval church made some serious attempts to put into practice, and which was eventually, centuries later, to be taken up as their own by some of the early protestant reformers.

Additional note: for a full discussion see K. Guth, *Guibert von Nogent und die hochmittelalterliche Kritik an der Reliquienverehrung* (Ottobeuren 1970) which was unfortunately not available at the time of the preparation of this paper.

[1] 1, 3, col 623.
[2] *Liber quo ordine sermo fieri debeat*, attached as a preface to the Commentary on Genesis, cols 21–32, especially col 27.
[3] 1, 2, col 619.

THE MAKING OF A TWELFTH-CENTURY RELIC COLLECTION

by DENIS BETHELL

T HE present communication derives from an attempt to make an edition of the list of relics of Reading Abbey to be found in one of the abbey's cartularies, British Museum MS Egerton 3031, fols 6v–8r. This is a list of no less than 242 relics, a collection which must have been formed between the founding of the abbey in the 1120s and the writing of the cartulary in the 1190s. It can be supplemented by a much shorter list of 24 relics made by the Dissolution commissioner, Dr London,[1] which however only adds one relic not present in the twelfth-century list, a bone of St Osmund of Salisbury, canonised in 1457. If we add the 'head' of the apostle Philip, given by king John, and added to the cartulary in a slightly later hand, we can be fairly safe in saying that the abbey acquired all but two of its relics in the first seventy years of its existence, and the list, which is very full and comparatively early as such lists go, has much to tell us of how such collections were made.

English lists of relics have been little studied. As far as I know there is no catalogue of them, and no principles have been laid down for their edition. It is the purpose of this communication to suggest some ways in which they can be used as historical documents, to put forward some suggestions as to how they should be edited, and to give some general conclusions as to how in particular Reading made its collection.

Many people find the subject of relics itself is both repulsive and peripheral. Much depends on a point of view: at its lowest level the collection of relics has more to be said for it than the collection of stamps. Relics are the physical, tangible reminders of what the saints of God have been: they stand as symbols, like the Eucharist itself, as reminders that the saints were men and women as we are, as important examples. Of course with the cult of relics there has always been a great

---

[1] [Thomas] Wright (ed), [*Three Chapters of Letters relating to the Suppression of the Monasteries, Cam. S*, XXVI (London 1843)] pp 225–7. A variant of the list will be found in Gonville and Caius College Cambridge MS 607, fol 279r. This adds one more relic, of St Mary Salome.

deal of superstition, of magical belief, of fraud, of profit from super-stition. However, there is perhaps no manifestation of piety towards which less sympathy has been shown by historians, and before we dismiss any belief which can be shown to have been of importance to large numbers of men it is our duty to understand before we judge. There can be no doubt that the collection of relics and their cult is among the oldest of christian practices. Anthropology has taught us to look with a great deal of patience and understanding at African witch-doctors: we might well spare some of this sympathy for our own christian forbears.

Such considerations must have special force when we study the twelfth century, for there can be little doubt that the twelfth century was the greatest age of the cult of relics in England. Saints' Lives and miracle collections make it plain that the great focus of popular piety was in the shrines: that there was no surer way for an abbey to attract the worship of peasantry and nobility than to possess an important relic, and the century is full of translations, revivals of hitherto utterly obscure cults, 'discoveries', and local canonisations. Some of the least attractive aspects of popular piety – like anti-semitism, and some of the most attractive – devotions of the Passion – can be shown to have their origins in certain relics and shrines. Only in the thirteenth century was devotion more surely directed to the Eucharist, and that in itself required monstrances, feast days, and processions to make it attractive – as a relic. If we consider how much more thirteenth-century piety was directed to Our Lord and His mother we may note how much this is done through relics: the rood of Bromholm, the precious blood of Hailes, Our Lady's milk at Walsingham. Both these tendencies of the twelfth and thirteenth centuries require further study. Historians of piety and religious devotion have yet much to tell us, and questions to answer. What is the religious importance of relics? What is the impor-tance of collecting relics, of showing them, of making pilgrimages to them, as social functions?[1] The collection and examination of relic lists is a necessary task for the solution of many such questions which rise from the realisation of how ancient, widespead, and important the cult of relics has been.

Relic lists have their uses for other sorts of historian. For historians of

---

[1] Two articles which discuss such questions are P. Heliot and M. L. Chastang, 'Quêtes et voyages de reliques au profit des églises françaises au moyen âge', *RHE*, LIX (1964) pp 789–823 and LX (1965) pp 5–53; and B. Toepfer, 'Reliquienkult und Pilgerbewegung zur Zeit der Klosterreform im burgundisch-aquitänischen Gebiet', *Vom Mittelalter zur Neuzeit. Zum 65 Geburtstag von H. Sproemberg* (Berlin 1956) pp 420–39.

literature and culture, these lists tell us of the foreign contacts and interests of a great abbey, and they are important auxiliaries to the study of
hagiography in ages when hagiography was an important literary
genre and a major literary activity.

For social and economic historians, it is clear that the possession by a
great abbey of certain relics affected its kalendar and its liturgical year.
Since the great feasts of an abbey were those of its district and possessions, they affected economic life by determining the dates of fairs and
markets. Since a new altar requires a relic, an abbey's collection of relics
affected the dedications of its subject churches and chapels: and the
cults which they represented gave a particular bent to local devotions.
Finally, a relic collection represents a conspicuous consumption
of wealth, and, since shrines were often melted and pawned, of
investment.

For historians of art, relic lists give a glimpse into church treasuries:
they give evidence of the artistic interests not only of the religious
communities, but of the royal and aristocratic families from whose
chapels and *haligdome* such relics often came. This is particularly important for English historians, whose greatest loss through the Dissolution
of the monasteries has been that of art and architecture. A visit to any
surviving twelfth-century abbey or cathedral must make a visit to the
Reading Abbey ruins in the Forbury Gardens seem tragic in the waste
and destruction they represent. Above all, the great loss has been that of
the glass, statuary, and treasuries of the great abbeys. Here and there in
England are to be found a few fragments of glass and embroidery: but
we have no glass or vestments from Reading. Here and there are a
few statues and fragments of statues. But what became of the most
beautiful Lady Statue in Christendom which the Bohemian traveller
Leo of Rozmital saw in Reading in the fifteenth century?[1] Or the statue
of the Holy Child Jesus which was given to Reading by Eleanor of
Aquitaine's father, the troubadour poet, William X, duke of Aquitaine?[2]

[1] *The Travels of Rozmital 1465–7*, ed M. Letts, *Hakluyt Society* 2 Series, CVIII (Cambridge
1957, for 1955) p 56;: 'I have never seen its equal nor shall I ever see one to compare with
it if I progress to the ends of the earth.'

[2] Egerton 3031, in a later hand: 'Dux Aquitanie dedit puerum regi Henrico fundatori
monasterii Rading.' This is explained in a note in Lambeth MS 371, printed by M. R.
James and C. Jenkins, *A Descriptive Catalogue of the MSS in the Library of Lambeth Palace*
(Cambridge 1932) p 503, in a thirteenth–century hand: 'Mem. quod in prima creacione
monasterii Rading dedit dux aquitannie Regi henrico fundatore quendam puerum ad
ecclesie': verses on p 513 show that the image was known as the 'Child of Grace': that
it had a chapel where miracles were worked, and that the cult still existed in the late
fifteenth century, since the verses consist of a prayer for prince Arthur (d 1502).

As for the great works in metal which are the glory of so many European cathedrals, especially in Germany, the all but solitary survival of one candlestick from Gloucester can convey scarcely anything of what was lost from England for ever in the 1530s. Here alas the Reading list is not as full as one could wish it to be: there are none of the elaborate descriptions of shrines and reliquaries such as we find in the relic lists of Christ Church Canterbury or St Paul's, nor any list of donors such as we find at Rochester, where the list of benefactors tells of the silver folding chairs given by king Harold's mother, and the ivory horn given by William the Conqueror. It is only by accidental reference that we learn that king John gave St Philip's 'head' to Reading,[1] or that a certain cross came from the chapel of Henry II's son-in-law, Henry the Lion, duke of Saxony and Bavaria, who stayed at Reading after his disgrace by Frederick Barbarossa.[2]

So much, briefly, for the use of relic lists. How should they be edited? The following seem to me to be the principles to be observed:

1. The saint concerned should be identified.
2. It should be noted whether the saint's feast occurs in the kalendars of the church concerned. This is sometimes the only way in which it can be determined which saint of the same name is intended.
3. It should be collated as far as possible with other relic lists, so that some idea can be obtained of how widespread the possession of a particular relic was.
4. Where additional information as to the provenance or possible provenance of a relic has been obtained it should be embodied in footnotes.

The attempt to follow such principles in editing the Reading list has been one reason for making this communication, since I wish to appeal for assistance in compiling a catalogue of English relic lists, and in identifying some of Reading's more obscure saints.

[1] 'Johannes rex Anglie dedit nobis caput Philippi apostoli venerandum. Et nobis nundinas ipso die concessit habere'. The 'head' is not the whole head of the apostle, but a head-shaped reliquary. There can be little doubt that this was part of the loot of the fourth crusade, c 1190 it was believed that the body of St Philip had been brought from Hierapolis in Syria to Constantinople: the body was in the Bucoleon chapel, the head in the church of All Saints. After 1204 both were dismembered and distributed in the West. For fuller references see C. Riant, *Exuviae Sacrae Constantinopolitanae* (Geneva 1878) I, pp 20, 121; II, pp 64–5, 115–16, 131–2, 175–6, 178, 199, 213, 217, 223, 227, 235–6, 237.

[2] 'De ligno Domini crux que fuit de capella Ducis Saxonie'. Henry the Lion made the Holy Land pilgrimage and was a considerable relic collector.

A twelfth-century relic collection

It remains to give what brief remarks can at the moment be made as to how Reading made its impressive collection of some twenty-nine relics of Our Lord, six of Our Lady, nineteen of patriarchs and prophets, fourteen of apostles, seventy-three of martyrs, fifty-one of confessors and forty-nine of virgins during the twelfth century.

First of all it must be said that Reading's collection relies in part on older collections. The abbey was definitely founded as an attempt to revive the piety and glories of three ancient Anglo-Saxon houses – Reading, Cholsey, and Leominster. We do not know what relics were possessed by the Old English communities of Reading and Cholsey: but we possess a relic list from Leominster.[1] Leominster had been an Anglo-Saxon nunnery, and there are grounds for supposing that it was founded as a community from king Alfred's great foundation of Shaftesbury.[2] This supposition is strengthened into certainty when we look at the Leominster list. Leominster possessed very considerable relics of king Edward the Martyr, Shaftesbury's chief saint, which came to Reading. When we find relics of queen Aelfgyfu, his grandmother, in the Reading list, although she does not appear in that of Leominster we shall be justified in thinking that they came via Leominster, since we know she was buried at Shaftesbury.[3] It is no surprise to find that four other relics of Old English nuns came from Leominster, and the other two are of St Frideswide from Oxford, up river from Reading, where a relic may have been obtained when her shrine was opened in 1180. Apart from these the Leominster list contains a collection of Irish, Breton, and Cornish saints. These represent the ancient shrines of Devon, Cornwall, and Dorset, and in particular the piety and interests of the court of king Athelstan. The final conquest of Cornwall, the lordship asserted over the Welsh and Scots, the presence of Irish and Welsh scholars at Athelstan's court all go some way to explain its interests. But Athelstan was also without doubt the greatest collector of relics among English kings: his interests and endowments were strongly marked in the collections of Wessex. From Wessex in the tenth century they came to Leominster: and from Leominster in the twelfth century to Reading. Among relics which travelled in this way were certainly

[1] A (not always reliable) study of the Leominster list was made by G. H. Doble, 'The Leominster Relic List', *Transactions of the Woolhope Naturalists' Field Club*, XXXI (London 1942–7) pp 58–65.

[2] Leland, quoted *Monasticon Anglicanum*, IV, p 55: cf William of Malmesbury, *De Gestis Pontificum*, ed N. E. S. A. Hamilton (London 1870) p 188.

[3] 'Quoddam magnum os sancte Aelfgive regine avie sancti Edwardi regis et martiris' (d 944). See [F.] Liebermann, [*Die Heiligen Englands*] (Hanover 1889) p 17.

those of St Aethelmod,[1] St Branwalator, the rib and bone of St David,[2] St Aelueva,[3] St Haemma, first abbot of Leominster,[4] and the mysterious 'St Exaudius, archbishop'. It is probable that the relic of St Samson also travelled to Reading in this way. The only other relic of a West English saint is that of St Petroc. Reading had 'some of St Petroc, and some of the cloth in which his body was wound'. Now Petroc is not in the Leominster list, and it is probable that his presence at Reading is due to one of the two occasions when his relics were brought to court in the twelfth century: once when the canons carried the shrine from Bodmin to Henry I, 'he venerated the body, fondled the shrine, and kissed it... and he remitted the unjust exactions of his henchmen'. In 1177 we are specifically told that Henry II took some relics for himself when they were brought to him at Winchester after their theft and removal to Brittany – events which were not without their political repercussions.[5] As we shall see, Reading could be quick to act on such occasions.

The second element in the list consists of what may be described as a standard old-fashioned English relic collection. It is clear from Reading's list that at its foundation or during the century a number of older houses were persuaded to give relics to the new community. Winchester was generous: Reading obtained relics of Birinus, Birstan, Swithin, Hedda, and Machutus. Most other houses were not: Bury gave a piece of cloth from the shrine of St Edmund; Durham two pieces of cloth from the shrine of St Cuthbert – though possibly Reading obtained its relic of Oswald from Durham; St Alban's gave a piece of cloth, though two bones of St Alban were also obtained, possibly when the shrine was opened in 1129; Westminster, always jealous for the relics of Edward the Confessor, simply gave a bit of the tomb. Canterbury was moderately generous: a piece of cloth from St Dunstan, a relic of St Lanfranc – no less – witnessing to an unusual cult of the great archbishop, and probably relics of St Salvius and St Blaise.

[1] [F. A. Gasquet and E. Bishop,] *The Bosworth Psalter* (London 1908) pp 165, 168, suggest that he is probably Aethelmod bishop of Sherborne c 772–81. A fuller note would be required than is here possible, but briefly his cult in the West Country is well established by pre-conquest liturgical evidence, and this with the evidence of the Reading list seems decisive against the treatise on the *Resting Places of the English Saints* (Liebermann, pp 13–14) which says that St Ethelred lies at Leominster.

[2] Not in the Leominster list, but a series of indulgences to the arm of St David in the Leominster cartulary (British Museum MS Cotton Domitian A III, fols 72r–3r) show that the arm of St David was generally accepted to be at Leominster, even by bishop Iorwerth of St David's (1215–29).

[3] ? Aethelgifu, Alfred's daughter, first abbess of Shaftesbury, died c 896, feast day 9 Dec.

[4] On him see *The Bosworth Psalter*, p 167.

[5] See P. Grosjean, 'Vie et miracles de S. Petroc', *An Bol*, LXXIV (1956) pp 172–3, 174–84.

A twelfth-century relic collection

If we look at the list of roughly sixty-seven relics which Reading shared with other English houses and which might be said in sum to be an average black monk collection, there are two other groups of relics which stand out: those from Constantinople, and those from Rome. One sub-group is particularly interesting: seventeen of Reading's fifty-four relics of Our Lord, Our Lady, and the patriarchs and prophets. These all share the same characteristics. They are highly improbable: Our Lord's shoe, swaddling-clothes, and blood and water from His side; bread from the feeding of the five thousand and the Last Supper; Veronica's veil and the shroud; Our Lady's hair, bed and belt; the rods of Moses and Aaron; relics of John the Baptist, St Anne and Symeon. All were available in Constantinople in the twelfth century. Many seem to have come to England in the tenth and eleventh centuries, if we are to trust lists from the older English houses, which often ascribe the gift of them to Athelstan, Edgar, Ethelred, or Edward the Confessor. It comes as no surprise to find that four of Reading's came from Leominster. For some of them it can be hazarded that their presence at Reading was the result of an early twelfth-century importation – like the hair of Our Lady to which the Egerton scribe wisely adds 'ut putatur'.[1] But their original source was almost certainly Constantinople, and they can be traced back to aged frauds of the third to sixth centuries. The same may be said of Reading's relics of the apostles. The greatest of these was the hand of St James which was given by the empress Matilda, who had stolen it from the German imperial chapel, whence it had come by a long route from Constantinople. The next was king John's head of St Philip, which was a piece of Constantinople loot of the fourth crusade. Of another seven minor relics of apostles it may be repeated what was said above: they were all available in Constantinople – in the church of the Holy Apostles – they were in all the older English collections, and two came to Reading from Leominster. Much the same may be said of a group of relics of virgins and martyrs: they were extremely widely spead, their source was probably Constantinople, they include some highly dubious and semi-fictitious saints, there are so many examples of their relics that any establishment of provenance is out of the question, and at the root of their cults lie the extravagances of early Syrian devotional practices.

[1] Eadmeri, *Historia Novorum*, ed M. Rule *RS*, 81 (1884) p 181, describes the arrival in England of hairs of Our Lady which had been obtained by Bohemund of Antioch from Constantinople; but the relic was common early in the west. Athelstan gave such hairs to Exeter, Edward the Confessor to Westminster, and Henry of Blois to both Glastonbury and Winchester.

The relics of the Roman martyrs belong to a very similar category. It would appear that such relics were early distributed by popes and early forged by pedlars. These relics were extremely common, and Reading shared possession of them with most English abbeys whose lists we have. A small group of French martyrs is in much the same case: Quentin, Lucian, Julian, Leodegar – and three confessors, Leonard, Giles and Germanus of Auxerre.

The third element in the list might be expected to be stronger than in fact it is. Reading was founded from the cluniac priory of St Pancras of Lewes, and it received a kalendar which marks it as clearly cluniac. There are a number of relics which Reading shares with Cluny, but they might equally have come from anywhere: it had its relic of St Pancras, but that is not distinctive either; the only relics which strongly suggest Cluny are those of the martyr, Arnulf of Tours (translated in 1103 in the presence of St Hugh of Cluny) and St Walter of Pontoise (d 1095).

These then are what may be called the derivative elements in the collection. In what may be called the 'original' parts of the collection we find that first of all Reading was 'up-to-date' in its collecting. Relics were carefully acquired of new saints. The most striking example is the magnificent list of relics of St Thomas Becket: but the relics of other contemporary saints were also acquired: St Bernard of Clairvaux and St Malachy of Armagh, and the boy saints William of Norwich and Robert of Bury St Edmunds, who were supposed to have been martyred by the Jews. We may note, too, Reading's interest in recent discoveries and excavations – in St Amphibalus 'discovered' at St Alban's in 1177, and perhaps in St Brigid 'discovered' at Downpatrick in 1185. It must, in passing, be asked why Reading possessed such considerable relics of St Brigid: head, jawbone, vestments, rib, hair. We know that Reginald, abbot of Reading, whom Henry II deposed, and who became abbot of Walden, had a brief unsuccessful Irish adventure in the 1170s and was still alive in the 1190s: was it his acquaintances who were in a position to obtain so much of the saint when she was discovered?[1] Or was it one of those campaigners in Ireland for whom the hand of St James worked miracles?[2] Some exceptional contact must lie behind this acquisition. (And where did Reading obtain the relic of St Brendan of Birr?)

[1] H. G. Richardson, 'Some Norman monastic foundations in Ireland', *Medieval Studies presented to Aubrey Gwynn S. J.*, ed J. A. Watt, J. B. Morrall, F. X. Martin (Dublin 1961) pp 29–44.
[2] See the miracles of the hand of St James in MS Gloucester Cathedral 1.

Secondly, there are a number of byzantine relics. Henry I sent an embassy to Constantinople about 1118 to acquire relics.[1] At least one of Reading's relics of the true cross is specifically said to have been sent to Henry I by the eastern emperor,[2] and another to have come from Constantinople.[3] Of a number of other relics it can be said that they must have come from the east; St Constantine, the emperor, St John the Almsgiver, St Cyril of Alexandria, St Auxentius, St Mardarius, St Philotheus and St Gerotheus. There is an interesting little group of Salonika relics which were possibly collected by Henry I's embassy: the oil of St Demetrius, the relics of St Nestor and St Irene of Salonika.

Thirdly, there is what may be called an all but complete set of Holy Land tour souvenirs, reminding us of the force of count Riant's remark: 'cathedral sacristies were the equivalents of our contemporary museums'. They represent the sites which were shown to pilgrims in the twelfth century: they include one of the latest references to the place where Our Lady traditionally bathed Our Lord in the church of the Nativity at Bethlehem.[4]

There are, however, a number of relics which fall outside any of these classifications. In some cases it is possible to make a tentative guess at the identification of particular twelfth-century donors. Thus, it was the empress Matilda who gave Reading what was without any doubt its chief relic, the hand of St James the apostle, St James the Great, and it seems reasonable, therefore, to suppose that the belt of Our Lady given by Matilda to Monkton Farleigh,[5] a cluniac foundation of the 1130s, is connected with Reading's belt of Our Lady. Then we may note that Henry I's first queen, Matilda of Scotland, was interested in relics of St Mary Magdalen. Such relics are unlikely to have come anywhere but from the cluniac abbey of Vézelay, and we may note too that Cluniacs pioneered dedications to her in England: thus the dedication of Reading's leper hospital and the abbey's possession of a relic represent the interests of both Henry I's court and the Cluniacs as we might expect.[6] Seffrid, abbot of Glastonbury, and later bishop of

---

[1] For this embassy see the Aldgate Chronicle, London Guildhall MS 122, IV, fol 16.

[2] 'Preputium Domini vel illud quod ab umbilico pueri Jhesu precisum est creditur esse, cum cruce de ligno Domini in textu quem imperator Constantin' misit Henr' regi Anglorum primo.'

[3] 'Crux quedam que de Constantinop' allata est deaurata, in VI capitibus auro quod oblatum fuerit Jhesu Christo.'

[4] 'De aqua in qua Dominus apud Bethleem balneatus est, ac diende ipsa aqua conversa est in manna usque in hodiernum diem'.   [5] Wright, p 58.

[6] V. Saxer, *Le culte de Marie Madeleine en Occident des origines à la fin du moyen âge* (Auxerre 1959). Saxer dates the 'discovery' at Vézelay to 1037–52, that at Aix to between

Chichester gave relics of St Nympha of Palermo to Glastonbury Abbey.[1] Now St Nympha was translated to the church of St Chrysogonus in Rome in 1123,[2] when both Seffrid and Reading monks were in Rome: and John of Crema, cardinal of St Chrysogonus, came to England as papal legate in 1125. We can see the links which brought this improbable and obscure Italian saint to Berkshire. A guess which is distinctly wilder, but which is interesting, may be made as to Reading's relic of Thomas the apostle – a piece of his pallium. Now English relics of St Thomas are not common. Only one other English list that I know contains a relic: Durham, also a piece of cloth – his 'vestment'.[3] On 16 May 1122, Odo, abbot of St Remy at Rheims, wrote to a friend to describe how an Indian patriarch had appeared in Rome and gave an account of the Indian shrine of St Thomas.[4] Monks of Reading and Durham were certainly at Rome early in 1123, and an English delegation was there in 1122. They must certainly have heard of the Indian patriarch, and would have been in a position to acquire secondary relics – cloths which had touched the Indian shrine. Other instances could be given showing a similar range of possibilities.[5] In other cases the provenance of a particular relic has been difficult or impossible to trace.[6]

1195 and 1205. For queen Matilda's gifts to Westminster see John Flete, *The History of Westminster Abbey*, ed J. Armitage Robinson (Cambridge 1959) p 68. The priory of Holy Trinity, Aldgate, founded under her patronage, was in fact dedicated to the True Cross and St Mary Magdalen.

[1] *Johannis Confratris et Monachi Glastoniensis Chronica sive Historia de Rebus Glastoniensibus*, ed T. Hearne (Oxford 1726) I, p 165.

[2] *Bibliotheca Sanctorum*, Institute Giovanni XXIII nella Pontificia Università Lateranense (Rome 1961–8) VIII (1966) *s.v.* Nympha.

[3] Otto Lehmann-Brockhaus, *Lateinische Schriftsquellen zur Kunst in England, Wales, und Schottland vom Jahre 901 bis zum Jahre 1307* (Munich 1955) IV, no 1491, p 403.

[4] Paul Devos, 'Le Miracle Posthume de St Thomas l'Apôtre', *An Bol*, LXVI (1948) pp 231–68.

[5] Relics of St Agnes the martyr are so common that there is really very little way of telling how Reading acquired its relic of St Agnes: but one twelfth-century translation should be drawn to the attention of English historians. The inscription on the shrine at Mont St Michel as read in 1640 was 'Anno domini 1184 Robertus abbas hanc dexteram fecit componi auro et argento et lapidis pretiosis in qua reposuit grande os de brachio sanctae Agnetis virginis et martyris, quod translatus fuit apud nos de capella regii Regis Sicilie per manum Thomae Brui qui fuit cancellarius predicti regis', D. Dubois, 'Le Trésor des reliques de Mont St Michel', *Millenaire Monastique de Mont St Michel*, ed J. Laporte (Paris 1967) I, p 562.

[6] It may be permissible to list a few puzzles here with a request for assistance. Among the martyrs: Who was 'St Theonost'? Can 'the tooth of St Reginald the martyr' conceivably refer to Reynald of Châtillon, executed by Saladin (1187)? Among the confessors: What was 'the ring of St Nicodemus'? Who was 'St Frinolaus'? Among the virgins: Who was 'St Willa'?

A twelfth-century relic collection

One question which is bound to be raised with regard to provenance is the question of the genuineness of the relics concerned. If the collection still existed this would be a proper question for those who exposed it for public veneration. Since it does not, the question must be posed differently. Is there any reason to suppose that the monks of Reading in the twelfth century made little enquiry as to provenance, so that we may regard this list not as evidence of foreign contact and traditional piety, but simply of gullibility and fraud? In the long run, of course, many of these relics were fraudulent, but the frauds they represented were already ancient and respectable in the twelfth century. In the main they were the result of the extravagances, enthusiasms, and credulities of, in particular, Syria and Egypt in the post-Constantinian age. Certain others – those of contemporaries – were certainly genuine. Nor is there much reason to suppose that in the case of its Old English saints Reading did not have what it claimed to have. It should be remembered too how small many of these relics were; as the Dissolution commissioners said scornfully, 'a multitude of small bonys, laces, stonys, and ermys'; that the mention of an 'arm' or a 'head' in a relic list means a metal 'arm' or 'head' often containing a small bone only. It can, for instance, be demonstrated how the supposed bones of the apostle Philip were broken up after the fourth crusade: king John knew well that he was only presenting a piece of the skull to Reading. It should also be recalled that many relics were secondary – cloths or oil – the oils of Demetrius, Catharine, Cosmas and Damian, are all mentioned in this list: any respectable pilgrim to Rome or Constantinople could obtain such relics – as today they can buy the small pieces of the earth of the catacombs sold in modern rosaries. It can only be an impression, but my impression is that in fact the twelfth century was not a great age of relic forgery in the sense that itinerant vendors of pigs' bones were readily received by great abbots. In the west the golden age of relic forgery in this sense seems to have been eighth-century Germany, where recent German converts fell ready victims to Italian salesmen:[1] a further age of massive forgery was the thirteenth century, when the fall of Constantinople with its vast treasury of relics to the 'crusaders' of the fourth Crusade both flooded the market and made imposture difficult to detect, while major relics in the hands of unscrupu-

[1] J. Guiraud, 'Le commerce des reliques du commencement du IXe siècle, *Mélanges G. B. de Rossi*, supplement to *Mélanges d'archéologie et d'histoire*, XII, Ecole Française de Rome (Paris 1892) pp 73–95; W. Hotzelt, 'Translationen von Martyrer–reliquien aus Rom nach Bayern im 8 Jhrdt.', *Studien und Mitteilungen zur Geschichte des Benediktiner Ordens und seiner Zweige*, LIII (Munich 1935) pp 286ff.

ious pedlars were both a fact and a likelihood. It may be that the very lnflation of the market then helped to lower the status of relics, and that the very large numbers of relics of Our Lord and Our Lady then made available had a significant effect on directions given to popular devotion. There were without doubt local canonisations of an extremely dubious kind in the twelfth century, and inventions of long dead saints in places where a lively imagination might well suppose them to be. There were resounding impostures like those at Glastonbury. Examples can certainly be found of deliberate deception and bottomless credulity. Nonetheless there was also scepticism. Hugh of Reading was a notable detector of forged charters. On the whole it is probable that the monks of Reading took some care that their relics should have some sort of pedigree and provenance.

INNOCENT III's TREATMENT OF THE
HUMILIATI

by BRENDA BOLTON

MANIFESTATIONS of popular religion both in conscious and less conscious opposition to the official hierarchical church were frequent by the early thirteenth century. Such movements, generated by a new and exciting interpretation of apostolic life among the laity, often expressed particular social and economic needs. This evangelical awakening emphasised urban and fraternal Christianity and was welcomed by those in the towns who were untouched by the ministrations of the local clergy.[1] Strong religious sentiment led them to practise a literal and christocentric piety through corporeal works of mercy and personal experience of poverty. Real spiritual devotion was no longer confined to monastic-enclosed communities but was centred on the domestic family unit, in which women too played a valuable rôle. Yet this spontaneous expression of lay piety represented a threat which could not be ignored. It was also a challenge which Innocent III met, during the seventeen years of his pontificate, by attempting to harness the untapped reserve of religious enthusiasm and vitality and to divert it into an orthodox channel which affected not merely acknowledged heretics but many of his own clergy.[2]

One such group of enthusiasts were the *Humiliati* of Lombardy whose wide popular appeal led to the establishment of their houses in Milan, Como, Lodi, Pavia, Piacenza, Bra, Brescia, Bergamo, Monza, Cremona and Verona.[3] Legend places their origin in the eleventh century but they

[1] G. W. O. Addleshaw, *The Early Parochial System and the Divine Office* (London 1957) deals in particular with the problems of the first foundation or baptismal churches of Northern Italy in the twelfth century. Here, a whole city often formed one parish, and the clergy, who led semi-communal lives, performed liturgical as well as pastoral duties.

[2] Lothar de Segni 1198–1216. Innocent's interest in religious movements has been dealt with most recently in [M]. Maccarrone, 'Riforma e sviluppo della vita religiosa [con Innocenzo III], R[ivista di storia della] C[hiesa in] I[talia] xvi (Rome 1962) pp 29–72. Also useful are the two relevant volumes by A. Luchaire, *Innocent III. Le concile de Latran et la réforme de l'Eglise* (Paris 1908) and *La Croisade des Albigeois* (Paris 1911).

[3] G. Tiraboschi, *V[etera] H[umiliatorum] M[onumenta]*, 3 vols (Milan 1766–8) contains the main collection of documents on the *Humiliati*. Important secondary works are [L.] Zanoni, *Gli Umiliati [nei loro rapporti con l'eresia, l'industria della lana ed i communi nei*

are first named officially in the general condemnation of 4 November
1184 by which Lucius III anathematised a whole group of sects classed
as heretical.[1] The *Humiliati* of Vibaldono near Milan appear to have been
reinstated in 1186, although their request for permission to preach was
refused.[2] In 1198 or 1199, two leading members of the *Humiliati*,
James de Rondineto and Lanfranc de Lodi, came to Innocent to seek
approval and recognition of their way of life.[3] His treatment of them
merits detailed consideration as it contrasts with his predecessors'
failure to face the very real problems posed by these popular religious
fraternities. He asked that they should present a short statement or
propositum to indicate their willingness to devote themselves to a life of
christian piety. Some characteristic features of the movement may be
established by an examination, not only of their *proposita*, but also of
Innocent's letters concerning them, and of chronicle evidence.[4]

By 1200, the *Humiliati* seem to have organised themselves into three
groups, which are referred to as orders.[5] The first and second orders,
led by *praepositi* and *praelati* respectively, were composed of unmarried
men and women living separate and ascetic lives in religious communities according to a form of rule unrecognised by authority. The
third order comprised a group of laymen living at home with their
families and practising strict evangelical precepts. These were the
Tertiaries who caught the eye and imagination of several chroniclers.
One couplet runs: 'Sunt in Italia fratres humiliati, Quijurare renuunt et
sunt uxorati.'[6] The *Chronicle of Laon* substantiates the importance to
them of family life, prayer, preaching and mutual support and emphasises their refusal to swear an oath.[7] Burchard, abbot of Ursperg, refers

secoli xii e xiii], Biblioteca historica italia, Serie II, 2 (Milan 1911); A. de Stefano, 'Delle
origini e della natura del primitivo movimento degli Umiliati', *Archivium Romanicum*,
II, (Geneva 1927) pp 31–75; [G.] Volpe, *Movimenti religiosi [e sette ereticali nella
società medievale italiana secoli x–xiv*], Biblioteca Storica Sansoni, NS, XXXVII (Florence
1961). Most valuable of all has been [H.] Grundmann, *Religiöse Bewegungen [im Mit-
telalter]* (2 ed Hildesheim 1961) especially pp 70–97 and pp 487–538.
1 *VHM*, I, p 79; C. J. Héfèle et H. Leclercq, *Histoire des Conciles*, V, 2 (Paris 1913) pp
1119–26.   2 *VHM*, II, pp 123–5.
3 *PL*, CCXIV (1855) col 921; *VHM*, II, p 139.
4 A most useful general introduction to Innocent's letters and the Papal Chancery may be
found in *The Letters of Pope Innocent III (1198–1216) concerning England and Wales*
ed C. R. and M. G. Cheney (Oxford 1967) especially pp ix–xviii, xxiii–iv, See also
PL, CCXIV–CCXVI (1855); [*Die*] *Regi[ster] Inn[ocenz III 1198–99*], ed O. Hageneder and
A. Haidacher (Graz/Köln 1964) and *R[egesta] P[ontificum] R[omanorum]* ed A. Potthast,
2 vols (Berlin 1874).   5 *VHM*, II, pp 128, 135, 139.
6 E. Comba, *History of the Waldenses of Italy*, trans T. E. Comba (London 1889) p 69.
7 *Chronicon Universale Anonymi Laudunensis*, ed A. Cartellieri et W. Stechèle (Paris
1909) pp 28–30.

scathingly to them as *rudes et illiterati*,[1] while Humbert de Romans considered them aptly named since they led a humble life of manual work.[2] Their *propositum* indicates that they ate and prayed in common, dressed soberly and sought to lead lives of apostolic purity and piety.[3] They felt that their *raison d'être* was preaching, but this had been forbidden to them by Alexander III and Lucius III, a prohibition strictly enforced on a local level by diocesan bishops.[4] The third order is addressed as *societas, fraternitas,* and *universitas,* possibly indicating that its members already formed some loose association or rudimentary guild organisation.[5]

That Innocent was conscious of the fundamental importance of the growth of religious sentiment is apparent from the *arenga* of his letters to the *Humiliati*. His policy was to establish the *distinctio* between irrevocable heretics and believers, and thereby to draw a line between heresy and orthodox piety. Whereas he insisted on condign punishment for heretics, likening himself to a doctor forced to amputate a malignant limb to save the body, he maintained that the cure is all important, the method by which it is achieved far less so.[6] The regeneration of clerical elements within the church was a matter of great urgency and Innocent's contact with the *Humiliati* showed him that such movements, carefully controlled, could be of use. There was much to be gained by adopting the more successful of their methods and thus bringing them back like lost sheep into the fold. His attitude towards them was therefore cautious but conciliatory: he did not wish to punish the innocent and was prepared to overlook minor deviations.[7]

On 6 December 1199, he wrote to Adelard, bishop of Verona, to warn him that the *Humiliati* in his diocese were being indiscriminately excommunicated and classed with Cathars, Arnaldists and Poor Men of

---

[1] *Burchardi et Cuonradi Urspergensium Chronicon,* ed O. Abel–L. Weiland, *MGH SS,* XXIII (Hanover 1874) p 377; *VHM,* I, pp 107–8.

[2] Printed in Zanoni, *Gli Umiliati,* pp 261–3.

[3] *VHM,* II, pp 132–3.

[4] *Mansi,* XX, p 476; *VHM,* I, p 79. The decree *ad abolendam* distinguished between those who preached privately or in public without papal or episcopal consent and those who taught false doctrines. The *Humiliati* were guilty of the former error.

[5] *VHM,* II, pp 128, 157.

[6] *Ibid,* p 139.

[7] 'Quia vero non est nostrae intentionis innoxios cum nocentibus condemnare', *PL,* CCXIV, col 789. On medieval heresy in general see A. Dondaine, 'L'origine de l'hérésie médiévale', *RCI,* VI (1952) pp 47–78; J. Russell, 'The Origins of medieval heresy', *M[edieval] S[tudies],* XXV (1963) pp 26–53; C. N. L. Brooke, 'Heresy and Religious Sentiment 1000–1250', *BIHR,* XLII (1968) pp 115–31; C. Thouzellier, *Catharisme et Valdéisme en Languedoc à la fin du xiie siècle* (2 ed Louvain 1969).

Lyons.[1] He ordered that measures against them should cease. Those of their views which were apparently orthodox should be reconsidered, and even when they appeared to stray from orthodoxy, they should be given the benefit of absolution if prepared to acknowledge such error and to submit. At much the same time he was confronted by their request for recognition.[2] He felt that the *Humiliati* could be a useful weapon with which to fight heresy. However, he declared himself unable to grant their request without deep thought and considerable investigation, because the character of their life, although analogous to that of other pious associations, was vastly different from that followed by any existing religious community.[3] So he established a special commission, composed of the bishop of Vercelli, a regular canon from the community of Mortara, and the cistercian abbots of Lodi and Cerreto. This was to receive, examine and pronounce authoritatively on the *proposita* of the *Humiliati*.[4]

Innocent originally planned to bring the *Humiliati* within the church by uniting them in a single rule, a *propositum regulare*, although he made it clear that he did not intend to discipline the community with the characteristic obligations of either monks or regular canons.[5] But the evidence collected by the commission, after two years of complicated and detailed investigation, appears to have pointed to the impossibility of placing the community under one rule. In 1201, their *proposita* received papal confirmation in three documents. Separate letters were sent to the Tertiaries and to the second order while the first order received a privilege similar to that granted to religious institutions.[6] The movement appears already to have had a definite form and known leadership since Innocent addressed some of the *praepositi*, *praelati*, and

---

[1] *PL*, CCXIV (1855) col 789.

[2] *Ibid*, cols 921–2.

[3] In a bull of 1091, Urban II confirmed the *vita communis* of certain laymen according to the form of the early church: *PL*, CLI (1858) col 336. Bernold of Constance lists three categories of convert to this primitive life, both men and women who had vowed obedience, celibacy and poverty in a communal life and married couples who lived according to strict religious precepts: *PL*, CXLVIII (1853) cols 1407–8. Similar groups sprang up during the twelfth century and in 1188 a community was founded at St Didier near Vicenza: G. G. Meersseman et E. Adda, 'Pénitents ruraux communitaires', *RHE*, XLIX (1954) pp 343–90, especially p 363, n 1. The problem of differentiation between such communities and religious orders is dealt with by M. D. Chenu, 'Moines, clercs, laïcs au carrefour de la vie évangelique (xiie siècle)', *RHE*, XLIX (1954) pp 59–89.

[4] *VHM*, II, p 136. *PL*, CCXIV (1855) col 922.

[5] *Ibid*, 'non tam locum quam votum, non tam habitum quam affectum'.

[6] The letters to the third and second orders are dated respectively 7 and 12 June, 1201: *VHM*, II, pp 128–38. The privilege to the first order was sent on 16 June: *ibid*, pp 139–48.

ministri by name.[1] Seemingly the task of the commission had been merely to indicate future lines of development, not to lay down totally new forms.

All three documents deal with the *Humiliati's* rejection of oath-taking. In common with the Cathars, they based this rejection on the Epistle of St James.[2] Innocent realised that such an interpretation of the New Testament was theologically dangerous, for the *Humiliati* were implicitly putting themselves in the same category as clerics, for clerics did not swear, and thus for the *Humiliati* to imitate them in this would be to behave heretically. Using extensive biblical justification, he attempted to compromise with all three orders by requiring them to recognise oaths in urgent cases but freeing them from the obligation to take those which were unnecessary and worthless.[3]

The question of tithe payments could not be resolved in one formula common to the whole movement. Each document, therefore, contains instructions appropriate to lay or clerical elements. The Tertiaries, as laymen, could neither possess tithes nor refuse to pay them to their diocesan bishops.[4] The second order was free from payments on its own lands and from its animal husbandry, but was still obliged to pay tithes when due to the church.[5] The first order was granted remission according to the formula *sane novalium* and, with diocesan permission, was allowed to possess tithes for its own use.[6]

A unique provision for the Tertiaries allowed them to gather every Sunday in a suitable place at which those 'wise in faith and expert in religion' could preach as long as they ignored theological questions and dealt only with exhortations to a pious and earnest life. Episcopal licence was necessary for this but the bishops were expressly commanded not to refuse. Such qualifications do not affect the importance of this provision. Although Innocent took care to distinguish between the preaching of ordained priests and that of pious lay groups, he was prepared to modify the fundamental law that no-one might preach without ordination. The *Humiliati*, preaching on their experience of christian life, were thus allowed an existence within the church.[7]

---

[1] The *praepositi* are named as James de Rondineto, Lanfranc de Vibaldono, Tancred de Mealono and Lanfranc de Lodi: *ibid*, p 139. Guy de Porta Orientalis is the only *minister* whose title is given in full: *ibid*, p 128; *PL*, CCXIV (1855) col 921. The *praelati* and *ministri* are simply listed according to their houses: *VHM*, II, pp 128, 135.

[2] Jas. 5: 12.   [3] *VHM*, II, pp 131-2, 137-8, 145-6.

[4] *Ibid*, pp 131-2.   [5] *Ibid*, pp 136-7.   [6] *Ibid*, pp 141-2.

[7] *Ibid*, pp 133-4. Grundmann, *Religiöse Bewegungen*, p 81, thinks it unlikely that the *Humiliati* had attempted to expound dogma because they were more interested in moral questions, but sees a new distinction between clerical and lay sermons.

The situation was difficult for a juridical mind such as Innocent's; the *Humiliati* did not represent, at least from the church's point of view, an homogeneous entity, since the movements contained both lay and clerical elements, living only partially in *vita communis*. The Tertiaries received papal approval of their *norma vivendi* but, possibly because of their married state, were never accepted into the church as *religiosi*.[1] Innocent's original proposal for a single *propositum regulare* came nearest to fulfilment in his treatment of the second order. Its *institutio regularis* was approved by the Holy See and conceded to the unmarried laity the jurisdictional status of *religiosi*.[2] The first order was specifically confirmed as a religious community and its obligations and privileges were recognised in its *ordo canonicus*.[3] Its members were to be tonsured and were granted the right to wear a habit *ut laicos litteratos*, presumably similar to that worn by Italian civil lawyers.[4] They were to be cloistered, but an instruction was given that if anyone tried to leave, he was not be be restrained.[5] They were allowed to build their own churches with episcopal permission but were not to prejudice those already in existence.[6] Although their rule contained elements of benedictine and augustinian monasticism, they were specifically to follow the liturgical customs of the canonical congregation of Mortara from which the bishop of Vercelli came.[7] The form of visitation and the relationship between the houses were based on the cistercian pattern. The letter to the first order contains elaborate details and instructions. The four superiors of the order, the *praepositi majores* of Rondineto, Vibaldone, Vigalono and Lodi, were to visit each other in turn. Furthermore, together with the four leaders of each of the other two orders, they were to consult together at least annually in a general chapter which was to deal with matters of business and religion. Laymen were specifically excluded from *spiritualia* although they had parity with clerics in temporal affairs. Any one of the *praepositi majores* could be deposed by the other three, and provision was made for a new election conducted by an arbiter from the community, assisted by one lay and two clerical electors. After a three-day fast, the whole community of brothers and sisters was to vote, and the successful *praepositus* then sought the confirmation of his diocesan bishop. His appointment was for life or until deposition.[8]

[1] Maccarrone, 'Riforma e sviluppo della vita religiosa', pp 47–9.
[2] *Ibid*, p 49, n 46; *VHM*, II, p 136.
[3] 'In primis siquidem statuentes ut in ecclesiis vestris *ordo canonicus* secundem Deum et institutionem vestram per sedem apostolicam approbatum, perpetuis temporibus observetur.' *VHM*, II, p 139.   [4] *Ibid*, p 142.   [5] *Ibid*, pp 141–2.
[6] *Ibid*, p 142.   [7] *Ibid*, p 143.   [8] *Ibid*, pp 143–5.

The composition of the movement, its place in the general pattern of heresy, lay piety and the formation of new orders are open questions, although some tentative suggestions may be made. The first order of priests appears to have been mainly aristocratic. Its members provided leadership for the movement and possibly recruits to the *praelati* and *ministri* of the second and third orders. Guy de Porta Orientalis, *minister* of the Tertiaries, is described as *vir nobilis* and *capitanei*.[1] In Lombardy there was a strong tradition of alienation among the lesser nobility, especially the *vavassours* who were usually excluded from any positive rôle in either political or ecclesiastical affairs. Just as some had supported the Patarines of the eleventh century, so others may have been tempted to join the *Humiliati* among whom they could more easily achieve the eminence denied to them by the church.[2] The houses of this order were well endowed with lands and possessions, possibly given by aristocratic patrons.[3] Perhaps this order also contained priests who had broken away from the church.

The movement appears to have had a strong lower-class base. Pious lay fraternities sprang up at a time of considerable urban expansion. They reacted not only against the pressures of anonymity and overcrowding, but also against the increase of wealth in direct contradiction to the primary demand of the Gospels for poverty. Some of the Tertiaries were evidently artisans, for Innocent showed concern that they should not be required to fast if they were at work.[4] To avoid any preoccupation with riches they were instructed to observe christian precepts and to give to the indigent all income in excess of their own needs.[5] But even at an early date, they may have given the impression that they were far from poor since, in 1214, Innocent urged the Lombard towns not to tax their communities too heavily.[6] By the middle

---

[1] 'nobili viro, Guidoni de Porta Orientali,' *PL*, ccxiv (1855) col 921; 'Guidonis dei Capitaneis portae orientalis,' *VHM*, i, p 44.

[2] Zanoni, *Gli Umiliati*, pp 19 ff. believed that religious reform movements emanated from the lower classes, but C. Violante, *La Società Milanese nell'età precommunale* (Bari 1953) pp 176ff. believes that the reaction was experienced by a wider cross-section of society. On the Patarine movement see *ibid*, pp 135, 198–204; C. Violante, *La Pataria Milanese e la riforma ecclesiastica* (Rome 1955) pp 105ff.; H. E. J. Cowdrey, 'The Papacy, the Patarines and the Church of Milan', *TRHS*, 5 Series, xviii (1968) pp 25–48.

[3] I am most grateful to Dr Janet Nelson for her valuable suggestions on this point. It is possible that such possessions and lands which belonged to the *Humiliati* may have continued to bear the names of their aristocratic donors. If this is so, the lords could have exerted considerable influence over the estates which were farmed and tenanted by the first and second orders. Much detailed research has yet to be undertaken before a clear idea of the social structure of the movement emerges. I am also indebted to my colleague, Dr Colin Tite, for his patient and constructive criticism of many points.

[4] *VHM*, ii, p 132.   [5] *Ibid*, p 133.   [6] *RPR*, i, no 4944, p 431.

of the thirteenth century they were established in a profitable wool industry, partly worked on a domestic basis but also involving the second order who, after the canonical hours, hurried away to their separate cloisters to exercise this skill *pro communi commoditate*.[1] They seem to have turned gradually from humble manual work to a quasi-capitalistic organisation, the existence of which the movement's chroniclers, John de Brera and Marcus Bossius, both writing in the fifteenth century, made vigorous attempts to justify.[2]

Even after their recognition by Innocent in 1201, the *Humiliati* still encountered strong resentment from the secular church. In 1203, at Cerea in the diocese of Verona, they were not only expelled but saw their goods granted away by licence from the archdeacon.[3] Although they were referred to as heretics, there is no evidence that they were not completely orthodox. Innocent always took great care to provide that, on the particular matters of preaching, church-building and tithe payments, permission should be sought from the diocesan bishop. The secular clergy could not understand why Innocent accorded favours to these repentant heretics whom they regarded as tares among the wheat. To attack heresy with such recently converted men and women seemed to them to be equivocal and to create a dangerous precedent. But Innocent was well aware of the deficiencies of his clergy. In 1199, he had overruled the bishop of Metz and had allowed a group of laymen to read the Scriptures in the vernacular 'lest these simple people should be forced into heresy'.[4] He recognised the positive contribution of christian example which such groups could provide, and attempted to defend them against the hatred and fear of the secular clergy.

The *Humiliati* were, in many respects, remarkably similar to the Franciscans. Both movements lived according to the *forma primitivae ecclesiae*, surrounded by lay Tertiaries and communities of women. Both were deeply mistrusted by the secular church. The *Humiliati* even shared some of the friars' success. Jacques de Vitry, visiting the heretical city of Milan in 1216, was able to report that the *Humiliati* were *alone* in resisting and, indeed, in actively working against heresy through conventicles and at least 150 conventual groups.[5] But there were vital

---

[1] *VHM*, II, p 156.

[2] *Chronicle of John de Brera 1421*, printed in Zanoni, *Gli Umiliati*, pp 336–44; *Chronicle of Marcus Bossius 1493, ibid*, pp 345–52.

[3] C. Cipolla, 'Statuti rurali veronesi', *Archivio veneto*, XXXVII (Venice 1889) pp 341–5.

[4] *PL*, CCXIV (1855) col 699.

[5] P. Sabatier, *Collection de Documents pour l'histoire réligieuse et littéraire du Moyen Age* (Paris 1898) pp 297–8.

differences between the two: the *Humiliati* had no outstanding leader and no Cardinal Protector to defend them against their enemies or to vouch for their orthodoxy.[1] The *Humiliati* were bound by a compromise rule which was an amalgam of diverse elements. The friars had the advantage of entering the church several years later with a rule that was entirely their own. Possibly the *Humiliati* were becoming rich and less attractive to the idealistic recruits who sought to experience real poverty.

Between 1200 and 1215, there was a proliferation of religious groups, penitential, pious, charitable and military, in places as far apart as Languedoc and Livonia.[2] Innocent examined each one with the care that he had accorded the *Humiliati*, taking some within the church as *religiosi* and authorising others to preach under the immediate vigilance of the diocesan bishop. His action may have provided a stimulus to episcopal preaching but it also seems to have provoked a strong response from the secular clergy. In 1215, at the Fourth Lateran Council, it was decreed that there were to be no new religious orders. Furthermore, anyone wishing to refound a religious house had to make sure that the rules and institutions were those of an approved order.[3] This may mark the victory of the 'conservative' bishops rather than the policy of Innocent himself. It is difficult to understand why he should have undergone such a complete *volte-face* unless considerable pressure was placed upon him. The bishops, fearing the contamination of their people and the exposure of clerical deficiencies, sought to create a situation in which heretics would, in future, stand out sharply from the rest of the flock. The Lateran Council crystallised the pattern which had become apparent after 1201. It was preferable that groups of clergy and laity

---

[1] R. B. Brooke, *Early Franciscan Government* (Cambridge 1959) p 62.

[2] On 22 April 1198 the Hospitallers of the Holy Spirit were founded by Guy de Montpellier: *PL*, CCXIV (1855) cols 83–4; *Reg Inn*, no 97, pp 141–4; *RPR*, I, no 96, p 11. On 17 December 1198 the Order of Trinitarians was founded to cure the sick and to liberate enslaved Christians: *PL*, CCXIV, col 215; *Reg Inn*, no 481, pp 703–8; *RPR*, I, no 483, p 46. On 19 February 1199 the Teutonic Order received confirmation of apostolic protection: *PL*, CCXIV, col 525; *RPR*, I, no 606, p 58. On 18 June 1204 the Hospital of St Maria in Sassia in Rome was recognised as a community of clergy: *PL*, CCXIV, cols 376–80; *RPR*, I, no 2248, p 194. On 18 December 1208 Durand de Huesca and the Poor Catholics were reconciled with the church: *PL*, CCXV, cols 1510–14; *RPR*, I, nos 3571–3, p 308 On 14 May 1210 Bernard Primus and his followers were reconciled with the church: *RPR*, I, nos 4014, 4015, p 346. On 20 October 1210 an evangelical and crusading order was founded in Livonia by bishop Albert of Riga: *PL*, CCXVI (1855) cols 326–7; *RPR*, I, no 4104, p 353.

[3] Cap 13, Lateran IV, in *Conciliorum Oecumenicorum decreta*, ed J. Alberigo *et al* (2 ed Freiburg 1962) p 218. See also Maccarrone, 'Riforma e sviluppo della vita religiosa' pp 60–9.

living in common should be persuaded to adopt the traditional rules of regular canons or hospitallers than that new rules should be created. Episcopal pressure seems to have led to the affirmation of a new principle. After 1215, canonical legislation to regulate and discipline new orders was brought within the competence of the Holy See.

No community was ever again organised on quite the lines laid down by Innocent for the *Humiliati*. He had shown flexibility by retaining the essential form of the movement when it would possibly have been easier to absorb the first order into an existing rule and to ignore the third. He had demonstrated his practical concern by allowing the Tertiaries to preach and by rewarding the devotion not only of men but of women. Yet he sowed the seeds of their destruction as a primitive evangelical movement. Outside the church, they were valuable critics, and their emphasis on communal work and the family unit put them in a strong position to convert. Once they had shown that they could win adherents, Innocent, with his love of institutions, disciplined, regulated and absorbed this spontaneous lay movement into the church. After 1201, they were forced into a diocesan structure which led to the ultimate vitiation of their early form. In some respects, they antedated the friars but their movement lacked the clarity, precision and leadership which would have made it a decisive force for the future. By 1214, Innocent himself was aware that they were no longer the eager representatives of a literal and christocentric interpretation of piety, although their movement continued to attract recruits for some long time after.[1] But this is not to underrate Innocent's achievement: from an undifferentiated *corpus* of religious sentiment, he enabled distinctive and valuable movements to emerge and ensured that they were perpetually harnessed in the service of the church.

[1] 'Humiliatos per Lombardiam in fide catholica et devotione apostolica constitutos monet et hortatur, ut attendentes "quod no habetis hic manentem civitatem" cum timore ac tremore incolatus sui tempore studeant conversari, eam re ipsa humiliatatem sectantes, ut securi expectare possint beatam spem et adventum gloriae magni Dei.' *RPR*, I, no 4945, p 431.

PIETY AND IMPIETY IN
THIRTEENTH-CENTURY ITALY

by ALEXANDER MURRAY

EVERYONE is familiar with the notion of an 'Age of Faith'.
It is the idea that, at some time in the past, everyone believed
what religious authority told them to believe. In this paper I
propose to test the truth of this idea, in one period, and one region.

I have chosen thirteenth-century Italy. The Middle Ages stand, *par
excellence*, as the Age of Faith; and the thirteenth century, late enough
not to starve us of evidence, was still early enough to be safely medieval.
Italy, too, chooses itself: its documents, and its debates, yield the
historian a clearer picture than he would get elsewhere. Whether
Italy was typical of latin Christendom is a question that would call, not
for another paper, but for another conference. But hints of her position
will appear in the course of our enquiry. Some sources singled her out,
some did not – giving an assurance, between them, that any difference
between Italy and the rest was a difference between shades of grey.

Italy, then, in the thirteenth century, is our field; and we shall be
enquiring in it not, now, about kinds of belief, but about *degrees* of it.
How far were our predecessors, in the time and place chosen, in the
modern sense 'religious'?

Innocent III; St Francis; St Clare; Bonaventura; Aquinas; Dante: Italy
supplied more than her share of the adornments of thirteenth-century
Christendom. Family records reveal, too, in Italian cities, a firm block
of more elusive lay sanctity, inspired by, and supporting, the church
and the religious orders. The piety of these saints, canonised and un-
canonised, is for us familiar ground. Mainly clerical sources, worked
over by mainly clerical historians, have made it so. In what follows, it
will be taken for granted. It will attend our proceedings; but as an
invisible spirit. The outcome of the proceedings will be, indeed, to exalt
the saints. But that will be achieved, not by rehearsing their legends
over again, but by revealing the obstacles they had to contend with.

Piety, then, implicitly; impiety, explicitly, will be our subject. Nor will every kind of impiety concern us. To parade the chronicled crimes of thirteenth-century Italy would be to re-write the *Inferno*. The sins we shall look for were less spectacular, and more radical, than the atrocities of Guelf and Ghibelline. Matthew Paris, with a curl on his northern lip, referred to the inhabitants of Italian cities as *semi-Christiani*,[1] and he meant, not mere sinners, but voluntary outsiders, in that measure, to any christian scheme. These voluntary outsiders will be our quarry; and their traces seen, on one hand, in unrelieved contempt for christian morals and observance, and, on the other, in express declarations of unbelief. We shall be explorers, in a word, to the antipodes: the antipodes of the Age of Faith.

Now explorers have to know where to start. For us, that presents an immediate problem. Familiar sources – letters, official acts, annals, legends – may mention the odd godless ghibelline magnate, but say little, below that level, of *semi-Christiani*.[2] Their relative silence may deter us. There are, however, plenty of explanations for it. Half-Christians were rarely 'news'. As for unbelief, there were reasons – including, it can be shown, a degree of ignorance – why respectable sources should not advertise it, especially to modern eyes. The relative dumbness of the main literary witnesses, is, then, no bar to our search. But it is no help either. The question remains, where to explore?

It is a geographical question. So a map can help answer it. The map shows six typical large Italian towns shortly after the end of the thirteenth century. The outlines involve some guesswork (shown by thinner lines). But wars did history this good turn, that cities had to build annular rings, marking their growth in stone. Thus the unbroken line shows the city circumference at the time of Barbarossa's wars, in the third quarter of the twelfth century. The broken line marks the outer wall as it may be surmised to have stood at the time of the Black Death, in 1348 – the demographic high-water mark of most medieval Italian cities.[3]

---

[1] *Chronica Maiora*, ed H. R. Luard, *RS*, 57, V (London 1880) p 170.

[2] The godless magnates can be pursued through Dante, *Inferno*, x, and commentaries on it.

[3] Sources for the map: (1) G. Braun and F. Hohenberg, *Urbium Praecipuarum mundi theatrum quintum* (Cologne 1593); (2) maps made available to me by the Istituto Geografico Militare in Florence: Verona (1819), Pisa (1793); (3) C. Hardie, 'The origin and plan of Roman Florence, *JRS*, LV, (1965) pp 122–40, map on p 133; (4) *Storia di Milano* (Treccani degli Alfieri, Milan) IV (1954) p 706 ('Milan in 1300' by Monneret de Villard); (5) tourist maps and personal inspection; (6) information on town walls from *Enciclopedia Italiana* (Rome 1949). Thanks are due to Professors D. A. Bullough and M. G. R. Conzen for their advice in connection with these maps; the responsibility for any inaccuracies rests with the author.

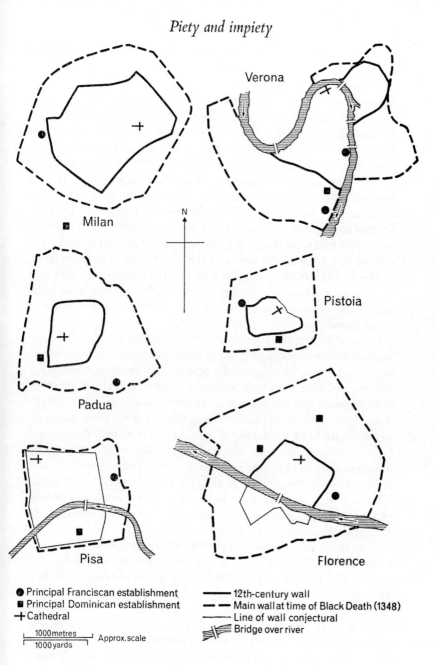

Verona

Milan

N

Pistoia

Padua

Pisa

Florence

● Principal Franciscan establishment
■ Principal Dominican establishment
+ Cathedral

——— 12th-century wall
– – – Main wall at time of Black Death (1348)
——— Line of wall conjectural
⇒⇐ Bridge over river

1000 metres
1000 yards
Approx. scale

Six Italian cities in the early fourteenth century showing position of mendicant convents

Now our familiar, silent sources were mostly written by and about people in the inner city: in the *palazzo* of a Villani, or a Della Scala, or of a bishop. But the bulk of the immigrants who swelled thirteenth-century towns lived outside the twelfth-century wall, in what would now be the housing estates. The centre of gravity of our problem lies, therefore, not in the middle of the old town, but round its periphery. It lies, in fact, where those circles and squares are, ranged just outside, or just inside, the twelfth-century wall: like bastions defending the old cathedral city against an immigrant siege. Bastions, in a sense, is what they were. For they represent convents of mendicant friars – the circles franciscan, the squares dominican – the church's response to the challenge of town growth. Their position betrays an intention: to reach the new populations, for whom the diocesan church did not provide. We shall be glimpsing in the course of this paper how limited the friars' success in this intention was. But now it is the intention by itself that matters, as expressed on the map: the friars faced towards the laity, particularly those sections of the laity not in some way already captives of the church.

Facing the laity, the friars betray its features to us. How? A main function of the friars was preaching. Some sermons were given extempore, and are lost. More generally, preachers made notes, more or less full. Some of these notes went into convent libraries; and some of these, in turn, passed into the national manuscript collections. There we can study them – almost, in places, hearing the words the friars spoke. As an historical source, these notes of sermons may have their dangers and their limitations. But they also have a peculiar value. For popular preachers, did not, like preachers to clergy, command a captive audience, professionally bound to hear pieties. They had to win their listeners. Ideas, as well as language, must be vernacular. The sermons of mendicant friars in this way reflect, from a religious angle, opinions and manners in their lay environment.

Sermons by thirteenth-century Italian friars will furnish the material for this study. Six Italian friars have been chosen, spread out over the century from the 1220s to 1305. The list begins with St Antony of Padua. This friend of St Francis was Portuguese by birth, but his great preaching career was spent mainly in northern Italy, between 1221 and his death in 1231. Antony of Padua left one main, wholly authentic collection of sermons, which has been printed. (They were given to friars, not to the people; but poverty of material from these early years of the century bids us overlook that fault, which does not touch the others.)[1] At the other extremity of Italy, and of fame, was Luca of Bitonto, an apulian Franciscan mentioned by Salimbene's Chronicle as having preached on the death of Henry of Hohenstaufen in 1233, and as having died in 1241. One book of Luca's sermons survives, a neat little pack of biblical quotations, with, nevertheless, a few passages of historical value joining the quotations together.[2] A third Franciscan, Albertino of Verona, is attractively drawn – also by Salimbene – preaching in Emilia in 1249–50: a critical moment for the friars in Italy, as we shall see later. One volume of Albertino's sermons survives, from an early franciscan convent in Tuscany.[3] Our fourth preacher, and first Dominican, is James of Varagine, the famous compiler of *The Golden Legend,* who spent his life in the dominican convent of Genoa, where he died as archbishop in 1298, at nearly seventy. James of Varagine's *Sunday Sermons,* which we shall be using, were composed in 1255.[4] Lastly come a pair of tuscan preachers, both Dominicans. Remigio de' Girolami was the leading preacher of the florentine convent, Santa Maria Novella, from 1266 until the end of the century. His *Sermons on Divers Matters* were composed in late 1281, or 1282, his *Lenten Sermons* probably a little earlier.[5] His successor as leading tuscan preacher was the Blessed Giordano of Rivalto, or of Pisa, who entered the dominican convent of Pisa in 1280, and died in Piacenza in 1311. Giordano preached in Florence for three and a half years. In that period, alone, his sermons were recorded, mostly in shorthand. They fill over a dozen volumes, printed and un-

[1] Antony [of Padua, *Sermones dominicales et in solemnitatibus*], ed Fr Locatelli, 3 vols (Padua 1895–1903). For their audience, see especially pp 39–54. Biography: J. Toussaert, *Antonius von Padua, Versuch einer kritischen Biographie* (Cologne 1967).

[2] Luca [de Bitonto, *Sermones dominicales*], MS Florence, *Bibl naz, Conv[enti] soppr[essi]* C 7.236 (ex S. Croce). Salimbene [de Adam, *Cronica*], ed G. Scalia (Bari 1966) p 122 line 27 – p 123 line 3; p 262 line 30 – p 263 line 2 (for 1233, 1247). The study of this and the other manuscripts in Florence was made possible for me by a grant from the research fund of the university of Newcastle upon Tyne, to which I here acknowledge my indebtedness.

[3] Albertinus [de Verona, *Sermones in festis sanctorum necnon in maioribus solemnitatibus coram populo habendi*], MS Florence, *Bibl laur, Conv soppr,* 548 (ex Bosco de' Frati) fols 1r–126r. Salimbene, p 480 lines 14–22 (also p 199 line 1).

[4] [Jacobus a] Voragine (= Varagine), [*Sermones dominicales*], MS Florence, *Bibl naz Conv soppr,* J 10.35. E. C. Richardson, *Materials for a Life of Jacopo de Varagine* (New York 1935) I, pp ix–xiii; II, pp 4, 40–54. On the proper spelling of his name, *ibid,* I, p x. I believe, against Richardson (II, pp 79–80), that the text we have of the *Sunday Sermons* is an abbreviation of the sermons as given.

[5] Remigius, [*Sermones*] *quadr[agesimales]*, MS Florence, *Bibl naz Conv soppr* G 7.939 (ex S. Maria Novella); [*Sermones*] *de div[ersis] mat[eriis]*, MS Florence, *Bibl naz Conv soppr,* G 4.936 (ex S. Maria Novella) fols 243ra – 404ra. For the date of *de div mat* see fol 404rb; compare fols 283vb–408va (death of Laurence, OP, confessor to Philip III). Biography and extracts: [R.] Davidsohn, [*Geschichte von Florenz*], IV (Berlin 1927) III, pp 67–9.

printed. Among the latter, I have chosen, as appropriate to our subject, a cycle given on the Creed during Lent, 1305.[1]

An extraneous burgundian friar has been intruded on our Italians, to speak on church attendance. Much of Humbert of Romans's life was spent in France. But he was provincial prior of the Dominicans in and near Rome from 1238 to c 1241, so there is every reason to include Italy among the sources of his experience. The special value of his testimony will be explained when we come to it.[2]

These, then, are our guides: three Franciscans, three or, in all, four Dominicans, spread out between 1221 and 1305, and, geographically, between Padua and Genoa in the north, and Apulia in the south. These friars were among the loftiest representatives of Italian Catholicism in their time. What, now, can they tell us of its antipodes?

It is a commonplace that preachers preach about sin, and are against it. Their text, the Bible, would oblige them to do so even if they were personally unacquainted with it. But each preacher handles the subject in a different way, and some of that difference betrays the effect of actual sins in the preacher's milieu.

Our own six Italian preachers were no exception to the rule. All expatiated on the contemporary prevalence of sin. Whenever it came to the matter of the thorns that choked the good seed, or king Herod, the wicked husbandmen, the clouds on Mount Sinai, the Egyptian bondage, or any other of the hundred biblical texts which pointed, literally or allegorically, at the wicked, a friar could be counted on to jump on his chance, and denounce, in the present tense, the violent, the vain, the greedy, the false and the sensual, who polluted the very air his audience breathed.

That it was real sinners the friars meant, not mere characters from the Bible, is plain from the phraseology used. 'Plenty of such enemies of God and the Virgin are to be discovered today.'[3] 'Many choose the broad path of carnal lust, or of honours, or of pleasures.'[4] 'Alas, what

---

[1] Giordano, *Prediche*, MS Florence, *Bibl naz*, xxxv, 222, cited as Giordano, *Credo; Prediche del Beato F. Giordano da Rivalto*, ed D. M. Manni, 7 vols (Bologna 1820) cited as *Giordano*, Manni; *Prediche inedite del Beato Giordano da Rivalto*, ed E. Narducci (Bologna 1867) cited as *Giordano*, Narducci. For a list of MSS and editions, *Giordano*, Narducci, p xxvi. Biography and further bibliography, [P. G.] Colombi, [Introduction to *Giordano da Rivalto, Prediche Scelte*], ed P. G. Colombi (Florence 1924) pp 7–29. Extracts in Davidsohn, pp 69–76.

[2] Biography in *Lexicon für Theologie und Kirche* (Freiburg 1957–67) under 'Humbertus'.

[3] Albertinus, fol 11a: 'cum tales hodie multi invenirentur lapidandi hostes dei et beatae virginis' (De S. Stephano).

[4] *Ibid*, fol 11b: 'set econtra multi eligerunt viam latam voluptatis carnis, sive honorum delitiarum.'

bad vassals does Jesus, King of Kings, have now; look around you, and see the malevolence of Christ's vassals!'[1] 'Alas, nowadays many use their tongues like pens of the devil.'[2] These remarks, their metaphors echoing some allegory in their context, are only a few of those to be gleaned, in this sense, from a single one of our group of preachers, Albertino of Verona. The same could be had from the others. In all, the extent, and contemporary character, of the wickedness are repeatedly made clear: it is always *multi* or *quanti*, *hodie* or *in istis diebus*. 'I find one fault in this world', said Giordano, 'and it is general to all peoples. It is an evil love of the world.'[3]

Our focus on sin becomes clearer when the particular sins which the preachers picked out are considered. Dante, it will be recalled, was scared in the darkness of his forest by three wild beasts: a leopard, a lion and a wolf: lust, pride and avarice – the sins, respectively, of youth, middle- and old-age.[4] As elsewhere, Dante allegorises a tradition. These were a familiar trio in friars' sermons, appearing in those of James of Varagine, in particular, with the regularity of faith, hope and charity. Other sins, certainly, get attention. In Antony of Padua, the trio scarcely appears as such: *gula* replaced *luxuria* in the threefold sin of Adam; and the saint dilates on *ira*, *invidia*, *hypocrisia*, *adulatio*, and a menagery of other sins.[5] But at the other extreme, the two tuscan Dominicans from the end of the century tend to merge the *ira* of partisan violence into pride, *gula* into a more general sensual worldliness.

The trio of lust, pride and avarice reflected scholastic ethics. It also reflected contemporary society; and this can be told, once again, from the detail, and stresses, given by the preachers. It can be told above all by the precedence given, within the trio, to the last, *avaritia*, which meant, not just hoarding, but money-mindedness. There is every reason, quite apart from sermons, for believing that thirteenth-century Italy saw a growth in a competitive spirit, of a kind finding special outlet in money-making. The friars' life was a reaction to this spirit, and their sermons staunchly confirm its prevalence. All our six preachers revert frequently, and at length, to 'avarice' and 'usury' (terms often used interchangeably). For avarice worked under many disguises, and on every level of

---

[1] *Ibid*, fol 11r b: 'set heu quam pessimos vasallos habet hodie re [*sic*] regum iesus nazarenus vide et considera malitiam vasallorum Christi.'

[2] *Ibid*, fol 57r a: 'Sed heu multi habent hodie linguas suas quasi calamos diaboli.'

[3] Giordano, *Credo*, fol 160v: 'Uno errore truovo io al mondo..., ed è generale errore di tutte le genti, e questo sie il malo amore mondano.'

[4] *Inferno*, I, 31–54; compare Jer. 5:6.

[5] Antony, p 42 b (Adam's sin); p 373 b (a list of sins).

society. Antony of Padua explained how usury admitted degrees of flagrancy: secret, blatant, or, in between, just secret enough to maintain the culprit in a reputation for benevolence.[1] Remigio de' Girolami exposed the different masks usury hid under: 'usurers blush to call themselves that. So they are called lenders, or changers, or even merchants; and their usury, "merit", "profit", or "fruit"'.[2] Albertino, for his part, pointed out how – *pace* Dante's leopard of youth, etc. – avarice touched all ages: 'other sinners stop sinning when illness or age blocks their path. Not the usurer. Healthy or sick, young or old, he persists in his wickedness.'[3] Similarly, the sin touched every class: 'High and low, all are out for gain.' The words are Jeremiah's. But James of Varagine found no difficulty in fitting the text to his own milieu.[4] For it was not just the big money-changers who were embraced in the preachers' glare, but notaries, advocates, and indeed a whole host of dependants: 'Where else will you find fair and noble women nowadays', asked Albertino, 'but in the homes of usurers?'[5] Finally, avarice poisoned every level of a man's activity: his thoughts, as he thinks 'ceaselessly, day and night, how to get money'; his intentions, since money becomes the aim of all he does; and his tastes, since he loves only what money can buy.[6]

It would turn our study into a thirteenth-century sermon, and a long one, to follow further our sources' deprecations of money-mindedness. But we have heard enough from these defenders of the faith, to learn which affection they regarded as the greatest affront to it. It was, indeed,

[1] Antony, p 28 *a*.

[2] Remigius, *De div mat*, fol 409v *a*: 'Unde usarii per verecundiam fetoris infamie se non vocant usarios sed prestitores vel campsores vel etiam mercatores et lucrum usarim non vocant usura sed meritum vel profectum vel fructum cum tamen sunt magnum demeritum et magnum danpnum.' This sermon is added to the volume of Remigio's sermons by another hand; but there is no reason to deprive him of its authorship.

[3] Albertinus, fol 94r *b*: 'Ceteri enim peccatores desistunt peccare impediente infirmitate vel senectute, set usuarius non sic: sive sanus sive infirmus, sive iuvenis sive senex, in malitia perseverat.'

[4] Varagine, fol 71v: ' "A maiore usque ad minorem omnes avaricie student." Sunt maiores, minores et mediocres. Per minores intelliguntur layci, per mediocres clerici, per maiores prelati.'

[5] Albertinus, fol 94r *b*: 'Ubi enim invenies hodie pulcras mulieres et nobiles et dextrarios fortes nisi in domo usurariorum?' For a list of cursed professions, Remigius, *Quadr*, fol 64r: 'Set non quidam hoc [*scil* subvenire pauperi] faciunt raptores, usurarii, advocati, iudices inpietatis, notarii Florentini, mercatores subdoli, qui expolliant domos viduarum.'

[6] Varagine, fol 71v: 'quia die ac nocte cogitare non cessant qualiter lucra acquirere possint et pecuniam augere... Alii sunt quorum avaricia est in intencionibus quia in omnibus quae dicunt et faciunt semper ad lucrum vel emolumentum temporale intendunt... Alii sunt quorum avaricia est in affectionibus quia temporalia ardenter diligunt et spiritualia parvipendunt.'

more than an affection. Cupidity was becoming a doctrine. Professor Baron has shown how, in the age of the friars, wealth was being defended by some lay writers as accessory to virtue.[1] We hear the same, spoken earlier, and from clergy: Antony of Padua, in the 1220s, denounced those 'contemporary priests' who urge their charges to acquire wealth, as no bar to salvation.[2] Luca of Bitonto similarly, makes the spirit of avarice, whose voice he had doubtless heard round him, enumerate the noble and charitable things that could only be done with wealth.[3] Money was no mere marginal temptation in the Italy of the friars. It transformed the very idea of virtue.

Italy, then, abounded in wickedness; not only in the public sort, that found its way into the chronicles and history books; but in the more diffuse kind, which gave the pious an impression they lived in sinful times. Lust, pride and avarice, were what they saw around them; and the greatest of these was avarice.

Wickedness, and lack of faith, are not the same thing. St Antony of Padua and the Blessed Giordano of Pisa, like other priests, confessed each morning that they had sinned exceedingly; and many of the ills convulsing politics in Innocent IV's time were no doubt perpetrated with a bad conscience. Nevertheless, where wickedness became habitual it put blocks in the way of piety which, to follow our preachers, could jeopardise a man's title to be called a Christian at all.

The blocks arose because wrongdoing absorbed a man. Giordano painted a droll sketch, for example, of the demands of libertinism: 'we see some wordly men who, to get a woman, will go out at night, forgetting about food, and endangering their persons, things not even a hermit would do for love of God'.[4] Libertinism, though, like other bodily sins, had natural limits. The quest for money and honour knew none. We heard James of Genoa scorning those who thought 'ceaselessly, day and night' of money.[5] Remigio de' Girolami said it was plain, from the lives of merchants, how heavy a toll wordly allurements exacted.[6] Giordano caricatured these devotees of 'the world' as

---

[1] H. Baron, 'Franciscan Poverty and Civic Wealth as Factors in the Rise of Humanistic Thought', *Speculum*, XIII (1938) pp 1–37. Baron's earliest instance of a writer advocating wealth as instrumental to virtue is Albertano of Brescia (1238).   [2] Antony, p 392 *b*.

[3] Luca, fol 271r *b*: 'spiritus cupiditatis veniens ad cor hominis dicens: acquire quantum potes, dum iuvenis es et mercare, atque excute solers... ut habeas quid filiis tuis dimites, quid pauperibus pro dando tribuas, quia redemptio anime viri divitie sunt.'

[4] *Giordano*, Narducci, p 17.   [5] See p 90 n 6 above.

[6] Remigius, *Quadr*, fol 12v: 'mundus quidquid promittit promittit cum labore et deceptione. Quod promittit cum labore patet in alexandro, romanis et aliis regibus qui regna

'throwing themselves into it all day, all day struggling to get rich, doing nothing, day or night, but fret and calculate'.[1] Libertinism, greed, honour; how vain the world was! Yet how men worked for it! 'There is no saying', exclaimed Giordano, 'what labours are undergone by those who seek riches, or carnal delights, or worldly honours.'[2]

The first block that this absorption put in the way of a man's piety was a practical one. Busy men could not spare time for church. How far mere shortage of time, by itself, accounted for low church attendance no-one can judge. Certainly, antipathy to sacred holidays as an obstacle to work was vigorous long before the thirteenth century.[3] Whatever the reasons it is clear that in thirteenth-century Italy much less use was made of churches than might have been.

Estimates in this matter can only be approximate. It is safer to express them in general remarks, in the medieval way, than to put them in modern percentages. Preachers, concerned as they were to reach as large audiences as they could, had a fair idea of who came to church and who not. Their findings, however, were of more direct concern to themselves than to their lay flocks. The clearest remarks on church attendance are therefore to be found, not in a sermon, but in a book on how to preach, written by one preacher for others: in Humbert of Romans's *On the Teaching of Preachers*.[4] The domestic character of this book gives it the added recommendation, as a source, of innocence of propaganda: it was no sermon, but a practical handbook, to be relied on by the most up-to-date preaching body in Christendom.

It has been important to take stock of Humbert of Romans's credentials. For we have scarcely another witness for the stark lesson he gives us: namely, that substantial sections of thirteenth-century society hardly attended church at all. It is not merely that the technique Humbert recommends to preachers for reaching the laity involves catching them at markets and tournaments, in ships, and so on – a fair enough sign that they were not to be caught in churches. Humbert goes

et provincias et totum illud quod habuerunt acquisiverunt cum magno labore corporis et periculis...idem patet in mercatoribus...Pugnat ergo mundus contra hominem per promissiones deceptorias et sic non permittit homines in quiete. Set occupat se homo totum in laboribus sine fructu, nihil de Deo aut celestibus cogitans, et per consequens cum moritur transit de labore in laborem.'

[1] *Giordano*, Narducci, p 133. [2] *Ibid*, p 129.

[3] G. G. Coulton, *Five Centuries of Religion*, I (Cambridge 1929) pp 234-46; *Medieval Panorama* (Cambridge 1938) pp 181-5.

[4] Humbertus de Romanis, *De erud[itione] praed[icatorum]*, *Maxima Bibliotheca Veterum Patrum*, xxv (Lyon 1677) pp 456-567.

so far as to explain why. A chapter on 'The Poor', for example, starts
with the bald assertion: 'It must be noted that the poor rarely go to
church, and rarely to sermons; so that they know little of what pertains
to their salvation.'[1] The author will say much the same of magnates:
'men placed in high station are rarely accustomed to hear sermons'.[2]
Among persons between the top and bottom classes, it is familiars of
big households, in particular, that Humbert picks out as bad attenders:
'this sort of *familia*, because of various occupations, is rarely accustomed
to gather in church, unless perhaps it be on the great feasts, and then for
morning mass'.[3] Ladies' maids, especially, were ill-placed for church-
going,[4] although their lapse was surpassed by that of some men-
servants who, urged on by wicked masters, omitted to go to church at
all, ever, and violated feast-days into the bargain.[5] Finally, as if the
laity were not bad enough, some of the clergy spent so much time in
gaming, pleasure and 'worse things' that these, too, Humbert observed, 'scarcely come to church'.[6]

This professor of preaching, then, Humbert of Romans, leaves a thin
estimate of church attendance. The two extremities of society, and
some groups in between – he mentions servants and reprobate clergy –
went to church rarely. Some never went. Humbert's impression is
singular for its clarity. However, corroboration can be found in our
preachers. So let us hear them.

'The just', said Albertino of Verona, 'should hear sermons, confess
frequently, and often visit church' – as if many people did not.[7] One
piece of the devil's mischief, Albertino complained on another occasion,
was to bind people's feet, so that they did not go to church.[8] Giordano,
at the end of the century, gives the same impression. He refers, as a
subject of common knowledge, to people who, through negligence or
presumption, do not attend the Eucharist, or make no attempt to fast in
Lent.[9] One day, Giordano relates, he suggested to a woman that she
take her daughter to church on feast-days, for the daughter's improve-

---

[1] *De erud praed*, II, Tract I, Ch 86, p 499 A.   [2] *Ibid*, Ch 83, p 497 C.
[3] *Ibid*, Ch 76, p 493 G.   [4] *Ibid*, Ch 98, p 505 C.
[5] *Ibid*, Ch 76, p 494 AB.   [6] *Ibid*, Tract II, Ch 2, p 508 C.
[7] Albertinus, fol 10v b: 'debent enim iusti venire ad predicationem et frequenter confiteri et ecclesiam sepius visitare.'
[8] *Ibid*, fol 73r b: 'Alligat autem diabolus homines…in pedibus per otium ne ad ecclesiam vel predicationem vadat.'
[9] Giordano, *Credo*, fol 146r: 'se tu non fai nulla bona opera, non andra al sacramento o prediche non darai limosine non perdonerai e userai mali modi.' *Ibid*, fols 112v – 13r: 'ora comincio frate Giordano a rimprendere i vitii delle donne e di quelle che non digiunano e disse / ne molto le quegli non iscrivo.'

ment. 'It is not the custom', the woman replied. The preacher told her to start one.[1]

Sacramental confession was a matter of special interest to authority. In 1215, the Fourth Lateran Council had made annual confession obligatory. It was little enough, preachers agreed. A few years after the decree, St Antony of Padua protested that while many people limited themselves to this annual, obligatory confession,[2] 'scarcely anyone', whether or not he confessed more frequently, did penance properly.[3] Two or three generations later, not only did Remigio and Giordano agree that many people made no confession 'in their heart',[4] but Remigio, from his experience in Santa Maria Novella, felt able to declare that 'There are many who confess neither in their hearts nor with their lips'; nor had they done so, it seems, for ten or twenty years.[5]

Whatever the neglect of sacraments, it was failure to attend sermons that preachers returned to most cordially. Here the Lombard, Albertino, picks up, among non-attenders, a class left out by the burgundian, Humbert: business-men. 'Some men', said Albertino, 'have hated the light of preaching: like usurers, seizers of goods, and greybeards who have grown old in wickedness... For when the lamp of preaching appears, usurers and others who want to persist in their wickedness hide themselves away.'[6] Remigio, in a similar tone, carped at the 'many' who 'do not want to hear God's word',[7] and Giordano, at 'men who never go to a single sermon'.[8] Giordano, in another address, used a phrase which may give us some index of the proportion of non-attenders: 'Blessed are they,' he said, 'who come to sermons, and read good books and Scripture; but especially, come to sermons.'[9] Hearing sermons,

---

[1] *Giordano*, Manni, II p 24 (20 Dec. 1304, Sunday morning, S. Maria Novella).

[2] Antony, p 276*b*.

[3] Antony, p 347*a*: 'fere hodie nullus est, qui veram agat poenitentiam'. Compare pp 50*a*, 75*b*, 224*b*, etc.

[4] Remigius, *Quadr*, fol 82v: 'multi confitentur ore set non corde.' *Giordano*, Narducci, p 149: 'Sono molti e molte che vengono a confessione, e non hanno pensato nulla innanzi.' Compare Giordano, *Credo*, fol 116r: 'Chomandamento è della chiesa che ogni christiano si confessi almeno una volta lanno. Ma il comandamento diddio è maggiore però che tu se tenuto di chonfessarti incontanente che tu sei in peccato mortale, il piu tosto che puoi.'

[5] Remigius, *Quadr*, fol 82v: 'Nam multi sunt qui nec corde nec ore confitentur equidem [?] per x annos per xx annos.'

[6] Albertinus, fol 55v *ab*: 'aliqui oderunt lucem predicationis, sicut usurarii et / raptores et senes antiquiti in malitiis... quia apparente luce predicationis abscondunt se usurarii et alii qui volunt perseverare in malitia sua.'

[7] Remigius, *Quadr*, fol 75r: 'set multi nollunt audire verbum dei.'

[8] *Giordano*, Narducci, p 134: 'uomini che non vanno a predica mai.'

[9] Giordano, *Credo*, fols 17v – 18r: 'beati quelli keccio fanno ke vengono a prediche e legono i buoni libri e le scripture [*sic*] ma specialmente / d'usare le prediche.'

reading; the two occupations are named in one breath, as if listeners to sermons did not outnumber the literate. The impressions of Humbert of Romans, then, are confirmed by popular preachers; in the matters of sacraments and of sermons, many people went to church rarely; a few, not at all.

Wickedness, by absorbing men's attention, erected this practical block to their life of faith: there was no time for devotion. It raised a second block, less palpable, but more radical in its effects. Absorption in the world ended by deforming the mind: it destroyed faith. For our preachers leave no doubt that, in their world, faith, like conduct, left much to be desired.

To begin with, it was a familiar theme in sermons that habitual action, good or bad, had its appropriate effect on a man's thoughts. St Antony of Padua, explaining a scriptural story, spoke of habitual sin as like the 'droppings of swallows' which blind a man's reason and intellect.[1] Gluttony was one such sin.[2] But lust, St Antony felt, was a particular enemy to faith.[3] In pursuit of the same idea, Fra Albertino used the image of a veil, which the various sins – lust, usury, robbery – lowered between Christ and the soul.[4] James of Genoa described the devil, once admitted to the soul, as 'shutting the ears of the heart', so that God's word could not penetrate.[5] Remigio observed that each man was prone to defend the sins he habitually committed, and this 'entombed' the soul.[6] Pride, especially, blinded one: 'as too much wind swells the eyes, so that they cannot see clearly, so men blown up with pride cannot see clearly, – and for a state this is disastrous'.[7] Giordano, finally, conveyed the idea by an anecdote. A king, besieging a city, demanded the right eyes of all the defenders. The defenders, whose cavalry tactics depended on good vision on the right, wisely refused,

[1] Antony, p 34*a*. Compare p 153*b*.

[2] *Ibid*, p 34*a*.

[3] *Ibid*, pp 34*a*, 252*b*, and especially 187*a*.

[4] Albertinus, fol 35v*b*.

[5] Varagine, fol 92r–v: 'diabolus in domu anime ingressus claudit aures cordis / ne verbum dei audiat.'

[6] Remigius, *Quadr*, fol 73r: 'Ex talia consuetudine peccandi cadit homo in necessitatem. Nam ipsa consuetudo altera natura est sive alterans naturam...Nam ex tali necessitate homo cadit in defensionem ipsius peccati vollens statum sui sceleris excusare. Sepe enim inveniuntur homines scelerati dicentes, quod peccatum non est usuria, assignantes rationes suas. Alii dicunt quod peccatum non est inter solutum et solutam. Alii dicunt quod peccatum non est ire in al[*sic*, a vulgarism?] excommunicatis...In ista tali defensione peccati sepellitur anima.'

[7] Remigius, *Quadr*, fol 45v: 'sicut enim nimius ventus tumefacit oculos ut clare videre non possint, sic superbia inflati clare non possunt videre, et hoc est valde periculosum in civitate.'

and finished by winning a pitched battle. The king, explained Fra Giordano, was the devil. He wanted us blind, to beat us more easily.[1]

Sin, then, by itself, affected the mind, lowering a veil across it. So the world's wickedness was itself the first testimony against its faith. However, there is other, more direct, testimony. In the first place, absorption in sin led a man, the preachers said, to ignore the question of his salvation. Luca of Bitonto spoke of sinners as plunged in a 'sleep of death', from which they were awakened, he said, 'neither by the preacher's cry, nor by the thunder of warning, nor by the scourges God deigns to send them'; a sleep the more culpable, in the case of supposed Christians, for taking place in daylight.[2] It is characteristic of preachers to hold human mortality before the eyes of their audience. Among our six, it was Remigio who developed this theme most fully, and it may profit us to hear his words:

A man sees to it that he is fit and well. Then he sets aside fear of sudden death, so that he can postpone doing good. It does not enter his head that man is vanity, or that, when death arrives, he simply ceases to exist. Such a person rules out the possibility of sudden death – whether by sword or rope – in his own case. He forgets that he is as it were sailing over death's rock, ready to be wrecked on it, and plunged into the depths of hell.[3]

It comes as no surprise to learn where the worst of this negligence was to be found:

The miser and usurer, who toils, and runs hither and thither, does not consider the brevity of human life. For he makes no attempt either to do penance, or give alms. If he did consider it, he would not sin...Schemers, fraudsters, tricksters, sodomites, and others of this sort, who sin in secret, give no thought to the approach of death; for if they did, they would not sin.[4]

The friar appends a chilling list of kinds of death – fever, hunger, falling buildings, wreck, beheading, hanging, and so on.

Many lived oblivious of their destiny. Whether that necessarily

---

[1] *Giordano*, Narducci, pp 29–32.

[2] Luca, fol 7vb: 'Multi dormiunt, ut illi qui diu in peccato morantur. Tales ad modum letargiae nec ad clamorem predicatoris, nec ad tonitrui comminationis, nec ad flagella divine animadversionis excitantur a somno mortis.'

[3] Remigius, *Quadr*, fol 59v: 'fecit se sanum et incolumen, non timet tam cito mori et sic tardat bene facere et non respiciunt [*sic*] quia nullus sit homo, cessat iam mortis [*sic*], nec cogitat si subito vel gladio vel fune esset sibi possibile mori, et non perpendit quia ipse est sicut scopulum mortis, et frangitur, et submergitur in profundum inferni.'

[4] Remigius, *De div mat*, fol 400vb: 'Istam brevitatem non cogitat avarus et usarius qui discurrit laborat et cetera nec penitentiam vel elemosinam vult facere. Si enim cogitaret non peccaret.' *Ibid.* fol 401ra: 'hoc non cogitant dolosi, fraudulenti, deceptores, sodomite et huiusmodi in occulto peccantes. Quia si bene cogitaret nunquam peccaret.'

Piety and impiety

meant they lived oblivious of God is debatable. But the implication was frequently drawn in those terms. 'Those whose eyes are not turned to Christ cannot see him'[1] 'Man occupies himself wholly in fruitless toil, never giving a thought to God or heavenly things';[2] 'bad men never think of heavenly things, no, and care nothing for them';[3] 'misers who abandon God...'[4] These are typical phrases. Remigio, whose 'hellfire' flavour has just been tasted, spoke in the same style of the multitude – 'how many, alas, in our city and in the world' – who went down to 'Egypt', the devil's kingdom: 'You will say, "who are these people?" I answer, first and foremost they go down to Egypt who worship idols of gold and silver. These are the misers and hoarders, who all their lives forget God, directing all their mind, all their intention to the piling-up of perishable and worldly wealth.'[5] *Tota vita sua Dei obliviscentes*: worldly preoccupation led to neglect, not only of death, but of God and all things invisible.

To write down even the most inveterate neglecter of God as an atheist is to slight the subtleties of religious psychology; and before we pass to evidence of disbelief in God, it must be recognised that our preachers – whose business religious psychology was – did not make this mistake. Sin might, for them, imply lack of faith. But it was an implication, no more; and that reserve is repeatedly made clear. Varagine will speak, for example, of 'the impious who *seem* to have no faith';[6] Remigio, of 'sinners, who believe in Christ, whose lips, and perhaps whose hearts, confess him, yet who disbelieve him, nay deny him, in their *acts*'.[7] Giordano will say that 'to wallow in sin is nothing other than to say *you wish* God did not exist'.[8] Even the toughened

---

[1] Albertinus, fol 35vb: 'non ergo possunt Christum cognoscere multi quorum oculi ad christum non aspiciunt.' Compare Luca, fol 270rb: 'Alii nec corde nec ore nec opere vocant deum, qui semper vana cogitant, mala loquuntur, et operantur perversa.'

[2] See p 91 n 6 above, last sentence.

[3] Giordano, *Credo*, fol 16or: 'Male genti non pensano di queste cosi [= i beni di paradiso] no, non si ne curano.' [4] *Giordano*, Narducci, p 40: 'gli avari, che abbandonano Iddio.'

[5] Remigius, *Quadr*, fol 38v: 'set heu quot sunt in civitate et mundo qui non ascendunt cum salvatore in ierusalem set potius in inpetu horribili in egyptum descendunt...Et si dicas qui sunt tales, respondeo quod quidam descendunt in egyptum ydola aurea et argentea adorant, et isti sunt miseri et avari, qui tota vita sua dei obliviscentes totam mentem totam intencionem in aggregandis diviciis deficientibus et terrenis expenderunt similes facti serpentibus qui ventrem terrae habentes terram comedunt.'

[6] Varagine, fol 51v (see Matt. 13:7): 'spinae vero sunt homines impii qui nec fidem videntur habere nec opera et insuper bonos persequantur.'

[7] Remigius, *Quadr*, fol 83v: 'peccatores qui licet credant in christum et confitentur christum ore et forte corde, operibus tamen non credunt, set negant.'

[8] *Giordano*, Narducci, p 9: 'istando tu in peccato, e piacendoti, non è altro a dire, se che tu disideri che Iddio non sia.'

sinner, paradoxically, could still believe. It was Giordano – whether because he thought more, or said more, or was written down more – who has left us the most penetrating description of this paradox: 'The sinner is divided in himself. He believes, and does not believe. He wants, and does not want. He acts, and does not know how to act. He is in a tangle, and cannot identify his will.'[1] Such a sinner, oscillating between extremes of belief and unbelief, might settle eventually into a state of 'half-belief'. Remigio called this *fides modica*, and he put it, duly, mid-way between 'living' and 'dead' faith. He gave as an example people who were always fretting about money: obviously, he said, such worriers lacked full faith in a God who provided life's necessities.[2] Whether because of alternation between belief and unbelief, then, or because of a steady half-belief, a godless life did not invariably signal bankruptcy in faith.

It did not invariably do so. But it could. The assurance that our sources did not leap to easy conclusions must enhance the value of their direct references to failures in belief; and it is these we now have to consider. It should be noted, first, that even the best faith was vulnerable. Everyone who had thought seriously of the virtue of *fides* realised, like Remigio with his *fides modica*, that it varied by degree. You might speak broadly, in public, of faithful and infidel, as divided by a great gulf. But experience – not to mention the New Testament – taught that the faithful themselves could have more or less faith. This lesson was increasingly learned during the thirteenth century, as awareness spread among the educated of the complexity of their own minds. Preachers knew it better than most. Giordano began his cycle of sermons on the Creed: 'Let us start with the first word of the Creed, namely *Credo*. This word is not an article of faith. Rather, it articulates the other articles and statements. And it says "I believe". And this word would make a big subject by itself.'[3] There is reason to think, from the way that it is written in the manuscript, that Giordano went

---

[1] *Ibid*, p 180: 'il peccatore è diviso e partito in sè medesimo. Crede e non crede, vuole e non vuole, fa e non sa che si fare, avolgesi e non sa che si vuole.'

[2] Remigius, *Quadr*, fol 31v: 'haec est in hominibus qui non habent tantam fidem ut credant deum qui dedit homini corpus et anima et omnia elementa et quae in eis sunt...et ideo continue laborant in acquirendo et cumulando divicias.'

[3] Giordano, *Credo*, fol 8r: 'Et comminceremci ala prima parola. Non è articolo di fede. Anci è articolo degli altri articoli e cose. Et dicie credo. Et questa parola die grande materia in se.' The sign ✠ follows, and the text proceeds on a new argument. The sign does not appear elsewhere in the MS (though a similar one appears on fol 120r). The scribe frequently breaks off in this way, usually remarking simply, for instance, 'e disse f.G. sopra queste cose molte parole molte' (fol 119r).

on to say more on the 'big subject', which the scribe did not see
fit to put down. At all events, all our preachers, Giordano included,
knew that believers had difficulties. One was prayer. You might
think your prayer unheard, and be tempted to give up praying. So Fra
Remigio told his hearers, if so affected, not to despair: even St Paul was
not always heard at once, and he was 'a saint, as you are not'.[1] It is for
our good that we should have to wait for consolation. A Christian who
does not read and trust the writings of the saints, Remigio said, will often
be troubled, because his faith is incomplete.[2] Besides prayer, two of the
church's miraculous doctrines presented a special obstacle. For the status
of transubstantiation in our preachers' milieu it will be enough to cite
Giordano:

It is a big thing [he admitted] to think of, that the bread and wine become
Christ's true body and blood...It is a big thing to think of, that it should be in
so many places, on all the altars, in heaven and on earth, in over 100,000 places
...But God is there to help our faith, so that a man must not say: ' What is
this that I am supposed to believe?'[3]

Grande cosa è a pensare. The eucharistic miracle, Giordano admitted,
'appears hard to believe'.[4] He went on to parade examples of metamor-
phoses and multiplications in nature, to make it seem less of a freak.

Faith, if it needed strengthening about the Eucharist, might also feel
what St Antony of Padua called *pia dubitatio*[5] about the resurrection of
the flesh – Christ's or ours. The model for this pious doubt was the
apostle Thomas, and sermons on this subject generally came up at
Easter, when the story of doubting Thomas was read. 'Therefore do
not be incredulous,' St Antony finished, 'O Thomas, O Christian, but
believe.'[6] 'Let the incredulous, then,' urged Albertino of Verona,
'themselves look into Christ's hands.'[7] Remigio, who, like Giordano,
had drunk at aristotelian fountains, went to some lengths to prove that
bodily resurrection was 'natural' – on the grounds that nature made
nothing in vain.[8] And it was 'not impossible' for a resurrected body to

[1] Remigius, *Quadr*, fol 31v: 'ergo tu cum non sis sanctus, sapiens et dignus sicut christus
et virgo maria et paulus, non desperes si statim non exauderis et consolaberis, quia
inducie sunt tibi ad meritum.'
[2] *Ibid*, fol 67v: 'si homo non respiceret et crederet scripturas sanctorum sepe turbaretur,
quae accidit quia [?] non esset beatissimus in fide...Et una causa est quia vidimus bonos
et castos et amicos dei satis plus tribulari et affligi in isto mundo quam malos ymo
quasi[?] consolantur mali.' [3] *Giordano*, Narducci, p 102.
[4] *Ibid*, p 103: 'questo pare dura cosa a credere.'
[5] Antony, p 141. [6] *Ibid*, p 142a.
[7] Albertinus, fol 36vb: 'aspiciant igitur increduli in manibus christi.'
[8] Remigius, *Quadr*, fols 102v – 107r.

pass, as Christ's did, through solid walls. Remigio ended, 'Why, then, are you astonished?'[1]

Temptations to doubt, in prayer, or about the most palpably miraculous of the church's doctrines – transubstantiation and resurrection – were one more class of weapon by which the devil sought to prise Christians away from their God. They were temptations to be resisted. Like any other temptations, however, they might not be resisted. Persons unused to resisting temptations in general might easily give way on this one. Not all sinners, it was agreed, were unbelievers. But some were. Our sources, whose delicacy of expression has been amply demonstrated, say so too often for their testimony to be brushed away.

The unbelief they speak of appears on two levels. The lower and less articulate was that found among the habitual sinners we have already met. It was unbelief, so to speak, of the heart, not the head. St Antony of Padua referred to the 'chill of unbelief' as a current evil,[2] and denounced bishops for ousting their fledgelings, by bad example, from 'the nest of faith'.[3] St Antony saw the sin of fornication as an almost automatic solvent of faith.[4] James of Genoa, for his part, referred to spiritual 'paralytics', 'who have neither faith nor works' to offer.[5] In connection with another parable, James spoke of dead vine-branches 'who neither stick to the stem by faith, nor bear fruit in works'.[6] The devil, he said, having shut the ears of the heart so that the soul does not hear God's word, 'extinguishes the light of faith'.[7] What St Antony saw in the north-east, James in the north-west, Remigio recognised in Florence. While Remigio admitted that not all his sinners were unbelievers, the faith of some was 'dead'.[8] For when concupiscence and habit, like tyrants, have bound a man, and he is caught in the vortex of desire, 'the fool, taking leave of his reason, oblivious of the name of God, says in his heart, "There is no God."'[9] Giordano spoke, or was recorded, more fully:

---

[1] Ibid, fol 107v: 'nec videatur hoc impossibile...quare miraris?'

[2] Antony, p 788a: 'frigus infidelitatis'.

[3] Ibid, pp 348b – 9a This passage refers partly, but only partly, to formal heresy.

[4] Ibid, p 187a: 'propter fornicationem amittitur fides.' See p 95 n 3 above.

[5] Varagine, fol 42v: 'alii sunt paralitici quantum ad utrumque qui nec fidem habent nec opera.'

[6] Ibid, fol 55r: 'palmite...qui non viti adherent per fidem nec fructificant per operationem.

[7] Ibid, fol 92v: 'dyabolus...extinguit lumen fidei.'

[8] Remigius, Quadr, fol 32r: 'fides mortua...'

[9] Ibid, fol 3v: 'concupiscentia reviviscente et invalescente ligat consuetudo et ratio consopitur et sic trahitur homo in profundum, malorum tyrannidi, vitiorum ira, et carnalium voragine desideriorum; absortus [?] rationis sue, divini nominis oblitus, dicit insipiens in corde suo, non est deus.'

Tell me now, how many of these unbelievers exist? Who nowadays believes
in the good things unseen, the good things of paradise? Who cares about them?
People do not care about them at all. They do not know what they are...
Today the whole world is full of this sin...Nowadays, they feel no fear of the
threats and pains of hell, they simply do not believe in them...they do not
place hope in any other life than the present.[1]

Chi crede oggi i beni invisibili...chissine cura?

One sort of 'fool' denied God with his heart. Other fools – Giordano
often called them *matti*[2] – made more articulate objections. Rational
demurs to faith, mere temptations to God's chosen, could become
philosophical corner-stones to the undevout. Remigio expressly relates
some unbelief to book-learning. There are men, he says, 'who, while
they believe the books of kings, princes and merchants, and even the
writings of pagans – who often say false and doubtful things – nevertheless refuse to believe Christ's words'.[3] It was not Fra Remigio's
business, in that sermon, to specify which of Christ's words made the
stumbling-block. But other preachers suggest answers. The eucharistic
miracle, we know, had long been disputed. As for the resurrection of
the flesh, we hear from St Antony of Padua, in the 1220s, of those
'unbelieving and hard of heart, who disbelieve it today', and who,
denying the general resurrection of the flesh, go on, naturally, to
'disbelieve that Christ rose from the dead'.[4] Rather than read traces
of manichean dualism in these *increduli et corde duri*, we may relate their
incredulity to a dogmatic materialism, a denial that any other world
than the present one exists. Giordano refers to this latter position, treat-
ing it naturally – regardless of theological paradox – as a rump surviving from Manicheism. Mani's 'madness', he said, had long vanished
from the world,

but there still remained from this heresy, among other wicked pagans, and
wicked Christians, that heresy above all which believed there was no other
world than this. These were pagan, worldly and carnal men. It is for this reason

---

[1] Giordano, *Credo*, fol 158v: 'Or mi di, quanti cia di questi infideli? Chi crede oggi i
beni invisibili, i beni di paradiso, chissine cura? Non si ne curan le genti. Non sanno che
se... Ma oggi ne pieno tutto il mondo di questo peccato...' *Ibid*, fol 159v: 'ogi, sicuri
delle minaccie e delle pene dininferno, nullo non credono.'

[2] *Giordano*, Narducci, pp 181, 261; p 102 n 3 below; etc.

[3] Remigius, *Quadr*, fol 80v: 'Quanta est ergo stultitia hominum qui cum credant libris
regum, principum, mercatorum et etiam scripturas paganorum, sepe falsa dubiaque
dicencium, nollunt credere verbum Christi, a quo necessario exclusum est omne falsum.'

[4] Antony, p 888 *a b*: 'Resurrexisse a mortuis Christum non credunt qui resurrectionem
corporum futuram negant.../...In illa corporum resurrectione generali Deus expro-
babit et condemnabit incredulos et corde duros, qui modo eam futuram non credunt.'

that the creed says 'and of things invisible'. There are many people today who do not believe there is another life, or that things could be better than in this one.[1]

Disbelief in Christ's words, denial of the Eucharist, denial of resurrection and of another world: these views, confirming each other, were familiar to the mendicant preachers, as articulate objections to the faith.

If tradition, whether as books by princes, or as heresy, fed one side of the rational antipathy to faith, it combined with day-to-day events in feeding another: a denial of Providence. Heretics might point to the injustices of the world as proof that the world was ruled by a bad God. It could equally well show there was no God at all – or, at least, none that had any interest below heaven. Remigio spoke in the imperfect tense of philosophers who had denied God's providence, and the utility of prayer; but it was in the present tense that he convicted them: 'those who speak thus', he said, 'do God a great injustice'.[2] Giordano echoed him. Ancient sages, he said, saw some things which seemed to imply God's existence, others which seemed to belie it. They had wondered, for example, why bad men were often exalted, good ones abased. 'What is this?', they had asked, 'how can it be that God exists? How could he sustain so many ills?' The preacher ends, 'in our own time, still, this question is put by madmen every day'.[3] Misfortunes, for individuals, and for society, were always there to provoke these 'madmen'. Nothing makes their rôle clearer than Giordano's reference to the buffets Christendom suffered in the second half of the thirteenth century. 'Should we lose our faith', he asked, 'because we hear that some new heretic has arisen? Tell me now!' And, he asks again, 'should you lose and abandon the faith because Acre was taken and sacked, and because so many other cities were taken similarly – Acre, and Tripoli, and Damietta, and Antioch, and other cities and castles? It is no

---

[1] Giordano, *Credo*, fol 96v: 'tuttavia ancora n'è rimasa di questa resia in altri mali paghani e neli mali christiani espetialmente di quella resia che non credeterro che altro mondo fosse che questo. Questi furo homini paghani, mondani e carnali, e pero dice "*invisibilium*". Molti ne sono ogi i quali non credono che altra vita sia o che melglo vi possa essere che in questa...'

[2] Remigius, *Quadr*, fol 67v: 'Aliqui fuerunt qui reputabantur sapientes apud homines huius mundi qui dicebant quod non oportebat orare nec rogare deum et allegabant ad hoc unam talem rationem: dicunt enim mundum non regi secundum providenciam dei, quia deus non fuit conditor istorum inferiorum...Quod refutandum est genesi... Ideo sic dicentes faciunt iniuriam magnam deo.'

[3] Giordano, *Credo*, fol 47r: 'sike dixero, che è questo? Non potrebe essere ke iddio fosse. Kome potrebbe sostenere tanti mali, e tante kose pessime? E ancora ogi si fa questa questione per li matti tuttodie.'

new thing that God should chastise his people.'[1] Not only did the
world and the flesh, then, create a dumb unbelief of the heart, a *frigus
infidelitatis*; central christian doctrines could be articulately denied.
Tradition fed one side of the denial; experience, belying God's Providence, the other.

Popular sermons reflect many aspects of contemporary manners. We
have looked only at religion, and, in religion, at its negative side. But the
sermons have revealed hidden things. A general prevalence of sin was
the first fact on which our preachers agreed. Lust, arrogance, and an
unbridled thirst for money, in ascending order, were the crimes they
put first. Religious observance, correspondingly, was low, both in and
out of church: some people never heard a sermon, some never went
to church, some never prayed. Behind these outward manifestations –
sin and low church observance – lay, finally, a variety of degrees of
faith. While the faithful struggled with doubt, the faithless could vaunt
scepticism. In a word: religion in thirteenth-century Italy suffered
most sorts of imperfection.

The picture we have drawn has suffered two main limitations. It has
lacked geographical distinction: all Italy has been treated at once. It may
be asked if godlessness varied from place to place. Individual cities,
certainly, had private reputations: Florence, already, for pride;[2] Siena,
for vain frivolity;[3] Pavia, for lust.[4] In ghibelline cities, the church might
suffer interdict, or government persecution. But in the long term these
differences evened each other out. For all their city-loyalties, business-
men and churchmen moved house more freely than Dante's bitterness
in exile might suggest. Our preachers have been picked from all over
Italy; all travelled; their impressions are general; and, taking into account the difference in scale in the records of their sermons, their impressions counterbalance each other.

---

[1] *Ibid*, fol 162r: 'Dovem noi perdere la fede per che noi udiamo alcuna novella dalcuno
eretico che si levi? Or mi di! Or dei però perdere la fede e lasciarla, perche acri fue
preso e disfatto, e preso allora cotante cittadi – acri, e tripoli di barberia, e dammiata, e
antioccia, e altri cittadi e castella? Non è cosa nuova che dio batta il popolo suo, non è
cosa nuova.' It would appear that 'di barberia' is Giordano's error.

[2] Benvenuto de Rambaldis [de Imola, *Comentum super...Dantis Comoediam*, ed J. P.
Lacaita], 5 vols (Florence 1887) III, p 530: 'eo tempore Florentia erat...inflata superbia'
(that is, at the time of Charles of Valois's entry, 1301). Compare Dino Compagni,
Cronaca, Bk I, Chs 1, 2, etc.

[3] Benvenuto de Rambaldis, II, p 409: 'senenses, vanissimos omnium'.

[4] Archipoeta, *Estuans intrinsecus*, line 30, (ed K. Langosh [= text of H. Watenphul],
Stuttgart 1965, p 48): 'Quis Papie commorans...castus habeatur?'

More important than any difference between city and city is the question of a difference between country and town. However, since the thirteenth century was a time of substantial migration from one to the other, this question must be considered in relation to a second fault in our picture. The picture has been static. Strung out from 1221 to 1305, the sermons have been treated as a block. Fra Giordano's mention of Acre, just now, must recall us to a sense of time. The thirteenth century, like others, was one of change, and it must be asked whether these changes permanently affected christian faith, for better or worse.

Fra Giordano's mention of Acre also recalls us to the more conspicuous of the two changes that need our attention. The crusading catastrophe that ended at Acre in 1292 had begun with the collapse of St Louis's crusade before Damietta in 1249. It was Matthew Paris, writing in St Albans, who described the earthquake that defeat had caused in popular faith in the west. Bishops thought it 'the worst crisis for Christianity since Mohammed'.[1] In Italy, 'the most noble city of Venice, and the other cities of Italy, whose inhabitants are half-Christians would have fallen into apostasy, had they not been strengthened by the succour of bishops and holy men in orders'. By these efforts, Matthew Paris says, 'the indignation of some was allayed, but not of all'.[2]

In St Louis's time, latin Christendom had for over two hundred years grown used to holding its own with Islam. Now, in the east – Italians cared little yet for christian victories in Spain – the balance of power was permanently shifting in favour of Islam. In 1250, as the hohenstaufen Antichrist, whose shadow had darkened Italy for the first half of the century, was dying in Apulia, the eastern Antichrist began a triumphal march up the Levant, a march which ended with the massacre at Acre. English chronicler and pisan preacher both witness to the shock this shift sent through christian minds.

But the shock of change, in thirteenth-century Italy, probably went deeper than chronicler or preacher understood. Astrologers would look back on the year 1240 as having started an increase in avarice – among other vices.[3] They put it down to an eclipse. History, accepting the fact, prefers an earthly explanation. With Frederick II, in 1250, died, after years of illness, the last serious medieval attempt at an Italian

---

[1] *Chronica Maiora*, p 254.
[2] *Ibid*, p 170, 'Et sic vix quievit aliquorum, non tamen omnium, indignatio.'
[3] Petrus de Abano, *Conciliator, Differentia*, IX (Venice 1526) fol 14 E. An eclipse of the sun, total in northern Italy, occurred on 3 June 1239; see F. J. Schröter, *Sonnenfinsternisse von* [A.D.] *600 bis 1800* (Christiana 1923) Chart 78 b.

monarchy. In just these decades, furthermore, while Germany fell, France and England were rising to replace her hegemony, offering Italian commerce a fatter market than any it had known before. In the middle years of the thirteenth century, in other words, Italy lost a master, and gained two customers. The demographic explosion of Italian cities was a response to these conditions.

The explosion lands us back with the countryman and the townsman. In our century, the one was fast becoming the other. A difference in outlook of town and country had already been noticed. Humbert of Romans said townsmen were worse.[1] Humanists, with their scorn for *rustici*, had long said the opposite.[2] Whatever the subtleties of that debate, a change, and a relatively fast one, from country to town, may be surmised to have had an effect on the immigrant. From a rural hamlet, with surviving pagan rhythms, he came to a packed, competitive society where neither his own habits, nor the old diocesan church, equipped him to resist the new temptations confronting him. The avarice, and perhaps some of the irreligion, that we have heard about, correspond to these conditions; Dante agreed:

> It was always the mixing-together of persons
> Which caused evil in the city,
> As heaped-on food does in the body.[3]

That conservative outburst may show, after all, an accurate insight.

Crusading failure; commercial success; from outside, and at home, the hold of faith was challenged. Matthew Paris and Giordano of Pisa both spoke of apostasy. Are we then, after all, to return to the view of an 'Age of Faith', and only date its decline a century or two earlier? Two considerations can be urged against this view. One is the distribution of evidence. Given the difference in scale of records, our preachers' references to unbelief are as solid for the early part of the century – for instance, in St Antony of Padua[4] – as for the later.

But there is a second reason for caution. Friars were not mere historical sources. They were the most vital element in the church of their time; and sermons were the spearhead of their campaign. Evidence

---

[1] *De erud praed*, fol 491 H.

[2] 'Rusticus' was a term of contempt used by the educated for the uneducated in Italy from the early eleventh century. For example, Ademar of Chabannes, *Epistola de Apostolatu S. Martialis* (*c* 1030), PL, CXLI, (1880) cols 91 C, 107 D, etc. Arnulph, *Historia Mediolanensis*, ed L. Muratori, *Rerum Italicarum Scriptores*, O.S. IV (Muratori, *LA*, 4 (Milan 1723)) Bk III, Ch I, p 20B, on archbishop Guido (1038): idiotam et a rure venientem'.

[3] *Paradiso*, XVI, 67–9. [4] Pp 100 nn 2–4 above.

abounds of the effect of these sermons. Who could tell, it was asked, how many Francis and Dominic had converted? As many, surely, as Paul and Augustine.[1] Salimbene tells of a poor woman who happened to give birth during a friar's sermon; a few words from the friar, and an ass had to be fetched to carry the gifts that were showered on her by the crowd.[2] Fra Giordano's sermons, it was claimed in Pisa, made enemies friends, loose women pure, the vice-ridden virtuous.[3] Sermons have been used here as mirrors. In their time they were lamps. The very words which tell us of godlessness acted to cure it.

The perpetual challenges, then, that confronted faith, from crusades, and everything else, evoked as perpetual a response, from persons whose concern it was, as it is no longer ours, to battle for the salvation of their contemporaries. We have been intruders, indeed, in a duel; a duel between piety and impiety. It was an elusive battle, fought behind the clamorous debates of thirteenth-century Italy – Guelf and Ghibelline, noble and commoner: elusive, but fierce, and enduring.

We have intruded, then; but with profit, if the background to St Francis and his friends has become clearer. The friars were not typical figures in a freakish age, but, morally, freakish figures in a typical age. Their mendicant life was a lasting wonder to contemporaries.[4] They were a small minority: 'Virgins are few, martyrs are few, preachers are few', said Fra Giordano.[5] It is the many who have concerned us; and we have seen a varied picture.

The scientific enlightenment was tempted to conceive faith not as a virtue, but as an original sin, from which the Messiah of knowledge came to rescue it. It follows from that view that, in the olden days, men must have believed all the Church told them. This paper has tried to shake the historical part of that conception. This distribution of faith, implicit or explicit, in thirteenth-century Italy was not uniform; but resembled, in its unevenness, the distribution of most other virtues.

[1] *Giordano*, Narducci, p 46: 'Di S Domenico e di S Francesco non si potrebbe dire.'
[2] Salimbene, p 103, lines 15–22.
[3] Quoted by Colombi, pp 10–11 from *Croniche Pisane*, ed G. Bonaini (Florence 1848) II, p 451.
[4] Albertinus, fol 97a: 'multi timent quando vident fratres minores ambulari nudis pedibus, et obstupescunt qualiter vivere possunt'; Salimbene, p 117, lines 11–15; *Giordano*, Narducci, pp 249, 256.
[5] Giordano, *Credo*, fol 162v: 'pochi sono i vergini e pochi i martiri e pochi i predicatori.' On the subject of *martiri*, I would like to thank my colleagues Mr B. W. Beckingsale, Dr D. J. A. Matthew and Dr W. A. Speck for reading this paper in draft, and making suggestions.

SOME POPULAR PROPHECIES FROM THE FOURTEENTH TO THE SEVENTEENTH CENTURIES[1]

by MARJORIE E. REEVES

IN the summer of 1304 the leaders of the Spiritual Franciscan party in Italy, Fra Angelo Clareno and Fra Liberato, were gathered with their followers in Perugia. They had recently returned from exile in the east. Benedict XI was dead and western Christendom awaited the outcome of what was to be one of the most crucial papal elections in the later Middle Ages. It was to be a trial of strength between the pro- and anti-French parties, accompanied by much political manœuvring, rumour and bargaining. In the interval, while the political groups were mustering their forces, there appeared a set of prophecies of the popes, called the *Vaticinia de summis pontificibus*, which can with some confidence be ascribed to the little group at Perugia.[2] Seldom in history can the gap between hope and political reality have been wider. The Spiritual Franciscans were thinking in terms of *heilsgeschichte*, and for them the crisis of all history was at hand, while cardinals Napoleone degli Orsini, Nicholas of Prato, and others were laying down the tortuous lines of the intrigues which resulted in the election of Clement V and the removal of the papacy to Avignon. It is only through these prophecies that we can discern the high expectations and pent-up emotion with which this moment was approached by some at least. Though the

---

[1] For permission to reproduce illustrations used in this paper the author and publisher are grateful to: the Bodleian Library, Oxford for reproductions from the MS Douce 88 and the MS Barocci 170 (both of which are available on the Bodleian colour filmstrips 'Oracles of Leo the Wise' roll 190E and 'Prophecies of the Popes' roll 218.10); and to the Biblioteca Riccardiana, Florence for reproductions from the MS Riccardi 1222B.

[2] The pioneer work on these prophecies was done by [H.] Grundmann, ['Die Papst-prophetien des Mittelalters',] A[rchiv für] K[ulturgeschichte], XIX (Berlin 1929) pp 77–159; ['Die Liber de Flore',] H[istorisches] J[ahrbuch], XLIX (Munich 1929) pp 33–91. This paper assumes that he was right in ascribing the *Vaticinia* to Clareno and his group in 1304. This ascription and date are, however, not quite certain. The *terminus ante quem* is given by Pipini's reference (below, p 111). Since pictures and text follow the Byzantine model closely, captions are the best internal guide for dating. These suggest a date after the election of Celestine V (1294) but the evidence is sufficiently ambiguous to leave a possibility that they were composed before Boniface VIII was elected.

moment passed and salvation drew not nigh, there was some powerful force of attraction in these prophecies: they were seized on immediately, quickly disseminated and imitated. Why was this?

The crisis expected by the Italian Spirituals was seen as the passage of the Church across Jordan into the Promised Land. Under this figure the abbot Joachim of Fiore had prophesied the transition from the second *status* of history to the third, the Age of the Holy Ghost.[1] By the beginning of the fourteenth century Joachim's ideas had undergone considerable modification but his fundamental tenet about history – the juxtaposition of the greatest tribulation and the greatest liberation, to be expected shortly – had entered deeply into the thinking of Spiritual Franciscans. Fra Angelo saw the persecutions endured by the Spirituals as the rising crescendo of evil which must prelude the new age.[2] The election of the hermit-pope, Celestine V, was probably hailed by many as the advent of the angelic pope, at that time just beginning to appear in prophecy.[3] But with his swift supersession by Boniface VIII the dawn was snatched away and the darkness of persecution supervened until the milder rule of Benedict XI gave a short respite. Belief in St Francis as the harbinger of the new age made the Spirituals certain of winning through, but their experience, with its alternate hopes and setbacks, had apparently convinced them that a dramatic break in history was necessary. This was not the break expected by a revolutionary group like the Apostolic Brethren,[4] with the violent overthrow of existing institutions, but a divine intervention forcing men to treat the Church on God's terms. The institution thus to be recreated was the papacy, but the continuity of this divinely ordained office was emphasised by the fact that the expected break was to come in the middle of a historical series.

Such a divine intervention could only be invoked through prophecy. The device of a prophetic series, ascribed to one of the great prophetic names of the past, enabled the authors to maintain the necessary continuity and pass over to the new order at the moment where *post-eventum* statement ended and real prophecy began. So the original *Vaticinia de summis pontificibus* was a series of fifteen prophecies, each one describing a pope in picture, caption and oracular text, the whole circulating generally under the name of the abbot Joachim. The series

---

[1] See Joachim of Fiore, *Liber Concordie* (Venice 1519) fols 6r, 21r–22r, 58r, 89v–90r, 106v; *Expositio in Apocalypsim* (Venice 1527) fols 95v, 195r.

[2] See [M.] Reeves, *The Influence of Prophecy [in the Later Middle Ages]* (Oxford 1969) pp 191–4.

[3] *Ibid*, p 401.   [4] *Ibid*, pp 242–8.

begins with the Orsini pope, Nicholas III, and in the following sequence Celestine V is clearly indicated by the caption.[1] The last historic pope is probably Benedict XI, and from this point onwards, it would seem, the language of genuine prophecy begins. By ascribing the series to Joachim, freedom for a sharp attack could be gained, while revolutionary hopes could be concealed under the guise of prophecy.

So far as I can discover, this production introduced a new type of prophecy into the west. Professor Grundmann – to whose studies in this subject I am deeply indebted[2]– has shown that the authors of the *Vaticinia* derived their model from the so-called *Oracles* of Leo the Wise, that is, the Byzantine emperor Leo VI (886–912) whose reputation became conflated with that of Leo the Philosopher.[3] A number of oracles on the future of the Byzantine empire were later attributed to him and of these the series which concerns us was probably in circulation in the twelfth century. The Greek historian Nicetas Choniates refers to several of them as having been applied by contemporaries to the death of John II (1143) and other emperors down to Isaac II (1185–95).[4] These references, together with the evidence of the *Vaticinia*, make it clear that – in spite of the absence of early manuscripts – the oracles were a product of the Comnenian period and not – as some scholars have thought – of the latest Byzantine period.[5] Possibly they were collected and edited *c* 1180.[6]

The *Oracles* of Leo consist of sixteen symbolic pictures, each with a caption and a verse (see Table, pp 132–3). The first, in the version I have used,[7] shows a serpent whose eyes are being attacked by two crows

---

[1] The tradition that the first prophecy was intended for Nicholas III is universal from Pipini onwards. See below, p 115, for the caption to Celestine V.

[2] Grundmann, *AK*, XIX (1929) p 107; *HJ*, XLIX (1929) p 41. The clue to the source of the *Vaticinia* was given by a sixteenth-century editor who rejected the suggestion (below, p 124).

[3] See [C.] Mango, ['The Legend of Leo the Wise'], *Recueil* [*des travaux de l'Institut d'études byzantines*], VI (Belgrade 1960) pp 59–93; B. Knös, 'Les oracles [de Léon le Sage', ΑΦΙΕΡѠΜΑΣΤΗ ΜΝΗΜΗ ΤΟΥ ΜΑΝΟΛΗ ΤΡΙΑΝΤΑΦΥΛΛΙΔΗ] (Salonica 1960) pp 155–88. Knös wrote his article on a newly identified MS of the *Oracles* in the Royal Library at Stockholm without knowledge of their use in the *Vaticinia*. Thus he believes that the later oracles were written after the fall of Constantinople in 1453. Both the above articles reproduce the pictures of the *Oracles*.   [4] Mango, *Recueil*, VI (1960) pp 62–4.

[5] *Ibid*, p 65, where it is argued that these were not *post eventum* prophecies but already in circulation when applied to specific emperors. The argument in itself does not seem quite conclusive, but finds support if the legend of pope Gregory was derived from this source (see below, p 131), since this would provide evidence for the circulation of one of the *Oracles*, at least, in France by the second half of the twelfth century.   [6] *Ibid*, p 65.

[7] No MSS earlier than the fourteenth century appear to have survived (see Mango, *ibid*, pp 79–80). The version I have chiefly used is that edited by P. Lambecius for G. Codinus, *Excerpte de Antiquitatibus Constantinopolitanis* (Venice 1729).

(Pl 1), the second an eagle bearing a cross in his mouth,[1] the third a unicorn (Pl 2). The fourth, the head of a man with a carefully drawn, non-imperial head-dress, is connected with a question to which we shall return later.[2] The fifth shows a robed man with a sickle in his right hand and a rose in his left, while an angel places a crown on his head (Pl 3).[3] This, as we shall see, becomes a crucial figure, notable for the fact that, through all the changes of interpretation and vagaries of draughtsmanship, its essential characteristics remain unchanged. The sixth is of a bull or cow and two heads of young men (Pl 4),[4] the seventh, of a bear suckling its young (Pl 5), and the eighth of a city with a head on a dish in the foreground (Pl 6). In the ninth picture the caption – Gratiarum Actio – seems to indicate a shift in tone, although the picture of a running fox with three standards before it has nothing unworldly about it (Pl 7). The tenth – of an empty throne and a hand with or without a sceptre (Pl 8) – suggests the beginnings of a spiritual revolution and, although the unicorn of the eleventh does not seem to follow this up,[5] the twelfth clearly marks the initiation of a search for a holy ruler (Pl 9). Under the caption Pietas it depicts a half-naked man seated on a rock or tomb and approached with reverence by a robed man.[6] In the next (Pl 10), the holy emperor has actually to be sought among the dead: he lies on two animals, bound in grave clothes, while an angel hovers over his head.[7] In the fourteenth the emperor stands crowned and holding the sceptre, while in the fifteenth an angel offers the crown to an emperor[8] (Pl 11) and in the last, emperor and patriarch stand side by side in the full panoply of their authority. The concluding

---

[1] The serpent and crows is a motif found elsewhere, the birds perhaps symbolising the perpetual enemies of Byzantium from east and west. The eagle symbolises the Byzantine empire (see Knös, Les Oracles, pp 166–9).

[2] Below, p 113 n 1.

[3] In some versions the rose is replaced by a candlestick. See below, p 112, for the connection of this figure with Andronicus I.

[4] Nicetas says that Isaac II Angelus resembled a bull and applied this prophecy to himself. The text is based on verses which, Nicetas says, were circulating at the time (see Mango, Recueil, VI (1960) p 63; Knös, Les Oracles, p 175).

[5] Since it carries a crescent on its flank, this unicorn should signify the Mohammedan power.

[6] Knös, Les Oracles, pp 181–2, interprets this figure as a young woman representing Constantinople weeping over her fate, but the main manuscript tradition seems clearly to indicate a male hermit, as does its use in the Vaticinia.

[7] In all versions the 'mummified' emperor lies supported on the backs of two animals, a detail which survives in curious forms in some early versions of the Vaticinia. The angel is usually holding a crown, but in the Stockholm MS is anointing the emperor with nard (Knös, Les Oracles, p 182).

[8] Again, in the Stockholm MS (ibid, p 185) the angel pours nard over the emperor.

sequence of captions – *Innocentia, Praehonoratio, Electio,* in contrast to such earlier ones as *Sanguis, Confusio, Membrorum Divisio* – emphasises the new quality of ruler expected.

Thus it seems that the original series itself embodied a revolutionary change from corruption and ruin to spiritual revival through the revelation of a saviour-ruler. I suggest that this was possibly why the Spiritual Franciscans seized upon the *Oracles,* discovered probably during their previous exile. They placed themselves, as it were, about half-way through, at the point where the first shift in tone towards the future occurs. Taking Benedict XI as the last of the old régime, the next one would be the ninth in the Leo series with the captions of this and the next two indicating the beginning of the new age. Then, with the twelfth, the angelic series would become open. Working backwards, they would find that, miraculously, the man with the sickle and rose fell to Celestine V – the only one in the first half of the Leo series who receives the attention of an angel. They then, it would seem, picked out the bear picture as appropriate to the Orsini pope Nicholas III and placed it first. There is, indeed, a good deal of adaptation in reworking the *Oracles* to make the *Vaticinia,* but the faithfulness with which some features are reproduced remains the most striking characteristic of the adaptation.

For studying how this adaptation was done I have used four early manuscripts and the testimony of Francesco Pipini, the Dominican writer (see Table, pp 132–3).[1] Concluding his chronicle as he does in 1314, his description of eight of the pictures is our earliest dated evidence. Pipini knew that the series was meant to start with Nicholas III and he applied each figure to successive popes down to his contemporary, Clement V. His detailed descriptions enable us to trace the way in which the Leo pictures have been handled. The bear with three young has become a mitred pope with one bear above his head and two clamouring at his knees. Martin IV is shown in association with a griffin or flying serpent and a bird, clearly a relic of the serpent attacked by two crows which is the first Leo picture. Honorius III has an eagle above his head and an animal, called by Pipini a rhinoceros, pawing him at one side.

---

[1] F. Pipini, *Chronica, Rerum Italicarum Scriptores,* old series, IX (Milan 1721) cols 724, 726, 727, 728, 736, 741, 747, 751. On authorship Pipini says: *Fertur a nonnullis Abbatem Joachimum libelli huius spiritu prophetico fuisse auctorem.* For the MSS, see table, pp 132–3. There is, apparently, another early MS at Palermo, but I have been unable to study this, or to see A. Danen-Lattanzi's article on it – 'I "Vaticinia de Pontificibus" ed un codice monrealese del sec. XIII–XIV', *Atti della Reale Accademia di Scienze Lettere e Arti di Palermo,* 4 Series, III, pt 2, fasc 4 (Palermo 1944) pp 757–92 and plates I–IV.

This combines the eagle and unicorn of the second and third Leo pictures. The fourth (Nicholas IV) seems to make a break from the *Oracles* of Leo, showing three columns, from two of which protrude heads, while from the third issues a hand with a scimitar. I shall return to this later. In the next, the king with rose, sickle and angel is now a tonsured monk to represent Celestine V. Boniface VIII appears with the cow (bull) and the two heads which form one Leo picture. For Benedict XI a version of the bear-picture is repeated and in the eighth Clement V is associated with the fox and three standards. Here Pipini stops.

His descriptions tally in the main with the earliest manuscript versions, although two of these in particular, one in the Biblioteca Riccardiana and the other a Douce manuscript in Bodley, represent an earlier stage of adaptation.[1] They are both very crude in execution. In the first picture the pope stands apart from the bears, a figure merely added to, not yet combined with, the original (Pl 12). In the second, the serpent attacked by the crow appears almost exactly as in the Leo picture, again with the pope standing beside (Pl 13). In the third the animal is clearly a unicorn, and in the Douce copy the eagle on the pope's head still has the cross of the Leo model in its mouth (Pl 14). When we come to the next picture we meet the problem of the three columns introduced by Pipini. The Douce copy has nothing corresponding to this and, as it only gives fourteen figures in all, this one was probably missed out because of an uncertain tradition. The Riccardi manuscript has here the bust of a monk in a vessel over-arched by a strange feature like a waterspout (Pl 15). Another early manuscript in the Vatican, Latin 3819, already has two flanking pillars with a crowned head on one and a hand issuing from the other, but the middle object is clearly a development of the Riccardi figure in which the over-arching feature has become a flying fish that leaps over the bust to attack the king's head on the left pillar. In later versions the curved thing finally becomes a scimitar in a hand slashing at one of the heads on the other pillars. I think a clue to this and to the sickle in the hand of the next figure may be found in Nicetas's account of how Andronicus I (1182–5) caused a portrait of himself to be set up, in peasant dress holding a sickle which curved over the bust of a youth. In the Douce version of this the man with the sickle carries on his head a jagged instrument surmounted by a severed head. Whatever the original connection between the *Oracles* and Andronicus's portrait, these two *Vaticinia* pictures seem to have in-

[1] See table, pp 132–3.

LEO ORACLES

1 Serpent and two crows. MS Bar fol 6v
2 Unicorn. 1729 ed p 165
3 King with sickle and rose. 1596 ed p 40
4 Bull with two heads. 1729 ed p 168
5 Bear with young. MS Bar fol 10v
6 City and head in vessel. 1729 ed p 170

7

8

9

10

11

12

LEO ORACLES

7 Fox with three standards. 1729 ed p 171
8 Empty throne. 1729 ed p 172
9 Hermit summoned forth. 1596 ed p 60
10 'Mummified' ruler. 1729 ed p 175
11 Angel offering crown. 1596 ed p 74
12 POPE PROPHECY: pope and bear. MS Douce fol 140r

13

14

15

16

17

18

POPE PROPHECIES

13 Pope, serpent and crows. MS Douce fol 140v
14 Pope, unicorn and eagle. MS Douce fol 141r
15 Head in a vessel. MS Ricc fol 2v
16 Monk with sickle. MS Ricc fol 3r
17 Pope and bull. MS Douce fol 142r
18 Pope and 'fox'. MS Douce fol 143v

19

20

21

22

23

24

POPE PROPHECIES
19　Empty throne. MS Douce fol 144r
20　Hermit summoned forth. MS Ricc fol 6r
21　Angel on mound. MS Douce fol 145r
22　Angel on tomb. MS Ricc fol 6v
23　Angel crowning pope. MS Douce fol 145v
24　Pope and human-faced animal. MS Ricc fol 8r

corporated details derived from a figure like this.[1] I have not discovered a source for the flanking pillars.

Whether or not it was originally related to Andronicus I, number five was universally understood to be an angelic type. The king becomes a tonsured monk but he is always presented with the sickle, the rose and the angel blessing him (Pl 16). For the sixth we have the original cow or bull with the two heads usually (but not invariably) reproduced at top left and the figure of a pope added (Pl 17). The seventh is the bear suckling its young from the *Oracles*, with a figure added, though in the Douce version this is still a king instead of the pope it is becoming. In the second half the order varies somewhat, but the eighth in the Riccardi and Vatican copies is the besieged city, with or without the head on a vessel, and the ninth is the fox with three standards to which the pope has been added (Pl 18). The Douce manuscript then reproduces the empty throne and a hand from the *Oracles* of Leo (Pl 19), but the other early examples all substitute a second fortified city with menacing hands threatening it from outside. The angelic sequence proper starts with the eleventh picture, which is universally of a naked or half-naked hermit either seated on or issuing forth from a rock or tomb and reverentially greeted by a man (Pl 20). The essential gestures, especially the hermit's hand raised in blessing, hardly vary at all, while a sun and moon, derived from the Leo original, appear in many versions. The evolution of the next picture is most interesting. In the Leo series the angel seeks out the emperor, sepulchred and bound in grave clothes, who must rise again. As we have seen,[2] a curious feature of the original is that the body is supported by two animals. In the Douce version this picture becomes an angel seated on a green mound supported by animals (Pl 21). The Riccardi artist has the angel supported by fierce heads above a sarcophagus (Pl 22), while the Vatican copy (Latin 3819) gives yet another version with a tonsured man seated on the right holding a mitre and on the left a curious arrangement of rabbits which is obviously a relic of the original animals. Perhaps the original theme of the mummified emperor was too obscure, for in later examples it is superseded by a quite different picture of an angelic pope holding his mitre over the flock. The final Angelic pictures follow a clear convention: the thirteenth shows an angel crowning the

---

[1] For Nicetas's reference, see Mango, *Recueil*, VI (1960) p 65. On Mango's argument Andronicus would have been applying the prophecies to himself, but if they were in the making in the later twelfth century the influence could be the other way round. The head of the man in civilian head-dress also, I suggest, bears a relation to Andronicus' portrait.　　　　　　　　[2] Above, p 110, n 7.

pope (Pl 23); the fourteenth, two angels supporting the pope, and the fifteenth, a pope holding a mitre, in place of emperor and patriarch in the *Oracles*.[1] In the Riccardi version he holds it over a four-legged animal with a human face and a headgear like a Red Indian's (Pl 24). In Vatican MS Latin 3819 a sixteenth picture shows a crowned animal with a human face. I think these two became amalgamated, for the later tradition of the fifteenth picture is of a pope holding his mitre over a crowned or horned animal which always has a human face. The meaning is uncertain: the animal may be the Lamb of God but sometimes it looks like a secular ruler or even Antichrist.[2]

Since we do not know what version of the *Oracles* was used by the authors of the *Vaticinia*, it is impossible to speak precisely about their adaptation of the text. They certainly used some of the original single-word captions; in Vatican MS Latin 3822, which gives us the earliest version of the text, these appear as in the original, for example *Sanguis, Confusio, Elatio*, but almost at once the short sentences must have been added which appear in almost all later versions, thus: *Occisio. Filii Balaae sectabuntur*, or *Bona gratia. Simonia cessabit*. The relationship of the prose text accompanying each picture to the original Greek verses of the Leo Oracle is more difficult to establish, since there were a number of latin translations from the Greek. The text of the *Vaticinia* as we have it in the earliest manuscripts does not correspond verbally to any of the latin Leo versions I have been able to use, but it is easy to detect a common original behind differing latin translations and one can therefore establish beyond a doubt that the texts of the papal prophecies are derived – with omissions and additions – almost entirely from the Leo texts. The enigmatic style of the oracles made their transfer to another context quite simple, but, on the other hand, made corruptions and attempted corrections all the more likely, since they often seemed unintelligible. Thus many variations appeared both in the latin version of the Leo *Oracles* and the prophecies of the popes. Emendations continued down to the sixteenth century when some editors declared that they had collated all possible sources in order to construct the correct text.[3]

The Spiritual Franciscans thus appropriated a strange set of symbols. They used all of them in one way or another, although sometimes putting two together and twice over repeating a symbol. In most cases they added the figure of a pope or turned an emperor into a pope.

[1] In some of these last pictures the mitre appears to be derived from the bowl from which the angel pours nard in one version of the *Oracles* of Leo.
[2] See below, p 123, for differing interpretations of this figure.
[3] See below, pp 123, 125.

How much did they understand of these enigmatic figures and texts? Many details are faithfully reproduced with apparently little meaning, for example, the two heads in number six and the three standards arranged in a certain pattern beside the fox in number nine. Some features appear simply because the text has been derived from the *Oracles* of Leo, while both remain completely obscure. An example of this is the serpent and crows. The bears must have been quickly related to the Orsini and become symbols of nepotism, but what is the significance of the unicorn, the cow and the fox placed in relation to the popes? If the details remain unintelligible, however, the main thrust of the prophecies is clear. These Joachites were able, through these symbols, to make a veiled but bitter commentary on the contemporary papacy and then to highlight the Joachimist expectation. Whatever the sickle and rose were meant to imply, this figure, which clearly represented an angelic interlude, expressed exactly the myth of Celestine V, which the authors emphasised in the caption which they added: *Elacio paupertatis. Obediencia. Castitatis Temperacio. Ypocritarum Destructor.* It was the original source, too, which gave them the concept of the angelic pope who was to be sought out by divine revelation as expressed in the pictures of the empty throne, the hermit on the rock, and the sepulchred emperor. In the *Vaticinia* this expectation of divine revelation is focused on the hermit figure who issues from the tomb or gives the blessing from the rock. The caption and text – both in part drawn from the original – emphasise this crucial moment in history: *Bona honoracio. Et revelabitur unctus qui habet prenomen monachi, petram habitans.* The full flowering of a new age is expressed in the culminating angelic series which still receives its main inspiration from the Leo *Oracles* emphasised again in the captions: *Bona intentio. Caritas abundabit. Prehonoratio. Concordia erit. Bona Occasio. Reverentia. Devotio augmentabitur.* The ambiguity of the final picture, however, does not derive from the Leo *Oracles*.

The *Vaticinia* belong to a small group of prophetic tracts all probably emanating from the same source in 1304–5. One of these, the *Liber de Flore*, is a second series of pope prophecies, without pictures and more historical in character. It appears to follow no model.[1] It starts unmistakably with Gregory IX (probably because the Spiritual Franciscans believed that the dilution of the Franciscan Rule was initiated by him) and, in place of the enigmatic Byzantine texts, gives more straightforward political details. Even the angelic portraits are more specific and more closely related to the contemporary scene than the *Vaticinia*. But

---

[1] On the *Liber de Flore*, see Grundmann, *HJ*, XLIX (1929) pp 33–91.

the angelic series begins with the same theme of the hermit, *pauper et nudus*, who must be sought out and crowned by the angel. After this the political alignment of these prophecies emerges strongly, for the angelic pope will form an alliance with a '*rex generosus*' from the line of Pipin the Frank. Together they will conquer east and west, recover Jerusalem, and bring the Greek Church back to its true obedience. The pope will create the French king emperor, while renouncing all temporal wealth for the Roman See and for the clergy generally. Here is the first sign of a holy alliance between the papacy and the French monarchy which becomes a recurring theme in popular prophecy over the next three centuries. The next angelic pope will be a Frenchman and will reform Germany. The third will be an Italian Franciscan and the last a Gascon who will make long pilgrimages throughout the world. Finally in Palestine the two barbarous peoples, Gog and Magog, will meet him with palms and songs and he will rule the world until the end. Here was a splendid programme, embodying the passionate hopes of that moment in 1304–5, but it did not wear well, for it was too rash in its specific detail. The enigmas of the *Vaticinia*, on the other hand, could provide unending attraction in the attempts to make them fit. So the *Liber de Flore* exists today in only three known manuscripts, while there are about seventy known manuscripts and printed editions of the *Vaticinia*.[1]

The popularity was in defiance of the fact that the real prophetic message of the *Vaticinia* soon proved to be a myth. Francesco Pipini in 1314 was concerned to apply the prophecies up to date, and it must be remembered that all were still probably *post-eventum* except the one for Clement V. Hugh of Newcastle, writing in 1319 a tract *De victoria Christi contra Antichristum*, was interested rather in looking forward to the *nudum pontificem* who would renew the dignity of the papacy.[2] The contemporary who most nearly shared the expectations of the authors was the provençal Franciscan, Bernard Délicieux. The evidence here is a little confusing. He was accused of having foretold the death of Benedict XI and this prophecy was connected with his possession of a book in which were *multae characteres et multae rotae et diversae scripturae in suis circumferentiis*.[3] Although it has been assumed so, this may not have

[1] For MSS of the *Liber de Flore*, see Reeves, *Influence of Prophecy*, p 523; of the *Vaticinia*, see [F.] Russo, *Bibliografia [Gioachimita]* (Florence 1954) pp 41–8.
[2] *De victoria Christi contra Antichristum* (Nuremberg 1471) unpaged, Ch XXVIII.
[3] See [M. de] Dmitrewski, ['Fr. Bernard Délicieux, O.F.M., sa lutte contra l'Inquisition de Carcassonne et d'Albi, son procès, 1297–1319], A[rchivum] F[ranciscanum] H[istoricum] XVII (Quaracchi 1924) p 472.

been the *Vaticinia*, first, because in the earliest versions this contains no wheels, and secondly, because it was probably written after Benedict's death.[1] There may have been another tract of this type circulating. But Bernard's reliance on the *Vaticinia* for future hope emerges clearly in 1319 when he was being taken into custody from Avignon to Toulouse. He talked openly of a '*papalarius*' by Joachim in which past and future popes were represented in pictures.[2] He had, it would seem, been able to apply what were probably the first two real prophecies in the series to Clement V and John XXII, for they were enigmatic and ambivalent in tone. But he believed that John would die within two years and that he would be succeeded by a pope with the name of *Bonagrazia*. This is, in fact, the caption of a prophecy in the *Vaticinia*.[3] It points towards the angelic series about to begin and Bernard Délicieux clearly expected the next pope to begin the new age of the Church. Thus, to this Spiritual Franciscan, the *Vaticinia* were not a curiosity of prophecy fulfilled, but a strength and incitement for the future. The greatness of his prophet had been proved – 'Isaiah and Joachim, how did *they* know the future?' was his retort to sceptics[4] – and therefore could be trusted for the rest to come.

Before 1356 a second series of *Vaticinia de summis pontificibus* had been produced and attributed to the abbot Joachim. Professor Grundmann thought that this emanated from a group of florentine Fraticelli and this seems quite likely.[5] The series follows the same general design as the earlier one but its dependence on the *Oracles* of Leo is slighter. The first picture is clearly based on the same bear-theme as the first in the previous series; the seventh utilises again the serpent attacked by a bird; the eighth is copied from another Leo picture. For the rest I have found no direct source. The series begins again with Nicholas III, the Orsini pope. The tradition on Celestine V and Boniface VIII seems to have sharpened with time: the first is shown piously kneeling before a tree from which emerges a hand in benediction, but behind a fox pulls

---

[1] In *Influence of Prophecy*, p 202, I assumed wrongly that this referred to the *Vaticinia*. Since the precise date of the *Vaticinia* is uncertain, there is a possibility that they were composed earlier than the date I have suggested here but no early MSS contain wheels. On the other hand, the *Vaticinia* do appear in wheel form in sixteenth-century editions (below, p 127), so possibly there was an early model for these which should be connected with another work in this group, the *Horoscopus* mentioned by Grundmann, *AK*, XIX (1929) p 107; *HJ*, XLIX (1929) p 40.

[2] See Dmitrewski, *AFH*, XVII (1924) p 332.

[3] Either the ninth or the tenth in the series.

[4] Dmitrewski, *AFH*, XVII (1924) p 332, n 3.

[5] Grundmann, *AK*, XIX (1929) pp 117–24. Printed editions are numerous.

at the pope's sleeve. The caption says *Voce vulpina perdet principatum*, while the text begins: *Benedictus qui venit in nomine Domini.*[1] Boniface is shown attacked by a cock, piercing a second bird and fending off a third, while a monk sits disconsolately behind. The caption is *Fraudulenter intrasti, potenter regnasti, gemens morieris.*[2] The eighth shows an interesting adaptation of a Leo picture which is not in the series used by the first adaptors but which I have found in one Leo manuscript.[3] In the original a king rides away with a hawk on his wrist watched by a queen standing in a doorway. To fit the theme of Clement V's removal to Avignon, this now becomes a mitred pope riding away with his hand raised in benediction, watched by a distraught widow in a church doorway. John XXII is represented with a sword which issues from his mouth to pierce the Lamb of God, while an agitated dove protests.[4] *Contra columbam hec ymago turpissima clericorum pugnabit*, says the caption – a strong indication that this series emanated from a Fraticelli group. The *terminus ante quem* for this series is set by a reference to these prophecies by Jean de Roquetaillade in 1356,[5] but it is not altogether easy to fix a moment of writing, that is, the moment when history turns into prophecy. I think myself that the portraits are historical down to the tenth, which is Benedict XII (1334–42). The eleventh, with the caption *Stolam suam in sanguine agni dealbabit* seems to indicate an angelic pope in the text and so does the twelfth, with the caption *Lupus habitabit cum agno, pariterque cibabit*, though neither of these has the clear indications of spiritual revolution as expressed in the earlier set. The thirteenth clearly shows an angelic pope, but the last two seem to represent a deteriorating situation. In the fourteenth a pope is attacked by an armed soldier, while the last is obviously intended for Antichrist, representing the dragon of the Apocalypse which pulls down the stars.[6] The caption reads *Terribilis es et quis resistet tibi?*, while the text begins: *Haec est ultima fera aspectu terribilis.* Thus the second set of pope prophecies embodies a more pessimistic outlook than the first. Although Joachimist expectation never denied a final deterioration, its programme placed the greatest onslaught of Antichrist before the spiritual revolution and emphasised the apotheosis of history in the spirtual glory of the third age. Here a more conventional view of history has supervened, reducing in importance the expectation of angelic popes.

---

[1] Number five in the series.
[2] Number six.
[3] See below, p 126.
[4] Number nine in the series.
[5] Jean de Roquetaillade (Rupescissa), *Vade Mecum*, ed E. Brown, *Appendix ad Fasciculum Rerum Expetendarum et Fugiendarum ab Orthuino Gratio editum Coloniae MDXXXV*, II (London 1690) p 501.
[6] Rev. 12:4.

Perhaps this is the reason why, in the second half of the fourteenth century, the two sets were put together, making thirty in all, with the second series placed first. This meant that the figure of Antichrist became less menacing in the middle of the sequence and that it culminated in the clear angelic portraits of the first series. By the time number fifteen (i.e. 'Antichrist') was reached in actuality it could be interpreted as Urban VI and associated with the Schism. Thus the form in which these prophecies achieved their greatest popularity in the fifteenth and sixteenth centuries was in this inverted order, the first fifteen (i.e. the later set) being ascribed to Joachim, while the second half (i.e. the first set) was, in this new form, ascribed to a mythical Anselm, bishop of Marsico.

The variety and widespread distribution of the manuscripts of these prophecies is one of their most interesting features. They were reproduced in every sort of style, from crude pen-and-ink sketches to elaborate illuminations. As successive popes appeared they were identified – the enigmatic style of the prophecies making this quite feasible – and the names were written in. A characteristic of both manuscripts and the later printed editions are the annotations of names added by eager readers of a later time. I propose to mention a few examples to illustrate the variety of style. At Yale there is a fourteenth-century French manuscript, with the title *De Imperatore*, which, among other prophetic material, has the whole of the earlier set of prophecies, both pictures and text.[1] The figures are tidy, clear drawings with all the features we have discussed, except that nearly all the animals have been turned into neat little dogs. The fact that only the earlier set is given suggests a date before 1350, but not too early, for the figure with the three columns appears in its established form. In the second half of the fourteenth century, Henry of Kirkestede made for Bury St Edmunds a considerable prophetic anthology which is now in Cambridge. Perhaps the two sets of the *Vaticinia* had not yet been put together, for he includes them separately.[2] First he gives the last five of the later set under the heading *prophecie Joachim de papis*. These five, according to my dating, are the properly prophetic ones. Henry probably had the whole fifteen, for he knew that they started with Nicholas III. He identified number eleven as Clement VI, in whose pontificate he was writing, and then gave the last four under the headings: *De papa futuro post eum* (twice), and then *De penultimo papa, De ultimo papa*. The last, of course, is the prophecy of

[1] Yale, University Library MS, T. E. Marston Coll. 225, fols 16–23.
[2] Corpus Christi College, Cambridge, MS 404, fols 41r, 88r–95r.

the *fera ultima aspectu terribilis*. Thus it is clear that Henry of Kirkestede expected an imminent climax in history and, it would seem, the end of the papacy. There are no pictures here, but later in his anthology Henry incorporates the whole set of the earlier fifteen with clear pen-and-ink drawings of an individual style. In a later hand the popes are all named down to Urban VI. This last is a remarkable picture of a black animal which appears to be a mixture of a bear and a beaver. It must be a corrupt version of the horned animal over which the last pope should be holding his mitre.[1] It looks as if Henry took a pessimistic view of the future, and yet two of the previous pictures show the usual angelic popes, crowned or supported by angels.

In the British Museum MS Arundel 117 – a fifteenth-century manuscript – has the whole thirty, with the text and crudely painted pictures.[2] The last named pope is John XXIII. Harley 1340 is a superb Renaissance manuscript with miniatures which have been claimed by Berenson to be by the Master of the San Miniato altar-piece.[3] Here the last-named pope is Eugenius IV. Yet another copy in the British Museum was made in the mid-century with delicate illuminations in pen and colour.[4] Eugenius IV is the last-named pope in the original hand, but in a later hand both Felix VI and Nicholas V are added.

In the same period there was a group in Venice in which prophecies were circulating. About 1454 a Venetian, Domenico Mauroceno, compiled an anthology of prophecies which inspired a Dominican, Fr Rusticianus, to enlarge and edit it. This in turn was copied by Andreas, a monk of St Cyprian's, from a copy belonging to St Georgio Maggiore. This last copy is now in the Biblioteca Marciana at Venice.[5] The core of this collection is a Joachimist tract produced at the end of the fourteenth century by a disciple of Joachim, Telesphorus of Cosenza.[6] This tract deals with the greatest tribulation of all time in the form of a great schism, with pseudo-pope and tyrant in wicked alliance, followed

---

[1] Fol 95r, cf above, p 114.

[2] British Museum MS Arundel 117, fols 137r–52r. This MS was compiled by someone interested in the past and future of the papacy. He included in it, besides the *Vaticinia*, several pontifical histories and lists, the Joachimist work of Telesphorus of Cosenza, prophesying schism and *renovatio* under the angelic popes, and Henry of Langenstein's refutation of this work.

[3] British Museum MS Harley 1340, fols 1r – 15v. See B. Berenson, 'Miniatures probably by the Master of the San Miniato altar piece', *Essays in honour of George Swarzenski* (Chicago 1951) pp 96–102.

[4] British Museum Additional MS 15691, fols 1r – 15v.

[5] Venice, [Biblioteca Marciana] MS [Lat. C1. III, 177]. On the contents of this MS see Reeves, *Influence of Prophecy*, pp 173, 343–5, 431–2.

[6] On Telesphorus of Cosenza, see *ibid*, pp 325–8, 343–5, 423–4.

by the sabbath of the Church under the angelic popes. Telesphorus took his portraits of the angelic popes from the *Liber de Flore*, but in the St Cyprian compilation Telesphorus's tract is preceded by some crude and startling pictures by a priest, Lazarus of Pavia, which include some of the *Vaticinia*. One shows the pope and the emperor locked in a wrestling match while balanced on a lion, a wheel and a boat which represent, with other symbols, the political powers of Europe.[1] Another picture is of a huge bull-figure which represents Antichrist.[2] The pope prophecies included are numbers twenty-seven to thirty, that is four of the angelic portraits from the earlier series.[3] Here Pius II and Paul II are identified, and then follow two clear angelicals who are still expected. In the latter part of this manuscript another hand takes up the work in 1476 with a collection of short prophecies, and then there are more sequences of pope prophecies in different hands at various dates. The latest is an imitative series ascribed to St Malachy which I shall mention later. Obviously this manuscript represents a continuing interest in these prophecies, though perhaps a note on Andreas, the original copyist, written by the abbot in 1495[4] to stress his prudence and good reputation, suggests that some thought this was dangerous stuff. In the same year Pietro Delphino, the general of the Camaldolesi and himself a Venetian, wrote to a monk, Hieronymus, asking him to get in touch with Domenico Mauroceno to copy a *papalista* about the angelic pope which he possessed.[5] Delphino's interest had been sparked off by a visit from the humanist Accaiuoli who had brought with him another prophecy about the angelic pope. Thus we catch an echo of the way in which pope prophecies were circulating and being discussed at the end of the fifteenth century.

The new medium of print quickened both circulation and discussion. The first extant editions were printed in 1515 in Latin and Italian by Leander Alberti, a Dominican of Bologna. Now we begin to get learned excuses for the unfailing popularity of the *Vaticinia* and scholarly attempts to discuss their interpretation critically. Alberti, in his preface, speaks of the consuming curiosity of mortals to know the future and lists all the various methods by which they seek to satisfy it. Montaigne picks up the same theme later in his essay on prognostica-

[1] Venice MS fol 10v, cf below, p 130, for another example of this picture.
[2] Venice MS fol 11r.
[3] *Ibid*, fols 13r – 15r. On fols 13v – 14v there are interesting extensions of the prophecies.
[4] *Ibid*, fol 42v.
[5] E. Martene et V. Durand, *Veterum Scriptorum et Monumentorum Historicorum, Dogmaticorum, Moralium...Amplissima Collectio*, 9 vols (Paris 1724–33) III, cols 1152–3.

tions.[1] He reflects on the way in which men are deceived by the ambiguities of prophecies, but nonetheless declares his desire to see for himself two marvels: Joachim's book foretelling all the future popes, their names and shapes, and that of Leo the Wise. We have no reason to think that Montaigne knew of the connection between these two, but, as we shall see, the *Oracles* were certainly circulating at this time. Montaigne further pointed out that men were easily enticed into interpreting prophecies to suit their own ends. This was exactly what happened to the *Vaticinia de summis pontificibus* in the sixteenth century.

The first to appropriate these prophecies for a cause was apparently Andreas Osiander, the lutheran minister of St Lawrence church in Nuremberg. He found two copies of the *Vaticinia* in Nuremberg and published an edition with a German commentary and a verse for each picture by Hans Sachs, in 1527.[2] It was easy to see in these pictures denunciations of papal worldliness, simony and political intrigue, and Osiander was able to use these medieval prophecies as a telling polemic against the papacy in general terms. He did, however, recognise the original portrait of Celestine V as belonging to a different category and immediately applied it to Martin Luther, an identification commented on by both Luther himself and Melanchthon.[3] He did not recognise the culminating series of angelic popes at all, but in any case, for Osiander, the papacy would not have an angelic future.

A reply to this protestant view of the *Vaticinia* came from Paracelsus in another Nuremberg edition *c* 1530.[4] This again does not apply the prophecies to individual popes but treats them as a general statement. His position might be termed catholic revolutionary, for he makes full use of the earlier prophecies to sharpen the denunciation of papal sins,

[1] *Essais* (Paris 1598) p 36.
[2] *Eyn wunderliche Weyssagung von dem Babstumb, wie es ihm biz an das endt der welt gehen sol, in figuren oder, gemal begriffen, gefunden zu Nürmberg in Cartheuser Closter, und ist seher alt* (Nuremberg 1527), unpaged. In 1528 J. Adrasder published a latin edition linked with Osiander's, see Reeves, *Influence of Prophecy*, p 454 n 1.

Since writing this paper I have found an English protestant version of the pope prophecies in a pamphlet dedicated to king Edward VI and Edward, duke of Somerset, Lord Proctector, by Gwalter Lynne: *The beginnynge and endynge of all popery, or popische kyngedome* (London 1548) unpaged. This uses selected pictures from both series of prophecies, without original captions or text, but with an anti-papal commentary which purports to be translated from the German. It is not derived from Osiander's edition and requires further study. I owe this reference to Mr Bauckmann.

[3] This portrait was now number xx in the series. For the comments of Luther and Melanchthon, see Reeves, *Influence of Prophecy*, p 490.
[4] *Expositio Vera Harum Imaginum olim Nurenbergae repertarum...* (Nuremberg *c* 1530). I have used an edition of 1570 (no place of publ).

yet still expects the revolution from which the angelic pope will emerge, stressing the fact that in the new régime the pope will be chosen and crowned by God through His angel, not through men.[1] The final picture he interprets, not as Antichrist, but as the seven-horned Lamb of God to whom the pope relinquishes his mitre, when all the sheep will be brought into one fold.[2] But the catholic revolutionary himself must receive an orthodox counter-blast. This came in 1570 from Paul Scaliger who wrote specifically against the false, vain, fictitious and seditious interpretation of the pseudo-magician, Paracelsus.[3] In order to free these prophecies from dangerous interpretations Scaliger goes back to the original interpretation, starting with Nicholas III and applying each prophecy to successive popes. But this means that the whole series of thirty has run out with Innocent VIII and that the concluding angelic portraits must be applied to actual fifteenth-century pontiffs. This Scaliger does with great ingenuity. Indeed, his application of an angelic portrait to Sixtus IV is most amusing.[4] By this method, of course, he drained the prophecies of anything but a strictly historical meaning. To Scaliger, Joachim was a true prophet, because he forecast actual popes, not because he foreknew the shape of history and delineated the angelic agents of an approaching *renovatio mundi*.

Finally, the full weight of scholarship was brought to bear on the problem of the *Vaticinia* by another Venetian, Pasqualino Regiselmo, with that mixture of credulity and science which seems to characterise much of sixteenth-century scholarship.[5] Regiselmo bases his claim to give the true interpretation on his scholarly researches. He parades the fact that he has examined eight manuscripts and seven printed editions in order to eliminate corruptions and false interpretations. These included that compilation of Domenico Mauroceno which had stimulated interest in Joachimist prophecy in Venice 130 years ago.[6] He all but stumbles on the real origin of the *Vaticinia*, for he has heard the view of some recent Greeks that the originals of these figures could be found

---

[1] Number xxviii (fol 44r).

[2] *Ibid*, fol 46r–v. For further reference to Paracelsus's interest in prophecy, see Reeves, *Influence of Prophecy*, pp 455–6.

[3] *Vaticiniorum et imaginum Joachimi...super statu summorum Pontificum... contra falsam iniquam, vanam, confictam et seditiosam cuiusdam Pseudomagi, quae nuper nomine Theophrasti Paracelsi in lucem prodiit, pseudomagicam expositionem vera, certa, et indubitata explanatio* (Cologne 1570).

[4] Quoted Reeves, *Influence of Prophecy*, p 457, n 2.

[5] *Vaticinia sive Prophetiae Abbatis Joachimi et Anselmi Episcopi Marsicani* (Venice 1589) unpaged, in Latin and Italian.

[6] *Ibid*, preface. For Mauroceno, see above, p 120.

under the name of Leo in Constantinople. Alas – he dismisses this as a foolish tale.[1] He resolves the dilemma of interpretation by maintaining that the *Vaticinia* do apply to individual popes, not the papacy in general, but not in continuous sequence. They occur at intervals by some secret mathematical principle and therefore extend into the future.[2] By this method Regiselmo – while countering the protestant line on the *Vaticinia* – is enabled to give full reign to a continuing prophetic hope in the angelic popes of the future.

We notice that both the erudite Regiselmo and Montaigne mention the *Oracles* of Leo and it is clear that this was also a subject of interest at this time. Most of the extant manuscripts belong to the sixteenth century. In 1596 an edition was published in Brescia which, so the title promised,[3] showed that the Turkish rule would end in the time of the present sultan. There are sixteen figures with notes in Latin and Italian. The figures show how little their forms must have changed over the centuries, for one can quickly recognise all the elements which went to the making of the *Vaticinia* in the fourteenth century: the serpent attacked by crows, the eagle with the cross, the cavorting unicorn, the bull, the bear with young. A figure such as the fox with three standards behind his back appears in exactly the same arrangement, although the beast looks more like a griffin than a fox. The angelic pictures are there too: the first one of the king with sickle and rose and the final sequence of the emperor swathed in grave clothes who has to be resurrected, the hermit called forth from his rocky retreat and the concluding angelic portraits. A link with Regiselmo's edition of the pope prophecies actually exists in a Turkish prophecy which occurs in both books with exactly the same picture and text.[4] It is strange that Regiselmo did not connect the two sequences of prophecies. The significant thing about this publication of the *Oracles* of Leo is that its interpreter expresses a similar prophetic hope for the future as in the case of the *Vaticinia*. The great need at the end of the sixteenth century was not for a spiritual revolution in Byzantium, but for a political one to destroy the Turk and restore a line of christian emperors. The current interpretation of the

---

[1] *Ibid*. Note to preface where Regiselmo dismisses a theory that the *Oracles* had been carved on a column in Constantinople. For a medieval reference to this legend see Knös, *Les Oracles*, p 167, n 2; for a further Renaissance reference see [Oxford, Bodleian Library MS] Barocci 170, fol 2v.

[2] *Ibid*, note to fig. XV.

[3] *Vaticinium Severi et Leonis Imperatorum in quo videtur Finis Turcarum in praesenti eorum Imperatore...* (Brescia 1596).

[4] *Ibid*, pp 79–80, cf Regiselmo, *Vaticinia*, at the end of both the Latin and Italian sections.

Oracles provided this hope. Each figure is made to cover a whole period of history. The fall of Constantinople is reached in figure three, where the unicorn with a crescent on his flank represents sultan Mahomet II.[1] The king with sickle and rose is interpreted as Soleyman the Magnificent, who is treated as a good emperor.[2] The next four are taken together as representing the ruin of the Ottoman empire.[3] The swathed and sepulchred emperor whom the angel summons indicates the beginning of hope. To his great satisfaction the commentator is able to interpret the text to show that this saviour will be sought and found in the west, not the east, and that he will be *vir catholicus*.[4] The rest of the sequence works out the promised deliverance in detail. The fourteenth figure breaks away from the usual subject to show a shepherd rescuing a lamb from a wolf. The wolf is the Turk and the shepherd the *Sanctissimus Pontifex* who will intervene to save the flock and show where the true emperor will be found. These crucial events are expected now, in the reign of Mahomet III, for the words of the oracle can be interpreted to show that, as Constantinople was conquered by a Mahomet, so it will be lost by one.[5] Then the supreme pontiff, the catholic princes and the newly-discovered emperor will take over. The last two figures are interpreted as the apotheosis of the restored christian *Imperium et Sacerdotium*.[6]

There are other indications of the value set on the *Oracles* of Leo in this period. On the Ides of April, 1577, in Crete, Francesco Barocci finished a dedicatory letter in which he presented to Iacopo Foscari, consul of Crete, a most magnificent manuscript copy of the *Vaticinia Leonis Imperatoris*.[7] It is a gorgeous production. A mutilated Greek version had come to light and Foscari had asked Barocci to restore and translate it into Latin. Barocci claims to have lavished much scholarship and labour on it in order to remove the errors and obscurities of which those who first transcribed the figures and verses from the marble column had been guilty. In this beautiful copy each figure occupies a whole page, richly illuminated with much elaborate detail. The text is given opposite in verse, Greek and Latin. The earlier figures all contain the usual elements, though with some variations. For instance, the eagle now stands on the unicorn's back; the man with sickle and rose is a turbaned eastern ruler standing in a battlefield of dead; the bull (or cow) is on an island towards which a fleet is sailing;

---

[1] *Vaticinium Leonis*, pp 24–5.
[2] *Ibid*, pp 40–1.
[3] *Ibid*, pp 46–55.
[4] *Ibid*, pp 56–9.
[5] *Ibid*, pp 68–71.
[6] *Ibid*, pp 74–8.
[7] MS Barozzi 170.

the walled city is on a sea-front which is being attacked by serried ranks of galleys.[1] Everything is more elaborate: the half-naked hermit sits on his rock in the usual attitude, but is being sought out by a long procession of citizens issuing from a distant town; the angel crowns the emperor amid an elaborate scene of church leaders.[2] From the twelfth figure onwards the series departs from the usual one, so that the end of the angelic sequence is lost. Instead we have thirteen more pictures of which there is no trace in other versions of the *Oracles* of Leo I have seen. None the less, one figure is clearly the source for the eighth figure in the second series of the *Vaticinia*, so this extended set, or some of it, must have been in circulation much earlier.[3] There is no culminating angelic hope in Barocci's version. The final pictures concern Antichrist, leading up to a magnificent double-page Last Judgement.[4] The scholarship and art expended on this book were apparently inspired, not by a prophetic hope, but by the fascination of the mysterious and the terrible.

The taste for prophecy in the sixteenth century is expressed in a number of collections, both printed and in manuscript. One of the most important in the first category was the *Mirabilis Liber*, first published in Venice in 1514 and subsequently in Paris in 1522 and 1530. Its main purpose, according to the long title-page and preface, was to claim the glories of the prophetic future for the French crown in a holy partnership with a pontiff of shining saintliness.[5] Thus it revives and restates what may be called the French version of the Joachimist future. Here prophecies are collected from many quarters. All the thirty *Vaticinia* are included, that is, text and captions but no pictures.[6] The interesting point here is that the two sets are given in the right order, instead of the later set first, and are drawn from different manuscripts. The note preceding the first says that this prophecy was found – with figures which have been omitted for the sake of brevity – in the library of St Victor of Paris. A similar note for the later set names the library of Cluny as the source. In neither case is an author given, but dates of composition are hazarded as round about 1040 and 1100 respectively. These are followed by an extract from the *libellus* of Telesphorus of Cosenza. This is headed *De angelico pastore et eius bonitate* and is described as taken from

---

[1] *Ibid*, fols 7v, 8v, 9v, 11v.   [2] *Ibid*, fols 14v, 15v.
[3] *Ibid*, fol 19v, cf above, p 118.   [4] *Ibid*, fols 27v – 8r.
[5] Ex his prophetiis et revelationibus intimis oculis perlustratis facile cognosci poterit pontificem maximum vite sanctitate perfulgentem brevi ex religiosissimo Francorum regno futurum, qui...pacem inter christicolas omnes componere statusque hominum... diligentissime reformare curabit...Super omnes reges et excellentia regna terrena habetur Gallorum rex cum regno omnium religiossimus....
[6] *Mirabilis Liber*, fols xxxv – xxxiii v.

a book of the abbot Joachim in the St Victor library.[1] Then come more miscellaneous prophecies and accounts of prophets, including Joachim. The first part, which is in Latin, ends with the revelations of the fourteenth-century franciscan Joachite, Jean de Roquetaillade, or Rupescissa.[2] The second part, which is in French, is again in praise of the holy pair, French king and angelic pope, who are to come. This compilation shows us a scholar, or scholars, seriously searching libraries and other places for prophecies to which, as a rule, the sources are carefully appended. The national bias given to the collection is clear, and this publication forms an important item in a group of French prophetic works of the sixteenth century. It is quoted by several other writers, including the compiler of a French manuscript anthology of prophecy to which I shall refer shortly.

One of the curiosities of the later sixteenth century is the craze for imitating the prophecies of the popes. These circulated, not only in print, but in manuscript. In the most extensive collection there are nine such imitative series and these do not include the most famous of all, the prophecies attributed to St Malachy. These series are sometimes expressed in the form of wheels with the names of popes and symbols between the spokes; sometimes in enigmatic captions only; sometimes in captions and pictures in the style of the original *Vaticinia*. All identify the popes up to a certain point and are then projected into the future. A typical product in print is an edition of 1600 in Venice of the *rotae* of six illustrious men of whom five are named: Joachim, Anselm, Iodochus Palmerius, Egidius Polonus and a Johannes Abbas.[3] Joachim's wheel is said to have foretold the pontiffs from Nicholas III to Urban VI. The captions accompanying it are those of the later fifteen *Vaticinia* attributed to Joachim and the small emblems representing each pope are based on the figures of the same set.[4] The second wheel contains the captions of the earlier set of *Vaticinia*, now attributed to the mythical Anselm, bishop of Marsico and said to run from Boniface IX to Pius III, but in this case only one emblem, that of the bear suckling its young, can be connected with the original series.[5] The next is an anonymous *Rota Hieroglyphica* which starts with Sixtus IV and has twenty-six divisions, with notes expounding the popes as far as Clement VIII (1592).[6] The *Rota* of Iodochus Palmerius, who died in 1544, has sixteen

---

[1] *Ibid*, fol xxxiiii r. [2] *Ibid*, fols lxvii r – lxviii v.

[3] *Vaticinia seu Praedictiones Illustrium Virorum Sex Rotis. . .cum declarationibus et annotationibus Hieronymi Ioannini* (Venice 1600).

[4] *Ibid*, fols 4 v–5 r. [5] *Ibid*, fols 6 v, 7 r.

[6] *Ibid*, fols 8 v–10 r.

symbols and identifies popes from Marcellus II (1555) to Clement VIII (1592).[1] The series under the name of Egidius Polonus was supposed to have been sent by John of Capestrano of Aeneas Silvius Piccolomini before he became pope and of course the series runs from Pius II onwards.[2] Johannes Abbas is unknown.[3] A full edition of the thirty Vaticinia published in Venice and Ferrara in 1593 adds all these series. This was republished in Venice in 1600, in Padua in 1625 and again in Venice as late as 1646.[4] These imitative series do not embody much of the Joachimist prophetic hope; their main point seems to be the game of making enigmatic symbols and oracles fit actual popes under the pretence of prophecy. Most of them run out soon after the end of the sixteenth century.

The popularity of the so-called prophecies of St Malachy is probably due to the fact that this is a longer sequence, extending to 111 in all.[5] There are no pictures but a series of captions or mottos which, for the historical past, simply form plays on words, often the family names of the popes. This series first appeared in print when published by the Cistercian Arnold Wion in 1595 and it seems most likely that it was, in fact, concocted at the time of the election of Gregory XIV in 1590.[6] Whether the immediate purpose was to canvass for a particular candidate is not clear, but in this case the ultimate aim is obviously to proclaim the eventual appearance of the angelic pope, as the final prophecies show.[7] Perhaps this also was a factor in their popularity.

That this type of prophecy was still being taken seriously at the end of the sixteenth century is further shown by three manuscript anthologies which I have studied. One – a Philips MS recently acquired by Bodley – is entirely devoted to various series of pope prophecies, all of them illustrated in pen and ink and colour wash.[8] There is a tree with thirteen branches, each bearing a caption for a pope. Ten are named, from Paul III to Gregory XIV. There is a wheel and a series of initial letters with

---

[1] Ibid, fols 12r/v. [2] Ibid, fols 25r–6v.

[3] Rota Vaticiniorum B. Ioannis Abbatis, ibid. fols 19r–20v.

[4] For other editions, see Russo, Bibliografia, pp 46–8.

[5] On the prophecies of St Malachy, see J. Schmidlin, 'Die Papstweissagung des hl. Malachias', Festgabe... Heinrich Finke (Münster 1904) pp 3–40.

[6] Ibid, pp 32–4.

[7] Ibid, p 39; 'Fides intrepida, Pastor angelicus, Pastor et nauta, Flos florum, De medietate lunae, De labore solis De gloria olivae.'

[8] Oxford, Bodleian Library MS, Ital. c. 73 (olim Phillipps 1726). The enthusiasm for prophecy which produced MS versions in an age of printing is further illustrated by British Museum MS Harley 3483 which is a copy of Regiselmo's 1589 edition of the Vaticinia, complete with all his annotations.

symbols, but most of the series are in the style of the *Vaticinia*, that is, of popes with symbols and captions, but, in this case, no text. The whole forms the strangest collection of symbolic pictures that I have seen. The *Vaticinia* are placed first, preceded by a picture of Joachim with his monks. After this, fantasy seems to run riot in eight further sequences, in which lions, dragons, eagles, serpents, falling towers and churches, armed men, kings and queens, a burning tree, a tree bearing cardinals' hats, and many other things, appear. It does not seem that the whole compilation was designed to proclaim the angelic popes, but again and again this motif does appear. In some sequences, it is true, the pessimistic view of history prevails, with an ending in Antichrist, but some certainly culminate in the angelic concept. The problem, however, is to understand what overall purpose the book was intended to serve. It certainly reveals a continuing interest in this method of forecasting the future of the papacy. In some of the series the last-named pope is Gregory XIV (1590-1); in two it is Innocent IX (1591) and in two it is Clement VIII (1592-1605). Thus all these series were probably being produced in the period 1590-5, along with the various wheels I have already mentioned and the prophecies of St Malachy. This particular manuscript was apparently compiled in the pontificate of Clement VIII.

Another manuscript anthology which is now in Bodley was owned by archbishop Laud.[1] This is also of Italian origin but a very different production from the previous one. On the one hand, it is more extensive in its range, including many more texts, instead of giving only the pictorial series of pope prophecies. On the other hand, the pictures it does include are ridiculous little pen and ink scribbles of a very primitive kind. Its main subject, however, is the same, namely, prophecies of popes past and future, and there is clearly some connection between the two manuscripts, for similar material of a not so obvious kind is found in both, for instance, the tree of the popes, drawn in identical style.[2] In Laud's book the first substantial piece is a pope prophecy which I have not so far mentioned: the vision of the blessed Amadeus in which the angel Gabriel revealed to him secrets concerning the angelic pope to come.[3] This had a considerable vogue in the early sixteenth century and an Italian version was published in Venice by Paolo Angelo of Byzantium. I have not seen a latin text except in this Laud manuscript, but

---

[1] [Oxford, Bodleian Library MS], Laud Misc. 588.
[2] Laud Misc. 588, fol 47v.
[3] For Amadeus and his prophecies see Reeves, *Influence of Prophecy*, pp 233-4, 440-1, 461-2.

the work is easily identified from the parts given by Angelo. After this follow prophecies under various well-known names – St Columbinus, St Hildegarde, St Bridget – and then, once again, a jungle of prophetic sequences. St Malachy's series is there, and others attributed to St Vincent Ferrer, Nicholas of Toledo and Simon of Holland. Again the series under the names of Iodochus Palmerius and Egidius Polonus appear with other anonymous ones found in various mysterious circumstances, for instance: *carmina inventa in quodam muro Abbatiae ruinato in Inghilterra*. Some are in the form of wheels and there is one extraordinary picture which is apparently cut out of a printed book but which I have only met before in manuscript form, in the venetian compilation of the fifteenth century to which I have referred.[1] Towards the end the whole thirty of the *Vaticinia* are given under the names of Joachim and Anselm, but without pictures. It was an extraordinary activity to put together all these puzzling oracles, especially since there appears to be no artistic motive. The little scribbled figures could not have attracted anyone. But more clearly than in the other anthologies the motif of the angelic pope does stand out as the main purpose of the compilation. As for date, again the latest series is one in which Clement VIII is the last-named pope, leaving four empty spaces beyond. The tree of the popes also goes as far as Clement VIII, leaving one more branch portentously labelled *Petrus sedebit*.

The third anthology I want to describe briefly is at Carpentras in the south of France.[2] It has a beautiful title-page in French which clearly belongs to the sixteenth century and reads: *Les Propheties Qui sont vulgairement attribuées à L'Abbé Joachim*. But, in fact, all the first part of the book consists of a splendid fourteenth-century copy of the *Vaticinia* which has been cut up and put into a scrapbook. The whole thirty prophecies are there, so it belongs to the later fourteenth century, but the earlier sequence is given in an early form and with a commentary by one 'Rabanus' which goes back to the original group of writings but is usually dropped in later versions.[3] Then, introduced again by a beautiful title-page, large portions of Regiselmo's edition of 1589 are copied out, including the preceding life of Joachim by Gabriel Barrio and Regiselmo's annotations.[4] This is followed by extracts from the *Mirabilis Liber* on the angelic pope and some from the pseudo-Joachimist

---

[1] Cf above, p 121.

[2] Carpentras, Bibliothèque Imguimbertine, MS 340. I am indebted to Mr John Fleming for calling my attention to this manuscript.

[3] On 'Rabanus' see Grundmann, *AK*, XIX (1929) p 107; *HJ*, XLIX (1929) p 40.

[4] Fols 35r–51r (in my foliation). On G. Barrio, see Reeves, *Influence of Prophecy*, p 118.

Some popular prophecies

Super Hieremiam.[1] Finally, the last part of this anthology brings us back to the *Oracles* of Leo again. Here are the earlier pictures of the serpent and birds, the unicorn and so on, together with all the captions and texts of the series which once inspired the *Vaticinia*.[2] Two interpretations are given for each figure. Most of these focus on the Turkish rulers, but the end of the Ottoman empire is envisaged in the prophetic future. There is no indication that the compiler of this anthology knew of the connection between the *Oracles* and the *Vaticinia*. It is a strange coincidence that a later sixteenth-century collector of prophecies should have brought together, without apparently any knowledge of the connection, the original model and the imitative series it had inspired in the fourteenth century.

These anthologies belong to an age which appears utterly removed from the emotional crisis which led that little group of Spiritual Franciscans to produce the *Vaticinia* in 1304. The question, to which I have no answer, is: what in the final decade or so of the sixteenth century sparked off these imitative series of pope prophecies and stimulated the production of these manuscript anthologies? What was the main interest? Was it just that of playing with intriguing puzzles? The theme of the angelic series and the *renovatio mundi* seems to be partially submerged, but never wholly and, in the case of the Laud Collection, was, I think, certainly the main purpose of the anthology. I have tried to show elsewhere that at the end of the sixteenth century the hope of an angelic pope was still current.[3] The evidence of the continuing circulation of the *Vaticinia* supports the view that even in an attenuated form, some people still speculated on the possibility of a spiritual revolution.

In all the printed editions and late manuscripts one of the unchanging themes is that of the hermit who is sought out among the rocks under divine guidance, to be made the supreme leader of the *renovatio mundi*. This theme deserves further investigation. It certainly goes back to the *Oracles* of Leo and it appears in the west quite independently of the *Vaticinia* in the legend of the mythical pope Gregory which is found in French literature from the last third of the twelfth century.[4] Here, as in the *Oracles*, when a pope has to be elected, God's voice directs men to the rocky retreat from which the emaciated penitent, Gregory, is brought

---

[1] Fols 51 v–57 v.

[2] Fols 57 v–75 v; the later pictures are not drawn in.

[3] Reeves, *Influence of Prophecy*, pp 468–72, 499–500.

[4] See G. Ehrismann, *Geschichte der Deutschen Literatur bis zum Ausgang des Mittelalters*, II, 2 (Munich 1927) pp 184–8. I am indebted to Dr R. Harvey for drawing my attention to the parallel between this legend and the *Oracles* of Leo.

	ORACLES OF LEO			PROPHECIES OF POPES				
	1596 ed	1729 ed	MS Barocci	MS Douce	MS Riccardi	MS Vat Lat 1	MS Vat Lat 2	Pipini
1	serpent & crows	serpent & crows	bear & young	bear & young & pope	pope & bear	serpent & crows & ? cleric	bears & pope	bears & pope
2	eagle & cross	eagle & cross	serpent & crows	serpent & crows & pope	serpent & crows & pope	text	serpent & bird & pope & dragon	griffin & bird & pope
3	unicorn & man	unicorn & man	unicorn & eagle & cross	unicorn & eagle & cross & pope	unicorn & eagle & pope	unicorn & eagle & pope	unicorn & eagle & pope	unicorn & eagle & pope
4	bull & two heads	head of man	king & sickle & rose		head of man in a vessel	text	three columns	three columns
5	bear & young	man & sickle & rose	bull & two heads	man & sickle & rose & two heads & severed head	monk & sickle & rose	man & sickle & rose	monk & sickle & rose	monk & sickle & rose
6	king & sickle & rose	cow & two heads	bear & young	cow & pope	bull or cow & two heads & pope	cow & pope	cow & pope & two heads	cow & pope & two heads
7	city & head	bear & young	city	bear & young & king	bear & young & pope	bear & young & king	bear & young & pope	bear & young & pope
8	fox & flags	city & head	fox & flags	city & head	city	city	city	fox & flags & pope
9	empty throne	fox & flags	mummified emperor	fox & flags & pope	fox & flags & pope		fox & flags & pope	
10	unicorn & crescent	empty throne	hermit & sun, moon etc	empty throne	city		city	

11	mummified emperor	unicorn & crescent	angel crowning emperor	hermit etc	hermit etc	hermit etc
12	hermit & sun, moon etc	hermit & sun, moon etc		derived from mummified emperor	derived from mummified emperor	derived from mummified emperor
13	king with sceptre	mummified emperor	series continues with different pictures numbering 23 in all	angel crowning pope	angel crowning pope	angel crowning pope
14	shepherd & lamb	king with sceptre		pope & angels	pope & angels	pope & angels
15	angel & crown	angel & crown		mitred pope & mitre	pope holding mitre over animal	pope holding mitre
16	emperor & patriarch	emperor & patriarch				? Lamb of God crowned

SOURCES

Oracles of Leo: Vaticinium Severi et Leonis Imperatorum in quo videtur Finis Turcarum in praesenti eorum Imperatore, una cum aliis nonnullis in hac re Vaticiniis (Brescia 1596); G. Codinus, *Excerpta de Antiquitatibus Constantino-politanis*, ed P. Lambecius, *De Imperatore Leone eiusque Oraculis* (Venice 1729) pp 161–79; Oxford, Bodleian Library MS Barocci 170.

Prophecies of Popes: Oxford, Bodleian Library MS Douce 58, fols 140r–6v; Florence, Biblioteca Riccardiana MS 1222B, fols 1r–8v; Rome, Vatican Library MS Latin 3822, fols 5v–6v [Vat Lat 1] (text and description of some figures only); Rome, Vatican Library MS Latin 3819, fols 147r–50v [Vat Lat 2]; F. Pipini, *Chronica, Rerum Italicarum Scriptores*, old series, IX (Milan 1721) cols 724, 726, 727, 728, 736, 741, 747, 751 (description only of figures).

forth to become the ideal pope. This might have been derived from the *Oracles* more than a century before the same theme was taken up in the Joachimist *Vaticinia*.[1] I have found another independent echo of this theme from the *Oracles* of Leo in a little prophetic tract, *Ve mundo in centum annis*, written in 1300 by a certain Gentile.[2] He refers to a prophecy which points to a future crucial papal election when, to those assembled as electors, the voice of God will speak directing them to go to the west of the seven hills and seek out *pauperum nudum meum* who will become the first pope-reformer. The words of the *Oracles* are directly quoted here, though without a hint of their source. There may well be other examples. I leave this question for the future and conclude with one general reflection: popular prophecy is seen here as a means of bringing an ideal hopefully nearer, and divine intervention as a method of revolutionising an institution whose authority cannot be impugned. The exaltation of the hermit amid the rocks is a medieval expression of the Magnificat theme and a striking affirmation of belief that the spiritual revolution must inevitably take place.

[1] See above, p 109, n 5, for the possible relation of this legend to the problem of dating the *Oracles*.
[2] H. Finke, *Aus den Tagen Bonifaz VIII* (Münster 1902) p 220, n 1.

BELIEF AND PRACTICE
AS ILLUSTRATED BY JOHN XXII's
EXCOMMUNICATION OF
ROBERT BRUCE

by ROSALIND M. T. HILL

THE sentence of excommunication was the ultimate spiritual deterrent available to the medieval Church. It was designed to be completely terrifying, and to the devout mind it probably was. In theory, it cut the offender off not only from his hope of eternal salvation but, as many a person found to his cost, from all contacts which made mortal life bearable, or indeed possible. But theory, as father Logan has shown us, is not the same thing as practice. The effectiveness of the sentence was limited both by the character of the person afflicted and, to some extent, by his social position. A king could get away with a good deal, and, for lesser men, the existence of the writ *de excommunicato capiendo* tacitly acknowledged the fact that a royal prison might be a more effective inducement to repentance than the terrors of the Church's ban. To some extent the Church itself had asked for trouble by cheapening the sentence. Many a modern librarian must wish for a suitably unpleasant punishment for those who borrow books and fail to return them, but when we find a bishop of Lincoln ordering the excommunication, after *trina monitio*, of all those who have failed to return a book borrowed from Master John of Dersingham,[1] we may wonder whether a sledgehammer were not being used to crack a nut.

John XXII's excommunication, in 1318, of Robert Bruce certainly does not fall into the category of excommunication for trivial causes, whatever one may think of the rights of the case, but the way in which the pope attempted, and Bruce frustrated, the execution of the sentence provides an interesting example of the difference between theory and practice in matters of ecclesiastical administration. The pope started from the assumption that Bruce was a lawful and distinguished subject of the king of England who had regrettably defected from his allegiance.

[1] *Rolls and Register of Bishop Oliver Sutton*, III, ed R. M. T. Hill, *LRS*, XLVIII (Lincoln 1954) pp 200–1.

Writing in March 1317 he praised the beauties of peace, now disturbed by 'the horrible seed of dissension blown abroad by Satan's pestiferous breath', and charged 'the illustrious Edward, king of England' and 'our beloved son that noble man Robert Bruce, at present ruling the kingdom of Scotland' to cease from fighting, 'upon pain of excommunication and interdict.'[1] Edward, with memories of Bannockburn, had no wish to fight, though he would not recognise Scottish independence. The initiative in the conflict lay with Bruce, who was supported not only by the people of Scotland but also by all its effective bishops. Failing their cooperation, how was the papal warning to be delivered?

The papal legates in England, Gaucelin and Luke, had already suffered at the hands of 'rank reivers' on the English side of the border, and were, understandably, unwilling to go up in person into the Lowland hills in order to bell so large and ferocious a cat. On the plea that 'they did not know where the noble Robert Bruce now governing the kingdom of Scotland kept his house (*larem tunc fovebat*) nor could they reach him or the kingdom of Scotland because of divers obstructions',[2] they deputed the embassy to the bishop of Carlisle and the archdeacon of Ely. These, 'not without labour and peril and great difficulty', managed to obtain from Bruce a safe-conduct as far as Roxburgh. Here they encountered James Douglas and Alexander Seton, who demanded to see the letters which they carried and showed them strong hostility. At length, after long argument, 'a certain clerk of the said Robert' guided them as far as Melrose, where they found Bruce encamped *campestriter*. Their troubles were not yet over. Bruce looked at the superscription of the papal letters and declared 'with indignation and ire' that they were addressed not to him as king of Scotland but to a certain 'Robert Bruce now governing the kingdom of Scotland' whose identity he did not know. He therefore refused to read them.

The legates made a second attempt to deliver the papal letters, this time by brother Adam, guardian of the Franciscans at Berwick. Adam, having obtained a safe-conduct, entered Scotland and was met by Alexander Seton 'calling himself seneschal of the said Robert', who, after presenting his letters to Bruce, returned and warned him that 'on peril of his life he should take himself off from the land and realm of Scotland'. Seeing his discomfiture, many of the Scots who were present fell upon the wretched Adam 'in a sacrilegious and hostile

---

[1] York, Borthwick Institute of Historical Research MS R. I. 9, Reg[ister of archbishop] Mel[ton] (rebound in two volumes 1968) fol 499 v.

[2] Reg Mel, fol 500 v.

manner', stole his letters, and stripped him even of the garments of his poverty and the provisions which he carried. They spared his life, and he was able to return to the legates and tell his story.[1]

Such treatment of papal messengers, coupled with Bruce's action in capturing Berwick, was bound to provoke the threatened sentence of excommunication. On 28 May 1318, the pope declared that since Bruce 'like a deaf adder' had refused to listen to papal monitions he and all his followers, supporters and accomplices, together with those helping him with gifts of money, horses and arms, or showing him counsel or favour, were to be excommunicated after a *trina monitio* spread over the exceptionally short period of ten days. The legates received this letter and published it from Nottingham on 13 August. They commanded that the warning and sentence should be published by every arch-bishop and bishop in the kingdoms of England, Scotland, Ireland and Wales, and directed that copies 'sealed with their great seal' were to be affixed to cathedral doors and to 'columns and lampstands' (an unusual and lively illustration of the verb *publicare*).[2]

What happened? Upon the ecclesiastical front, curiously little. Bruce, whose bishops stood solidly loyal behind him, declared and quite clearly believed that he had never been excommunicated because he was not the person described in the papal letters. When in 1319 the pope wrote to suggest that the Scots should treat with the archbishop of York and the bishops of Ely and Carlisle concerning absolution and the restoration of peace, he disregarded the whole affair. In January 1320 the pope fell back upon the convenient, if fictitious, explanation that Bruce and his supporters had been prevented from coming to Rome by their fear of military attack upon the journey, and he therefore issued for them an impressive safe-conduct, addressed to all the clergy and laity of western Europe. This document was sent to archbishop Melton with instructions that he was to forward it to Bruce. Melton, reasonably enough, passed on the letters to his frontier suffragan, Lewis de Beau-mont, bishop of Durham. Lewis reported that he had directed Alexan-der of Carlisle, guardian of the Franciscans of Newcastle, to carry out the mission.[3]

Nothing came of it – nothing, at least, which John XXII could regard as satisfactory. On 6 April 1320, the barons and community of the realm of Scotland answered the pope in the magnificent letter known as the Declaration of Arbroath, but they did so in the clear consciousness of the righteousness of their cause in the eyes of God and the Church. They

[1] *Ibid.*   [2] *Ibid*, fols 502–3 v.   [3] *Ibid*, fols 504 v, 507 v.

did not hesitate to point out, effectively but deliberately, that although Rome was the see of St Peter, it was St Peter's elder brother St Andrew who was responsible for the conversion of the Scots, 'although they were settled at the outermost ends of the earth'. Bruce never regarded himself as lawfully excommunicated, and never showed any intention of going to Rome to explain himself. He was a man of deep if somewhat peculiar piety; the murder of Comyn in a church he seems to have taken in his stride, but he venerated the saints and was remembered as a benefactor of churches. On his deathbed he charged his friend James Douglas to take his place on the crusade and carry his heart into battle against the infidel – a charge which was duly carried out.

A few minor repercussions of the excommunication can be traced in northern England. Roger Delhull, priest, who had been ordained under duress by a Scottish bishop,[1] and William of Brauncewell, clerk, who had attended a mass said by a Scottish priest,[2] duly sought archbishop Melton to obtain absolution from sentences of excommunication which they had inadvertently incurred. In 1321 four people from Ravenser Odd in the East Riding of Yorkshire (one of them a woman) complained that 'because against their will they had been compelled to communicate with Scots, the parishioners of the place in which they now dwelt regarded them as excommunicate, avoided them, and refused to sell them food or other necessities of life'.[3] As so often happens in a war, it was the civilians who were caught in the cross-fire.

[1] *Ibid*, fol 449. [2] *Ibid*, fol 511. [3] *Ibid*.

BACON AND EGGS:
BISHOP BUCKINGHAM AND SUPERSTITION
IN LINCOLNSHIRE

by DOROTHY M. OWEN

I HAVE recently read through almost all the surviving medieval registers of the diocese of Lincoln, while collecting material for a book on the church in medieval Lincolnshire society. As may be imagined, a good many interesting patterns are emerging from this and other sources; this short note results from the examination of one such pattern.

John Buckingham, who like so many other bishops of the fourteenth century, had been a civil servant, ruled over the see of Lincoln, with conspicuous industry and attention to detail, for the twenty-six years between 1362 and 1398. His career is the subject of a doctoral thesis, on which Miss Alison McHardy is now engaged, and I do not propose to discuss it here. Instead, I want to consider in detail one or two incidents in his episcopate which are, I believe, of some relevance to the theme of this conference.

Professor Hamilton Thompson has discussed at some length the administrative aftermath of the Black Death in the diocese of Lincoln, and the difficulties experienced by the authorities in persuading parochial chaplains to reside, and to accept their former stipends, are well known.[1] No-one has mentioned, so far as I know, some of the popular religious manifestations which were also the outcome of this time of disturbance and unease. Professor Ward and Professor Momigliano have each reminded us of the religious remedies resorted to in times of disturbance, and my theme is similar to theirs: there seem to have been in Lincolnshire some manifestations of a desire on the one hand for intensified religious observance, and on the other, for supernatural reassurance. How far these were spontaneous, how far they were cunningly exploited for profit, I find it difficult to decide, but they undoubtedly existed, and they equally undoubtedly came into conflict, at some points at least, with the diocesan government.

[1] A. Hamilton Thompson, 'The episcopal registers of Bishop John Gynwell, 1349–50'), *Archaeological Journal*, LXVIII (London 1911) pp 301–61.

The temper of the age was already apparent during the episcopate of Buckingham's predecessor, John Gynwell. In 1360 Gynwell admonished the archdeacon of Lincoln to forbid his subjects to regard Saturday, or any part of it, as a festival, and to order them to continue work on that day until vespers. This may, of course, be symptomatic merely of labour shortages, yet Lincolnshire had always had a tendency to over-strict observances of this sort, going back at least as far as 1202, and this may have been a resurgence of earlier practices.[1] At the same time Gynwell found it necessary to forbid the carrying of parochial banners in the Whitsuntide processions, because they had recently led to disturbance, violence, and even homicide. The register of Buckingham shows little sign, until the last ten years of the episcopate, that he was disturbed by similar manifestations, but a passage in the *Nova Legenda Anglie*, appearing under the year 1376, suggests that something was going on.[2] It concerns a ruinous chapel of St Edmund, which had been founded in the twelfth century on land in Wainfleet, on the Lincolnshire coast.

A certain Alan, named Wastelere, of Wainfleet, who worked as a roofer, in various materials, lay on his bed in the silence of the night, and had the following vision in a dream. He seemed to see the image of St. Edmund, which is placed in the chapel of the monks of St. Edmund at Wainfleet, coming to him, and saying 'Alan, where have you arranged to work next?' To which he replied 'For the lord of Kyme, with whom I have contracted to work speedily, at Burwell.' The image responded, 'You know that my chapel is almost ruinous, and urgently needs repair. Drop everything, and apply yourself to the work that is necessary.' Alan protested, saying that he could not break his contract, but the image persisted: 'Go, and contradict me no further. Put my service first, and, have no fear, I will reward you'. Alan, thus spurred on, on the morrow set about roofing the chapel, expecting no wages for it, but doing a good job, and in the end he had not less, but more, of food and all other necessaries.

This story is followed by a series of miracles performed in or near Wainfleet on crippled or blind people: sixteen sailors are rescued from a storm while sailing across the Wash, another is saved from a perilous deep in the fen called Rabwater. Several times the name of John de Hayton appears as an agent recommending the saint and his works; it is hard to avoid the conclusion that he was the promoter of the incidents. Whatever his rôle, the campaign succeeded, for the chapel survived until 1534 at least.

[1] L[incoln] E[piscopal] R[egister], Reg. 7, fol 149r; *The earliest Lincolnshire Assize Rolls*, ed D. M. Stenton, *LRS*, XXII (Lincoln 1926) p xi.
[2] C. Horstmann, *Nova Legenda Anglie* (Oxford 1901) pp 677–81.

There is no record that the bishop took any action for or against the Wainfleet occurrences, but there are two explicit cases in which religious or superstitious practices not unlike these were firmly condemned by him. The first concerned a wayside cross in Rippingale: in 1386 Buckingham's register records a mandate for the holding of an inquiry.[1]

A serious complaint has reached us that many of our subjects have made for themselves a pretended statue vulgarly known as Jurdon Cros, in the fields of Rippingale, and have begun to adore it, and to report that many miracles are done there. They are preaching and ringing bells and holding processions, for the deception of the people and the increase of gain, and laymen are said to be converting the offerings to their own uses.

The bishop evidently received an unfavourable report; he condemned the cross and its adorers and refused them permission to erect a chapel near it. They were not deterred: in the papal registers for 1392 there is this entry:

Licence at the petition of Robert Joneson de Morton, rector of two portions of Repynghale, in the diocese of Lincoln...for him and the parishioners and any others, without the licence of the ordinary, to found and build a chapel of Holy Cross, and to have mass and other divine offices celebrated therein, upon the spot in certain fields within the parish bounds near the high road, on which for a hundred years has stood and still stands, a certain wooden cross, whither, by reason of the miracles wrought there, great multitudes with offerings resort from the said diocese and from other parts of England. Bishop John, for a reason unknown, has forbidden such offerings to be made there, on account of which the cross is not held in due and wonted devotion.[2]

Note how the age of the miracle-working statue has increased and note also, that the promoter of the project is again closely connected with the parish church.

The other example turns from miracle-working to a revival of something like pagan practices, which, while interesting enough in itself, is probably symptomatic of some popular religious feeling of the time:[3]

John etc...to my dear son William of Banbury, rector of the parish church of Nettleham, which is of my collation and in my diocese...I heard some time ago that in your church, the cure of which I entrusted to you, a very foul abuse, hateful to God, had blinded the minds of your parishioners so that in the most

[1] *LER*, Reg 12, fol 331 v.
[2] *Calendar of...Papal Registers: Papal Letters*, IV (London 1902) p 368.
[3] *LER*, Reg 12, fol 450 r.

holy ceremonies of Easter, when the sacrifice of the Spotless Lamb, that is, of Christ the Redeemer of mankind, having been offered on the altar, is distributed to the faithful, before the body and blood have been tasted they each year cause to be blessed solemnly by the priest, in church, swine's flesh commonly called Bacun, (which the Chosen People were forbidden in the Old Testament to eat because it was impure) and many shelled hardboiled eggs. These, which are provided at your expense, are carried to every house in the parish as a sort of holy offering, to the great scandal and dishonour of the Church of Christ and its sacraments, to the danger of the souls of these idolaters and, by example, to the souls of others.

Here, you will note, the culprits are the people of the parish, and not the incumbent, and it is hard to avoid the feeling that the strength of such manifestations lay more in those who were ready to take part in them than in the clerical exploiters. There are no more references to such practices in Buckingham's register, but it is in his time, or very soon after, that several local pilgrimage cults began, for example to the Good Rood of Boston – there is even a pilgrim token for it – and to the statue of St Petronella at Boultham near Lincoln.[1] I do not think that I am exaggerating when I say that in the second half of the fourteenth century there was something of a revival of popular religion in Lincolnshire.

What is equally interesting, and here one reverts to Professor Momigliano, is the official attitude to these practices. Less than a century earlier bishops Sutton and Dalderby were condoning local customs very like the Nettleham one, especially meinport, which was bread brought into church on Easter Tuesday by the married women of the parish, whereas Buckingham had plainly set his face against them.[2] We know that he condemned these two samples; there is a case of a clerk doing penance for sorcery in 1376, and it seems probable that in unrecorded visitations many smaller manifestations were put down. In 1391 he had occasion to rebuke the proctors of the consistory for unseemly behaviour, including *fastuosas locuciones et supersticiosas*, which suggests that there, at least, he was fighting against an overwhelming movement, which his successors did not even try to control.[3]

[1] P. Thompson, *History and Antiquities of Boston* (2 ed, Boston 1856) pp 134, 300; *LER*, Reg. 20 fol 8 v.

[2] *Rolls and Register of Bishop Oliver Sutton*, ed R. M. T. Hill, III, *LRS*, XLVIII (1954) p 110; v, *LRS*, LX (1965) p 140; *LER*, Reg. 3, fols 154 r, 291 v.

[3] *LER*, Reg 12, fols 161 r, 389 r.

'WILDE WITTES AND WILFULNES': JOHN SWETSTOCK'S ATTACK ON THOSE 'POYSWUNMONGERES', THE LOLLARDS

by ROY M. HAINES

UNTIL the pioneer work of Dr G. R. Owst in the 1920s and 1930s English sermon literature was a neglected field. Even today Owst's two general studies[1] remain largely isolated monuments, the starting-point of those who would pursue the sermon, but not, perhaps, so influential in related fields as their intrinsic worth and astonishing thoroughness would appear to merit.

As Owst pointed out,[2] James Gairdner's four-volume work on Lollardy[3] failed to take account both of unpublished material in episcopal registers[4] and of an extensive sermon literature in manuscript. It was by means of the sermon that Owst himself was able to recreate much of the social background of fourteenth and fifteenth-century England. A prominent element in that background was Lollardy.

The most recent account of the Lollards,[5] by relying principally on

[1] *Preaching in Medieval England: [An Introduction to the Sermon Manuscripts of the Period c. 1350–1450]* (Cambridge 1926); *Literature and Pulpit [in Medieval England]* (Cambridge 1933, 2 ed Oxford 1961). He added a postscript with the publication of his lecture: *The Destructorium Viciorum of Alexander Carpenter, [a Fifteenth-Century Sequel to Literature and Pulpit in Medieval England]* (London 1952).

[2] *Preaching in Medieval England*, p 130: 'When Dr Gairdner wrote his learned study from a ripe acquaintance with almost every kind of document that might be associated with ecclesiastical and public records [*note*: Except the Registers, I understand, which he confessedly had not studied], it is safe to say that the rich contemporary evidence of great orthodox sermon collections in this country had not lain open before him, nor probably anyone else.'

[3] *Lollardy and the Reformation in England* (London 1908, repr New York n.d.).

[4] Foxe, of course, had used the registers as well as other manuscript sources. [*The*] *Acts and Monuments [of John Foxe]*, ed the Reverend S. R. Cattley, with a preliminary dissertation by the Reverend G. Townsend, 8 vols (London 1837–41), is the edition quoted in this paper.

[5] J. A. F. Thomson, *The Later Lollards 1414–1520* (Oxford 1965). See also: M. E. Aston, 'Lollardy and the Reformation: Survival or Revival?', *History*, XLIX (London 1964) pp 149–70; A. G. Dickens, *Lollards and Protestants in the Diocese of York 1509–1558* (London 1959).

the evidence of the registers and such ecclesiastical and secular court records as survive, has filled in that portion of the *lacuna* in Gairdner's sources and demonstrated the survival of Lollardy into the sixteenth century. But there is no mention of sermon literature. A balanced history of the Lollards, which makes use of all the available material, has still to be written.

It is arguable that the sermon, a combination of schematic arrangement, well-worn exempla, and stereotyped allegory, and, moreover, often difficult to date, can add little to the picture already built up from other literary sources and from administrative and judicial records. This may prove to be so, but judgement could with advantage be suspended until more of the sermon material has been sifted.[1]

In his *Literature and Pulpit in Medieval England*, Owst draws some of his more striking illustrations from an early fifteenth-century collection of sermons in the Bodleian Library, Bodley MS 649.[2] This is written in a single hand and attributed in the 1602 catalogue to a John Swetstock, whose name, now virtually erased, could be read[3] on folio 8r,[4] and can still be seen in abbreviated form on folio 48r.[5] As Owst suggested,[6] Swetstock – or whoever the author was – may have been a monk, for he identifies himself with the possessioners.[7] But in any case, the sermons

---

[1] Surprisingly few latin sermons from late medieval England are available in print. Most notable are: *The Sermons of Thomas Brinton, Bishop of Rochester (1373–1389)*, ed Sister Mary Aquinas Devlin, Camden 3 series, LXXXV–VI (London 1954). See H. G. Richardson's comments on the date of composition and authorship of the sermons, some of which he considers to be wrongly attributed to Brinton: *Speculum*, XXX (Cambridge, Mass., 1955) pp 267–71. But W. J. Brandt argues for Brinton's authorship of all the sermons in the original which lies behind the Harleian MS: 'Remarks on Thomas Brinton's Authorship of the Sermons in MS. Harley 3760', *Mediaeval Studies*, XXI (1959) pp 291–6

[2] The MS comprises 216 folios. The first part is numbered 1–134; numbers 33 and 99 are omitted from the foliation; fols 133v, 134r–v, are blank (apart from some later writing on fol 134v); fols 111 v–12 v are devoted to hymns. The second part of the MS is numbered 145–228; there are two fols 164 but the next one is correctly numbered 166. Thus 131 folios are written on in part one, 84 in part two, a total of 215.

[3] I am told that the inscription can no longer be read even by ultra-violet light. It could well be that Swetstock, whom I have not come across elsewhere, was merely the scribe. Dr R. W. Hunt is of this opinion. I am grateful to him for inspecting the manuscript.

[4] Bodleian Library, summary catalogue no 2293. The entry quotes the 1602 MS catalogue (Bodleian Library, MS Rawlinson Q. e. 31, fol 117v): 'Jo. Swetstock sermones anglicolat. MS in 4to.' This (earliest) catalogue is described by G. W. Wheeler, *The Earliest Catalogues of the Bodleian Library* (Oxford 1928) Ch 1. The Swetstock entry, which must surely refer to the present manuscript was an addition to the original list, being placed under the folio titles for the letter 'S' (Libri Theolog: in fol. lit. S.).

[5] 'q[uod] Jo[hannes] S[wetstock] [?]'.   [6] *Literature and Pulpit*, p 84.

[7] Fols 35r, 125r. Though a broader meaning of the term would include secular clerks who were beneficed.

seem to fall into two groups, the first of which, covering 130 folios[1] and incorporating twenty-five sermons addressed principally to the secular clergy,[2] appears homogeneous, with an obvious coherence of style and subject matter, as well as the same macaronic form. A notable feature of this series is the writer's creation of atmosphere by repeated topical allusion. He exhibits a pronounced patriotism, hero-worships that celestial knight, Henry V, whom God has sent to strike down Lollards on the one hand, the French on the other, and fiercely attacks that cancer in the realm – Lollardy.[3]

It is possible that this first group of sermons belongs in its entirety to Henry V's reign. At least three of them make mention of him as the ruling monarch.[4] From internal evidence the final sermon can be dated between the duke of Clarence's death, 22 March 1421,[5] and that of Henry V himself, 31 August – 1 September 1422.[6]

The times are clearly out of joint. On the theme *Nunc dies salutis*,[7] rendered in English, 'Alle seke and woful come to weele, now is a day of gostle hele', the preacher expands the plaint common to religious enthusiasts of all ages – devotion is not what it was. He bemoans the fact that today's cloth is of a different colour – things are not what they were in the time of the 'ancient fathers'. As for preaching and theology (*doctrina*), where, he asks, are they nowadays? Heresy and Lollardy are rife, the number of Lollards increases, other sins run wild. There is no correction, or very little. A Lollard, or any other vicious person, can

---

[1] That is, discounting one folio for the hymns – *Salve festa dies* (fols 111 v–12 v).

[2] Four of them are added after the hymns. The first group is not rubricated, but the themes of the earlier sermons are taken from the epistles or gospels for the Sundays in Lent. There is some rubrication in the second group, which consists mainly of sermons for saints' days and other festivals.

[3] Cf Foxe, *Acts and Monuments*, III, p 397: 'whereby we have to understand more clearly both what were the proceedings of the king in the said parliament [of 1413], and also what was the blind affection of monks and priests at that time towards their king and prince, who was then called *Princeps sacerdotum*, in condemning and destroying the poor Lollards,' The political aspect is stressed by M. E. Aston, 'Lollardy and Sedition 1381–1431', *PP*, XVII (1960) pp 1–44. See also G. Leff, *Heresy in the Later Middle Ages* (Manchester 1967) II, pp 586–605.

[4] No 6, fol 35r, 'dominus noster [MS 'nostri'?] rex quem Deus misit nobis in defensionem ecclesie et salvacionem tocius regni'; no 22, fol 112 v, 'florem tocius milicie militum Dei ligium dominum nostrum qui nunc est qui statuitur supra pinnaculum perfeccionis et virtutis ut apparet per opera'; no 25, fol 130 v, 'noster graciosus rex nunc cepit super se gubernacula navis', and fol 132r, 'our maistour mariner our' worthi prince'.

[5] For an illustration of the descent of Fortune's wheel one need go no further, the preacher suggests, than the sad story 'insignis principis ducis Clarenc. cuius anime propicietur Deus' (fol 131r).

[6] *Handbook of British Chronology*, ed R. M. Powicke and E. B. Fryde (2 ed London 1961) pp 37, 422.   [7] 2 Corinthians 6:2.

readily find protectors. His Ordinary will not dare to correct him for fear of his life. Significantly, the preacher forbears to dwell on the topic of the fickleness of man's devotion to the Church. It is there for all to see.[1]

The theme *Assumpsit in civitatem*[2] gave opportunity for the preacher to develop an allegory of the fortified town, in which the *civitas misericordie* is contrasted with that *maledicta civitas*, Jericho. In that city of sin, on the tower of pride, stand priests decked out in secular garments ready to discharge their arrows of evil speaking. With them are laymen sporting huge triple liripipes and 'wastful cloþinge', and women with hanging tails and horns large enough to 'punche þe and put þe of' the city's wall. Then there is that great army of Lollards, obstinate in their malice, who would rather be burned than give up the devil's city. Also on the walls are seculars and regulars from every sect, some with arrows of bitter words, others with devices of evil deeds, and all prepared to stand and defend their malice. Clerks pack the towers: indeed, so full of soldiers is the city that it surpasses the art of heralds to count that sinful populace.[3]

Social criticism sprang readily from the theme '*Jesus abiit*'[4] – joyful summer (*iocunda estas*) has given place to the unhappy winter of sorrow and misery (*miserabilis yemps doloris et miserie*). The affliction of the times is manifest. There can be no greater woe than that of the English nation, in which people rise against people, brother against brother, son against father,[5] and in which there is such 'dilful debate', shedding of blood and killing. So run down is the kingdom that the slightest breeze from Wales is likely to blow it over. All this is ascribed to the serpentine venom of Lollardy.[6] The preacher concludes by gathering up his metaphors:[7] the eagle, the king of birds, is

---

[1] The preacher interprets the story of Exodus 17. Aaron is the spirituality ('prelati, curati et alii viri ecclesiastici'), Hur (Ur) the temporality ('domini temporales, milites et divites communes') – the twin supporters of Moses (fol 1v). 'Quam brevis est eorum ad ecclesiam devocio pertranseo, de hoc plus loqui non cupio, demonstrat ad oculum res gesta' (fol 2r). The same refrain is taken up at a number of points, e.g. fols 55r, 76v.

[2] Matthew 4: 5.   [3] Fols 10v–11r.

[4] John 6: 1; sermon no 9, fols 54r ff.   [5] Cf Matthew 10: 21; 24: 7.

[6] 'Sed que est causa *istius* tocius doloris? Creditis certe serpentinum venenum inferni execrata lollardria que flatur inter nos...þe fidris diviciarum ar blowen a way, potentes rami civitatum separantur, vix aliqua tenet cum alia, ur myti nidus in tantum debilitatur quod modicus ventus Wallie est in puncto to blowid don' (fol 55r).

[7] The preacher is interpreting '*moraliter*' the exemplum of the eagle who built her nest on a lofty crag. A serpent attempted to destroy the eagle's young by using the wind to carry poison, but its effect was counteracted by a special stone which the eagle placed in her nest. The story is among the *Gesta Romanorum*, ed Charles Swan, Broadway Transla-

God;[1] the eagle's nest is the English realm,[2] in which the clerimony has 'cast her plumme and lith in care and soroo', the *aves communitatis* have been visited with poverty, while the *aves chivalrie* have lost their lives. An objective observer cannot but conclude that the precious stone – Christ,[3] has dropped out of the nest. *Jesus abiit.*[4]

The pervasiveness of the Lollards weighs heavily on the preacher's mind – widespread dissemination of their beliefs is taken for granted. But it was not only the laity who spread heresy; clerics did likewise, even those with cure. In his view the christian faith had declined over a short period owing to the presumption of the laity and the negligence of *curati*.[5] Lollardy is seen as the first of the devil's messengers sent to reduce the human race to servitude – whose 'false heresys' have been published throughout the realm.[6]

To illustrate this 'historically' the preacher applies the story of king Antiochus Epiphanes – oppressor of the people of God – to his own times.[7] By king Antiochus is to be understood the devil who has long battled against the Church in the realm of England, bringing wars and dissension, spiritual and bodily death. He has gathered thousands of men and a great army against God and his ministers. This conflict has lasted from the time of Wycliffe – armed in heresy, the captain of the devil's war. In the preacher's own time numerous sharp attacks have been made on the Lord's house, Holy Church. First the Lollards discharged vicious words at the poor friars, ridiculing their poverty and order – which comprises many great clerks and good men. Then they dug a mine beneath the tower of the possessioners, whom they vilify, in an attempt to capture the Church's treasury. They find means for the temporal arm to take 'our' possessions and to snatch 'our' food. They

---

tions (London n.d.) tale xxxvii. It is sometimes wrongly attributed to Pliny, who does, however, mention the precious stone. See *C. Plini secundi Naturalis Historiae Libros Indices*, ed Otto Schneider (Hildesheim 1967) under Aquila, Aetites.

[1] 'Moraliter rex et imperator omnium creaturarum omnipotens pater celi' (fol 54v).

[2] 'pater celi...hath bild in foresta huius mundi calidum nidum et securum, nidum huius regni. I*ste* nidus non fuit ex lethy bowes nec modicis ramulis, sed ex stif braunchis et fortibus, ex pulcris villis et civitatibus ex fortibus castellis et turribus...' (fol 54v).

[3] 'Et quod nullum nobis infortunium accideret posuit inter nos preciosum lapidem ethitem [aetitem] per quem interpretatur noster salvator Jesus ...' (fols 54v–55r).

[4] 'Quisquis ergo intime consideret miserias que regna[n]t inter nos iam pro male fide, þe wele et honorem in quo stetimus perantea, potest sane dicere quod tunc in nido Anglie erat preciosus lapis et quod nu[n]c ab Anglicis Jesus abiit' (fol 55r).

[5] Fol 14r–v.

[6] 'Primus nuncius quod demon mittit ad genus humanum ad redigendum ipsum in servitutem est lollardria...' (fol 16r).

[7] Sermon no 6, fols 34r ff. The story of Antiochus Epiphanes and the white-robed horseman comes from 2 Macc. 11.

take no account of excommunication and the Church's censures, but throw conscience 'to the cock'.[1] They care not a straw for the pope and all his power. The machines of their malice are directed at all the towers – at the whole state of the Church. So numerous did they become, so bold and foolhardy, that they rebelled against the king. They attempted to make Lollards of the clergy, and even worse, to subvert the faith and God's laws.[2] Yet, though they hurl their machines against the castle of Christ in this English realm, it is much worse, the preacher comforts himself, in Bohemia. In conclusion he asks God in his mercy to change their hearts to the true faith and speedily to destroy their stubborn and obstinate malice.[3]

In the preacher's day a simple equation of cleric with *literatus*, layman with *illiteratus*, the two categories being quite distinct, was no longer tenable. The change from this idyllic state is bemoaned in two of his more extravagant allegories – those of the tree and of Mount Sinai.[4]

At one time the beautiful tree of the christian faith housed in its lofty branches the birds of heaven – the clergy and those with cure of souls. The clerimony flew about on the wings of contemplation, viewing the mysteries of God in the mirror of Holy Scripture. All terrestrial animals lay beneath the tree; that is, all illiterate seculars. There was then no doubt about the faith, no climbing too high: men received it in their hands and held to it. Under such order the christian faith was well served. But now that order is upset, the heavenly birds fly down to earth, the earthly animals climb up. Clerks and *curati* – the true mirror of sound doctrine and good living for the people – fly down, some teaching heresies and errors, others giving themselves to worldly occupations – taking more account of the loss of a shilling than that of a soul. Correspondingly, the layman who climbs too high, even if he does not know a letter in a book, wishes to dabble in the highest divinity and to give instruction on the sacrament of the altar, boldly intruding himself into the eternal wisdom of God, of which the apostle Paul feared to

---

[1] For this expression see *Proverbs*, [*Sentences, and Proverbial Phrases from English Writings mainly before 1500*] (Cambridge, Mass./London 1968) ed B. J. Whiting with H. W. Whiting, C353 'To cast to (at) the Cock'.

[2] Fol 35r. Much of this is repeated in sermon no 24, fol 125r. Cf *Literature and Pulpit*, p 84.

[3] 'sed multo peius circa Prage in regno Boemie, ut asseritur. Deus ex sua misericordia illorum convertat corda ad fidem veram vel cito destruat illorum pertinacem et obstinatam maliciam' (fol 125r). For a modern assessment of the situation see F. Šmahel, '*Doctor evangelicus super omnes evangelistas*: Wyclif's Fortune in Hussite Bohemia', *BIHR*, XLIII (1970) pp 16–34.

[4] Sermon no 3, fols 14r ff; nos. 13, 24, fols 79v ff, 124r ff. The story of the tree comes from Daniel 4; that of Moses from Exodus 21.

speak.[1] And so the fine leaves of the word of God begin to fall, the broad boughs – the articles of faith – break down, and the tree itself atrophies. *Non sic, domini mei, non sic.*[2]

The same idea is conveyed through the allegory of Moses – for the Middle Ages the model of the good pastor – and Mount Sinai. Only Moses was allowed to ascend the mountain to speak with God. A man who rises above the sea of the common people by letters and right living, by the excellence of clerimony and perfection of life, is a sovereign clerk. As a spiritual Moses he can ascend the mountain of faith. To him it pertains to treat of clerical matters, to deal with questions, to teach Holy Scripture and to inform the people of divine law. No layman should climb the mountain, meddle with Scripture or clerical business. He must wait at the foot, and the foot of faith is the *Credo* – the twelve articles.[3]

From the sermons as a whole one can gather much about the 'false opinions' attributed to the Lollards. Perhaps the most dangerous concern the sacrament of the altar. The Church teaches that the body of Christ is offered daily to the Father by the priest. It is the same body on each and every altar; although there are many hosts, there is but one body. After declaiming this orthodox doctrine the preacher tells the story of an event which he claims (conventionally) had taken place some two years before at Oxford. One of that sect – a false Lollard – entered a church to watch a sacring, not out of devotion to the sacrament, but, as afterwards transpired, from motives of disrespect. He waited until he had seen fifteen sacrings, for each of which he dropped a small pebble into the sleeve of his tunic. On leaving the church he met another of his sect. 'Look', he said, 'how many gods I have seen today.' Placing his hand in his sleeve to withdraw the pebbles he found, not fifteen, but one, yet his sleeve was quite undamaged. The stones could only have fallen by a miracle. Both Lollards went to confession and forswore their errors, from that moment believing in the sacrament like other Christians. And so, the preacher concludes, the blessed body is neither broken nor diminished by the fraction of the host.[4]

The same sermon contains another recent miracle – this time from

---

[1] Fol 14r–v. Romans 11: 33–6.

[2] An expression which recurs frequently in bishop Brinton's sermons.

[3] 'Sanctus Moises ascendit in montem sed cunctus expectabant [*sic*] deorsum ad pedem montis. Pes nostre fidei est tuum credo, hic est fundus nostre credulitatis, hoc est fundamentum tocius Christiane religionis, termini facti ad pedem montis sunt 12 articuli fidei quos apostoli plantaverunt in tuo credo per iussionem spiritus sancti' (fol 80r). The same allegory is used in a later sermon (no 24) fols 125v–6v.

[4] Sermon no 14, fols 89v–90r.

Nottingham – which further illustrates the power of the host.[1] It should be remembered, that in relating such 'genuine' miracles, the preacher was scoring points off the Lollards, who had nothing of the kind to their credit.[2]

Next in order of importance comes the Lollards' rejection of auricular confession. For them it was enough to confess in their hearts to God alone, whereas, the preacher urges, everyone ought to confess to the priest in God's house.[3] He has an *exemplum* to press home the point. There was once a great heretic on whom a saint had compassion, persuading him to amend his life. The youth went to confession and thereafter negotiated the ordeal of carrying a heated iron for a furlong. Emerging unscathed, he thus evaded both spiritual and bodily death, while his former companions went to the flames. The preacher despaired of telling this to the Lollards, who, he felt, would treat it with derision. No grace comes into their hearts because they do not admit the means of grace.[4] Allegedly they went even further, holding that confession serves no useful purpose and that no priest under the sun has the power of absolution. This, says the preacher, is contrary to an article of the Creed: 'I believe in the remission of sins.'[5]

Lollards also repudiated images, which the preacher upheld as a means of devotion. He urged his hearers to look on their 'kalendar' – to give heed to the cross,[6] genuflecting before it and wholeheartedly adoring God. Of course, Lollards will say: 'Why should I genuflect before a cross of stone or wood?' The answer is, that 'although the cross which you see with your bodily eyes is of stone or wood, it represents

---

[1] Fol 90 v. On the topic of images and the representation of saints see *Literature and Pulpit*, ch 3 'The Heavenly Host'.

[2] 'nullum miraculum ostenditur per eos. Deus nullum operatur pro eis' (fol 64 r). Cf fol 101 v: 'Ideo quicquid dixerint lollardi ne credatis eis sed honorate ymagines in precibus et oblacionibus'.

[3] Fol 37 r.

[4] 'faciet inde derisum, nulla bonitas potest eos movere et nec gracia sink in eorum corda, et non mirum, quia nolunt admittere gracie media. Precipuum remedium contra peccatum et medium gracie est sacramentum penitencie, ut predixi. Sed Illud vilipendunt est mere illis venenum, odiunt audire de *illo*' (fol 37 v).

[5] 'sicut dicunt lollardi, "Quid facerem ad confessionem? Scrift ad nichil servit. Nullus presbiter sub sole habet potestatem me absolvendi." Qui sic dicis male scis tuum credo' (fol 100 r).

[6] 'Quando veneris respicias super tuum kalendarium crucem, attende penas quas pro te sustinuit, flectamus utrumque genu ante crucem...' (fol 101 r): 'Respice tuum kalendarium sanctam crucem ubi videre poteris armatam tui regis' (fol 86 v). Cf William Thorpe's 'Examination', *Acts and Monuments*, III, p 266, where the use of images as 'kalenders' is criticised. See also *Middle English Dictionary*, ed H. Kurath and S. M. Kuhn (Ann Arbor 1956–) *s.v.* Calender.

the pains borne for you on that wood'. It is, he declares, the will of God to be honoured in such images, as appears from the miracles wrought there.[1]

Closely related to images is the intercession of saints. This means of grace the Lollards likewise decry, contending that the best saint in heaven has enough to do to pray for himself. To demonstrate their rejection of the saints' prayers they are said to have erased their names from the Litany.[2]

Their attitude to alms is seemingly ambivalent. He is no Lollard who gives alms in private to the honour of God, but he *is* one who gives alms so as to be accounted holy and to draw men from faith to error. Almsgiving of that kind is of no profit to the giver. Such alms are not offered on the altar of faith, and without faith they cannot be pleasing to God.[3]

The rejection of the pope is not ranked high among Lollard tenets, and we might be tempted to infer that a corollary of the preacher's emphasis on the English nation and realm is his disinterested attitude to the denial of papal authority. That Lollards cared nothing for the pope is twice condemned, but the second occasion is a mere duplication of the first.[4]

Exceptionally dangerous to the preacher's mind was the Lollards' assumption that they were entitled to meddle with doctrine. 'Be not to bold ne to besy *movere questiones*', he cautions in his macaronic way, 'be not to curious *cognoscere Dei concilium*, go not to fer, *potes de leni errare et exire viam rectam.*' Lollards do not accept the Church's ruling, but in 'wilde wittes and wilfulnes' fly so far that they no longer know where they are.[5]

But not only do these heretics spread their opinions informally, they also preach out of their own heads on matters of faith. Curates are warned to beware of such men and their painted words.[6]

---

[1] See p 150 nn 1, 2 above.

[2] 'asserentes quod suppremus sanctus in celo satis habet orare pro seipso et in signum quod desiderant illud medium non cupiunt oraciones sanctorum, ut dicitur raserunt omnia sanctorum nomina in latenia extra suos libros...' (fol 37 v).

[3] 'Non voco ipsum lollardum qui dat elemosinam privatam ad honorem Dei, quia est actus valde meritorius et multum acceptus Deo, sed *iste* est lollardus qui dat elemosinam to be holldyn holi and to draw men a fide in suos er*rores*. Elemosina data is*t*omodo non proficit datori, non offertur super aram fidei et sine fide impossibile est placere Deo' (fol 64 v).

[4] '*þ*ai set not i cirpum per papam et totam eius potestatem' (fol 35 r). The remark is repeated at fol 125 r.

[5] Fol 38 v.

[6] 'Isti [lollardi] despiciunt sacramenta ecclesie and heltful customes quos apostoli ordinaverunt... Isti ex proprio capite predicant contrarium et inficiunt populum' (fol 43 v).

It was bad enough for illiterate laymen to intrude as far as a master of theology,[1] but how could one stomach the women with their English books and smattering of clergy? The question had even been posed: 'Why should not women be priested and enabled to celebrate and preach like men?' To this outrageous suggestion there was a ready answer, for Our Lady, though sinless and full of grace, was given no such powers. The preacher's advice to the weaker sex is unequivocal: 'tak þe to þi distaff, coveyt not to be a prest ne prechour, schal never cloc henne be wel crowing cok'.[2]

Such were some of the beliefs and practices with which the author of these sermons reproached the Lollards. But his task of controverting them was no light one. Lollardy might be 'wind and words', but such words did not come directly to the hearers. Errors, he complained, are not told straight, but circulated covertly in 'gay *verbis* in derke sentens *sacre scripture*'.[3] They are subtle too, these 'poyswunmongeres', they do many good works, give much alms, pay their debts, and abstain from great oaths and swearing. These are good works in themselves, but behind them lie false opinions. The Lollard is like the poisoner, who does not administer his poison neat, but mixed with sweet-tasting food and medicine.[4]

The preacher is irritated by the outward aspect of Lollardy – 'wrappet in holines, *magnam sanctitatem*'. Lollards appear ascetic, they adopt simple clothing, talk little, and look pale. These are the marks of holiness, but 'all is not gold that glitters'.[5] Despite the *tristis ymago* of the Lollard, who lowers under his hood, hanging his head and looking forlorn, one must beware the sword hidden beneath the cloak.[6]

Perhaps then, it would be right to end on a note of exasperation. The preacher saw the Lollard everywhere in the 1420s, and for his insidious poison could prescribe no quick-acting antidote. But at least he had the satisfaction of having taken up preaching, one of the principal anti-Lollard weapons.[7] Nobly did he carry out his own advice to the clergy:

[1] As the preacher was only too well aware, there was also the *literate* layman, who likewise had to exercise restraint. 'Ideo qui es laicus et licet bene litteratus tene te deorsum ad pedem montis, serva te infra limites fidei' (fol 98 r).

[2] Fol 98 r–v.   [3] Fol 70 v.

[4] Fol 64 v.

[5] 'Ista sunt signa sanctitatis, sed non est totum aurum quod splendet' (fol 16 r). Cf *Proverbs*, G 282.

[6] Fol 16 r. On the attribution of 'feigned piety' to the Lollards, see *Preaching in Medieval England*, pp 138–40.

[7] 'non tantum demonstret ei his utmast rigour but medie his mercy cum iusticia clamat sibi toto corde et dicit Domine adiuva me sicut I tok to my prechynge' (fol 21 v). It

'Lift up your voice like a trumpet. . . sound forth against heretics and Lollards.'[1]

would doubtless be possible to substantiate the preacher's pessimistic assessment. At Exeter, for instance, the disturbed state of affairs is demonstrated by a mandate which was not registered in archbishop Chichele's register but preserved locally: R. Foreville, 'Manifestations de Lollardisme à Exeter en 1421?', *Le Moyen Age*, LXIX (Paris 1963) pp 691–706. Likewise, in Lincoln diocese, bishop Repingdon was concerned by the spread of Lollardy, which 'continued to be promulgated in sermons, tracts and conventicles and to attract many supporters among both clergy and laity': *The Register of Bishop Philip Repingdon 1405–1419*, ed M. Archer, LRS, LVII (Hereford 1963) pp xxxii–xxxvii (esp p xxxvii).

1 Fol 11r – inspired by Isaiah 58:1. It was, of course, a ready-made rallying cry for preachers. Cf *The Destructorium Viciorum of Alexander Carpenter*, p 40.

PROTESTANT SPIRITUALITY
IN THE FIRST AGE
OF THE REFORMATION

by GORDON RUPP

PIRITUALITY is a catholic word, beginning to dissolve into ecumenese, but it is much better than 'piety' with its nineteenth-century overtones, or the rather better eighteenth-century phrase 'inward religion'. And it suggests, as I should wish to do, some of the continuities between medieval and protestant religion.

The fifteenth century is still for historians a very misty valley, but we are coming to see some things more clearly, and one thing is that late medieval thought and devotion is not to be written off or talked down as preparing for the Reformation because it was in fact religion run to seed, and in the field of devotion characterised by a morbid and individualistic pietism. Preaching, for example, was of growing importance. We have not yet the full story of the number of preacherships founded in German towns in the fifteenth century and their significance. We know that this was accompanied by a stress on the importance of hearing the Word, almost to the point of disparaging the sacrament of the altar, and not only Wessel Gansfort but Gabriel Biel can be quoted at this point. Again, the lay study of a vernacular Bible ante-dates the reformers. Much as John Bunyan echoed the older English of the puritan Geneva Bible, so that astonishing market-gardener among the prophets, Clement Ziegler of Strasbourg, is steeped in the pre-Reformation Bible which appeared in 1466.

Again, the fundamental literature of protestant instruction, the exposition for the laity of the Creed, Commandments and the Lord's Prayer is rooted in the chain of medieval primers.[1] There are important questions which we cannot yet answer: one is what was the strength and character of the 'modern devotion' at the end of the fifteenth century – it seems that at Cologne it was strong enough to lay its mark on students like John Staupitz and the young Bullinger – and there is a similar unanswered question about the lay diaspora of

[1] C. Butterworth, *The English Primers* (Philadelphia 1953).

Rhineland mysticism among the 'Friends of God'.[1] I intend to by-pass Erasmus, but of course the influence of his writings was seminal among the first Protestants: negatively, his criticism of the externalised and mechanical devotion of contemporary religion – criticism with more gall even than Tyndale and Karlstadt, who in these matters simply echo him; and positively the effect of his edifying discourses, the *Enchiridion*, the *Adagia*, the *Colloquies*, his *Paraclesis*, and above all, in England at least, his paraphrases of the Scriptures.

I suppose a history of medieval spirituality might well end with three reformers, Johannes Oecolampadius, Martin Luther, Thomas Müntzer.

Oecolampadius was by temperament and training an addict of late medieval devotion, growing up into the spiritualism of his teacher, Jacob Wimpfeling, and of his lay friends Pirckheimer, the brothers Adelmann, and Conrad Peutinger, a kind of Teutonic Thomas More. He turned to the study of the Greek Fathers, to translate whom be-. came his life's intellectual work. As a young preacher he was much in demand at patronal festivals of nunneries, and one of his more success-ful efforts was published as *Of the harmful and the fruitful winds that blow about the garden of the soul*. It says a good deal that as late as April 1521 he entered religion in the Briggitine house of Altomünster in Bavaria, though it was not long before he re-emerged to become the leader of the Reformation in Basel. There is discernible in him that spiritualism common to many of the South German humanists, and it was perhaps this which made him take his friend Zwingli's side against his old patron Luther in the eucharistic controversy. A man of noble character and scholarly temper with his own patterns of spirituality.[2]

The question, 'Luther and the Mystics', has too often been answered negatively – the last Luther Congress was a case in point – by narrowing the definition of 'mystic' so as to rule out his indebtedness to medieval religion. And the differences do exist. Von Loewenich summarises them as a radical repudiation of any kind of doctrine of merit, Scripture as the sole source of christian truth, and salvation through Christ alone.[3] But to leave it there is to invite the retort courteous of catholic scholars like Werner Hülsbusch who demonstrates the similarities between Luther and the 'Elements of a Theology of the Cross' in Saint Bonaventure.[4]

[1] J. Staedke, *Die Theologie des Jungen Bullingers* (Zürich 1962) pp 20ff.

[2] [E. G.] Rupp, *Patterns [of Reformation]* (London 1969) I.

[3] [W. von] Loewenich, [*Von Augustin zu Luther*] (Witten 1959) p 268.

[4] W. Hülsbusch, *Elemente einer Kreuzestheologie in der Spätschriften Bonaventuras* (Düsseldorf 1868) pp 9ff.

The phrase 'Theology of the Cross' has been used by scholars to denote stresses in Luther's theology which never disappeared from his thought, but which are prominent in the years 1516–18, which are implicit in the 95 Theses, and explicit in his Theses for the Heidelberg disputation in 1518.[1]

Luther's first publication, in 1516, was an edition of the fourteenth-century mystical writing which we now call the *Theologia Germanica*, and he reprinted it with a fuller text in 1518. On the frontispiece of the first edition, there is a picture of the crucifixion: on the second, of the resurrection. For it is the point of the treatise that the cross and the resurrection belong together, but not simply as historical events, to be viewed from without, but spiritual realities in which we participate as in us the old Adam is daily crucified, and the new man rises who grows into conformity with Christ.[2]

One of the lessons Luther learned from the book was the egocentric character of sin. In the margin of the 1516 edition he wrote *Meitas* – my-ness – i.e. *mei commodi affectus, quo ego meipsum quaero quanto decrescit ego hominis, tanto crescit in eis Ego divinum.*[3] At this time, too, he read with delight the sermons of John Tauler, and his copy with his marginal jottings has also survived. His debt to German devotion about the cross was wider than books. If he learned about the appeal to the 'wounds of Jesus' from his teacher John Staupitz, there were many Thuringian churches with some poignant carving of the sufferings of Christ, and in St George's Eisenach, which he attended as a boy, there is a group very like the first frontispiece of the *Theologia Germanica* – without these things Luther is no more to be explained than Matthias Grünewald. And we cannot but remember that it was among these very same Thuringian villages where Luther and Thomas Müntzer grew up that the great nuns, the Gertrudes and the Mechtilds, nourished this tradition of devotion to the sacred humanity of Christ. Of course, theology is a matter of proportions: we shall see how the radicals turned the same materials to very different use; and in Luther's case there are equally important elements: Augustine, the Psalms, St Paul, and so a stress on conscience, guilt, forgiveness, faith.

In the great matter of his prayers,[4] Von Loewenich has rightly stressed that Luther owed more to his monastic training than he ever knew. This is perhaps why Josef Lortz does more justice to Luther's prayers

---

[1] [E. G. Rupp, 'Luther's 95 Theses and the "Theology of the Cross"'], in *Luther for an Ecumenical Age*, ed C. S. Meyer (St Louis 1967).
[2] G. Baring, *Bibliographie der Ausgaben der 'Theologia Deutsch'* (Baden-Baden 1963).
[3] *Ibid*, p 27. [4] G. Wertelius, *Oratio Continua* (Luna 1970).

than most recent protestant writers. 'Luther possessed a mighty power of prayer. He was rooted in God...he never had to jump over any ditch before beginning to speak with God...There was a robust solidarity about Luther's prayer...he interpreted many things in the Bible in a quite inadmissibly private way, but he did not play at Christianity.'[1] In moments of great personal stress, he knew where to go: on the fateful night before his appearance at the diet of Worms; in the anxious days of the diet of Augsburg, when he had just to wait for news in the Castle Coburg, he spent three hours a day in prayer, standing, as he loved to do, with hands clasped at the open window, before him only the heavens and the dark spires of the pine-covered hills. And when, at this very time, there came news of his father's death, he simply said 'My father is dead' – and took his psalter to his room where he remained for two days alone in prayer.[2]

Here at the heart of the earthquake and the fire of controversy there was a simplicity which is the mark of spiritual greatness. When he wrote his classic little *Children's Catechism* he found that there were those, and some of his young pastors among them, who treated it as an ABC to be read through and done with. But he never got beyond it. From it he and his wife said their prayers to the end of their days, and in his penultimate letter to her he comforted her anxiety by saying, 'Read the Catechism, my dear, about which you once said – Why it's all about me!' In 1519 he printed a form of Commandments and the Lord's Prayer; in 1523 a collection of prayers, the *Betbüchlein* – some of which got into the English primers. Then in 1529, after the grim discovery of christian illiteracy among pastors and laity which came to light in the evangelical visitation of Saxony, he wrote the *Catechisms*, the larger intended for pastors and teachers, a handbook of evangelical religion. All these qualities and this experience he concentrated in 1535 in his marvellous little tract, *A simple advice how to pray, for his friend Peter the Barber*.[3] It is a simple mixture of spiritual wisdom, common sense and humour.

Dear Master Peter. I give you all I know – and tell you how I pray myself ...

First when I feel cold in heart or disinclined to pray I grab my book of Psalms and go to my room, or if there's time, into Church with the crowd and there, just as the children do, I say out loud – the Ten Commandments and the Creed and if there's time a word or two from Christ or Paul or the Psalms...[4]

---

[1] J. Lortz, *The Reformation in Germany*, trans R. Walls, 2 vols (London 1968) I, p 434.
[2] P. Smith, *Life and Letters of Martin Luther* (London 1911) p 250.
[3] *WA*, xxxviii, p 358, lines 1ff.   [4] *Ibid.*

It's a good thing to pray first thing in the morning and last at night. And watch out for deceitful thoughts that say 'Wait a little. I'll put in an hour at my prayers, but I must just do this or that' – in the end that prayer will be crowded out.[1]

And then, when speaking aloud has warmed your heart, and you have come to yourself, then either kneel down or stand with folded hands and say or think as briefly as ever you can – 'Heavenly Father I am not fit to pray…but thou hast commanded it, and promised to hear me and hast taught us both what to pray and how to pray, through thy dear Son, Our Lord Jesus Christ.'[2]

Luther then gives a very brief exposition, clause by clause, of the Lord's Prayer, with the final comment:

And see that you give it a good strong 'Amen' – and don't doubt that God most certainly hears you with all His grace, and remember that you are not just standing or kneeling by yourself but the whole Christian church and all good Christians are with you, and you among them in one united prayer which God cannot disregard. And don't go away from prayer until you have said or thought to yourself. 'Very Good, this prayer has been heard by God, that's for sure!' That's what 'Amen' means.[3] Not that you need to say all those words. But I mean the heart is to be stirred up in this way – for I myself am not tied to this or that word or syllable, but today this way and tomorrow that, so long as I am warm and in the mood, and yet I keep as near as I can to the same words and thought. And it often happens that I browse so richly in one single thought that I can leave all the other petitions, for when that happens the Holy Ghost himself is speaking and one word of his sermon is worth a thousand of our own prayers, and so I have often learned more in one prayer than I could myself think out of many.[4]

Make your heart ready and eager for prayer…what else is it but tempting God when your mouth babbles and the mind wanders to other thoughts, like the Priest who prayed 'Deus in adjutorium meum – Colin, did you unhitch those horses? – Domine ad adjuvandum me festina – Doris go and milk the cow. Gloria patri et filio et spiritui sancto. Hurry up boy, a pox on you!'[5]

No, you must concentrate – like a really busy barber – who has to fix his thoughts and his attention and his eyes on his razor and on his customer's hair and whether he is stropping or shaving – for if he is jabbering at one and bowing at another – he will slice off a bit of nose or gash a lip, or cut a throat …how much more in our prayers must the heart be one, and wholly devoted to its prayer.[6]

---

[1] *Ibid*, p 359, lines 4ff.
[2] *Ibid*, p 360, lines 1ff.
[3] *Ibid*, p 362, lines 30ff.
[4] *Ibid*, p 363, lines 4ff.
[5] *Ibid*, p 363, lines 21ff.
[6] *Ibid*, p 364, lines 7ff.

Then, if there is time after the Lord's Prayer take the Ten Commandments and make out of each a four fold posy – 'ein lerebuchlein – ein sangbuchlein – ein beichtbuchlein – ein betbuchlein'.[1]

After that, if there is still time take a creed or chapter of Scripture...any one Psalm, any one chapter of Scripture will make a good firelighter to kindle the heart.[2]

And Luther ends the treatise with short comments on the main divisions of the Creed: 'and now pray for a good strong faith that will endure until you come to where everything goes on for ever, that is, after the resurrection from the dead and on into eternal life'. Frederick Heiler thought Luther, with Jeremiah and Paul, as among the giants of prophetic prayer, and Luther certainly set great store on the examples in the Bible. 'I take on a great thing (*magnam rem presumo*) when I pray.' Once in a time of drought he pleaded with the Lord before the congregation – ending with an enormous sigh. And when Melanchthon collapsed in 1540, Luther strode to the window and prayed: 'Our Lord God could not but hear me – for I threw the sack before his door and rubbed God's ear with all his promises about hearing prayer.' That our deep human needs force us to pray earnestly is something Luther's world knew better than our affluent society. To read Kurt Dietrich Smith's lecture which he gave at Göttingen in December 1944 on these passages of Luther, is to remember that there is more at stake about prayer than philosophic problems.[3] Walther Köhler has well said, 'About Prayer there was no conflict in the camp of the Reformers – this inmost sanctuary they shared between them.'[4] Drawing on the same christian, and biblical, inheritance, it was natural that the reformers said much the same things – that 'Prayer is the exercise of faith', for example, is something to be found in Luther, Zwingli and Calvin. Melanchthon wrote his own *Catechism*, and composed many prayers. He devoted a chapter to prayer in the 1555 edition of his *Commonplaces*, and this was translated into English with a preface by John Bradford.[5] Three of Zwingli's 67 Theses deal with prayer, and he too devoted a chapter to the subject in his *Commentary of True and False religion*. As we might expect, Zwingli stresses the inwardness of prayer: 'Greetings,

[1] *Ibid*, p 372, lines 25ff. [2] *Ibid*, p 373, lines 7 ff.
[3] K. D. Schmidt, *Gesammelte Aufsätze* (Göttingen 1967), Luther lehrt beten; Loewenich, pp 261ff, 'Die Frömmigkeit Martin Luthers'.
[4] [W.] Köhler, [*Dogmengeschichte*] (Zürich 1951) p 430.
[5] C. L. Manschreck, *Melanchthon, The Quiet Reformer* (New York 1958) pp 311–13; *Melanchthon on Christian Doctrine*, ed C. L. Manschreck (New York 1965) pp 297ff.

thou godly, inward prayer which is awakened in the heart of the believing man – yea, a tiny sigh which lasts but a moment and then turns again to heed what God is saying.' But it is devotion truly earthed. 'The countryman may pray at his plough, and so the smith also at his anvil: if he looks to God in all he does...then he is praying without ceasing.'[1] Martin Bucer's rich doctrine of the Holy Spirit enabled him to keep hold of Luther's doctrine of christian liberty even when immersed in a practical programme of reform in Strasbourg.

I can no more prescribe how to bring yourself before God in meditation or penitence than you can make rules to teach a man to laugh and jump for joy who has no joy in his heart. To make such rules for everybody when most people have neither penitence or love of God can only lead to hypocrisy and in the end to blasphemy – for Christian people must have true freedom in the Spirit – and then the Christian congregation will get along.[2]

Elsewhere Bucer tells how the Spirit helps us to pray. 'First – we pray in the Spirit. Second, He assures us that our prayers are for the glory of God. Third, in the Spirit we will not doubt that God will grant our requests. Fourth, such prayers will be made with humility and resolution.'[3]

We sometimes forget that Calvin's massive *Institutes* are the theological dinosaur that got away, and that there were other important forerunners of the reformed tradition in the 1540s. Matthew Parker knew what he was doing when at the beginning of Elizabeth's reign he commissioned John Man, the warden of Merton, to translate the *Commonplaces of Wolfgang Musculus*. This includes a lucid and profound section about prayer. 'We are to pray for four reasons: God's Son commands us to pray to the Father: our necessity whereby we be compelled to pray: to exercise our faith: and the nature of the love which the godly disposed do bear to God.'[4] We need to find times and places for prayer because 'holy men have always been accustomed to appoint certain hours unto prayers at which times they might humbly pour out the heat and comber of their hearts to the sight of God'.[5]

Nonetheless, to turn from Musculus to chapter 20 of the third book of Calvin's *Institutes*, in which he treats prayer, is to believe in the survival of the fittest, even among theologians.[6] Those who like to read their

---

[1] Köhler, p 434.   [2] *Ibid.*

[3] Peter Stephens, *The Holy Spirit in the Theology of Martin Bucer* (Cambridge 1970) pp 89ff.

[4] *The Commonplaces of Wolfgang Musculus* (London 1561) fols 484ff.   [5] *Ibid*, p 485.

[6] John Calvin, *The Institution of Christian Religion*, trans Thomas Norton (London 1587) bk III, ch 20. See also his *Commentaries on the Psalms*; also R. S. Wallace, *Calvin's Doctrine of the Christian Life* (Edinburgh 1959) pp 270ff.

Calvin in doughty Thomas Norton's English will find some splendid passages. To Calvin, prayer is a mystery, and here we come close to his shy and sensitive heart. For if he is the first reformer to talk of rules and laws of prayer it is all within the context of the bounty and the love of God, given us in Jesus Christ, 'in whom the Lord willed the whole fulness of his largesse to rest, that from thence we should all draw as from out of a most plentiful fountain'. And so he contrasts those who 'do mumble up prayers without any musing of the mind on them' with 'the godly who must take heed that they never come into the sight of God to ask anything but because they do both boil with earnest affection of the heart, and do therewithal desire to obtain it of him'. These serene pages are full of comfortable words. 'It is wonderful that with so great sweetness of promise we are either but coldly, or not at all moved, that a great part of men, wandering about by compasses, had rather leaving the fountain of living waters to dig for themselves dry pits than to embrace the liberality of the Lord freely offered to them.'

Those who turn to the thirty-odd double-columned pages of reference to prayer in the Parker Society edition of the *English Reformers* will realise how impossible it is to select. I suppose Thomas Becon has claim on our attention because he wrote at length about prayer, as he wrote at length about everything. There is a section on prayer in that interminable catechism of 500 pages intended for the edification of a small boy of five, and we must be grateful for Dr T. H. L. Parker for reprinting Ponet's catechism which, with the Prayer Book catechism, shows us that English Protestants too could write real catechisms.[1] Becon's treatise, *The Pathway to Prayer*, is a very stony pathway. Instead let me quote from William Tyndale – that man for all weathers – as he summarises the Lord's Prayer in his, and Luther's, *Wicked Mammon*:

Prayer is a mourning, a longing and a desire of the spirit to God-ward, for that which she lacketh: as a sick man mourneth and sorroweth in his heart, longing for health: faith ever prayeth. For after that by faith we are reconciled to God and have received mercy and forgiveness of God, the spirit longeth and thirsteth for strength to do the will of God, and that God may be honoured, his name hallowed, and his pleasure and will fulfilled. The spirit waiteth and watcheth on the will of God and ever hath her own fragility and weakness before her eyes. And when she seeketh temptation and peril draw nigh, she turneth to God and to the testament that God hath made to all that believe and trust in

[1] *The English Reformers*, ed T. H. L. Parker, *Library of Christian Classics*, xxvi (London 1966).

Christ's blood: and desireth God for his mercy and truth and for the love he
hath to Christ that he will fulfil his promise and succour and help us and give
us strength, and that he will sanctify his name in us and fulfil his godly will in
us and that he will not look on our sin and iniquity but on his mercy and truth
and on the love that he oweth to his son Jesus Christ: and for his sake to keep
us from temptation that we be not overcome and that he will deliver us from
evil and whatsoever moveth us contrary to his godly will.[1]

In his *Liberty of a Christian Man*, Luther had established the bond
between spirituality and practical theology, in that we are to be
'Christs' to one another. This is how Tyndale says it:

In Christ there is neither French nor English: but the Frenchman is the Englishman's own self, and the Englishman the Frenchman's own self. In Christ
there is neither father nor son, neither master nor servant, neither king nor
subject, but the father is the son's self and the son the father's self: and the king
is the subject's own self and the subject is the king's self, and so forth. I am thou
thyself, and thou art I myself and can be no nearer of kin. We are all the sons
of God, all Christ's servants bought with his own blood and every man to other
Christ his own self – so Christ is the cause why I love thee and why I am ready
to do the uttermost in my power for thee, and why I pray for thee.[2]

In the 1520s the *Theologia Germanica* went through about the same
number of editions as the *Enchiridion* of Erasmus, and exercised deep
influence among the radical reformers. Andrew Karlstadt's training was
in the *via antiqua* at Cologne, and it is possible that there, like Staupitz
and Bullinger, he came into contact with the 'modern devotion'. He
was the sort of theologian who is always going through phases, and at
Wittenberg he was in turn a Thomist, a Scotist, an Augustinian and an
Erasmian. A trace of the Erasmian phase are his theses against the
Gregorian chant. The first two read: 'Prayer is the elevation of the
mind to God. This is best, when it is done from the heart, for God is
spirit.' Then follow:

But simply to do the Psalms in vigils and canonical hours is not to pray.
The song we call Gregorian chant removes the mind further from God.
For if the singing be well done it elevates the mind to pride,
And if bad, with hawking and coughing it moves the hearers to laughter.[3]

He corresponded with Thomas Müntzer, and after his break with
Luther in 1522 produced a series of mystical writings. His booklet

---

[1] W. Tyndale, *Doctrinal Treatises etc, Exposition and Notes etc: An Answer etc*, ed H.
Walter, 3 vols, *Parker Society* (Cambridge 1848–50) I, p 93.
[2] *Ibid*, pp 296–8.
[3] H. Barge, *Andreas Bodenstein von Karlstadt*, 2 vols (Leipzig 1905) I, p 492.

Concerning '*Gelassenheit*' was written for a layman, George Schenck, who had been trying to read the *Theologia Germanica*, and Karlstadt simply expounds its main argument with many direct citations. It had now become the vehicle for Karlstadt's spiritualism, an imbalance of law and spirit which wavered between mysticism and a legalistic puritanism. This new significance for the *Theologia Germanica* is seen by the fact that it was republished in 1526 with a preface by Hans Denck, the schoolmaster and chaplain of the Sebaldus Kirche, Nuremberg, and one of the more attractive anabaptist leaders. Denck drew heavily on St John's Gospel and on Tauler, as well as on the writings of Karlstadt and Müntzer, and develops his own emphasis on the inner word. Before his death in Basel in 1527, he wrote a moving confession, dedicated to 'all who seek salvation in Jesus Christ' and expressing his pain at having to separate from fellow Christians, 'whom I recognize as my brothers because they pray the same prayer which I pray and honour the same Father whom I honour'.[1]

But if Denck was a noble character, he kept dubious company. So he got drawn into the extraordinary affair of the so-called 'Godless Painters of Nuremberg'. The two brothers Bartholomew and Sebald Behaim were notable artists – there is one of their paintings in the National Gallery – but they were the centre of a rowdy group of artists who read and talked Karlstadt and Müntzer, hobnobbed with well-known Anabaptists, and generally gave trouble to the authorities in that firmly lutheran city. One night they came out with some outrageous statements – denying God, denying Christ, denying the sacraments, and saying rude things about the godly magistrates. It is tempting to see in them pioneers of the 'Death of God Theology'. As one of the brothers seems to have said that statements about Christ meant no more to him than the sentence, 'Duke Ernest has gone up the mountain', it is even more tempting to think of them as logical enquirers into nonverifiable theological statements. I think the truth is that they were blind drunk. But certainly after three days in gaol they were only half repentant, and the rather odd result was that their pastor, Hans Denck, was banished the city and the godless painters were allowed to go on with their godly paintings.[2]

Thomas Müntzer's theology is his spirituality. He was well read in

[1] Q[uellen und] F[orschungen zur] R[eformationsgeschichte], xxiv, Hans Denck, *Schriften*, ed G. Baring and W. Fellmann, *Quellen zur Geschichte der Täufer*, vi, 1–3 (Gütersloh 1955–60) ii, p 105.

[2] T. Kolde, 'Zum Prozess des Johannes Denck und der drei gottlosen Maler von Nurnberg, in *Beiträge zur Reformationsgeschichte* (Leipzig 1890).

the Fathers and in the more exotic theologians of the fifteenth century. He had read St Hildegard of Bingen and Mechtild of Hackeborn, and carried the sermons of John Tauler around with him. He knew well the works of Henry Suso and dabbled in such apocalyptic writings as the pseudo-Joachimite commentary on Jeremiah. From these elements he drew his theology, the emphasis on the 'Living Word', on the existential meaning of faith, and on the Spirit who works within the ground of our being, purging the soul from creaturely desires. Müntzer's even more than Luther's deserves to be called a 'Theology of the Cross' – 'for what', he asks, 'do the whole of the Scriptures teach other than the suffering Christ – in Head and Members'. He has, moreover, a plan of salvation, a pattern of sanctification, of christian experiences in successively active and passive phases from the first awakening of faith to the moment when the christian soul becomes the temple and the dwelling place of God. Partly this follows the classical pattern of purgation, illumination, union; partly it anticipates the gnostic mysticism of Paracelsus, Weigel and Böhme. But it is all soaked in the study of the Bible, and set within a sound trinitarian and christological frame.[1]

This remarkable theology has to be related to two sets of facts: his liturgical experiments, fully choral, by which he provided a German congregational version of Mattins and Evensong and his orders for a German mass, and his revolutionary programme of violence, a just revolution to be achieved by his apocalyptic bands of Covenanters, the 'Elect friends of God'.

The Strasbourg authorities in the 1530s had to deal with most of the radical leaders, and the record has recently been published of their dealings with two of the most interesting – and most awkward – of them, the brilliant engineer, Pilgram Marbeck, and the Silesian gentleman, Caspar Schwenckfeld. Marbeck was the great biblicist, and attention paid to him by Dr Klassen and others has concentrated on his hermeneutics.[2] Schwenckfeld owed much to the devotional writings of the young Luther – and then from 1530 onwards to the *Imitation of Christ*, to Tauler, and last of all, the *Theologia Germanica*. Marbeck and Schwenckfeld were that recognisable protestant type the leading layman who at the end of the day has become more an ecclesiastical parson than the parsons themselves, and both were rather prima donnas, so that

[1] Rupp, *Patterns*, III; E. W. Gritsch, *Reformer without a Church* (Philadelphia 1967); H. J. Goerters, *Innere und Aussere Ordnung in der Theologie Thomas Müntzers* (Leiden 1967).
[2] *QFR*, XXVI, *Quellen zur Geschichte der Taüfer*, VIII, 1–2, *Elsass*, ed H. G. Rott (Gütersloh 1960); G. J. Kiwiet, *Pilgram Marbeck* (Kassel 1958); W. Klassen, *Covenant and Community* (Kassel 1968).

the quarrels they began in prison in the thirties reverberated on through the forties, and perhaps engendered more heat than light.

That the reformers were at one about the importance of prayer is because they were united about the importance of faith and the dependence on God which it involves. This is what the reformers preached and taught by word and mouth and we have not to forget the stream of their apostles, the students going out from Wittenberg, the pastors from Geneva, the wandering prophets of the Anabaptists in Germany and Austria. But the printed word outstripped them, the great explosion which between 1518 and 1524 increased the sale of books sevenfold in Germany. Luther's thirty writings between 1517 and 1520 reached a third of a million copies with the major tracts going into a score of editions, to be pirated again and again. A great part of this was controversial and polemical. But Luther turned a little tract of a few pages into a weapon, and some of his shortest works, his *Sermon on Good Works* and his *Liberty of a Christian Man*, were among his most effective. Of larger works, it was the *Commentary on Galatians*, with its discussions of faith, law and gospel, and good works, which was most often translated into English. Not that the 'Theology of the Cross' had been forgotten. Dr Kingston Siggins has recently shown how Luther's study of christology continued to mature, and how important are his hundreds of sermons on Christ, where the Johannine element is as important as the Pauline in the treatment of justification. Luther's *Postills*, his simple sermons on the Epistle and Gospel for the day, had an immense circulation, so that until well on in the eighteenth century they did not need to be included in collected editions of Luther's works.

The question arises – how far was all this understood of the people, and misunderstanded of the little Luthers, the little Zwinglis, the little Calvins? Walther von Loewenich, in an essay on 'Self criticism of the Reformation in Luther's Larger Catechism', shows how much heart-searching and with what good cause Luther devoted to this question in his middle and later years.[1] But there is some evidence that in fact the reformers were able to get their message across at all levels of society, and that in that age of growing literacy there was an immense amount of reading in the Bible and the mass of catechetical and edifying literature. Urbanus Rhegius wrote to Erasmus in 1522, 'Recently I heard a matron who was able to discuss the relation between Law and Gospel in the Epistle to the Romans more learnedly than many of our great doctors.' On his return from Germany in 1537, bishop Edward Foxe told the

[1] Loewenich, pp 261ff.

English convocation, 'The lay people do now know the holy Scripture better than many of us, and the Germans have made the text of the
Bible so plain and easy with the Hebrew and the Greek that now many
things be better understood without any glosses at all than by all the
commentaries of the doctors.' Josef Lortz has testified to the superiority
over catholic forms of the new protestant catechisms, and of the important new helps for the education of the young, including music and the
teaching of hymns.

Some evidence, too, is provided by the tracts and broadsheets which
played hard to the popular gallery. Generally in these dialogues there is
a layman, a student, a peasant, a housewife, an Alf Garnett type whom
we must not confound with the real common man. One such, *A
conversation between a Father and his Son*, which appeared in 1523, has
recently been edited by Dr Carl Meyer. Imbedded in the roughage of
anti-clerical polemic there is a succinct exposition of justification by
faith:

When a person sins against God his Saviour, then the law as the Decalogue
comes and holds it in front of his nose...and says 'Pay what you owe' – and
see, at this a man cries to God and is in despair. Then God comes...with
grace...'Do you believe I can help you? If he believes, he is helped already and
thus God awakens him by his grace which is promised him in the gospel...
so you must believe that the righteousness of Christ is your righteousness.[1]

There is an interesting group of tracts in the early 1520s by Henry
Kettenbach of Ulm. It includes a remarkable sermon on the Church,
expounded in terms of predestination, and if it looks backward to St
Augustine, it looks forward also to the Scots Confession and to William
Perkins. He has a dialogue, more lively than the common run, between
'Brother Henry and a Little Old Mother from Ulm'. She is a rather
worried observer of the old pieties, not very quick on the uptake, for
after a page and a half of ranting anti-clericalism she says, 'Dear brother
Henry, I gather that you are annoyed.' It abounds in anti-clerical
asides, like 'What are you parsons doing about us poor lay folk?', and
'Why are you exempt from taxes unlike me who spin from morning
till night and often into the moonlight?' But here, too, is a plain exposition of salvation by faith.[2]

Old Mother: Why have I such pain in my heart – which neither Penance nor
Prayer nor Mass can relieve?

[1] *Luther for an Ecumenical Age*, pp 82ff *Flngschriften* [*aus der ersten Jahren der Reformation*],
ed O. Clemen (Berlin 1967) I, pp 21ff.   [2] *Flugschriften*, II, pp 1ff.

Brother Henry: Paul says, through faith we have peace with God. So now, if you want quiet and peace in your heart you must...ponder and believe that Christ has taken your sin on himself, and made satisfaction for it, done penance with his suffering – He gives you His godliness – His innocence – His suffering as though you were Christ Himself, and He what you are – for Christ is our Righteousness.[1]

The public worship of the new churches, with their emphasis on devout hearing of the Word, their congregational psalm and hymn singing, their prayers in the vernacular and the sacrament as the communion of the faithful, were the public frame of protestant spirituality. But hardly less important was the importance of the christian home. 'Ye be in your own homes bishops and kings', said John Knox, 'and so let there be worship of God morning and evening.' Many prayers and forms of devotion were printed with the godly household in mind. We know how at the court of Henry VIII and Edward VI devout ladies took the initiative, and we have one glimpse of a not-so-devout husband: 'I have heard say', said Latimer, 'when that good Queen that is gone had ordained in her house daily prayer before noon and after noon, the Admiral [Seymour] gets himself out of the way like a mole digging in the earth.'[2] The order of the day which Martin Bucer devised for his two student *famuli*, William and Martin, gives a vivid picture of a christian household, in essentials much the same as that of Sir Thomas More at Bucklersbury. We see them at their meals, reading and answering the post, and for the students a range of chores from getting up first in the morning, to taking it in turn to teach the maids their catechism. Latimer, in his Grimsthorpe sermons on the Lord's Prayer, tells the story of St Antony and the equally saintly cobbler in sixteenth-century dress:

In the morning his wife and he prayed together: then they went to their business, he in his shop, and she about her housewifery. At dinner time they had bread and cheese, wherewith they were well content and took it thankfully. Their children were well taught to fear God and to say their Paternoster and the Creed and the Ten Commandments.[3]

Nor may we forget the parson's home, since sons of the manse loom so large in the *Dictionary of National Biography*. One of the more pleasing pictures of the new parsonage is that of Urbanus Rhegius, with his wife Anne: a humble home was all they could provide for their thirteen

[1] *Ibid.*

[2] H. Latimer, *Works*, ed G. E. Corrie, 2 vols, *Parker Society* (Cambridge 1844–5) I, p 228.

[3] *Ibid*, p 393.

children but they aimed to make it a good one: a 'true house of God', he said, 'where at all times by me and mine, at home or abroad, the Word of God may be heard. I think the very angels might stoop to look at such a home.'[1] 'Such a home', he said, 'would indeed be a seminary for the Church, when man and wife both call upon the Name of the Lord, the one protecting the other, so that the faith of the one is concerned for the faith of the other.' Anne knew both Greek and Hebrew, and out of their family Bible study they wrote down a genuine dialogue, about the walk to Emmaus, which became a best seller and a minor devotional classic.

Olive Wyon once said to me how much she thought Protestantism had been impoverished by its too sharp rejection of so much of the catholic spiritual, and especially the contemplative, tradition. And it is true that the ruins of Fountains and Rievaulx and Tintern point to those splendid buildings not made with hands, the cathedrals of the human heart. And I think I would now say that it might have been a disaster had either the Reformation or the Counter-reformation completely triumphed everywhere, and that the stalemate turned out in the end for the progress of the gospel. What I said to Olive Wyon was that the Protestants did not try to turn common men into second-rate mystics, but to provide for wayfaring Christians a way to heaven and a frame on which faith, hope, love might grow. And this they did for many millions of souls, not without great signs and wonders of sound and action. Above all, these first years of the Reformation were, as regards spirituality, years of sowing. Luther, at his most disheartened, might have prayed Gerard Manley Hopkins's words – 'Give my roots rain.' We read the sombre picture which Philip Hughes gives, for example, of the state of the clergy and of religion, in the beginning of the reign of Elizabeth. But look ahead another twenty, thirty years: Martin Bucer's apparently hopeless pipe-dream, his vision of a christian England, is marvellously and almost exactly fulfilled by the Cambridge Puritans with their immense simplicities, their preaching, their pastoral care, their moral theology, their theology of experience; while on the other side Donne, and Herbert, and Little Gidding express a pattern of spiritual power rich and distinct from that of the Middle Ages or the catholic Reformation.

The priesthood of believers meant for the reformers that each had a never-dying soul to save: what they taught was not just propaganda, but as Luther said to Peter the Barber, 'this is what I do, this is how I

[1] Urbanus Rhegius, *Leben und ausgewählte Werke*, G. Uhlhorn (Elberfeld 1861) pp 330–3.

hope to be saved'. And it was for them not the sign of atomistic in-
dividualism, but the true priesthood which intercedes and prevails for
others. Let Luther have the last word:

Every single Christian is such a man as the Lord Christ was on earth, and so he
does great things – he rules the world in divine matters, he helps and uses all
other men, and he is really responsible for the greatest things that happen on
earth. For God reckons him as of more account than the whole earth which
God made and maintains for his sake, so that if there were no Christians on earth,
no city or land would be safe, yes in one day everything might be destroyed by
the Devil. But that corn grows, and that men live in peace and safety, for this
they have the Christians to thank. Poor beggars we are indeed, and that's sure:
but nevertheless, making many rich: having nothing we possess all things. And
it is also true that what Kings and Princes and citizens and peasants possess they
have – not for the sake of their nice blonde hair – but for the sake of Christ and
of his Christians.[1]

[1] *WA*, xlv, pp 532ff.

SOME THOUGHTS ON THE DEVELOPMENT OF A LAY RELIGIOUS CONSCIOUSNESS IN PRE-CIVIL-WAR ENGLAND

by MARC L. SCHWARZ

ONE of the most significant aspects of the religious literature written in England in the critical half-century before the Long Parliament was the considerable contribution made by lay writers. Whatever belief one chooses, Anglicanism, Puritanism, mysticism, skepticism, rationalism, deism, a lay representative can be found who espoused it. Whatever type of writing one selects, devotional books, spiritual biographies, polemics, ecclesiastical histories, legal studies, a search of the *Short Title Catalogue* would readily bring to light a layman who produced such works. From the pietist John Norden to the firebrand William Prynne, to the contemplative moderate Lucius Cary, Viscount Falkland, the age abounds with a rich variety of lay religious opinion.

That so many laymen now began to engage in religious writing should not surprise us. Beneficiaries of the great impulse that the Renaissance gave to lay education, many of these early seventeenth-century lay thinkers were products of the universities and the Inns of Court, creating a sophisticated lay society provided with the intellectual tools to embark upon systematic religious discussion. In addition, the English Reformation, with the extensive rôle it had bequeathed to the royal government and parliament in determining religious affairs, ensured a laity increasingly aware of its power within the Church. Though divines remained unsympathetic toward the notion of lay religious expression[1] and more than once urged upon their lay adherents the need to consult the clergy on such matters, the statistics of lay authorship during the period show that these warnings were not necessarily heeded.

---

[1] The persistence of this clerical attitude is noted in William Haller, *The Rise of Puritanism* (New York 1938) p 172, and Charles and Katherine George, *The Protestant Mind of the English Reformation, 1570–1640* (Princeton 1961) pp 325–6.

Yet the results of such statistical lay head-counting would be of limited value if lay theological thought differed not at all from that of the clergy, if lay religious spokesmen were no more than clerics in lay garb. However, the real significance of this phenomenon is that many of these writings were an expression of a unique and truly lay religious consciousness.

This lay consciousness is apparent when one looks at what the laymen themselves wrote about their relationship to the clergy.

Our first example is one in which the assertion of a lay point of view is partly hidden in a mixture of naiveness and humility. It is taken from the writings of the topographer and practical pietist, John Norden, whose devotional works gained a wide audience in the late sixteenth and early seventeenth centuries. The popularity of his *A Pensive Man's Practice*, for example, is attested to by the fact that it went through over forty editions between its publication in 1584 and 1627. In one of his other treatises, *A Sinfvll Mans Solace* (1585), Norden sought to explain in the epistle why he, as a layman, should aspire to write the kind of book one usually associated with the clergy. His remarks, though unassuming, are still important for our purposes. 'Although (perchance) it may be obiected against me', Norden stated, 'that I am of an other profession, vnlerned, without experience, a greene head, & of no judgement: I yeeld me guilty of all: onely my profession as a Christian I stand to defend: though not a professed Diuine, but a poore Pupil, that is willing to be instructed of more learned and godly diuines'.[1]

Despite Norden's apparent admission that his youth, ignorance and lack of formal theological training make his effort somewhat presumptuous he is firm on one point; that since he is a Christian he is entitled to make this attempt. The importance of this point should not be underestimated because it is surrounded by so much that is submissive and apologetic, for it is a notable plea that a lay Christian as well as a clergyman should be able to make his views known.[2] Moreover, earlier in this same epistle, Norden noted that while he wrote this book to benefit himself he also hoped that his readers would profit spiritually from it. Thus Norden was casting himself in the role of a religious adviser and comforter, a task normally thought to be the exclusive preserve of the clergy.

---

[1] John Norden, *A Sinfvill Mans Solace* (London 1585) 'The Epistle Dedicatorie'.

[2] See also A. W. Pollard, 'The Unity of John Norden: Surveyor and Religious Writer', *The Library*, VII, 3 (London 1926) pp 233–52, 240. Professor Pollard also points out that in Norden's later works he continued to dwell on this theme. *Ibid*, pp 248–9.

The opportunities and responsibilities of the christian layman, which we have seen Norden discuss, were also considered in one of the most eloquent works produced by a layman in the early seventeenth century. A much more personal work, not originally written for public consumption, Sir Thomas Browne's *Religio Medici*, composed in 1635, shares with Norden's work a number of features. It too is a work of deep humility filled as it was with acknowledgements of former mistakes and the feeling that reason should be made consonant with faith. Browne, a moderate Anglican, conceded that he had 'no Genius to disputes in Religion'.[1] Yet for all his modesty, he also showed that there was still a place for lay inquiry. At the outset of his essay, for example, Browne noted that while some might feel that a doctor like himself would have no competence in discussing religious matters, he would 'assume the honourable Stile of Christian'.[2] Sir Thomas thus believed, as Norden did, that the appellation of Christian had a wide meaning which included the layman as well as the cleric.

Yet, whereas Norden produced a conventional work of popular piety, Browne, of course, moved to the higher plane of individual religious reflection and concerned himself with the very foundations of his belief. Therefore, when Sir Thomas took up the title of Christian he made it clear that this choice was not the result of mere obedience to his upbringing or nationality, but because 'I find myself obliged by the Principles of Grace, and the Law of mine own Reason, to embrace no other name than this'.[3] His decision, therefore, was based on private discovery and reflection, not on the dictums of authority. Such a statement also illustrates quite well the inquisitive eye that a layman like Sir Thomas could focus on the study of religion.

Browne's emphasis on reason is echoed in a variety of ways by other lay thinkers. A number of them, for example, denounced religions that were based on blind obedience to doctrines rather than on the firmer foundations of knowledge and reason. In this connection, English laymen frequently derided Roman Catholicism for keeping its laity in a state of unhealthy ignorance. A good example of this kind of revealing observation may be found in Sir Francis Rous's *The Diseases of the Times* published in 1622. Rous, a leading puritan mystic, anti-Arminian and parliamentarian, took this occasion to condemn the Catholic Church for differing from the Protestant by preventing the mass of its people from learning the true teachings of God. Popery, Rous com-

---

[1] Sir Thomas Browne, *Religio Medici and Other Writings* (London 1965) p 7.
[2] *Ibid*, p 3.　　　　　　　　　　　　[3] *Ibid*.

plained, 'is generally a Religion very neere fitted for brute beasts, for it teacheth them to be saued in ignorance, and by beleeuing as the Church beleeues. Which is vpon the matter by beleeuing that which they know not, and by not knowing what they beleeue.'[1]

The Anglicans also criticised Catholicism for the same reasons. Sir Edwin Sandys, the famous parliamentarian and the son of the archbishop of York, provides us with a good illustration. In his *Evropae Specvlvm*, first published in 1605 but written in 1599, Sandys argued that the Roman clergy had convinced their people to surrender their minds to the collective opinion of the Church.[2]

However, Sir Edwin followed this condemnation with a fascinating passage in which he depicted an ideal kind of laity that would not be duped by clerical propaganda. These individuals, he declared, were the type that were of 'so sharp, deep, and strong discourse, that they yeild not their firme assent to any thing till they have found out either some proper demonstration for it, or some other certain proof whereon to ground it assuredly'.[3] Such intelligent and mature laymen, and certainly Sandys numbered himself among this group, would thus use reason to weigh and evaluate whatever ideas the clergy might attempt to enforce.

The efforts of other lay thinkers show that the high standard set for the laity by Sir Edwin was not a visionary hope but a firm reality. One only has to consider, for example, moderate anglican thinkers like Lord George Digby and Viscount Falkland who, in the 1630s put clerically-endorsed sources of religious authority like the writings of the Fathers and the decisions of church councils to the test of reason and found them wanting.[4] Even the outspoken puritan legalist and pamphleteer, William Prynne, asserted in an early tract that, 'The only infallible way to determine, to finde out the ancient, the vndoubted Doctrines of our Church, is to compare them with the Rules of triall.'[5] And we can imagine his thorough, if narrow, mind sifting through the different arguments and finally marshalling the evidence that appeared with such tiring regularity in the marginalia of his works.

---

[1] Sir Francis Rous, *The Diseases of the Time Attended by Their Remedies* (London 1622) pp 189–90.
[2] Sir Edwin Sandys, *Evropae Specvlvm, or a View or Survey of the State of Religion in the Westerne Parts of the World* (The Hague 1629) pp 27, 34. [3] *Ibid*, p 33.
[4] See *Letters between the Ld. George Digby and Sir Kenelm Digby Kt. Concerning Religion* (London 1651) p 4, and Lucius Cary, viscount Falkland, *Of the infallibtilitie of the Church of Rome* (Oxford 1645) pp 5–9.
[5] William Prynne, *Anri-Arminianisme or the Church of Englands old antithesis to New Arminianisme* (London 1630) 'Epistle Dedicatorie'.

The statement of Prynne also suggests another important factor that had led some laymen to rely increasingly on their own judgement. Where so much was still controversial in the early seventeenth century, where not only ancient authorities, but contemporary clergy as well, spoke in contradictory terms, the layman would ultimately be called upon to decide questions for himself. Such was the recommendation of the period's most uncompromising lay observer, John Selden. In his *Table Talk*, a book of great perception about the problems of his age, Selden urged that laymen should 'consult with divines on all sides, hear what they say, and make themselves masters of their reasons; as they do any other profession, when they have a difference before them.[1]' Thus Selden believed that lay self-reliance was needed in order to make sense out of religious controversy.

A similar view was advocated by another well-equipped lay theologian, the deist, Edward, Lord Herbert of Cherbury. In his historical study of Henry VIII, composed in the 1630s, Lord Herbert included, in his discussion of the parliament of 1529, a reply from an unidentified member of the Commons to a speech delivered in the Lords by John Fisher, bishop of Rochester, condemning the lower house for their lack of faith and their interference in religion. This anonymous reply, which appears in no other chronicle, is so close to Herbert's own views that a modern authority has suggested that he inserted it there as a format for expressing his own opinions.[2] However, in this answer we find this 'unknown' speaker arguing that, 'Laicks and Secular Persons' needed to investigate religion because 'so many Religions and different Sects (now conspicuously in the whole World) do not only vindicate unto themselves the name of the true Church, but labour betwixt Invitations and Threats for nothing more than to make us Resign our Faith to a simple Obedience'.[3] To Herbert, the layman, in the face of this conflicting religious scene, had to be ready to make the right choice for himself.

By 1640, therefore, laymen were beginning to exude confidence in their own abilities to understand religion and some began, even more significantly, to argue that they were better fitted to comprehend and explain certain aspects of these matters than were the clergy themselves. The ubiquitous William Prynne provides an illustration of both these

[1] *The Table Talk of John Selden*, ed Samuel H. Reynolds (Oxford 1892) p 175.
[2] *Lord Herbert of Cherbury's De Religione Laici*, ed Harold Hutcheson (New Haven 1944) pp 53–4.
[3] Edward, Lord Herbert of Cherbury, *The Life and Reigne of King Henry the Eighth* (London 1672) p 321.

points. Prynne was very conscious of the fact that he was a layman and did not fail to emphasise that point. Writing in 1628, for example, he defended the right of a layman to engage in religious debate by pointing out that, 'Laicks euen in the Primitiue Church', had 'written on points and matters of Diuinity with publike approbation,' noting that both St Augustine and Origen published theological works before they were ordained.[1] Prynne was also ready to enter the lists, he tells us, 'to anticipate the enuious and malignant Cauils of some peeuish Diuines who would monopolize Diuinity to themselves alone'.[2] Thus he became, in his own eyes, the defender of the faith eager to assail the false doctrines of arminian clerics who would impose their ideas on the English Church.

Nor did Prynne approach his task with any doubts about his capacity to carry it out. Though not a cleric he assured his readers of his competence in his first blast at the hierarchy published in 1626. Comparing his efforts to other books critical of the Arminians he came to the conclusion that:

Yea I may with modestie affirme it, without any pride, arrogance, or self-conceite, that there was neuer any hitherto who hath written of this controuersie that hath handled and discussed it, so fully and perspicuously, as I have done it here. I have produced many more arguments and reasons, and cited more quotations from *Scriptures, Fathers, Councells, Synods, Confessions, and modern Diuines* to confute this *Error,...*than any yet haue done that I could read or heare of.[3]

There is no sense of humility in this statement and Prynne obviously felt no qualms about his scholarly talents. Instead of issuing an apology, Prynne took the offensive, declaring himself, a layman, to be the best authority on his subject.

Another lay thinker whose work merits attention in this regard is John Selden. Undoubtedly Selden was a brilliant lawyer, and in 1618 he brought his legal abilities to bear on the Church in his *Historie of Tithes*. There is no place in this brief paper to discuss the full ramifications of this work. However, Selden's contention that tithes were based on common law and that clerical claims to tithes by divine right must remain unprovable speculations, caused an immediate uproar and outcry from churchmen. Accusations, in particular, were made that a

---

[1] William Prynne, *A Briefe Survey and Censure of Mr. Cozens His Couzening Devotions* (London 1628) 'The Epistle'.　　　　　[2] *Ibid.*

[3] William Prynne, *The Perpetvitie of a Regenerate Mans Estate* (London 1626) 'To the Christian Reader.' Some copies of the 1626 edition do not include this preface.

common lawyer had no business dealing with such a matter.[1] In the preface to his *Historie* Seldon took up these objections which had surfaced even before its publication. In the course of his discussion he made two important points; first there was nothing in a divine's course of study to equip him to investigate tithes and, secondly, only a common lawyer had this training. As he pointed out, the '*Practice of Paiment* and the laws Tithing...were alwaies and are part of the proper Obiect of his [the common lawyer's] studies'.[2]

The significance of Selden's work cannot be underestimated. By attacking the competence of the clergy to deal with a matter they had long considered under their own jurisdiction, he succeeded in removing a whole area of investigation from the control of churchmen and placed it under lay scrutiny. Such an achievement was due to Selden's emphatic defence of the common lawyer's expertise on this issue.

Another lay religious observer, the courtier, scientist and philosopher Sir Francis Bacon, offers us a further fascinating glimpse of this mood of lay superiority. As a counsellor to two monarchs, Bacon was called upon to give advice concerning English religious problems. In 1603, for example, he drew up a state paper for James I to provide the new king with a view of the religious situation in the realm and to propose some ideas toward its possible improvement. Bacon began this assessment with a discussion of why, he, as a layman, should take this task upon himself. Perhaps, Sir Francis suggested, the very fact that he was not a clergyman might enable him to look at religious subjects with a perspective that divines did not possess. Thus he noted that:

It is very true that these ecclesiastical matters are things not properly appertaining to my profession, which I was not so inconsiderate but to object to myself. But finding that it is many times seen that a man that standeth off, and somewhat removed from a plot of ground, doth better survey and discover it, than those which are upon it, I thought it not impossible, but that I, as a looker on, might cast mine eyes upon some things which the actors themselves (especially some being interested, some led and addicted, some declared and engaged) did not or would not see.[3]

Bacon makes the important point that the clergy, by the very nature of its professional position, had a vested interest in topics concerning the Church. The layman, on the other hand, free of this commitment, is better able to see such matters objectively. With Bacon, then, we have reached the ultimate conclusion; a layman's view of religion can be less biased and more perceptive than that of the clergy.

[1] John Selden, *The Historie of Tithes* (London 1618) p xvii.   [2] *Ibid*, p xx.
[3] *The Works of Sir Francis Bacon*, ed James Spedding, x (London 1868) p 103.

In this brief study we have only been able to mention a few of the important lay writers of the period. Others that come to mind, for example, are Sir Robert Cotton, Sir Symonds D'Ewes, John Bastwick, Sir Edward Bagshaw and Sir William Vaughan. Yet, it is fair to say that those whose ideas have been discussed are representative of a movement of great dimensions in pre-Civil-War England. No longer content to remain passive recipients of the clergy's teachings, laymen had entered into religious debate sometimes timidly, but more often with considerable confidence in their abilities. This movement, active and widespread as it was, may be regarded as the development of a truly lay religious consciousness in England. Starting before 1640, it laid the groundwork upon which great lay thinkers like John Milton, Robert Greville, Lord Brooke, Henry Parker and Thomas Hobbes, would make their contribution to English religious thought. What had occurred, in fact, was a striking intellectual revolution in which the layman moved from his pew to the pulpit in the debate over the Church which was not only the clergy's but his own as well.

THE SOCIAL TEACHING OF
ARCHBISHOP JOHN WILLIAMS

by R. BUICK KNOX

IN English history the seventeenth-century upheavals were of great importance in leading to parliamentary government, religious toleration and autonomous science. In both popular belief and scholarly teaching the Puritans have been given much credit for these developments.[1] However, the process was much more tentative and complex than has often been supposed. For example, Milton is remembered as a prophet of popular liberty but his experience in the practical affairs of government drove him to aim at government by a virtuous aristocracy which was most likely to arise from among those who had property and the consequent time to spare for political activity.[2] The recent awakening of interest in the more extreme sectarian and revolutionary movements on the Continent and in England has brought into sharper focus the relative conservatism of many of the Puritans and has given the English Civil War and its aftermath the appearance of a rift within the landowning and propertied classes. Science owed much to the current questioning of tradition and of authority but it also owed not a little to the diligence of several royalist clergy and laity who in their years of unemployment during the interregnum devoted themselves to scientific observations and experiments; the genius of Sir Christopher Wren was maturing during these years.[3] Families and individuals were often torn by conflicts of loyalties. There was the loyalty to the possibility of a better and more balanced society free from ecclesiastical impositions and from the exercise of power without responsibility; there was also the loyalty to the existing structure of society which, for all its faults, was a fence protecting the country from mob rule and communal chaos. Many changed from side to side in the years before, during and after the Civil War and they did so not simply out of a

---

[1] E.g. C. Hill, *Intellectual Origins of the English Revolution* (Oxford 1965).
[2] P. Zagorin, *A History of Political Thought in the English Revolution* (London 1954 pp 110ff; P. Zagorin, *The Court and the Country* (London 1969) esp Ch 6.
[3] B. J. Shapiro, *John Wilkins, 1614–1672* (California 1969) Ch 5.

prudential desire to be on the winning side but because they were apprehensive of the revolutionary trends in the movement in which they had got involved.

Churchmen were not immune from this uneasiness. Indeed, they were more open than most to the fear of chaos and the loss of their positions. It is their occupational hazard to see their privileges not as a traditional social inheritance but as the special and permanent ordinance of God, and therefore any threat to their position is liable to be regarded as sacrilege. They thus tend to have a vested interest in the preservation of a system wherein they have an assured position. So, while it is important to grasp the theological nuances of the teaching of archbishops such as Bancroft, Abbot and Laud, their political and social presuppositions cannot be ignored in seeking to assess their outlook, even if such presuppositions were not often overtly set forth in their sermons and writings. Archbishop John Williams had little of such reticence in setting forth his position and yet he usually receives scant attention in any survey of the social teachings current in his time. His influence was eroded by his personal flamboyance and by his habit of carrying out even very ordinary and unexceptionable policies by extraordinarily devious methods. Also, his stark defence of class distinctions and of the social privileges of the ruling classes was not entirely palatable even to those who shared his convictions. Though it was an age when personal privilege and mundane ambition were apt to be wrapped up in the language of piety and high principle, there was nevertheless a recoil from Williams's lush biblical quotations in support of the divine ordering of the hierarchical structure of Church and State. Later generations have found it difficult to digest the florid exaltation of Williams in the biography by John Hacket and so the extent of his gifts and of his meteoric rise has been much underrated.[1] It was not for nothing that he was made dean of Salisbury, lord-keeper of the Great Seal, dean of Westminster, bishop of Lincoln and archbishop of York. Moreover, he had a realistic grasp of the realities of political and social power and of the motives making for stability or for revolution.

His social outlook rested on a few basic assumptions. There is a providential order in the world, and prudence in conduct is rewarded by earthly prosperity. The stability of society is assured by the ready acceptance of the gradations in society as part of the divine order. There is a worldly pomp and glory which befits those in the higher orbits of power in both Church and State. It is part of Williams's

---

[1] [J.] Hacket, [*Scrinia Reserata*] (London 1692): Hacket was bishop of Lichfield, 1661–70.

curious genius that his exposition of these principles begins from scriptural texts which seem to teach the opposite. He often stressed the
Gospel warnings against worldly possessions which had a magnetic
power to draw attention away from the realm of eternal reality towards the fleeting pleasures of earthly power. In one of his early sermons
before King James and Prince Charles his text was the words of Christ
as given in Matt. 11: 8 – 'What went ye out to see? A man clothed in
soft raiment? Behold they that wear soft clothing are in Kings' houses.'[1]
He began with an encomium upon asceticism and stressed Jesus's
disapproval of 'our pride and excess in apparel' which drew the flat-
tering looks of 'idle people who spend their time in gaping, gazing and
going to see'. There were common people, 'private persons', who
pandered to this 'public humour' and in so doing they devalued the
beauty God had provided in the flowery carpet of earth, the spangled
canopy of the heavens, the wavy curtains of the air and the whole host
of the creatures; these were the wonders in which God intended men
to discern his greatness, but men, under the Devil's instigation, had
devalued these works of the Creator by preferring a diamond to the
sun, a mantle of estate to the glittering plumes of a peacock, the
colours of the court of Spain to the meanest butterfly, and King
Solomon in all his glory to the flower of the field. Indeed, people were
so easily deceived that when Herod appeared before his people in
royal apparel he was saluted as a god. Even more deplorable was the
sartorial display seen in churches. The glittering array made the eyes of
worshippers roll when they should be reading; the rustling of silks
made brains to swim when they should be thinking. Women were even
worse offenders for they sent to the ends of the earth for novelties but
had ceased to send to the coasts of heaven for the jewels of shame-
facedness and modesty; how could there be repentance when they were
adorned with satin instead of sackcloth, and with pearls instead of ashes?
All such display was a symptom of that vanity which made people yearn
for notice far beyond what was warranted by their station in life. Such
vanity insisted that 'we must have all the colours of the rainbow to
glitter about us' and to be 'a flag of pride to allure people to come out
and see'. All this grandiose show existed alongside the poverty of the
naked who needed clothing, of the hungry who needed feeding, of the
thirsty who needed refreshing and of the benumbed who needed tending. All these needs were ignored so that there might be a parade of
riches to advertise the wearers.

[1] J. Williams, *A Sermon of Apparell*, 22 February 1620 (London 1620).

The theme of mortification was also prominent in a sermon preached in 1628 before the House of Lords assembled in Westminster Abbey. By then he was feeling the wintry blasts of involuntary mortification as he was being crushed from his positions of influence by the ascendant Laud.[1] He took as his text Galatians 6: 14, wherein Paul prays that he may glory only in the Cross of Christ. Compared with the glories of the Cross of Christ earthly vanities are but crucified carcases and yet, even in their putrescence, they can still assail the regenerate person and can take the enticing form of riches, glory and greatness. Williams quoted classical and christian writers of antiquity who had pointed out the lures of pleasure and of 'all that makes a shining and glittering in the world'. 'The vayne pompe and glory of the world' needed to be renounced again and again and there was need of special watchfulness 'when the world fawnes upon us with honours, riches, greatness and favours'. The great of this world expected homage, but 'Christ poured out his blood to redeem thee, spread out his arms to embrace thee, bowed down his head to kiss thee, and yielded up the ghost to save thee'.

All this emphasis upon the perils of possessions might seem to be leading up to an appeal to the hearers to sell all that they had and give to the poor. Not at all. Williams was no Savonarola lashing the rich and giving a personal lead in renunciation. Nor did he really intend to alienate the throng of gaily-dressed courtiers and their ladies who listened to his sermons. The clue to his real intent has already been dropped in the reference to those who, in Williams's view, dressed above their station in life. He had in mind those who had no place of public eminence but who, having prospered in business, could afford to dress ostentatiously and out of keeping with their rank.[2] Magistrates and others in positions of authority in Church and State had need of the 'escutcheons of dignity'.[3] Christ approved the wearing of fine clothes by those who live in kings' houses by which Williams understood the tribunal of the judge, the tent of the captain, the province of the praetor and the consistory of the bishop and all places where those appointed to positions of authority in the king's realm carried out their duty. Contrary to the view of many exegetes who see in Christ's words a censure of the folly of royal finery Williams saw in these words an endorsement of the wearing of 'soft and precious' garments by those 'for whom they were meet and decent'. There

[1] J. Williams, *A Sermon in the Collegiate Church of S. Peter in Westminster*, 6 April 1628 (London 1628).

[2] J. Williams, *A Sermon of Apparell*, p 14.   [3] *Ibid*, pp 26 ff

was thus ample justification for the panoply of Abraham's jewels, Jacob's perfumes, Joseph's ring and fine linen, David's changes of apparel and Mordecai's stately clothes; such precedents, as well as Christ's words, ruled out any ground to 'censure the honourable clothing of men in place' which was worn not for 'the cockering and cherishing of their body but for the credit and countenance of their place and dignity'. Williams granted that those who rightfully wore regalia had need of faith, repentance and devotion because where the service of the Master in heaven was neglected by those in high places there was not likely to be true service of masters on earth. This, however, did not curtail the propriety of official magnificence and Williams felt justified in maintaining a lavish establishment not only in his deanery at Westminster but also in the rural remoteness of Buckden in Huntingdonshire where as bishop of Lincoln he provided a generous table and maintained a copious choral foundation with daily services and frequent musical entertainments; he held he could not spend to be beloved and to oblige out of a narrow revenue.[1] Williams was not naturally cast in the mould of a patient sufferer under affliction. In a sermon on Job he saw the key to the meaning of the story not so much in the patience as in the final outcome; 'The Lord blessed the latter end of Job more than his beginning'.[2] It was impolitic to drift into the dregs of desperation because in the end God must bestow outward blessings upon those who humbly seek his service; if he did not do so there would be no proof that he owned the world and its riches and it would be a cause for boasting among the ungodly if the righteous were invariably seen to have 'a thin and bare shelter' in the storms of adversity without 'an assured resolution of a happy issue in God's good time'. It was true that the trials and the rewards often seemed unfairly balanced but Augustine had made two helpful suggestions which threw some light upon the inequalities; first, if rewards were automatic many would then seek God not for his own sake but for the ensuing benefits; second, precisely balanced rewards would encourage legalism, and patience would be reduced to a 'carnal concupiscence' for the merited recompense. Williams therefore saw nothing disreputable in the possession of this world's goods which were God's gifts and he held it would be an insuperable stumbling-block to religion if the wicked had a monopoly of riches and it would also make a mockery of the command to practise charity and give alms to the fatherless, the poor and the

---

[1] Hacket, p 30.
[2] J. Williams, *Perseverantia Sanctorum*, 18 February 1628 (London 1628).

stranger. Augustine had said riches were a good without which we could not do good. Poor Lazarus was indeed in heaven but he was there in the bosom of the rich man Abraham. Earthly sufferings were a source of perplexity but just as an embroiderer out of a mangled pile of cloth of gold and silver produces 'his curious imagery, so God takes Princes and Nobles and mangles them with crosses and calamities and deep temptations and then makes them up again into angelical forms and images', and Job was remodelled into 'an eternal president of the reward of patience' and had a fame as far spread as the beams of the sun and the moon.

Kings were thus raised, cast down and restored by God and they had inalienable prerogatives which were not to be infringed by a rebellious people. Kings had to be careful not to permit their power 'to be prophaned by every bungler' and their commands were never lightly to be disobeyed. As was true of Archbishop Ussher, the doctrine of submission to royal commands became for Williams a means of justifying the position of the Stuart kings in England.[1] Parliament could affirm and declare the king's right to rule but it could not create what had behind it the authority of God.[2] Disobedience could only be justified when a command was contrary to a clear passage in the Word of God but such a situation was a hypothetical rarity. Some might have scruples about King James's *Book of Sports* but Williams counselled conformity because the king and his advisers were more able than any others to discern the consequences of their orders and it would be perilous to commit the sin of disobedience in order to prevent a probable but contingent inconveniency.[3] He was sure that King James merited full obedience. Williams owed his rise to James who had also protected him from the jealously of Laud, and when James died Williams knew he would be exposed to the full blast of disfavour and so his funeral oration over James was a glowing tribute to his sovereign whom he labelled as 'Great Britain's Solomon'.[4] James had combined so many gifts in himself that he was 'the most powerful speaker that ever swayed the sceptre of this kingdom' and his every action was 'a virtue, and a miracle to exempt him from any parallel amongst modern Kings and Princes'; he had survived so many perils and threats in Scotland and England that he was a 'Miracle of Kings and a King of Miracles'. He had to

[1] R. Buick Knox, *James Ussher, Archbishop of Armagh* (Wales 1967) Ch 9.
[2] J. Williams, *The Holy Table, Name and Thing* (printed for the diocese of Lincoln 1637) pp 22–5.
[3] *Ibid*, p 68.
[4] J. Williams, *Great Britain's Salomon*, 7 May 1625 (London 1625).

his credit outstanding achievements in his direction of religion, justice, war and peace. He had upheld the Church of England whose form of government had been received from Christ and the apostles and was 'the only discipline that ever agreed with the fundamental laws of any Christian monarchy'. Even if such laws had been of human origin Williams agreed with Whitgift that humble and meek spirits should submit themselves to the order appointed by lawful authority. He had little trust in the capacity of common people to make wise initiatives or decisions; they should obey 'those that have the chief care and government in the Church'. Whether in Church or State, the law was the 'quintessence of reason' and its critics manifested 'a humour which is the quintessence of fansie'.[1] Nor did he allow his misfortunes under Charles to make him waver in his advocacy of reverence for the 'higher powers whom God hath placed for the government of this world'. When preaching to the House of Lords he pled for a laying aside of the 'hopes, hatred, fear and flattery that have swayed but too much in Assemblies of this nature'.[2]

Williams was thus a defender of the existing social pattern. The crown, parliament and the ecclesiastical authorities had been placed in their positions by God; they knew the sweep and complexity of human affairs and had the data and the competence for making decisions. They ought to explain their policies as far as state security and the capacity of the people to assimilate it would allow but subjects ought also to recognise their subordinate rank and be content to live within the orb of obedience. His haughty spirit was exasperated by the rebellious spirit displayed during and after the Civil War and he died in dejection without having seen any heralds of the dawn of a new stability.

[1] J. Williams, *The Holy Table*, pp 136, 142.
[2] J. Williams, *A Sermon in the Collegiate Church of S. Peter*, p 39.

THE PURITAN PIETY OF MEMBERS
OF THE LONG PARLIAMENT

by G. S. S. YULE

ALTHOUGH most historians of the English Civil War pay lip service to Puritanism as one of its main ingredients, as a matter of fact, the analysis of religious conviction is rarely undertaken except, perhaps, in regard to the ministers. How deeply Puritanism impinged on the laity is either ignored or treated in an imprecise fashion or explained as rationalisation of deeper economic or social concerns. The Whig historians, who coined the phrase 'Puritan Revolution', really see Puritanism playing a general political role, leading to toleration, with the advanced exponents of liberty, like Cromwell, or as causing the opposition to clerical episcopal tyranny in the case of people like Prynne. Even so careful an historian as W. A. Shaw fails completely to understand Pym's use of biblical imagery and, I think, basically underplays the religiosity of the Parliament men.[1]

Oliver St John whose religious attitude is either completely disregarded or who at best is described as an Erastian trying to keep those fanatical puritan ministers in their place, had a private copy book in which he expounded the first two chapters of Ephesians in over one hundred folio pages.[2] This is not without precedent. John Harrington's copy book[3] had extracts from Twiss on 'Predestination', a pious excursus on the christian duties for a godly Parliamentarian, a short comment on Ephesians in Greek, a comparison of certain Johannine vocabulary in Greek and Arabic (headed rather mysteriously the 'Arabic Gospel of John'); some comments on the Old Testament in Hebrew, and then extensive essays combining classical and christian ethical attitudes, with passages from the Psalms and Seneca, being interwoven.

The author of the hard-hitting pamphlet *A Pack of Puritans* forbore

---

[1] W. A. Shaw, *A History of the English Church during the Civil War and under the Commonwealth* (London, 1900) I, p 50 n 1. Perceptive as he is, he fails to take full account of the biblicism or piety of the members of Parliament and so tends to read back the nineteenth-century politico-religious concerns into the seventeenth century.

[2] B[ritish] M[useum] Add[itional] MSS 25,285.   [3] BM Add MSS 10,114.

to quote passages from Luther and Calvin to support his argument as being too well known, but quoted freely from Athanasius, Ambrose, Augustine, the English reformers, Bullinger and Peter Martyr.[1]

The puritan members of Parliament spoke as if they were a compound of David and Nehemiah. 'We must preserve our religion entire and pure', said Sir John Wray the member for Lincolnshire, 'without the least compound of superstition or idolatry.'[2] Their arguments, like those of Say and Sele speaking on Separatism,[3] or Ireton at Whitehall speaking on Israel as a model for the state,[4] were theologically sophisticated and their biblical allusions, like those of Pym[5] subtle, and of Prynne encyclopedic.[6]

Biblical precedent is, I believe, the most important characteristic of puritan theology, and its effect on the laity was profound. Whereas for Luther the Bible was essentially Gospel, for the Puritan it was essentially a book of precedents, containing, it is true, good news for the elect, but this was because this good news happened to be part of the divine revelation along with precedents for reforming the Church and society. If one could show that a certain course of action was in accord with biblical precedent then that was that. In a remarkable passage Ludlow stated why he was in favour of executing the king. 'I am convinced', he said, 'by the express words of God's law. "That blood defileth the land, and the land cannot be cleansed of the blood that is shed therein but by the blood of him that shed it" (Numbers 35: 33). And therefore I could not consent to the counsels of those who were contented to leave the guilt of so much blood upon the nation and thereby to draw down the just vengeance of God upon all of us.'[7] And the Commonwealth's men, Ludlow said later, urged that monarchy was not good in itself 'from the 8th chapter and 8th verse of the first Book of Samuel, where rejecting of the Judges and the choice of a king, was charged upon the Israelites by God himself as a rejection of Him; and from another passage in the same book, where Samuel declares it to be a great wickedness, with divers more texts of scripture to the same effect'.[8]

[1] A Pack of Puritans (London 1641) pp 2, 14, 48, 54–6. S. Halkett and J. Laing, Dictionary of Anonymous and Pseudonymous English Literature (London 1926), ascribe the authorship to Sir Peter Wentworth.

[2] Eight Occasional Speeches made in this Parliament by Sir John Wray (London 1641) p 12.

[3] Say and Sele, A Speech concerning Liturgy and Separation (London 1641).

[4] In A. S. P. Woodhouse, Puritanism and Liberty (London 1938) pp 154–6.

[5] Pym's speech against Laud in William Prynne, Canterburies Doome (London 1646) p 30.

[6] William Prynne, Independency Examined (London 1644) for example, p 11.

[7] E. Ludlow, The Memoirs of Edmund Ludlow, ed C. H. Firth (Oxford 1894) I, p 207.

[8] Ibid, I, p 185.

Time and again the resort to biblical precedent as the final arbiter is made by Puritans in the Long Parliament. The constant theme of the puritan preachers to the members of the Long Parliament had been the reformation of Church and Society by the pure word of God, – 'to draw nakedly and clearly out of the Scriptures those clear truths concerning this new state [of the Church] as will not endure any quiddities or querks'.[1] This lesson the Parliamentarians learnt well. 'We meet not the name of an Archbishop or a Dean, or an Archdeacon in all the New Testament', argued Harbottle Grimston who was no radical.[2] 'The best means to distinguish between true and false religion', said John Hampden, 'is by searching the sacred writing of the Old and New Testament which is of itself pure and indited by the Spirit of God...In these two testaments is contained all things necessary to salvation...consequently any religion which joyneth with this doctrine of Christ and his Apostles, the traditions and inventions of men...cannot be true'.[3] William Prynne countered those who justified no further address to the king on the grounds of necessity, by direct appeal to scriptural precedent. 'No pious or honest intentions', he said, 'can justify or excuse any irregular actions...as is clear by the actions of the Bethsheemites, Uzza, Saul and others' (giving the references to 1 Sam. 6: 14, 15, 19, 20; 1 Sam. 15: 13; 1 Chron. 3: 9 and Matt. 6: 7).[4]

Perhaps the most striking illustration of the biblicism of members of the Long Parliament was in 1646 when they were arguing with the presbyterian divines of the Westminster Assembly over the question of the power of the lay eldership. They sent a series of questions to the Assembly and asked precisely for biblical warrant for the proposals of the divines –

whether by the Word of God the power of judging and declaring what are scandalous offences, for which persons guilty thereof are to be kept from the Sacrament of the Lord's Supper...is either in the Congregational Eldership, or Presbytery or any other eldership congregation or persons; and whether such powers are in them only, or any of them and in which of them, *Iure Divino*, and by the will and appointment of Jesus Christ.[5]

---

[1] Nathaniel Holmes, *The New Reformed Church* (London 1641) p 50.
[2] Harbottle Grimston, Speech in Parliament, 9 Nov. 1640, in J. Rushworth, *Historical Collections of Private Passages etc*, 4 vols in 7 (London 1659–1701) I, p 35.
[3] John Hampden, *His Speech in Parliament 4 Jan, 1641* (London 1642) p 2.
[4] William Prynne, *The substance of a speech made in the House of Commons, 4 Dec, 1648* (London 1648), Epistle to the reader, unnumbered pagination, p 8.
[5] *Questions propounded to the Assembly of Divines by the House of Commons, April ult, 1646* (London 1646) pp 5, 6.

With their intense concern for the Bible one of the most insistent cries of the early years of the Long Parliament was for a preaching ministry. 'Show your love', urged John Gauden in a sermon before the Commons, 'by using all means to plant and nourish truth by setting up the lights of good and painful preachers in the dark and obscure places of the land, where, God knows, many poor souls perish for want of knowledge [such I mean] as can and will rightly divide the word of truth.'[1] And this was a constant concern of the Long Parliament men. A main charge against Laud, said Pym, was that 'divers godly and orthodox preachers were suppressed in their persons and estates'.[2] Under the Laudian regime, protested Maynard, the ministers had become 'hoarse and dumb in their preaching.'[3] In his *Unbishoping of Timothy and Titus*, Prynne waxed vehement against 'the suppressing of Master John Rogers' lecture' at Dedham. 'Hath not the lecture been the greatest blessing that ever this town enjoyed?' he asked, 'the chief means that hath enriched it.'[4]

As patrons of livings the puritan gentry went to great pains to see that godly preaching ministers were installed. 'It is very well known', said Seth Wood at the funeral of Sir William Armine, member of Parliament for Grantham, 'that in all those places in his dispose he planted men of very good reputation, and abilities to preach the Gospel, and gave proportionable encouragement both for countenance and maintenance.'[5]

Lady Warwick, said Samuel Clarke, 'had a tender conscientious care to provide good ministers in places where she had anything to do... Leez, Braintree, Foulness may be witness of this',[6] while he extolled Nathaniel Barnardiston for 'his extraordinary endeavours constantly to present every living where he was patron, such as were right qualified and holy men'.[7]

This intense concern for the Bible and preaching over the years created a distinctive style of puritan spirituality. 'I meditated on the sermons and prayed them over', wrote Lady Warwick in her spiritual diary, 'And had also meditations', she continued, 'upon the joys of

---

[1] John Gauden, *The Love of Truth and Peace* (London 1641) p 24.

[2] John Pym, *A speech to the Lords on the delivery of articles against Laud* (London 1641) p 2.

[3] *Master Maynard His Speech at the Guildhall Jan 6, 1641*, p 3.

[4] *The Unbishoping of Timothy and Titus...by a well wisher to God's Truth* (London 1636) p 155.

[5] [Seth] Wood, [*A Saint's Entrance into Peace and Rest by Death*] (London 1651), A sermon preached at the Funeral of Sir William Armine, p 20.

[6] [Samuel] Clarke, [*Lives of Sundry Eminent Persons*] (London 1683) p 173.

[7] *Ibid*, p 113.

heaven with the thought of being ever freed from sin, and being ever with the Lord.'[1] 'Oh despise not the day of grace which is able to build you up and give you an inheritance among them which are sanctified', wrote Roger Hill, the member of Parliament for Bridport to his daughter. 'A prize is now put into your hands; improve it to the utmost, put it not off. This is the best day to work in before the troubles and cares of this world come upon you, give all diligence now to make sure of the Lord Jesus Christ...Seek the Lord daily as in private and public.'[2] 'Dear Ned', wrote Lady Harley to her son, 'let nothing hinder you from performing constant private duties of praying and reading. Experimentally I may say that private prayer is one of the best means to keep the heart close to God. O it is a sweet thing to pour out our heart to God as a friend.'[3] 'I have been often with him in private prayer in his closet,' said Edmund Calamy of the earl of Warwick, 'in which he was very zealous and devout, and hath left behind many religious collections, written with his own hand for the good of his soul.'[4]

The private devotions in no way displaced the public. The earl of Warwick showed his religion, said Calamy, 'in his frequent attendance when he was in London upon weekly lectures, and by his example and encouragement drawing many persons of quality to our congregations.'[5] Sir Robert Harley the leading puritan gentleman of Herefordshire 'would heartily feed upon the ordinances. He came with hunger to them and did afterwards digest them with real nutriment. How would his heart melt under the word, and dissolve into liquid tears.'[6] Lady Warwick[7] and Nathaniel Barnardiston also laid great stress on preparation for the sacrament

Though he ever exceeded the most in diligence and reverence in other duties of Gospel Worship, yet in his conscientious preparation for and fruitful improvement of the Lord's Supper he did exceed himself; for the most part he spent all the time he could redeem in a fourth night before the Sacrament, in his Closet in reading, praying and examination of his spiritual state, with other duties of preparation tending thereunto.[8]

This emphasis of the puritan laity on the sacrament, for which there are many other examples, should dispel the usual belief that the Puritans so

[1] *Ibid*, p 171.
[2] Roger Hill to his daughter Mrs Abigail Lockey, BM Add MSS 46;500, fol 48.
[3] [*Letters of Lady Brilliana*] *Harley*, ed R. T. Lewis, *Cam. S*, LVIII (1853) p 15.
[4] Edmund Calamy, *A pattern for all*, Sermon at funeral of the Earl of Warwick (1658) p 34
[5] *Ibid*, p 35.
[6] Thomas Froysell 'Funeral Sermon of Sir Robert Harley', in *Harley*, p xxxiii.
[7] Clarke, p 170.   [8] *Ibid*, p 112.

venerated preaching that they disregarded the sacraments. Such a belief comes from a post-1840 viewpoint, reading back positions, common perhaps in the nineteenth century, but which were never held by the main stream Puritans.

This life of personal piety had its effects, and the picture that emerges is rather different from the traditional and from much modern 'orthodox' historiography on the subject.

Sir Robert Harley 'was noble in his liberality to the saints in their want: their necessity was his opportunity'.[1] 'Give in secret', instructed Roger Hill to his daughter, '"tis the best evidence of sincerity.'[2] Seth Wood said of Sir William Armine that his works 'would tell how good a Land-Lord and benefactor he was to every tenant, and every poor body will be his orator to set forth his goodness of this kind'.[3] Lady Armine too 'was frequent and constant in giving to charitable causes. She gave large yearly contributions to promote the carrying on of the work begun in New England, for the conversion of the poor Indians.'[4]

Theologically they displayed a consistent style of evangelical piety. 'I never observed him', said Seth Wood of Armine, 'trust in the works of the flesh or of the law but in the alone mediation of Christ Jesus. I have heard him to disallow of the Romish Profession because it obtrudes a thousand vanities into the Mediatorship of Christ Jesus.'[5] Of the religiously reticent John Pym, Stephen Marshall said he 'was a faithful servant of Christ, one who long since was born of water and of the holy Ghost, engrafted into Christ, adopted to be the child of God, justified freely by his grace.'[6]

Outwardly they were strictly sabbatharians like Harley, who 'paid a dear devotion of love to the Lord's Day (that pearle of the week)',[7] while vice they attacked, like Sir William Armine, 'with a great gravity and severity'.[8]

Can one with safety generalise from these relatively few examples? The religious attitudes of these puritan gentry is not easy to come by, but one can see such a similarity of stance in the Parliamentary speeches of many puritan members on such subjects as abolishing ritual in worship, setting up preaching ministers, Sabbatharianism and anti-Popery, with that of those about whom much more detailed and intimate knowledge of their religious sensitivity remains that I myself am

---

[1] 'Funeral Sermon of Sir Robt, Harley', *Harley*, p xxxiii.
[2] BM Add MSS 46;500.   [3] Wood, p 21.
[4] Life of Lady Armine, in Clarke.   [5] Wood, p 17.
[6] Stephen Marshall, *The Churches Lamentation for the Good Man his losse* (London 1644) p 27.   [7] *Harley*, p xxxiv.   [8] Wood, p 19.

now strongly of the opinion that the intensity of the religious feelings of members of the Long Parliament has been greatly underestimated. For example in that excellent dictionary of Parliament men by Miss M. F. Keeler[1] one gains all kinds of information about their wealth and Parliamentary and military activity, but next to nothing about their Puritanism. Yet surely if one wants to understand the Civil War it is much more significant to know that a member of Parliament was an ardent and convinced Puritan than that he was on the Sewers Commission.

Professor Trevor Roper in his brilliant essay on the *Fast Sermons of the Long Parliament*[2] suggests that they were part of Pym's propaganda machine to gain support for particular policies of state. In most cases, particularly in the early years, this is what specifically they were not. The constant theme of these early sermons was the necessity to reform the Church before the State was reformed. In that most inflammatory of sermons *Meroz Cursed* his whole purpose, said Marshall, was 'to inflame your hearts after such a temper of spirit that you may be willing to give up yourselves to the help of the Lord and his Church'.[3] 'Now this is the great work that the Lord requireth at your hands of ye worthies of Israel', said Calamy (and he was here speaking of what he called a national reformation), 'to shut up all those unprofitable trees, to repair the breeches in God's House.'[4]

And this attitude was shared by many puritan members. 'We are assembled here', said Sir Benjamin Rudyard at the opening of the Long Parliament,

to do God's business and the King's, in which our own is included as we are Christians, as we are Subjects. Let us first fear God, then we shall honour the king the more...Let Religion be our *primum quaerite* for all things else are but *etcetera's* to it, yet we may have them too, sooner and surer, if we give God his Precedence.[5]

Gardiner's phrase 'The Puritan Revolution' was even more apposite than he thought.

In stressing as I am the religious outlook of many of the puritan members of Parliament I do not want to deny their political or social

[1] M. F. Keeler, *The Long Parliament, 1640–41; A Biographical study of its Members* (Philadelphia 1954).
[2] H. R. Trevor-Roper, 'The Fast Sermons of the Long Parliament', in *Essays in British History*, ed H. R. Trevor-Roper (London 1965).
[3] Stephen Marshall, *Meroz Cursed* (London 1641) p 25. See also p 49.
[4] Edmund Calamy, *England's Looking Glass* (London 1641) p 23.
[5] Rushworth, IV, p 24.

aspirations as factors in the conflict. What I wish to do is to begin to formulate the problem in their terms and not ours. One must begin to think back into a situation where Church and State formed one christian society, and the governors in that society saw themselves responsible for its total welfare. Consequently right religion was essential for the total health of that society and right politics would help maintain right religion. 'The State depends on Christ and on religion', said Sidrach Simpson to the Commons in 1643, 'as its first cause. Religion is the cause conservant of the State: this laurel keeps the Garland about the head of princes from being blasted or thunderstruck...If Religion be the supporter of the State then corruptions of religion are the greatest traitors; they strike at government and majesty by the root.'[1] Bernt Moeller[2] has explored this relationship in the South German and Swiss City States during the Reformation. If we would apply the same criteria to the Long Parliament, we might cease giving implausible rationalisations for puritan religious piety in terms of social and political expediency and begin to realise that for contemporaries this activity needed no special justification.[3]

[1] *A Sermon Preached at Westminster before Sundry of the House of Commons by S. Simpson* (London 1643) pp 19, 20.

[2] Bernt Moeller, *Reichstadt und Reformation* (Gütersloh 1962).

[3] I am indebted to the Nuffield Foundation, the Ian Potter Foundation and the Australian Humanities Research Council for grants to visit England for two periods of three months in 1967–70 when most of the research on this theme in preparation for a larger work was done.

'HE-GOATS BEFORE THE FLOCKS':
A NOTE ON THE PART PLAYED
BY WOMEN IN THE FOUNDING OF
SOME CIVIL WAR CHURCHES

by CLAIRE CROSS

R ECENT seventeenth-century historians have stressed the opportunities the disruption caused by the Civil War gave to
women to assert a new role for themselves, first in religion,
then in society in general.[1] There is much truth in this thesis: especially
among the more extreme sects like the Ranters, and, later, the Quakers,
women did publicly teach and evangelise, activities hitherto exclusively
reserved for men. Yet this emphasis upon radical women sectaries can
be misleading since it tends to obscure the importance of more sober
protestant matrons. For them the Civil War did not mark a new period
of spiritual awakening or intellectual enlightenment: rather it brought
to fruition a tradition of independent action by laywomen which can
be traced back at least to the days of the Henrician Reformation.

One day in 1640 five persons covenanted together to form a separatist church in Bristol, later known as the Broadmead church. This church
owed its foundation almost entirely to the initiative of a remarkable
woman, Dorothy Hazzard, whose story merits re-telling at some length
since it illustrates this continuity between popular protestantism of the
later sixteenth and early seventeenth centuries and the congregational
churches of the 1640s.[2] The seventeenth-century chronicler of the

[1] K. Thomas, 'Women and the Civil War Sects', *PP*, XIII (1958) pp 42–62. E. M.
Williams, 'Women Preachers in the Civil War', *JMH*, I (1929) pp 561–9. R. L. Greaves,
'The Ordination Controversy and the Spirit of Reform in Puritan England', *JEH*,
XXI (1970) pp 225–41.
[2] Professor Collinson has emphasised this tendency towards congregational independency
in Elizabethan popular protestantism. P. Collinson, 'The Godly: Aspect of Popular
Protestantism in Elizabethan England', *Past and Present* Conference Papers, July 1966,
typescript. The life of Dorothy Hazzard is taken from E. B. Underhill (ed), *The
Records of a Church of Christ meeting in Broadmead, Bristol, 1640–1687*, Hanserd Knollys
Society (London 1848) pp 8–32, 232. Hereafter *Broadmead Records*. Dr Nuttall recently
drew attention to Dorothy Hazzard: [G. F.] Nuttall, *Visible Saints*, [*The Congregational
Way 1640–1660*] (Oxford 1957) pp 45–8.

Bristol church, Edward Terrill, gives no details of Dorothy Hazzard's background; she first appears in his annals as the young wife of Anthony Kelly, a Bristol grocer and a follower of Mr Yeamans, the minister of St Philip's, Bristol. Yeamans held fasts for the godly in private houses 'where they did cry day and night to the Lord to pluck down the lordly prelates of the time, and the superstitions thereof' and Kelly became a ripe professor. In 1631 he died, but his widow persevered in godliness, renowned for her piety and zeal for reformation. She continued to run her husband's business, making a point of keeping the grocer's shop open at Christmas to demonstrate her abhorrence of the superstitions of those days. In the not entirely felicitous words of her biographer, like 'a he-goat before the flock' (Jer. 50: 8) she led the godly on to practise 'that truth of the Lord...namely, separation'.

After the death of Yeamans in 1633 the true professors in Bristol had no permanent minister, but they still met to repeat sermon notes and to fast and pray. Occasionally they could hear Mr Wroth, Mr Symonds or Mr Craddock, reforming ministers from the church at Llanvaches in South Wales.[1] Then a new minister, Matthew Hazzard, 'savouring of a puritanical spirit', came to lecture in the city. The good people of Bristol seem to have recognised a spiritual affinity between Hazzard and Dorothy Kelly and they persuaded her to marry the young man. Already Dorothy Hazzard was in serious trouble for her nonconformity, for when her parson had defended in the pulpit the use of pictures and images in worship, she had walked out of church, vowing never to hear him again. Only by moving out of the parish could she and her husband avoid citation by the ecclesiastical authorities. At this juncture the incumbency of St Ewins fell vacant and Matthew Hazzard secured the living which he held from 1639 until 1662.[2] A new period of profitable work within the church seemed to be opening for his wife. At St Ewins parsonage she sheltered godly families about to embark from Bristol for New England and provided a refuge for devout women at their lying-in so that they could avoid the ceremonies at their churching and at the baptism of their babies.

Yet even at this time of usefulness Dorothy Hazzard felt impelled to go forward. Her husband did not minister the sacrament promiscuously without examination to the whole parish, but he was bound by his position to read the book of Common Prayer which increasingly she

[1] For the church at Llanvaches and the surrounding area see G. F. Nuttall, *The Welsh Saints 1640–1660* (Cardiff 1957) pp 1–37, and Nuttall, *Visible Saints*, pp 34–6.
[2] A. G. Matthews, *Calamy Revised* (Oxford 1934) p 255.

considered to be ungodly. She faced a crisis of conscience. She knew it was her duty to set an example to the parish by attending her husband's services, she knew also she should not countenance the corruptions of the prayer book. One Sunday morning, as she agonised over whether to go to church or stay away, she picked up her Bible and read Revelation 14: 9, 10, 11. 'If any man worship the beast and his image, and receive his mark in his forehead, or in his hand, the same shall drink of the wine of the wrath of God.' In these words she recognised the voice of God and resolved never again to hear the Church of England service. With Goodman Atkins, a countryman, Goodman Cole, a Bristol butcher, Richard Moone, a farrier, and Mr Bacon, a young minister, she formed a covenanted church which met in her own house. At first the separatists compromised by going to the parish church after the set service had ended solely to hear Mr Hazzard preach, but then John Canne, the separatist, visited Bristol. Dorothy Hazzard sought him out to offer him hospitality. He in return instructed her and her companions on the difference between the church of Christ and Antichrist, and they decided to renounce entirely all ministers who did not come out of the antichristian worship. At this development Matthew Hazzard, the orthodox husband of a separatist wife, had to run the gauntlet of hostile clerical criticism. One Bristol colleague told him that as his wife had left his church so she would go on to abandon his bed; 'but she, approving her heart to the Lord, walked before him, with her husband, in his ordinances, blameless, to his death, near thirty years afterwards'.

The Broadmead church in Bristol grew quickly to a membership of one hundred and sixty after its separation. At first it had no minister, though occasionally Mr Wroth came over from Llanvaches and then, after his death, Dorothy Hazzard secured Mr Pennill to be their minister. On the surrender of Bristol to the royalists in 1643 the church migrated to London; it returned two years later when the city had been retaken by the parliamentarians and established a new covenant. After 1645 Dorothy Hazzard seems no longer to have maintained such an ascendancy over the church's life but she remained an active and honoured member until on 14 March 1675 at a great age she 'came to her grave a shock of corn fully ripe'.

As an individual Dorothy Hazzard was unique and yet her activities were not as unprecedented as might be supposed. For years puritan women in practice had frequently showed marked independence, a very different quality from the submissive meekness extolled by contemporary puritan writers.[1] When Dorothy Hazzard is compared with Elizabeth Bowes or Anne Locke, who both abandoned their husbands in the reign of Mary I to join John Knox on the continent, then her behaviour towards Matthew Hazzard appears less startling.[2] Indeed there is a particularly close parallel between Anne Locke and Dorothy Hazzard: both were widows of city merchants and came from that sector of late sixteenth and early seventeenth century society where Professor Notestein thought women were most emancipated; both chose for their second husbands young radical ministers.[3] When in the 1630s the wife of the dean of York, unbeknown to her husband, could encourage a York minister to hold puritan conventicles in the deanery, then again it is hardly an innovation to find Dorothy Hazzard more advanced in matters of church government than her clerical husband.[4] Although the most dominant, Dorothy Hazzard was by no means the only woman to influence the newly founded church in Bristol: on its return to Bristol in 1645 it met for a time in the house of Sister Griffen in Christmas Street. After the church dismissed Dr Ingello, not considering him sufficiently serious to continue as their minister, Mrs Nethway, a brewer's wife, took it upon herself to ride into Wales to hear Mr Ewins preach: 'she was the instrument, when she came home, to persuade the leading brethren of the congregation...to endeavour to get the said Mr Ewins to be teacher to this congregation'. Mr Ewins subsequently ministered to the church until his death in 1670. A list of the members of the Bristol church does not survive earlier than 1671 but then almost three quarters of the members of the church were women.[5]

An almost exact contemporary of Dorothy Hazzard was Katherine Chidley, another founder of separatist churches. Like her she came from an urban background, in this case London, though it is not definitely known to which 'church of God in London' she belonged. While little has been recorded about the life of Mrs Chidley, she stated

[1] L. L. Schücking, The Puritan Family (English translation London 1969) pp 1–96. The more the evidence becomes available about the behaviour of actual women in the early seventeenth century, the more it is possible to question the extent of the subjection of women in the 'typical' puritan household. The godly ministers seem to have been pursuing a mirage, far from reality.

[2] For Elizabeth Bowes and her daughter Marjory see J. Ridley, John Knox (Oxford 1968) pp 130–44. For Anne Locke, P. Collinson, 'The Role of Women in the English Reformation illustrated by the Life and Friendships of Anne Locke', SCH, II (1965) pp 258–72.

[3] W. Notestein, 'The English Woman 1580–1650', Studies in Social History, ed J. H. Plumb (London 1955) p 97.

[4] R. A. Marchant, Puritans and the Church Courts in the Diocese of York, 1560–1642 (London 1960) p 81.

[5] Broadmead Records, pp 32, 37–8, 135–6.

her opinions on church government clearly, logically and without equivocation in her first book, published in 1641, *The justification of the Independent Churches of Christ*. This was an answer to *Reasons against the Independent Government of particular Congregations* by Thomas Edwards who subsequently wrote *Gangraena*. Educated women had for the past century published translations of religious treatises; Anne Locke, to mention only one, had translated the *Sermons of John Calvin upon the songe that Ezechias made*... and Taffin's *Of the markes of the children of God* but it was not customary for women actually to engage in religious controversy. Katherine Chidley, however, made no apology for her new departure; she had absolute confidence in the rightness of separation.

It is, and hath been (for a long time) a question more enquired into than well weighed, whether it be lawful for such, who are informed of the evils of the church of England, to separate from it? For my own part, considering that the Church of England is governed by the canon laws (the discipline of Antichrist) and altogether wanteth the discipline of Christ, and that the most of them are ignorant what it is, and also do profess to worship God by a stinted service book, I hold it not only lawful, but also the duty of all those who are informed of such evils, to separate themselves from them, and such as do adhere unto them; and also to join together in the outward profession and practice of God's true worship, when God hath declared unto them what it is; and being thus informed in their minds of the knowledge of the will of God (by the teaching of his son Jesus Christ) it is their duty to put it in practice, not only in a land where they have toleration, but also where they are forbidden to preach, or teach in the name (or by the power) of the Lord Jesus.[1]

Above everything else she believed in the authority of the god-fearing layman. 'I tell you... [she later asserted in her argument] such honest souls (though they are not of the clergy, but of those whom you call the laity) are the fittest men on earth to make churches, and to choose their own ministers...though they be tradesmen, and such as these have dependency upon Christ alone, whose way is properly the sincere way of God.'[2]

The meagre evidence which remains for the activities of Katherine Chidley indicates that she did her best to carry out in her life the principles expressed so confidently here. Thomas Edwards, scarcely an

---

[1] K. Chidley, *The justification of the Independent Churches of Christ* (London 1641) unpaged, sig. *2. The spelling and punctuation have been modernised here, as in the quotations throughout this note.

[2] *Ibid*, pp 68–9.

impartial witness, said in 1646 that she had won converts to separatism in Stepney.[1] On 16 August 1646 at Bury St Edmunds she witnessed with her son Samuel the signing by five men and three women of a covenant establishing an Independent church there. Dr Nuttall considers she may well have been the chief impetus behind the foundation of this church whose members in unusually strong terms denounced the 'vain inventions,...human devices,...abominable idolatories' of those who continued to attend their parish churches or who worshipped in 'superstitious high places which were built and dedicated to idolatory.'[2] In the summer of the previous year she had apparently disputed in public with the minister of Stepney on this very matter as to whether an ecclesiastical building which had once been dedicated to a popish saint could ever be used for the reformed service of God.[3]

Katherine Chidley and Dorothy Hazzard were obviously women of great dynamism in their different localities: a third example of the influence of women in the founding of gathered churches comes from lower in society and is one of corporate, not individual action. At Bedford there was no one outstanding matron, but rather a company of godly women who assembled together to form the Bedford church in 1650 which a little later attracted John Bunyan into membership.[4] The four brothers and eight sisters who began the work at Bedford were 'Mr John Grew and his wife, Mr John Elston, the elder, Anthony Harrington and his wife, Mr John Gifford, Sister Coventon, Sister Bosworth, Sister Munnes, Sister Fenne, Sister Norton and Sister Spencer, all ancient and grave Christians'.[5] For the first few years after regular monthly records began to be kept in 1656 the church frequently commissioned its sisters to examine women seeking fellowship and to visit and exhort women members negligent in their attendance.[6] When the members of the church were listed about 1673 and again in 1693 there were twice as many women members as men.[7]

Yet it would be wrong to give the impression that women invariably or even usually dominated churches established during or just after the

[1] [T. Edwards], *Gangraena*, pt I (2 ed London 1646) p 25.
[2] Nuttall, *Visible Saints*, pp 27, 29. J. Browne, *History of Congregationalism...and Memorials of the Churches in Norfolk and Suffolk* (London 1877) p 394.
[3] *Gangraena*, pt I, p 25.
[4] J. Bunyan, *Grace Abounding to the Chief of Sinners*, ed R. Sharrock (Oxford 1962) pp 14–15, 83.
[5] G. B. Harrison (ed), *The Church Book of Bunyan Meeting 1650–1821* (London 1928) p 2.
[6] *Ibid*, pp 15–25.   [7] *Ibid*, pp 5–6.

Civil War: in the Huntingdonshire church of Fenstanton, founded by the baptist Henry Denne, men and women members were roughly equal, and at the baptist churches of Warboys, Huntingdonshire, and Hexham, Northumberland, men slightly outnumbered women.[1] Nor was it the case that women were necessarily drawn to those churches where their gifts might find the freest exercise or to those ministers who held more advanced views on women's rights. Elizabeth Warren, one of the most scholarly of the Civil War women writers, published an erudite tract on the duty owed by the laity to the godly parochial ministry.[2] Because of the spiritual fame of that most theologically and socially conservative of puritans, Richard Baxter, a pious gentlewoman, Mrs Hanmer, came to settle in Kidderminster in the late 1650s with her daughter, Margaret, and lived there 'as a blessing among the honest, poor weavers'.[3]

With Mrs Hanmer at Kidderminster history in the seventeenth century seems to be repeating itself. At the Restoration she and her daughter pursued Baxter to London, and in 1662 Margaret Charlton married him, an exact parallel to the association of Mrs Bowes and Marjory with Knox a hundred years earlier. Little, except time and social status, separates Dorothy Hazzard in Bristol from Lady Margaret Hoby labouring at Hackness in Yorkshire to instruct her extended family in protestant practice at the turn of the sixteenth century.[4] It is pertinent to distinguish between the godly, and relatively sober, women of the Civil War period like Katherine Chidley or Elizabeth Warren and the ecstatic visionaries such as Lady Eleanor Davies or Anna Trapnel; certainly their written work is utterly different.[5] The education of women seems to have penetrated deeper into society in the early seventeenth century than perhaps it did in the sixteenth century, though this is a subject that needs much further investigation. It may be that many of these women at least partially educated themselves; once they could read, by regular attendance at sermons and exercises and by diligent reading of the Bible and contemporary theological and devotional writers they attained to very considerable biblical

[1] E. B. Underhill (ed), *Records of the Church of Christ gathered at Fenstanton, Warboys and Hexham 1644–1720*, Hanserd Knollys Society (London 1854) pp 251–6, 283–4, 289–97.
[2] E. Warren, *The old and the good way vindicated* (London 1646).
[3] W. Orme, *The Practical Works of the Rev. Richard Baxter*, I (London 1830) pp 237–9. J. M. Lloyd Thomas (ed), *The Autobiography of Richard Baxter* (London 1925) pp 267–77.
[4] D. M. Meads (ed), *Diary of Lady Margaret Hoby* (London 1939).
[5] For excerpts from the writings of Lady Eleanor Davis see *Historical Manuscripts Commission Report, Hastings*, IV (London 1947) pp 343–5. A. Trapnel, *The cry of a stone* (London 1654).

learning. Whatever the puritan theory on the submissive place of women in society, no bushels could quench these lights. Godly women achieved so much influence in certain churches during the Civil War period not so much because of the revolutionary nature of the times as because the whole trend of puritan practice for at least the previous century had been preparing them for such action.

THE SOCIAL STATUS OF SOME
SEVENTEENTH-CENTURY RURAL
DISSENTERS

by MARGARET SPUFFORD

I FEEL I must ask the indulgence of this meeting for offering any contribution. I am primarily a social and economic historian, dealing with village communities in Cambridgeshire. Until very recently, I have been trying to establish the economic framework within which these communities worked – the way, in fact, they made their bread and butter, or rather, lard. But I am now trying to extend my terms of reference to include that part of the villagers' lives which revolved round the parish church, or, occasionally, the nonconformist chapel. As a first step I have been trying to discover the exact social status of villagers who were active members of nonconfomist groups in the later seventeenth century.

I must here stress the very strict limitations of my work. It is confined only to members of rural communities, and does not cover a large enough sample of dissenters to make any claim to statistical validity, unlike the work of Cole and Vann on the early Quakers.[1] Moreover, by confining myself to the village members of dissenting groups, I am, by some definitions, examining dissent only amongst 'the lower classes'. I am myself extremely chary of using the word 'class' of the many, and important, different strata within village communities, even by the end of the seventeenth century. Certainly there were clear and well-marked economic differences between yeomen, husbandmen, labourers and craftsmen, as the very different value of their goods at the time of their deaths shows.[2] These economic differences were becoming increasingly emphasised in upland Cambridgeshire by the polarisation of

---

[1] Alan Cole, 'The Social Origins of the Early Friends', *Journal of the Friends' Historical Society*, XLVIII (London 1957) pp 99–118 and [R. T.] Vann, 'Quakerism and the Social Structure [in the Interregnum]', *PP*, XLIII (1969) pp 71–91.

[2] The median wealth of the eighteen labourers whose inventories occur amongst those preserved in the Consistory Court of Ely records from the 1660s was £15. That of the twenty-four husbandmen was £30; that of the fifty-five craftsmen was £40, and that of the fifty-eight yeomen was £180.

agricultural society in the seventeenth century, as corn-growing became more and more an occupation for the farmer with over forty-five acres. Economic differences in themselves, however strong, do not necessarily make for social cleavage, however. The work I have recently done on inheritance customs in this county shows that fathers tried to provide all their younger sons with either an acre or so of land, or a cash sum with which to set up a cottage, even if the eldest was to inherit the main holding. This constant paternal effort to provide all the members of a family with at least a toehold on the land meant that the immediate members of a family could, and did, sprawl right across the economic divisions within a village, and comprehend, at one extreme, yeomen who were turning into gentry, and, at the other, landless labourers with only a cottage to their name.[1]

What I am now attempting to discover is whether dissent likewise gained an equally strong hold throughout the whole of certain village communities, or whether, for instance, yeomen, whose superior economic status led to a higher degree of literacy,[2] were more likely to adopt dissenting opinions.

The Compton Census of 1676[3] showed that the villages of Cambridgeshire contained between four and five per cent of nonconformists. This proportion was almost exactly typical of the country as a whole.[4] An average figure is very deceptive, however, because a detailed examination of the distribution of nonconformity shows that it had really taken root in some areas, and was almost completely unknown in others. There were twenty-five parishes which contained a group of ten or more dissenters. Two more were omitted from the Census which almost certainly, from other evidence, contained as active and large a body of dissenters.[5] These parishes were the ones in which religious issues played a strong part as a potentially divisive force, although naturally a group of this size had more impact in one of the upland or valley villages of the county, with fifty or so houses, than in one of the typical villages on the edge of the fens with over a hundred houses. It is

[1] Margaret Spufford, 'People, Land and Literacy in Cambridgeshire in the Sixteenth and Seventeenth Centuries', unpublished Ph.D. thesis, Leicester, 1970, pp 68–74, 107–20, 200–3.

[2] Margaret Spufford, 'The Schooling of the Peasantry in Cambridgeshire, 1575–1700', *Agricultural History Review*, XVIII (London 1970) pp 130–47.

[3] William Salt Library, Stafford. Soon to be printed in the Staffordshire Historical Collections, ed A. Whiteman,

[4] 4.4 per cent in Cambridgeshire; 4.5 per cent, or 1: 22, over the country.

[5] Margaret Spufford, 'The Dissenting Churches in Cambridgeshire from 1660 to 1700', P[roceedings of the] C[ambridge] [Antiquarian] S[ociety], LXI (Cambridge 1968) p 75.

the social position of the nonconformists in two of these parishes which I want to look at here.

Orwell is a small village on the clay uplands. When it was mapped in the 1670s, there were only fifty-five houses there, so the Hearth Tax of 1674 was not far out in taxing fifty-two of them.[1] Despite its size, Orwell had no less than fifty-eight nonconformists in 1676, a far larger number than any other parish in the county. Most of them were Congregationalists, although curiously enough there were also a few Muggletonians there. Orwell was one of the main centres where Francis Holcroft's team of helpers worked. It was noticed by the bishop in 1669, and a licence was issued for a meeting place there in 1672.[2] In 1675, a list was made of the members of Holcroft's church in Cambridgeshire which survives, in a very corrupt form in the Bodleian.[3] One of the sections of this list contains church members drawn from Orwell and three neighbouring villages. By comparing the Congregational list with the Hearth Tax taken a year earlier, it is possible to identify most members of the church from Orwell who were also heads of households. The uses of the Hearth Tax are not exhausted there, fortunately. There is no doubt that entries in the tax lists form a general, if not a precise guide, to the economic position of those taxed. In the seventeenth century, retired or declined yeoman farmers could be found, like their counterparts today, hanging on in houses they could not afford to keep up, but, as an overall guide, the tax is adequate.[4]

Nearly a quarter of the householders of Orwell who were taxed in 1674 on their hearths were identifiable as nonconformists.[5] This is an astonishingly large proportion if you remember that we are here con-

[1] PRO, E. 179/244/23.

[2] [G. Lyon] Turner, *Original Records [of Early Nonconformity under Persecution and Indulgence* (London/Leipzig 1911)] I, p 36, II, p 863.

[3] Bodleian Library, Oxford, MS Rawlinson D. 1480 fols 123–6.

[4] The median wealth of those who died in southern Cambridgeshire in the decade 1661–70 and can be identified in a Hearth Tax return as occupants of houses with one hearth was £24; that of a man occupying a house with two hearths was £60; that of a man with three hearths was £141, and that of a man with four or more hearths was £360. Compare with the figures in n 2, p 203 above. Margaret Spufford, 'The Significance of the Cambridgeshire Hearth Tax', *PCAS*, LV (1962) pp 53–64.

[5] Twelve out of fifty-two householders. I have throughout, in identifying nonconformists, used a combination of the 1674 Hearth Tax, with Turner, *Original Records*, the Congregational church list of 1675, and, where there were Quakers, the Volume of Sufferings, I, pp 101–35 in the Friends' Meeting House, London and the Quaker Register for Cambridgeshire, PRO, R. G/6/1219. I have also used as supplementary evidence two episcopal visitations, of 1679 and 1682, which contain many names of parishioners presented for attending conventicles, without, of course, their adherence. Cambridge University Library, Ely Diocesan Records, B 2/6 fols 13–28 v and 39–53 v.

sidering heads of households alone. The amount of trouble caused by
the dissenters of Orwell is indicated by a couple of entries in the churchwardens' accounts. Between Michaelmas 1668 and Michaelmas 1669,
and again in the following year, no less than seven applications were
made for a 'warrant for the phanaticks'. The parish register, too,
gives ample evidence of the amount of nonconformity there, for the
deaths of dissenters were sometimes recorded even though they were
not buried in the churchyard. It was not always possible to carry the
corpses elsewhere, and the disgusted scribe recorded several times in the
later seventeenth century that someone had been 'buried with the burial
of an asse' in a close or orchard.

Who then were these Orwell dissenters? A comparison of the size of
their houses recorded in the Hearth Tax with those of the remainder of
the community shows that they were distributed throughout every
layer of village society from the top to the bottom, and that there were,
if anything, slightly more poor men among them than among their
conforming fellows. (See Table, p. 211) John Howard, senior, who paid
tax on five hearths, and is therefore likely to have been a very considerable yeoman, was a dissenter. So was John Adams, who had a more
modest house with only two hearths. This had been one of the meeting
places of the conventicle in 1669. John Adams was one of the few
remaining small yeomen of Orwell who held only about twenty acres
of arable in the 1670s; most of them had been squeezed out in the en-
grossing process which had been going on throughout the century.
When he died, as an old man, in 1691, he left £91: a barely adequate
estate by yeoman standards. Three of the twelve dissenting householders
of Orwell who appeared in both the 1674 Hearth Tax returns and in
the rental of the 1670s were holders of half-yardlands like John Adams,
but another three were certainly cottagers with a very small acreage.
Half of the dissenters in the Hearth Tax returns paid on only one hearth.
There is no doubt that Congregational opinions had gained as much
hold on the poor, by village standards, as on the rich. Richard Barnard,
who has a cottage with one hearth in 1674, was constantly in trouble
with the ecclesiastical authorities for not going to the parish church.
He must have been a devoted adherent, for his orchard was commonly
used for Congregationalists' burials. He was described by his neighbours as a husbandman when he died in 1693, and was by then an impoverished one, for his goods were valued at £15. Edward Caldecot,
who likewise paid tax on one hearth in 1674, was also paying a cot-
tager's rent of 3s 4d in the 1670s, and was really poor, for he was pos-

sessed of goods worth only £5 when he died in 1690. Nonconformist opinions, and prosperity, bore no relationship at all to each other in Orwell.

Willingham, on the edge of the fens, was three times the size of Orwell. Its minister, Nathaniel Bradshaw, was a non-subscriber, whose proud boast it was that he had left 'four score and ten praying families' there at his deprivation.[1] By 1669, there was a flourishing Congregational conventicle there. It had about a hundred hearers, taught by Francis Holcroft and Joseph Oddy. Many of the members came from other places, and they were, in Bishop Laney's words 'all very meane, Excepte some few yeomen'. A licence was obtained for Willingham in 1672 and it remained a Congregational centre. A few Quakers appeared there in the 1670s also. The Congregational church list of 1675 again lumps together Willingham members with those from two neighbouring villages, but once again some of the householders can be identified by comparing the list with the Hearth Tax return of the year before. An agreement on the use of the Willingham fens was marked or signed by all of the commoners in 1677–8 and another comparison can be made with this.[2] It is unfortunate, for these purposes, that the membership of the church was predominantly female. Only twenty-two of the seventy Congregationalists in the Willingham section of the church list were men. All the remainder were, as usual, women and it is almost impossible to trace a woman's status unless her husband is named. However, of the twenty-two men in Francis Holcroft's church who came from Willingham, Oakington and Over, fourteen appeared in the Hearth Tax return, or in the commoners' agreement, or in a set of presentments made in 1673 for Willingham.[3] So about half the male membership of the church came from Willingham, and it is possible to examine their backgrounds and see if the bishop's judgement that they were 'all very meane' was a partial statement or not.

Willingham, like the other fen-edge villages, was pastoral. The social and economic structure of these villages was entirely different from that of the upland villages like Orwell. Whereas, on the uplands, the tenants of half-yardlands had been losing their holdings since the end of the sixteenth century because small-scale corn-growers were unable to withstand the continued pressures of the price-rise and bad harvests,

---

[1] *Calamy Revised*, ed A. G. Mathews (Oxford 1934) p 69.
[2] Cambridgeshire Record Office, R. 59/14/5/9 (f).
[3] See footnote 1, p 208.

here, on the edge of the fens, such men were men of substance, because of their common rights, and the cattle that went with their holdings. These villages were not economically polarised in the way that arable, upland, villages were. They had a lower proportion of the houses of landless or near-landless men, with only one hearth, and a much higher proportion of the houses of the moderately prosperous with two or three hearths. Commoners were more prosperous than their fellows, and were more likely to have larger houses, Every single one of the nine male Congregationalists named in Francis Holcroft's church list of 1675, who was identifiable in the tax list of 1674, lived in a house with two or three hearths. The Willingham Congregationalists were not, therefore, like their fellow members at Orwell, distributed throughout the village community. They were neither drawn from the poorer thirty-nine per cent of the villagers who lived in houses with only one hearth, nor from the most prosperous seven per cent of the house-holders who had bigger houses with four or more hearths. They came from the relatively comfortable and substantial middle section of this village community. All but one of them were also literate, in the sense that they could write their names, which usually seems to indicate the ability to read. Francis Duckins is a good example. He was one of the foremost of the church members, because his house was one of the meeting places of the conventicle in 1669, and was the one chosen to be licensed as a meeting place in 1672. It was taxed on three hearths in 1674. The bishop was plainly out of touch with the nuances of village society when he described these people as 'all very meane'. They were nothing of the kind; they were the small yeomen-graziers who formed the backbone of Willingham society.[1]

The same judgement applies to the Quakers of Willingham, about

[1] Since this paper was written, my attention has kindly been drawn by Mr Dennis Jeeps of Willingham, to a list of presentments of Willingham people in a book of miscellaneous court records in the Ely diocesan records in the Cambridge University Library (E.D.R. D/2/54 fols 39 v–40 v). This list made in 1673 gives more dissenters' names than I have drawn from the other sources listed in n 5, p 205 for Willingham, and adds no less than thirteen more men assessed in the Hearth Tax, some of whom were certainly Congregationalist according to the 1675 list, and most of whom were probably so. I fully expected that a more complete identification of the Willingham dissenters would destroy the contrast between it and the other villages, and show that nonconformist opinions were spread throughout Willingham society, as they were elsewhere. In fact, the contrast was confirmed. Even though two men in the 1673 presentments did live in houses with only one hearth, they were not representative, and the overwhelming majority (88 per cent) of the dissenters identified in the Hearth Tax lived in houses with two and three hearths. The table on p 211 has been adjusted to include these men, and any discrepancy between it and the text is accounted for by this late addition to the article.

whom the bishop wrote in even more deprecating terms than the Congregationalists. Four Quakers of Willingham can be identified in the 1674 Hearth Tax returns. Three of them had houses with two or three hearths, and one had an outstandingly large house with five hearths. The two Quakers who appear among the commoners could both sign their names. When the bishop wrote of the local dissenters in the terms he did he was either making a deliberate attempt to mini-mise their importance within their own communities, or he was genu-inely ignorant of the difference between a day labourer and a fenland yeoman.

A close look at the dissenting members of two village communities at the same date therefore gives a very different impression of their status. In one, nonconformist opinions had spread throughout the villagers, from the prosperous to the poor: in the other, these opinions were almost entirely confined to the comfortable middle stratum of smaller yeomen. I must admit that I am myself at a loss for an explana-tion. I am frankly surprised by the result. The most likely solution is that it ties in, in some way, with the very different social situation which I have already indicated in the upland and the pastoral villages. I still cannot understand why Congregational opinions should make no appeal to the poor of Willingham, while they did to the poor of Orwell.

As I said at the beginning, however, I have not been dealing with a group of statistical significance; a dozen Congregationalist and Muggle-tonian householders in Orwell and another dozen Congregationalist and Quaker householders in Willingham do not make a fair sample. I have had a brief look at the distribution of Congregational and Quaker opinions at Cottenham, which is both close to Willingham, and compar-able with it economically. A rather larger number of dissenters there seemed to be well-off than in the community at large, but the pheno-menon was not so clearly marked as at Willingham. I have also had a look at the Quakers in Swavesey, then a small port and market town on the edge of the fens. Swavesey was the nursery of Quakerism in this part of the county, and the early Quakers, involved in the mass arrests of 1661, were as usual, predominantly female; but they were also pre-dominantly poor. Four of the nine men involved were labourers, whilst three others were craftsmen. By 1674, the Quakers of Swavesey were better off, but two of the half dozen who appear in the 1674 Hearth Tax returns were still occupants of houses with only one hearth. This certainly does not tie in with the picture of Willingham dissenters as a prosperous group, nor, incidentally does it tie in with Vann's suggestion that first generation Quakers were more prosperous than converts after the Restoration.[1]

The obvious next step is to analyse the whole of the Congregational church list for Cambridgeshire, together with the Quaker records, and the pitifully small list of the General Baptists at this date who had managed to survive persecution, in conjunction with the whole of the 1674 Hearth Tax returns for the county. But unless this is done on a basis of the very different farming regions within the county, or any other county treated in this way, one will lose sight of the economic realities in the search for what Vann has splendidly called 'the protection of the law of large numbers'.[2] It is extremely dangerous to stick an arbitrary label on the tenant, farmer, owner or occupier of twenty acres and call him a 'yeoman', when in an upland area producing sheep and corn he is likely to have been a husbandman struggling along under severe pressures, and in the fens or the forests, a comfortable farmer enjoying reasonable spending power. If it is worthwhile looking at the distribution of Dissent amongst the peasantry at all, which is open to question, the structure of the communities concerned must first be fairly well known.

[1] Vann, 'Quakerism and the Social Structure', p 78.   [2] *Ibid*, p 91.

Distribution of Hearths 1674

	Orwell						Willingham					
	Identifiable dissenters		Others		All villagers		Identifiable male dissenters		Others		All villagers	
	No.	%	No.	%	No.	%	No.	%	No.	%	No.	%
Large houses – four hearths and over	3	25	8	20	11	21	1	4	9	7	10	7
Modest houses – two and three hearths	3	25	19	47	22	42	22	88	60	48	82	54
Small houses, cottages – one hearth	6	50	13	33	19	37	2	8	56	45	58	39
Totals	12	100	40	100	52	100	25	100	125	100	150	100

METHODISM AND THE MOB IN THE EIGHTEENTH CENTURY

by JOHN WALSH

EARLY Methodism is often studied as an example of a popular religious movement, but the purpose of this paper is to explore some of the reasons behind its unpopularity, for suffering and persecution characterised its early phases as well as growth and success. The persecution of Methodists took many forms. Perhaps the hardest to bear were those least often recorded, such as the eviction of society members from their homes and jobs, or the unnerving social ostracism which made life intolerable in many villages and families. The persecution usually described in the journals of the methodist pioneers, however, was that inflicted by 'the mob'. 'The mob' was an elastic term in their vocabulary and could range from a knot of village youths throwing stones to the ferocious urban crowds which cruelly assaulted worshippers in Exeter in 1745 and Norwich in 1752. 'Mobbing' too covered a gamut of activity. Much of it was rude horseplay, like the release of sparrows at the candles in a cottage meeting; some was petty malicious damage, like the breaking of windows. But not infrequently it erupted more violently. Preaching-houses at St Ives, Sheffield, Arborfield, Wolverhampton, Nantwich and Chester were pulled down, and others severely damaged. A number of houses, generally of poor people, were wrecked or sacked. Many persons, women and children among them, were cruelly beaten and some scarred or injured for life. A few, like William Seward, first blinded and then killed by a mob at Hay in 1741, paid for their beliefs with their lives. The knowledge of these ordeals, transmitted by biographies and oral tradition, gave the movement its equivalent of a martyrology and built up that image of heroic, primitive Methodism which, like the image of primitive Christianity itself, stimulated and reproved the piety of later, more comfortable generations.

The aim of this paper is to enquire into the causes of mob violence, rather than to describe the effects of persecution on the nascent methodist movement. It offers no more than a few tentative generalizations on a large and complex theme. There is no space here for consideration of regional variables (why, for instance, Scotland was as peaceable as Ireland was bloody) or comparisons between rural and urban cases.

It might help to begin by putting these disturbances into some kind of perspective. In their reaction of outrage the early preachers, and still more later historians, have tended to over-emphasise the singularity of these violent incidents. It takes only a casual perusal of the journals of the brothers Wesley to see that rioting was a commonplace, almost tradition-al means of group expression, whether as a form of social protest – like the corn riots, or the riots of clothworkers and colliers which the Wes-leys observed – or of celebration, like the noisy exuberance of crowds celebrating a military victory or an election result. In the absence of efficient police, public order was difficult to maintain. It was notoriously absent from local festive occasions like wakes, fairs and revels which attracted much drunkenness as well as some methodist preaching, and those who addressed such crowds put themselves deliberately into a dangerous situation. A good deal of the growth of early Methodism was in areas of scattered settlement, like the north country dales, or in new industrial settlements like those round the Kingswood collieries, where cultural isolation or squalid conditions removed the sanctions for law and order (such as they were) which existed in the tight-knit, nucleated parish. The religious nature of the persecution suffered by Wesley's followers did not make it unique. Through the series of 'popish plot' alarums in the seventeenth century, to the Gordon Riots of 1780, Roman Catholics had been the victims of mob hysteria: indeed, some of the early Methodists were attacked because they were believed to be papists in disguise. Protestant Nonconformists had undergone the legal persecution of the Clarendon Code, and even after the Toleration Act were not exempt from the violence of crowds, as the Sacheverell riots, the Jacobite riots of 1715, and the Priestley riots of 1791 were to prove. The violent persecution of religious dissidents was still alive in the nineteenth century in the shape of No Popery crowds or sporadic, brutal assaults on new sects such as the Bible Christians, Primitive Methodists and the Salvation Army. A nineteenth-century Bible Christian apostle to the Isle of Wight claimed to have been struck by enough stones and brickbats to build a chapel.[1]

Without denying the real ferocity of many attacks on Methodists one might suggest that accounts of them are occasionally overdrawn by

[1] J. Woolcock, *A History of the Bible Christian Churches on the Isle of Wight* (2 ed Newport 1897) p 12.

preachers accustomed in their homiletic practice to dramatise events for the benefit of an unlettered audience. In popular evangelicalism there was (as a friendly critic noted) a tendency to 'overstate dangers that it might magnify deliverances; and to give a little of its own colouring to facts'.[1] The more luridly the peril was depicted, the more strikingly could be portrayed the special providences which preserved the faithful Christian. There can be little doubt too that much of the hostility shown by crowds was intended to terrorise and intimidate rather than to inflict real physical damage. There is frequent discrepancy between the bloodcurdling threats shouted at victims and the amount of injury they actually incurred. One doubts the literal intent of the Thorpe woman who vowed to wash her hands in the heart's blood of the preacher.[2] Threats like these were, understandably, taken literally by the persecuted, who were terrified and outnumbered; they could hardly be expected to understand that their real destination was not the graveyard but the duckpond. Of the violence actually inflicted, a considerable portion was aimed at psychological humiliation rather than corporeal injury: this was the purpose of the stripping of clothes, the rolling in dungheaps and kennels. Its object was often a show of collective strength which would strike such terror into a preacher that he would pledge himself never to return to the parish. It says much for the fervour of the preachers that it very seldom worked. Finally, some threatening or violent behaviour was deliberately provocative, intended to incite counter-violence in angry or panic stricken individuals which might then justify the reading of the Riot Act, a legal prosecution, or might at least compromise the victim's claim to represent patterns of christian love and forbearance. Sometimes this tactic succeeded; more often it rebounded from the iron self-discipline and the obvious charity of the victims.

What caused this violence? How could the efforts of early Methodists to attain holiness and practise love be rewarded by such cruelty? The first preachers themselves were often content with a simple, diabolical interpretation. Those who mobbed God's children were 'sons of Belial', 'Satan's children', 'the beasts of the people', and a living object lesson in the evangelical doctrine of human depravity. Persecution was the inevitable response of the Devil when disturbed in his strongholds by the trumpet call of the Gospel. Modern studies of opposition to Methodism have tended to focus largely on the literary

---

[1] *The Christian Observer*, VII (London 1808) p 316.
[2] [*The*] *Journal of* [*the Rev*] *J*[*ohn*] *Wesley*, ed N. Curnock (London 1938) IV, p 231.

critique of the movement in sermons, episcopal charges and pamphlets. But studies of the establishmentarian mind, though valuable, do not always illuminate the grounds of popular hostility, which, though often strongly reflecting that of clergy and gentry, was not coterminous with it.

Nevertheless, the judgement of Henry Moore, Wesley's preacher and early biographer, carries weight. 'The lower orders of the people would never become riotous on account of religion, were they not excited to it under false pretences by persons who have some influence over them and who endeavour to keep behind the scene.'[1] In a great number of instances the action of hostile crowds was caused (to use Wesley's characteristic phrase) by 'the great Vulgar stirring up the small'.[2] The incitement came from clergymen, gentry or some 'blustering, influential farmer'.[3] It might take the form of inflammatory sermons on the traditional theme of 'Church in Danger'. It frequently involved the offer of free ale at the public-house to those who would join in, for the provision of alcohol had the two-fold effect of attracting the roisterous and sportive members of the community and also of providing them with the Dutch courage which they often needed before they marched out to attack passive and defenceless victims. The costs were defrayed by the instigators, but could be charged to the parish. The church accounts at Illogan in Cornwall show the entry 'expences ...on driving the Methodists ix s. oo d.'[4] There were other ways to raise a mob. John Nelson discovered at Horbury in Yorkshire that 'almost the whole town had agreed together that all the journeymen and apprentices should leave work as soon as the next preacher came'.[5] A mob in Waterford in Ireland was raised from the employees of local merchants.[6] In many instances, the instigators of mobs operated vicariously through agents or servants, not wishing to degrade themselves by a personal appearance. In Teesdale the Earl of Darlington was prevailed on by a local clergyman to set his servants on to the Methodists.[7] At Barnard Castle, the regular captain of the local mob was fitted out with a gold laced hat and sword by the gentry.[8] It is noticeable how frequently men in livery figure at the head of mobs. A gentleman's

[1] H. Moore, *The Life of the Rev John Wesley*, II (London 1825) p 269.
[2] *Journal of J. Wesley*, III, p 263.
[3] [T.] Cocking, [*The History of Wesleyan Methodism in Grantham*] (London 1836) p 133.
[4] *The Wesleys in Cornwall*, ed J. Pearce (Truro 1964) p 36.
[5] [*Lives of the*] *Early Methodist Preachers*, ed T. Jackson, I (3 ed London 1865) p 158.
[6] C. H. Crookshank, *History of Methodism in Ireland*, I (Belfast 1885) p 273.
[7] [A.] Steele, [*History of Methodism in Barnard Castle*] (London 1857) p 41.
[8] *Ibid*, p 32.

bailiff was a ring-leader in the Exeter riot of 1745 and in the riot at
Stratton in Wiltshire in 1741 John Cennick learned that the chief
clubber was 'that friend of the Devil', Sylvester Keen, a Swindon
bailiff.[1] In other instances the rough work was accomplished by the
parish clerk, the churchwardens, even the church singers, acting at the
behest of the parish clergyman. Not that genteel organisers were always so discreet: gentry were not above leading their retainers in person, and clergymen witnessed or led parish mobbings, occasionally in
full canonicals.

When the encouragement of social superiors was withdrawn, mobs
often disbanded. John Wesley observed of South Molton, 'when the
gentry would neither head nor pay the mob any more, the poor
rabble were quiet as lambs'.[2] As important as money payments or
alcoholic bribes, perhaps, was the sense of security given to a crowd
by the knowledge that they had the approval of those in authority.
This was more than a matter of mere deference; it was also a matter of
legitimation – an assurance was needed that the acts of violence in
question were not immoral, illegal or excessive, and that they had
received the sanction of the agents of local authority. In several instances,
the objects of crowd hostility were taken forcibly to the house of a local
magistrate – sometimes to his manifest embarrassment. Those who
wished to encourage crowds in their work often exhorted them with the
cry that 'there is no law for the Methodists'.[3] This popular assumption
was based on much ignorance, but also, perhaps, on the common knowledge that many of the early preaching-houses and preachers were not
licensed as they needed to be under the provisions of the Toleration Act.
There was also a strong suspicion that field preaching fell foul of the
Conventicle Act which still stood on the statute book.[4] But great encouragement was also given to mobs by the failure of some magistrates
to give protection to methodist victims of harassment or violence.
Some, indeed, gave active encouragment to the mobbers, like the
JP at Otley who told the crowd, 'do what you will to them so you
break no bones'.[5] Others dragged their feet or prevaricated, like those
who refused to grant licences to Methodists on the grounds that the

---

[1] [J.] Cennick, [An] Account of a late Riot [at Exeter] (London 1745) p 13; The Weekly
History, xxv, 19 Sept 1741, p 4.   [2] Journal of J. Wesley, iv, p 241.
[3] For example Early Methodist Preachers, i, p 191; [The] Journal of [the Rev] C[harles]
Wesley, intr T. Jackson (London 1849) i, p 346.
[4] J. S. Simon, 'The Conventicle Act and its Relation to early Methodism,' Proc[eedings of
the] Wesley Hist[orical] Soc[iety], xi (Burnley etc 1917) pp 82 ff.
[5] Journal of J. Wesley, iv, p 468.

Toleration Act was intended to cover protestant Dissenters, and could not be invoked by the Methodists, who still professed themselves members of the Church of England. Pusillanimous or conniving magistrates annoyed John Wesley greatly, and he attributed much methodist suffering to them. Of the disturbances at Gloucester in 1765 he wrote, 'all they do is to be imputed not so much to the rabble as to the Justices'.[1] He was convinced that whenever the law was enforced firmly, outrages faded rapidly away.

This resentment of gentry and clergy is not hard to explain. Methodism is often portrayed today as a counter-revolutionary force, inculcating submissiveness among the poor, but this is not how many of those in power saw it. They feared it as a challenge to public order and to the authority of their class. Two aspects of the movement gave especial cause for alarm. First, in an age when the agencies of government were decidedly weak and decentralised, Methodism looked the more sinister because of its highly articulated and nation-wide organisation. Secondly, it addressed itself primarily to the poor, whom it drilled into disciplined cadres which owed their allegiance to leaders far beyond the reach of any local authority. The societies were tended by itinerant agents, whose origins were unknown, whose persons were obscure, and who appeared to have no formal authorisation whatever. They were totally unamenable to the normal, localised social controls of squire or parson. Who could tell what the clandestine aims of these men might not be? The traumatic folk-memories of the Civil War and Commonwealth still troubled the minds of many churchmen and gentry. The Methodists looked alarmingly like the harbingers of a second and perhaps a more proletarian puritan revolution. The constable who arrested John Nelson in Nottingham during the hysteria of the '45 rising told him 'it hath been observed that there was always such a preaching, brawling people before any judgement came upon the land'.[2] Might not the cobblers and ploughboys whom Methodism inspired to preach and imbued with a sense of their own divine inspiration turn out to be a new generation of Levellers? It was reported – not without foundation – that the Methodists believed in the community of goods.[3] A gentleman at Middleton in Yorkshire picked up a bludgeon and joined a mob 'swearing most dreadfully that the Methodists should not take his land from him'.[4] The preacher undermined the patriarchal

[1] *Ibid*, v, p 250.   [2] *Early Methodist Preachers*, I, p 146.
[3] For example, A. Jephson, *A Friendly and compassionate Address to all serious and well-disposed Methodists* (London 1760).
[4] Steele, p 53.

authority of gentry and clergy alike by his scorching critique of the vices of the 'polite world' and of the worldliness of the 'carnal' clergy. His impudence seemed compounded by his lowly status, by the fact that he was usually not a resident of the parish whose morals he up-braided, and also, not infrequently, by his youth. Bishop Chandler complained of the preachers as insolent boys.[1] Moreover, when re-proved by local dignitaries, they were often irrepressible: they an-swered back to magistrates and bandied texts with parsons with such facility that it was sometimes alleged that they had printed Bibles of their own to support their novel teachings.[2]

It was the parish clergyman, who felt deeply his proprietary, patriar-chal status as the legal pastor of a territorial parish, who was most directly challenged by the arrival of Methodism. Those high churchmen who based their authority on divine right were especially affronted. The preachers, while professing themselves members of the Church of England, drew people away from the parish church and set up, if not as yet altar against altar, at least pulpit against pulpit, pastor against pastor, creating incipient schism in many parishes hitherto united as one flock. One can see the point of view of the curate of Eccles who complained to John Bennet that he had 'preached at his very door and under his nose, which had made him look but little'.[3] It goes without saying that the theology of the revival was extremely repugnant to most clergy-men, High Churchmen and Latitudinarians alike, particularly its doctrine of justification by faith alone, which seemed to many nervous churchmen a dangerous docrine that would cut at the very roots of common morality. The evangelical doctrine of conversion carried with it many ecclesiastical consequences, not least the implication that those ministers of religion who did not preach the doctrines of grace, and had not themselves experienced the forgiveness of sins, were blind guides, false prophets or dumb dogs that would not bark. Some prea-chers did not hesitate to apply such epithets to the parish parson and in so doing aroused a violent reaction. Often provoked, they were also provoking. Wesley's rule was 'no contempt, no bitterness to the clergy', but he admitted that some of his preachers broke it, and brought persecution upon their heads.[4] The alienation of the once friendly Mr Egginton, the parson at Wednesbury, had been an act of 'inexcusable

---

[1] *Proc Wesley Hist Soc*, xxviii (1951–2) p 49.
[2] [R. Burdsall, *Memoirs of the life of R.*] *Burdsall* (2 ed York 1811) p 63.
[3] Methodist Archives MSS, Journal of John Bennet, 13 April 1750.
[4] [*The*] *Works* [*of the Rev John Wesley*, ed T. Jackson] (repr 3 ed London 1872) xiii, p 229.

folly' and a contributory cause to the riots there; the same seems to have been the case at St Ives in Cornwall, Cork and elsewhere.[1] After John Nelson was beaten up at Ackham in Yorkshire, the parson's brother cursed him, crying, 'according to your preaching, you would prove our ministers to be blind guides and false prophets; but we will kill you as fast as you come'.[2]

As well as damaging the status or authority of some, methodist preaching threatened the livelihood of others. Dissenting ministers provide examples of men who might be threatened on either count, dependent as they were on the voluntary contributions of their hearers. The minister who set about John Smythe with a club in County Cavan in Ireland exclaimed 'how dare you go about preaching, setting the whole neighbourhood out of their senses, and thinning my congregation?'[3] While Dissenters usually recognized some consanguinity with the new sect, they figured in a few English and Irish mobs. Nonconformist acrimony against the competition of Methodism must have been sharpened by fears that the zeal of the new sect would reawaken the high church reaction that had only recently abated, and might (as indeed was to prove the case) lead some alarmed churchmen and politicians to contemplate an unfriendly revision of the Toleration Act. In both the Exeter and the Norwich riots, the 'Church rabble' showed an alarming proclivity to broaden their attack from one on the Methodists to one on nonconformist meeting-houses.[4] There were other groups whose secular livelihoods were hit by methodist preaching and whose representatives figure commonly in the front ranks of mobs. Noticeable were those who offered services or entertainment condemned as ungodly. Howell Harris in Wales, wrote Whitefield, 'made it his business to go to wakes, etc., to turn people from such lying vanities. Many alehouse people, fiddlers, harpers etc., (Demetrius-like) sadly cry out against him for spoiling their business.'[5] Alehouse keepers and brandysellers figure in several disturbances. It was from the encouraging doors of the alehouse that many mobs went out to meet their prey. Actors too had an intense professional dislike of Methodism. Charles Wesley's lodgings were besieged by 'those sons of Belial, the players' in 1740, threatening to burn down the house and murder him. He noted in his journal 'the ground of their quarrel with me is this, that the Gospel has

[1] *Ibid*, p 229.
[2] *Early Methodist Preachers*, I, p 162.
[3] [Methodist Archives MSS, D.] Smythe, [A Short Account of the late John Smythe].
[4] Cennick, *Account of a late Riot*, p 28; *Gentleman's Magazine*, XXII, 11 Feb 1752, p 90.
[5] [George] *Whitefield's Journals* (Banner of Truth Trust, London 1960) p 229.

starved them'.[1] It is probable that the theatres close to Whitefield's newly-built Long Acre Chapel in London put up the money for the mobs which disturbed its worship in 1755-6.[2] Was it an accident that the leader of the violent Cork riots was a ballad singer by profession, one Nicholas Butler?[3]

It would be unfair, however, to interpret group violence against early Methodism exclusively as the work of what professor Rudé has called 'hired bands operating on behalf of external interests'.[4] By no means all those who engaged in the harassment of Methodists were hirelings and mercenaries, or acting merely out of deference to social superiors. Mobbing might take place against the wishes of the local landlord – as with the crowd that dared to disturb worship at Lady Huntingdon's house in Ashby de la Zouch; or against the will of the parish minister – as with the enraged men who prevented Wesley from walking up to the pulpit of his friend John Milner of Chipping.[5] The size of some mobs suggests that if leaders were hired, they were engaged to perform actions commanding a good deal of popular support. When Dicky Burdsall rode into Kirk Douglas to begin preaching, he noted how the inhabitants poured out of their homes with indignation, 'like bees when the hive is disturbed'.[6] That these crowds, especially in large towns, contained their share of criminals, of psychopaths, of the shiftless, and of misfits, is highly probable, and indicated by the subsequent fate of some of their members (for local Methodists took care to scrutinize their careers for signs of God's providential judgement). The hooligan element is noticeable in the many instances of sexual assault or indecent behaviour to women. Mobbing also had undoubtedly an important recreational aspect. It was for many participators a field sport to be unselfconsciously enjoyed. But for all this, many of those who took their part in the mobbings were moved by ideas as well as irrational drives, and not infrequently felt their actions justified in terms of social necessity or religious duty. There were villagers who felt that the Church Militant had the right to use a certain amount of deterrent force against those who threatened it, and:

[1] *Journal of C. Wesley*, I, p 261.
[2] L. Tyerman, *The Life of the Rev George Whitefield* (2 ed London 1890) II, pp 355–65.
[3] *Journal of J. Wesley*, III, p 409.
[4] See E. P. Thompson, *The Making of the English Working Class* (London 1965) pp 68–9.
[5] *The Works of the Rev George Whitefield*, II (London 1771) p 350; *Journal of J. Wesley*, IV, p 59.
[6] *Burdsall*, p 160.

prove their doctrine orthodox
By apostolic blows and knocks.[1]

After mobbing the Methodists at Middleton, near Barnard Castle, the 'principal persecutors, probably supposing they had been doing God's service, repaired to the Church and received the sacrament'.[2] The early Methodists often had the whole village solidly against them. In the Lincolnshire village of Boothby, for a while it was a case of 'Boothby against John Mayfield and John Mayfield against Boothby'. When the village rioters escaped punishment at the Quarter Sessions (even though it was by the clemency of Mayfield himself) they received a heroes' welcome as they marched home to the village with ribbons in their hats, to the peal of the church bells.[3]

A root cause probably lay in the feelings of xenophobia and outraged traditionalism aroused by the 'new religion'. The preacher was an intruder, a stranger, and an agitator. 'He was', wrote Thomas Cocking, 'not of their *way*...He came among them as one of a strange tongue, and from a strange country'.[4] He was marked out by his dress, by the saddlebags on his horse and often by an outlandish accent. Sometimes he came with an escort of supporters, which lent his arrival something of the air of a hostile demonstration. Whitefield once rode into Tewkesbury with 'about one hundred and twenty' friends on horseback, to the great alarm of the inhabitants; John Cennick, at the time of the Stratton riot in 1741, had an escort of fifty on horseback and as many on foot.[5] The preacher was no ordinary traveller, but a man with a mission, bent, it seemed, on winning converts to a newfangled creed that conflicted at many points with the ordinary mores and activity of the community. The chief charge against him was that of 'disturbing the world',[6] of unleashing unwanted social and religious innovation. The villagers of Hanby in Lincolnshire, who flocked to the church in order to deprive the preachers of an audience, feared that Methodism would 'entail all kinds of evil upon them'; that 'men running about talking of God, hell and heaven, were tokens of dreadful judgement, or of the great day itself being at hand'.[7] The preachers upset many easy

[1] S. Butler, *Hudibras*, ed J. Wilders (Oxford 1967) p 7, (1st Part, Canto 1, lines 197–8).
[2] Steele, p 50.
[3] A. Watmough, *A History of Methodism in Lincoln* (London 1829) pp 35–6.
[4] Cocking, p 132.
[5] *Whitefield's Journals*, p 298; John Rylands Library, Manchester, Eng MS 1076/27, J. Cennick, *A Brief Account of the Great Awakening in Wiltshire etc.*, entry for 6 Sept 1741.
[6] *Early Methodist Preachers*, I, p 192.
[7] G. Barratt, *Recollections of Methodism and the Methodists in Lincoln* (Lincoln 1866) p 18.

assumptions and threatened many accepted norms of behaviour by raising drastically the standards of morality. They disturbed men's minds, folk grumbled, by 'pretending to be better than other people'.[1] A crowd complained to John Nelson in Leeds that the Methodists 'make people go mad; and we cannot get drunk, or swear, but every fool must correct us, as if we were to be taught by them'.[2] A man at Wentworth in Yorkshire grumbled 'after May Day we shall have nothing but praying and preaching; but I will make noise enough to stop it'.[3] It was, perhaps, against social change as much as evangelical religion that people fought. They realised that the intense commitment to holiness demanded by the methodist societies had important social repercussions. It might entail the weakening or even severance of attachment to the parish church, still possibly the most outstanding focus of communal life. It involved a revolution in leisure activities; the abandonment of familiar pastimes and customs, innocent as well as brutal, Morris dancing as well as bull-baiting; customs often woven deeply into the traditional fabric of life. The preacher was feared not only as 'an enemy to their pursuits of pleasure' but as a man who seemed bent on removing traditional landmarks of social life.[4] Most important of all, the new creed seemed disruptive of family life. The conversion of people – many of them young people – to the new and still despised sect brought (as Wesley allowed) many a literal fulfilment of the prophecy of Luke 12: 51–3: 'suppose ye that I came to send peace upon earth? I tell you nay, but rather division. For from henceforth there shall be five divided in one house; three against two, and two against three.'[5] The bitter family persecution that might result from conversion is a poignant theme in methodist biography. The other side of the process is seen there too in the furious incursions into Methodist worship made by the unconverted in search of members of their family 'perverted' to the new creed. Action of this kind was generally performed spontaneously by individuals, but it also contributed to violence on a larger scale. Another contributory cause of the Wednesbury riot of 1744 was said to be the story that a local man, who had missed his wife for some days, had found her with a favourite preacher at a methodist meeting.[6] When converts were relatives of gentry, there could be trouble. In a scene that could have come out of *Tom Jones*, the

---

[1] *Journal of J. Wesley*, III, p 20. [2] *Early Methodist Preachers*, I, p 103.
[3] *Journal of J. Wesley*, IV, p 231. [4] Cocking, p 132.
[5] *Works*, VIII, pp 122ff.
[6] *Some Papers Giving an Account of the Rise and Progress of Methodism in Wednesbury* (London 1744) pp 21-2

burly Mr Dearsby, horsewhip in hand and irate at the Methodism of his daughter and son-in-law, pushed John Valton's posterior against the bars of a fire and then delivered him up to a hired mob.[1] In County Fermanagh, the Henderson family, with a mob of a hundred, besieged the methodist Armstrongs for two days, to starve out two preachers who had converted their daughter.[2]

The indignation of mobs was at times kindled by rumour that the methodist preachers were motivated by sordid self-interest. In particular it was said that they captivated naive people – especially 'silly women' – in order to mulct them of their savings. In the Norwich riot of 1752 it was alleged that James Wheatley was ruining local families by demanding frequent collections and by insisting on attendance at a multitude of services which cut into the working day of breadwinners. 'Many journeymen', ran the complaint, 'who had worked hard till noon, going home, found their wives gone out to the *dear hearers*, and their children neglected and no dinner for them, and that by such avocations many mouths had come upon the parish.'[3] Though wild, these charges were plausible. The preachers were often travellers who had no visible means of support and could easily be confused with mountebanks who lived by their wits and their tongues.

The clandestine nature of society meetings generated much paranoid suspicion. If all could gain admission to the public services of the Methodists, class and band meetings were private, intimate occasions, confined to those who had submitted to the exacting rules of membership. Inevitably, these gatherings excited the curiosity of outsiders, titillating curiosity about what went on behind the locked doors. 'The rabble wanted sadly to know what they did at their private meetings.'[4] At times they broke in violently in order to find out. Here we encounter a phenomenon that has been explored by the historians of anti-catholic and anti-immigrant movements in the United States; the projection on to the persons of some alien group of the fantasies, particularly sexual, of the community around them.[5] The popular imagination in England luxuriated in the idea that the closed and often nocturnal

---

[1] Methodist Archives MSS, John Valton's Journal, 12 March 1767; cf *Early Methodist Preachers*, VI (1866) p 63.
[2] C. H. Crookshank, *A Methodist Pioneer. The Life and Labours of John Smith* (London 1881) p 75. John Smith is the same person as the John Smythe mentioned above.
[3] *Gentleman's Magazine*, XXII, March 1752, p 125.
[4] *Early Methodist Preachers*, II (1866) p 123.
[5] Cf D. B. Davies, 'Some Themes of Counter Subversion', *Mississippi Valley Historical Review*, XLVII (Cedar Rapids, Iowa, 1960).

gatherings of the Methodists were a cover for obscene practices. It was commonly reported, wrote Nicholas Manners, that 'when they were assembled together, they put out the candles and committed lewdness'.[1] The lovefeasts, by their very title, seemed to indicate this possibility. Occasionally Methodists fell under the suspicion of witchcraft through their habit of nocturnal meeting. At Barnard Castle people ran up to Catharine Graves with pins to draw her blood and immunise themselves from her magic.[2] The charge of sorcery might also be levelled at a successful revivalist preacher, whose strangely compelling power over his hearers could be ascribed to the influence not of the Holy Spirit but of the Devil. The fits and convulsions which occurred under the preaching of John Smythe earned him the name of 'the Conjuror' and helped to make him one of the most mobbed Methodists in Ireland.[3] He had the habit of reading his text through a magnifying glass and the rumour ran that 'whosoever he looked on thro' the glass was, by something like sorcery or necromancy, struck into fits, and that as a wizard or magician, he should be hanged, drowned or knocked on the head'.[4] The attribution of occult powers to Methodists must have been increased by the claim of some of them occasionally to foretell future events; still more by their successful prophecies of judgement on their opponents.

The astonishing and often rapid alteration wrought by methodist preaching on men's lives by conversion was – at least by those who disliked it – often seen as a kind of witchcraft, or as a weird and alarmingly contagious psychic disease. The Methodists, a man told John Pawson, 'are the most bewitching people upon earth; when once a person hears them, there is no possibility of persuading him to leave them again'.[5] The former friends of James Rogers 'gaped and stared at him as a monster...swearing that...if they did not keep from him he would convert them all, and make them as mad as himself'.[6] William Huntington found himself and his wife regarded by some as carriers of a 'religious infection'.[7] The frequency with which Methodists were described as 'mad dogs' probably symbolises this dread of the new religion as a type of spiritual rabies, bringing madness to those whom it infected.

---

[1] N. Manners, *Some Particulars of the Life and Experiences of N. Manners* (York 1785) p 6.
[2] Steele, pp 17–18.   [3] Smythe, p 26.
[4] *Ibid*, p 43. He was, in fact, murdered by a knock on the head.
[5] *Early Methodist Preachers*, IV (1866) p 11.
[6] *Ibid*, p 280.
[7] W. Huntington, *God the Guardian of the Poor* (10 ed London 1813) I, pp 49–50.

Methodism was associated with anti-national as well as anti-social qualities. A major ground for crowd violence against it was the fear that its gatherings and organisation were a cover for clandestine subversion. The movement had the misfortune to make its first, well-publicised appearance in many areas during the Jacobite scare of the 1740s. It fell foul of the spy mania and the deep fears of internal treachery engendered by the war of 1739–48 and still more by the Jacobite rising of the '45. Those years were the high-water mark of large anti-methodist riots. Fears that Methodists were Jacobites or even Catholics in disguise were surprisingly widespread. Lady Huntingdon fell under the same treasonable imputation as lowly itinerants. Persecution for alleged Jacobitism was suffered by the scattered Inghamite societies in the Yorkshire dales as well as by urban Methodists. There were rumours that the Wesleys were bribed by the Spaniards to raise a disloyal army among the poor. While the charges were ludicrous, they gained credence from the occasional ineptitude of the preachers. John Cennick and Charles Wesley both brought trouble on their heads by innocent but tactless prayers for the Lord's 'banished ones' or 'exiles'.[1] There were just enough catholic elements in the Wesleys' theology to raise suspicions even among their calvinistic methodist brothers that they were, indeed, popishly inclined. But the essentially paranoid and irrational nature of the political charges against Methodism is perhaps best illustrated by their contradictoriness. We have seen how Methodists were accused simultaneously of being puritanical precisians and orgiasts or devotees of witchcraft. So too they were attacked both as Levellers and as Jacobite exponents of authoritarian monarchy. The ironies of this situation were nice. The 'papistical Methodists' were victims of several murderous attacks by Irish Catholics who feared them as ultra-Protestants. The allegedly crypto-Jacobite Methodists were the *bêtes noires* of some real Jacobites in England. There was probably an element of vestigial Jacobitism in the Wednesbury mobbers of 1743–4, for Staffordshire still had the reputation of being dangerously jacobite. Some of the leading rioters significantly wore oak-leaf badges.[2] In Norwich, the riot of 1752 appears to have had a more explicitly jacobite tinge, led by a local Hell-fire club who styled themselves 'Jemmy's men' and sang jacobite songs during their roisterings.[3] But such information, even if widely known, would probably not have deterred

[1] *Weekly History*, XXVI, 26 Sept 1741, p 4; *Journal of C. Wesley*, I, p 361.
[2] *Works*, XIII, p 170, some were also anti-Jacobites.
[3] *A True and Particular Narrative of the Disturbances and Outrages in the City of Norwich* (London 1752) p 27.

the active opponents of Methodism. It was a commonplace of English anti-Catholicism that Jesuitry was always cunning and protean enough to assume the most improbable of shapes and the most impenetrable of disguises. It was not at all remarkable that it should don the mask of the 'mechanick preacher'. In fact, as outsiders, adherents of a new sect that was both little known and yet highly organised, the Methodists were cast for the role of scapegoats, on whom could be poured the vague and half-formulated anxieties of their fellows.[1] They were whipping-boys for those who felt a compelling need to demonstrate in aggressive fashion their loyalty to traditional national values.

These political suspicions soon began to diminish. In the next great national crisis, that of 1778–82, they were barely visible, despite the upheaval of the Gordon Riots. During the anti-Jacobin hysteria of the 1790s Methodism aroused a great deal of official suspicion, but this was seldom translated at the local level into rioting. Where the movement pushed into new terrain it still encountered violence, but not on the scale of the 1740s and 1750s. In many once troubled places Methodism was soon tolerated and even welcomed. Parishes learned to live with the uneasy dyarchy of church and chapel, parson and preacher. Ignorance and suspicion faded as the new religionists became familiar parts of the ecclesiastical landscape and symbolised their permanency by the bricks and mortar of a chapel. It was one thing to mob strangers speaking in the open air, but it required far more daring to assault well-known neighbours in a licensed preaching-house. The anti-methodist mob had revealed itself as a transitory phenomenon born of cultural shock and destined to fade rapidly as fears abated, anger cooled and the new movement itself began to acquire the aura of respectability.

[1] Cf J. Higham, *Strangers in the Land. Patterns of American Nativism 1860–1925* (New Brunswick, N. J. 1955) for some interesting parallels.

EVANGELICALISM AND WORLDLINESS
1770–1870

by MICHAEL HENNELL

'PURE religion and undefiled before God and the Father is this, To visit the fatherless and widows in their affliction, and to keep himself unspotted from the world.'[1] The carrying out of this injunction has been interpreted differently in different ages. Professor Rupp reminded us in an early book that sixteenth-century Puritans and Protestants were not Victorian Christians in period costume.[2] Calvin and Knox would have been hounded by the Lord's Day Observance Society if their views on Sunday games had been known to Victorian evangelicals. During the years 1770–1870 there was an increasing strictness and rigidity with regard to 'the world'. First of all there was the question did the world belong to God or the devil. Most evangelicals in 1770 would have said that it belonged to God, but by Victorian times they were not so certain. Abner Brown, speaking of one parson's wife, says: 'When her fine manly boys came home for the holidays, she would not allow them to stand at the window of their father's parsonage without making them turn their backs so as not to look at the romantic views by which the house was encircled, lest the loveliness of "Satan's earth" should alienate their affections from the better world to come.'[3] On the other hand Lord Mount Temple when censured by friends for attending the Queen's fancy-dress ball replied: 'This is God's world by right, and not the devil's. Our business is to subdue it to its lawful king, and not to abandon it to the enemy.'[4] With regard to pleasures and amusements there was a growing strictness; I was able to give an example of this with regard to the Venn family in *John Venn and the Clapham Sect*.[5]

John Venn once received a letter from his friend, Edward Edwards, asking for advice as to whether he should allow his children to be taught

[1] Jas. 1: 27.
[2] E. G. Rupp, *Is This a Christian Country?* (London 1941) p 12.
[3] Abner Brown, *Simeon's Conversation Parties* (London 1863) p 73.
[4] G. W. E. Russell, *A Short History of the Evangelical Movement* (London 1915) p 132.
[5] [M. M.] Hennell [*John Venn and the Clapham Sect*] (London 1958) p 158.

dancing and to be allowed to attend parties. Here is John Venn's reply (his eldest child was fifteen):

Your question about the education of children is very important. With respect to parties, they never go to any where cards and dancing are introduced, neither do they learn to dance. About the latter point I have had some doubts, my father had me taught to dance Minuets and the dancing master of his own accord chose to add country dances. My sister has had her children taught and several of my religious friends, others have not. I do not condemn those that do, but, on the whole I think it right to lean on the safe side...I have seen so many instances of children of professors by indulgence in this respect, enter into the vanities of the world, that I am afraid of giving them any liberty beyond the bounds of strictest prudence. With respect to the children themselves I make them my friends in the case and frankly tell them these my views and my desires, to arm their minds beforehand and I hope I shall teach them to bear the reproach of singularity and imputation of folly.

The next generation were even stricter, and the problem of whether children were sent to dances just did not arise. John Venn's grandson writes of his own father, Henry Venn, secretary of the Church Missionary Society from 1841–72: 'He shared to the full the old-fashioned distrust and aversion to "worldly amusements". Theatres, novel-reading, dancing, cards, etc., were never, to the best of my recollection, named or denounced, but the understanding was none the less clear that such things were not for him or his.' He adds that there was only one novel in the house, *Quentin Durward*. 'How it had effected an entrance I cannot say.' The answer is simple, John Venn of Clapham ordered and read all Scott's novels as they appeared and recommended them at least to his daughters. *Quentin Durward* must have escaped the Victorian purge, or maybe one of Henry's sisters had the rest.

Handel's oratorios came under suspicion of early evangelicals because his music was played at Ranelagh and Vauxhall along with fireworks, fencing displays and masquerades. In 1784 there was a Handel Commemoration in Westminster Abbey. John Newton 'improved' the situation by preaching fifty sermons at St Mary Woolnoth based on the Bible passages used in the libretto of the *Messiah*. He did not denounce the commemoration as some other preachers did, but he made it clear that he disapproved of scripture as 'the subject of a musical entertainment'.[1] Fifty years later a correspondent in the *Record* criticised Bishop Ryder of Lichfield for allowing his name to appear as a Vice-President of the Birmingham Music Festival. The festival consisted of

---

[1] Bernard Martin, *John Newton* (London 1950) p 299.

oratorios including the *Messiah* and ended with a fancy-dress ball. After some hesitation the editor published the letter and supported the writer in the ensuing correspondence. Those who took the opposite point of view held that oratorios were not positively sinful, that Joseph Milner, though not musical, had attended a music festival 'to show that a Christian was not debarred from this source of recreation', and an unnecessary slur was being cast on a godly evangelical bishop. The editor maintained that oratorios were positively sinful, that Christians should not listen to sacred music sung by opera singers of uneasy virtue; he, of course, respected the character of Bishop Ryder, but he doubted the authenticity of the Milner story, adding: 'If we are right in following John Newton, Legh Richmond, and we believe the great mass of real Christians of the present day, in considering Musical Festivals an awful and impious desecration of holy things by a giddy and perishing world, we are bound in duty to make the statement with all distinctness and faithfulness.'[1] But the argument did not end there, from the other side came:

I thank not a man to say at such a time, the person who sings is an adulterer, and he who plays a drunkard; upon them be their sins. I know and I desire to know nothing of them. I came not here to scrutinise, far less to patronise the characters of the performers. Their relation to me is simply that of an organ pipe and I lose almost all perception of their existence, while my mind is borne upwards upon the wings of heavenly music and heavenly love. The art is the Lord's and the praise is his.[2]

But this is unlikely to have been the majority view; Thomas Moseley, Rector of Birmingham and eleven dissenting ministers, including John Angel James, questioned the rightness of the Oratorios and wanted money for the General Hospital raised by direct appeal. On 9 October the *Record* reported that at the first day of the Festival the bishops of Rochester and Worcester were present 'but not, we are happy to observe, the bishop of Lichfield'.

With the theatre itself there was no compromise. On 7 March 1839 the *Record* made this comment on the closure of two large theatres on Wednesdays and Fridays in Lent:

For ourselves we could wish that the Queen and the Government of a professedly Christian country had nothing to do with such schools of profligacy as theatres. We could wish them shut altogether; and we have no sympathy with the religious or moral feelings of those who will not go to the theatre in Lent,

[1] *R[ecord]* (London, 15 September 1834).   [2] *R* (2 October 1834).

but who will go to it after Lent; who will not go on Wednesdays and Fridays but will take their wives and daughters on Thursdays and Saturdays to see a strumpet crowned with garlands and cheered to the echo by a demoralised multitude, because she has a pretty face, or a good voice, or captivates the fancy or admiration of the town.[1]

In 1839 the Theatre Royal in Cheltenham was burnt down. Francis Close's fulminations against the stage and his influence were so extensive that it was not rebuilt. Charades were considered harmless for children but not for clergy, as can be seen from this comment from a letter in the *Record*:

I should be sorry indeed to interfere with the innocent recreations of children *when they are left to themselves*, but I confess, that for a clergyman to be seen at one time standing at the altar, in the reading desk, or in the pulpit, speaking as a dying man to dying sinners, or administering the most solemn rites of religion, and on the next day to be seen enacting fictitious characters, assuming, perhaps, the gait of a buffoon, or, it may be of banditti, or some other criminal character, is, to my mind, nearly as inconsistent as appearing in a ballroom like one of your 'dancing clergy'.[2]

The *Record* counted and sometimes took names of clergy attending balls and hunts. The editor, writing of the Earl of March's coming-of-age ball, comments: 'On this hey-dey of giddy dissipation, we find the names of fifty-one clergymen given by the *Chronicle* as present.'[3] In the same year, 1839, eleven clergy had their names taken for attending a ball at Yoxford and a Suffolk clergyman who suggested that offending clergy at a Saxmundham ball should have been remonstrated 'privately and individually', was told 'no terms ought to be kept with these men who thus knowingly, in opposition to God's word, make their brethren to offend by their conformity to the world.'[4] The *Record* discovered from the *Dorset County Chronicle* that four clergy had taken part in a fashionable hunt:

It is sufficiently deplorable to witness country gentlemen devoting the greater part of their time to the boisterous amusements of the hunting field, and the revelry with which it is almost uniformly associated, but to see a clergyman booted and spurred with a jockey's cap and hunting coat turned up with black to denote the gravity of his vocation, to see him hallooing on the hounds and panting to be in at the death; to see him afterwards taking his place at the jovial board, to discuss over the brimming goblet the comparative merits of horses and dogs, or to participate in conversation more grovelling and debasing! But

[1] R (7 March 1839).   [2] R (21 January 1839).
[3] R (7 March 1839).   [4] R (24 January 1839).

we can pursue the subject no further – surely it becomes our ecclesiastical rulers to arouse themselves and put an end to these discreditable proceedings.[1]

Occasionally the other side is heard. On 27 September 1830 a correspondent, signing himself 'NEITHER DANCER NOR SPORTSMAN' wrote 'There may be vanity in a Bible Society, as well as humility in a ball-room.'[2] Dickens was not alone in seeing that the platform of a May Meeting could be turned into a stage.

By the 1830s the novel had come under the ban. The *Record* drew attention to Scott's popularity and significance at the time of his death in 1832, 'But, alas, we cannot look upon the Waverley novels with the feelings of approbation which are so universally entertained. On the contrary, we consider their scope and tendency as being within the highest degree injurious, eminently calculated to lead away the most powerful and cause men to set their affections on the things of the earth'.[3] In 1838 the evangelical world was distressed to discover from the biography of Wilberforce by his sons, that the evangelical saint read Shakespeare, Scott and Bulwer. One correspondent, signing himself 'FLAG OF DISTRESS' feared that Wilberforce's example would encourage parents to allow their children to read fiction, 'Who can calculate how many salutary impressions are effaced by novel-reading? The opportunities that retirement affords for reflection are lost, the subject that sermons afford for meditation are forgotten through novel-reading. A chain of connexion is by this means preserved with the world when at the greatest distance from it, and a relish is preserved for worldly intercourse when again restored to it.[4]

Smoking on the other hand does not seem to have been regarded as 'worldly' till the later part of the period; John Newton smoked a churchwarden pipe; Sir James Stephen, according to his son Leslie, 'once smoked a cigar, and found it so delicious that he never smoked again'.[5] The virtues of temperance and total abstinence were also late in being recognised as essential to the unworldly Christian. The British and Foreign Temperance Society, of which Blomfield was president and J. B. Sumner one of the vice-presidents, was not founded till 1831 and was directed against spirit drinking. Sir Thomas Fowell Buxton, Wilberforce's successor as the leading abolitionist, was a brewer. On the whole 'teetotalism' was disliked because of its emphasis on good works and, according to Brian Harrison, because of its working-class

---

[1] R (23 April 1832).   [2] R (27 September 1830).
[3] R (27 September 1832).   [4] R (5 July 1838).
[5] Leslie Stephen, *Life of Sir James Fitzjames Stephen* (London 1895) p 61.

radical support.[1] The Temperance Society came to an end in 1850 but three years later the United Kingdom Alliance was formed to work for prohibition and the Church of England Temperance Society came into being in 1862. By the sixties temperance had attained respectability under the motley leadership of Dean Close, Frederick Temple and Henry Manning. An early exception was Spencer Thornton who formed the Wendover branch of the Church of England Total Abstinence Society as early as 1841. 'We recommend the intemperate to join as their only safeguard; – the temperate, as an example and encouragement to others.'[2]

Though the Lord's Day Observance Society was not founded till 1831, evangelical sabbatarianism remained inflexible during the whole period. Henry Venn persuaded several shop-keepers at Huddersfield to accept Sunday closing and 'Venn people' patrolled the streets to see that all was quiet and to urge those they met to go to church.[3] Close at Cheltenham persuaded 500 shopkeepers not to open on Sundays; in the town as a whole only a few general shops refused to come into line. In 1809 the evangelical prime minister, Spencer Perceval, ceased to call parliament on Mondays so that members should not have to travel on the sabbath.[4] Melbourne and Peel were censured by the *Record* for holding Sunday cabinet meetings; the former was praised when he abandoned the practice in 1839. Young Queen Victoria was from the outset criticised for her failure in the matter of Sunday observance. On 21 June 1838 the *Record* complained: 'We have anew to repeat our deep regrets that Her Majesty is so ill-advised as to set so evil an example to her loyal subjects. The Opera till the morning of the Lord's Day. In the morning attendance at public worship. And in the afternoon Her Majesty presenting herself to the nation as the leader of that worldly show and vanity which the parks exhibit on the Sabbath.'[5]

Columns of letters and leading articles in the *Record* protest against Sunday opening of parks, the zoological gardens and museums. In 1838 there was a proposal to build a race-course and hippodrome at Notting Hill. Lord Teignmouth, a leading evangelical, was taken to task by the *Record* for making the alternative suggestion of purchasing Primrose Hill 'for purposes of public recreation, to be open free on Sundays and on weekdays for harmless games, such as cricket'.[6] In Parliament Sir

[1] Brian Harrison, 'Religion and Recreation in Nineteenth Century England', *PP*, xxxviii (1967) p 100.
[2] W. R. Freemantle, *Memoir of Spencer Thornton* (London 1850) p 101.
[3] Hennell, p 23.   [4] Asa Briggs, *The Age of Improvement* (London 1959) p 173.
[5] *R* (21 June 1838).   [6] *R* (23 April 1838).

Andrew Agnew and Mr J. P. Plumptre, both prominent on May Meeting platforms, constantly pressed for the suppression of Sunday train services, Sunday postal transmission and Sunday trade and business. In 1840 the Birmingham and Bristol railway was built through Cheltenham, but owing to Close's influence, none but two mail trains stopped at Cheltenham Station for six years. 'In Edinburgh Close was hailed as the Church of England cleric who had secured the best observance of the Sabbath outside Scotland.'[1]

In 1838 Edward Monro, an early Tractarian incumbent protested in the *Record* against Sunday excursions to Harrow Weald which disturbed church services and prevented railway employees from attending them.[2]

In 1838 Plumptre introduced a bill attempting to forbid 'trade and business' taking place on Sundays; this applied to coachmen, guards, ostlers, turnpike gatekeepers, waiters in inns, clubhouses and reading rooms, pastrycooks, hair-dressers, canalmen and sailors. The *Globe* commented that 'a policeman' would have to be 'planted at every house to see that the people obey' and added, 'If Plumptre will bring in a Bill that the National Gallery should be open on Sundays, and the galleries of the British Museum, and any other places where harmless amusements may be found, and higher tastes acquired, he will do more good than twenty restrictive Sabbath Bills.'[3]

The motives for Sunday observance were mixed; in part at least there was a genuine desire to gain for the worker a six day week, but there was also the stronger motive to prevent sabbath desecration. A Worcester clergyman writes of a bargee being summoned to work at 6 a.m. on a Sunday; he did so for four or five hours with a bad conscience, 'he knew it was not a right thing'. At 3 p.m. he was summoned again, but refused to work and was sacked. He had a wife and three children. The clergyman does not mention what he did for the man but his letter speaks of 'Sabbath desecration of our rivers and canals'.[4] Another letter tells of a gale on the Mersey, 'attended with much loss of life and property... on Sunday, the 6th instant, not a vessel belonging to the Mersey and Navigation was injured; the men, resting on the Sabbath day, according to the commandment, were in safety'.[5] The evangelical middle class were not beyond exploiting the evangelical domestic servant as this extract from an advertisement in the *Record* for a coach-

[1] G. Berwick, 'Close of Cheltenham: Parish Pope', *Theology*, XXXIX (London 1939) p 194.
[2] *R* (14 February 1839).   [3] Quoted *R* (2 July 1838).
[4] *R* (5 April 1838).   [5] *R* (27 January 1837).

man shows: 'High wages not given. A person who values Christian privileges will be much preferred.'[1] Presumably he would be allowed to attend church and family prayers.

After 1870 the gulf between the evangelical and the world became even greater, at least where Keswick piety and perfectionism insisted on withdrawal from political and social action and cultural activity.

[1] *R* (5th February 1835).

THE RELIGION OF THE PEOPLE AND THE PROBLEM OF CONTROL, 1790–1830

by W. R. WARD (*Presidential Address*)

THE generation about which I wish to speak was, I make no doubt, the most important single generation in the modern history not merely of English religion but of the whole Christian world. For despite the holy water sprinkled by the late Dean Sykes and his pupils, there seems no doubt that the effectiveness of the Church throughout Western Europe was undermined by the same forces which were everywhere sapping the *Ancien Régime*, the whole institutional complex of which the religious establishments were part. The great crisis of the French Revolution altered for ever the terms on which religious establishments must work, and in so doing it intensified everywhere a long-felt need for private action in the world of religion. It also brought out how the balance of institutions varied from one society to another. In Germany the Protestant establishments were able to absorb evangelicalism and though they could not assimilate Roman Catholic minorities, they had rendered them by 1918 as unable to manage rationally without a Protestant establishment as the Protestants themselves. In England the legal dependence of the Church upon the state disguised a real dependence of a weak state upon networks of informal influence including those of the Church. The English state had been too weak to put down dissent, too weak to allow its clergy to play at politics in their Convocation, too weak to plant the Anglican establishment in the American colonies. In the mid-nineties a Church entirely unequipped to meet the repercussions of the revolutionary crisis in France, had to face its moment of truth with no better state backing than the episcopalians of colonial America, not because, as bewildered clergy perpetually insisted, there was a peculiar perfidy in Tory politicians, but because there was no German-style concentration of power on which they could draw. As a working establishment the Church of England collapsed even more quickly than that of France, its fate epitomised by a great non-event, whose importance has been notably unsung by historians, the failure of government to put down itinerant

237

preaching and Sunday schools by a restriction of the Toleration Act in 1799 and 1800. Till 1870 the state owed some obligations to the Church, but already gave public notice that it could not save the day for it. In America the experience of colonial revolt had turned the sects into an informal religious establishment; the forces of public order being so much weaker and society so much more expansive even than in England, the Americans had to drive the machinery for reconstituting religious society much harder than it was ever driven by the English. But elasticity gave the American informal establishment an absorptive power greater even than the formal establishments of Germany. Methodism and the benevolent system, episcopalianism, and eventually even Roman Catholicism, were taken on board and made vehicles of American nationalism.

The problem of control in England therefore, turned upon a unique social balance; the English Church faced the new forces of the age with neither the institutional power of the German *Landeskirchen* nor the dynamism of the American churches. Concurrent endowment of different religious bodies was one of the great non-starters of the century; equally the supplanting of the formal establishment by an informal *Volkskirche* was one of its unrealised dreams. England failed to secure either a formal or informal establishment of real effectiveness. In the first decade of the century with the dismemberment of the old establishments proceeding apace, the prospect of a popular evangelical church seemed a real one. Since the mid-1790s the two growing points of the church order, the itinerancy and the Sunday schools, had undergone a remarkable development upon an undenominational basis, and if the Anglicans had dropped out of the one and were being rapidly displaced by popular pressure from the other, there were new reinforcements in an undenominational press and that great battery of Bible, Tract and Missionary Societies which formed a pattern of Christian progress all the way from Basel to New York. The sudden weakening of traditional communal indoctrination seemed to clear the decks for associational activity of all kinds. This seemed the way to Christianise the people, and also to create new networks of informal influence which English public institutions evidently needed. The substance of this new religion of the people as proclaimed in the prospectuses of the reviews and the trust deeds of a host of Sunday schools was the XXXIX Articles of the Church itself, and it was to prove that social tension like that which in the mid-1790s had caused the Church to cut adrift from the new movements, was to break up much of the associational mechanism, and change its frame of mind. Denominational loyalties came increasingly to be pressed as a counterpoise to class antagonism within the ranks, and while anathematising the out-groups had its uses in keeping the in-groups together, it converted a social conflict into that denominational contest which formed the main substance of the politics of the 'thirties and 'forties.

In the space of one paper, I can examine this process in one community only, the Wesleyan Methodists, and for only the first twenty years of the nineteenth century. Both community and date are, however, important, for not only were the Wesleyans the fastest growing of the evangelical communities, but their connexional constitution forced up their tensions into open and central conflict more readily than among the independents. Moreover it was in the first decade of the century and not, as the books sometimes say, in the years following the Tractarian débacle, that the Wesleyans aspired to become an informal Protestant establishment and felt assured that neither states[1] nor individuals which stood in their way would come to any good. Yet three successive and related challenges, religious, social and administrative, exposed their Achilles heel and set the problem of control within Methodism itself.

The first challenge came from revivalism, or as it is convenient to call it in an English context, from Ranterism. There is no need to repeat the oft-told tale of the Conference declaration against camp-meetings in 1807, and of the formation of the Primitive Methodist Connexion in which revivalism was in a measure institutionalised. But it is important to see why Conference acted as it did. For the doings on Mow Cop had no political significance; 1807 was a year of low social tension; and it was in any case the regular itinerancy which was under political fire at that moment. The truth is that Ranterism had a considerable pre-history both in the country and more recently in the great Northern towns.

For Ranterism challenged Wesleyanism hard where it teetered between form and formalism. Wesleyans had a firmly articulated schema of the Christian life, beginning with conviction of sin and finding liberty and working up to entire sanctification, which had its own imaginative appeal. It enabled the believer to judge his progress experimentally, and guided the Class-leaders through the official system of spiritual inquisition. Everyone understood its merits but there was no official recognition of its limitations, or of the signs, already

[1] R. Reece, *A compendious martyrology, containing an account of the sufferings and constancy of Christians in the different persecutions which have raged against them under pagan and popish governments* (London 1812–15) I, pp iii–iv

discernible, that the thing was becoming a bore. There was the same formalism about Wesleyan preaching. At the bottom were the exhorters. The exhortation consisted of reproving sin, pleading with the sinner to flee from the wrath to come, describing the speaker's own experience in these matters, and testifying to his present joy. The framework of the exhortation appears to have been rigid, held together by these topics, the main scope for individuality lying in the personal testimony. The distinction between exhorters and preachers, whether itinerant or local, lay in 'taking a text'. This was a public declaration that the speaker had ceased to 'exhort', and also that he accepted a new restraint, that of dealing with the specific doctrines brought out by his 'texts'.[1] John Phillips of Osset wrote: 'The doctrines I preach are, the fall of man, repentance towards God, faith in our Lord Jesus Christ, and the holiness without which no man can see the Lord.' In 1802 Joseph Entwisle emphasised that 'the Head of the Church has put great honor upon a few *leading truths* by wch. Methodist sermons are characterised, and a man need never lose sight of them for the sake of variety'.[2] The undertaking to preach 'our doctrines' still required regularly of Methodist itinerants, began with this technical sense, and applied to all those who had completed their apprenticeship as exhorters. One can feel the sense of relief when Hugh Bourne resolved to take his collier friends for a day's 'praying and shouting' on Mow Cop.

This system of instruction and control had little hope of containing a society as dynamic as that which was developing in the great towns, and even in the countryside the 1790's had shown that the crucial breakthrough was being made less by exhorting, preaching or class-leading, than by cottage prayer-meetings led by entirely unofficial persons. They exploited the new social solidarity of the lower orders in the villages, to enter private houses, and in prayer to incorporate their neighbours into the circle of the faithful.[3] It was characteristic that William Clowes, the great Primitive, was an unusually impressive man in prayer, even in silent prayer. Even in his Wesleyan days, he spared his class the official inquisition, and humanely encouraged their initiative in religious exercises of which they were capable.[4]

[1] Margaret Batty, Contribution of local preachers to the life of the Wesleyan Methodist Church until 1932, and to the Methodist Church after 1932 in England (Leeds MA thesis 1969) pp 39–40.
[2] M[ethodist] C[hurch] A[rchives] MSS. Joseph Entwisle to Joseph Benson, 21 June 1802.
[3] Despite confusion of terminology this is evidently what is referred to in a *Report from the clergy of a district in the diocese of Lincoln* (London 1800) pp 11–12.
[4] *The Journals of William Clowes* (London 1844) p 59.

The class rapidly increased until the house became so full, that there was hardly room to kneel. In leading my classes I used to get from six to ten to pray a minute or two each, and thus to get the whole up into the faith; then I found it a very easy matter to lead thirty or forty members in an hour and a quarter for I found that leading did not consist so much in talking to the members as in getting into the faith, and bringing down the cloud of God's glory, that the people might be truly blessed in their souls as well as instructed in divine things.

Of course (as he ingenuously reports) souls were converted in every room in the house, even in the larder.

Moreover a far-reaching process not only of political but of spiritual education was going on among working-men. Half the interest of the journals of Bourne and Clowes lies in the light they cast upon the progress of humble men for whom adherence to the Establishment was out of the question and official Wesleyanism offered no way forward. One day Bourne was struck down at one of those country corners where the saints so often wrestled with God or with Satan.[1]

Coming home at the praying place in Mr Heath's fields, I felt as if I was held by an irresistible power, and I sank down into nothing before it, and everything that I did was contrary to God. I felt it die away – I gave myself up to God. Immediately came 'the spirit of burning', and I was made 'a habitation of God through the Spirit.' I wondered at myself; I could scarcely believe what the Spirit witnessed.

But it was not all immediacy, for the men from the Potteries were in touch not only with American revivalists but with James Crawfoot and the Magic Methodists of Delamere Forest, who specialised in visions; with Peter Philips, a chair-maker of Warrington, who led the Quaker Methodists of that place into contact with the spirituality of the Society of Friends; with James Sigston, a school-master notorious in the annals of Leeds Methodism. The bizarre visions of pious women in their circle, establishing the celestial pecking-order of the prophets and seers of Cheshire and North Staffordshire,[2] reveal a lively awareness of a range of spiritual possibilities far beyond the Wesleyan discipline.

Then there was exorcism. Anglicans reproached Wesleyans with it, and Wesleyans the Ranters.[3] There is no doubt that exorcism went on in orthodox Methodism, but the Ranters did not blush to provide a service which was evidently in lively popular demand. As a young

---

[1] J. T. Wilkinson, *Hugh Bourne 1772–1852* (London 1952) p 42.

[2] Hartley-Victoria College, Manchester, MS Journals of Hugh Bourne F fol 131.

[3] *Ibid*, fol 121. The charge here was that they were actually *in* witchcraft.

man, Clowes could defeat though not destroy the notorious Kidsgrove bogget,[1] and by 1810 he and Bourne were grappling with a spirit world almost Methodistically organised.[2]

I visited Clowes [writes Bourne]. He has been terribly troubled by the woman we saw at Ramser. I believe she will prove to be a witch. These are the head labourers under Satan, like as the fathers are the head labourers under Jesus Christ. So we are fully engaged in the battle. These, I believe, cannot hurt Christ's little ones till the[y] have first combated the fathers. It appears that they have been engaged against James Crawfoot ever since he had a terrible time praying with and for a woman who was in witchcraft. For the witches throughout the world all meet and have connection with the power devil... Well the Lord is strong and we shall soon, I believe, have to cope with the chief powers of Hell...I am certain the Lord will give us the victory.

Revival was a rural phenomenon all the way from Pomerania and Swabia to Lincolnshire and Kentucky, but its progress might be speeded in areas where industrial employment replaced landlordism by forms of economic dependence not organised on a parochial basis.[3] This was especially the case where the extractive industries, mining, quarrying and fishing, created a close cohesion of their own, whether in Siegerland, Cornwall or County Durham, but it happened also where the putting-out system in the textile industries altered the character of the whole countrysides as in Wuppertal, parts of the Black Forest, the North Midlands or the West Riding. But the brakes rarely came off more suddenly than they did now for rural immigrants to the northern industrial towns, and amongst them came a series of outbreaks of Ranterism and clashes with the Wesleyan preachers. Here especially religious antagonism was sharpened by social conflict. The uninstitutional movements of God's grace so dear to the revivalists, evoked a powerful echo in men who were at the losing end of institutions and chilled the marrow of those with a stake in institutional stability. There were always men of substance who dabbled in revivalism, but everyone knew that men's leanings one way or the other were deeply coloured by their social standing.[4] Already there was little love lost between the revivalists and the little knot of wealthy intermarried Woods, Marsdens and Burtons with whom Bunting, the future architect of early Victorian Methodism, allied himself, and who maintained a cross bench position

---

[1] Clowes, *Journals*, pp 43–4.
[2] Hartley-Victoria College, Manchester, MS Journals of Hugh Bourne E fol 299.
[3] Cf R. A. Ingram, *The causes of the increase of Methodism and dissension* (London 1807) pp 85–6.
[4] T. P. Bunting, *The Life of Jabez Bunting* (London 1859–87) I, p 115.

between Methodism and the Church, with brothers in the ministry of each.

With the turn of the century the revivalists began to claim the same rights of private edification amongst Wesleyans as the latter had claimed in the Church. Separate places of worship began to go up, and secessions began in Preston, Stockport, and Macclesfield; in Leeds James Sigston and 300 of his friends were expelled and set up as the 'Kirkgate Screamers'.[1] The reactions of the Wesleyan preachers are vividly illustrated in the surviving correspondence about the Macclesfield men who published their rules as Christian Revivalists in 1803. The superintendent minister Joseph Entwisle, was a wise and kindly man whose 'simple and unaffected devotion'[2] was acknowledged far outside the connexion. He took a generally hopeful view of the circuit and ascribed its admittedly flat state partly to factory work which kept people much too late to attend weeknight meetings, and partly to the fact that the secession of the revivalists had evoked rather too much conservative backlash among 'the leading friends'.[3] But the junior preacher, Jabez Bunting, already regarded in the third year of his ministry as a preaching and organising prodigy, saw the whole matter in black-and-white terms.[4]

The people in this town are tired of parties and divisions: & in general equally of the rant & extravagancies of what is called Revivalism...Divisions *from* the church, though awful, are perhaps after all less to be dreaded than divisions *in* the church...Revivalism, as of late professed & practised was [likely if] not checked, to have gradually ruined genuine Methodism. [I a]m glad, however, that they have been the first to draw the sword. But as they have drawn it, I earnestly wish that our preachers would take the opportunity of returning fully to the spirit & discipline of ancient Methodism, & with that resolve to stand or fall. The temporary loss of numbers would probably be more than recompensed by the increase of real scriptural piety, the restoration of good order & the establishment of brotherly love.

Bunting's doctrinaire conviction that he was possessed of the Wesleyan tradition in some sense in which his elders who had travelled with the great man were not, was ominous for the future of Methodism. For the next generation the older men were generally more liberal than Bunting's young hard-liners, and in 1806 the conjunction of his appoint-

---

[1] Leeds Central Library, John [should be Thomas] Wray's MS. History of Methodism in Leeds, x, fols 145–7.
[2] J. Nightingale, *Portraiture of Methodism* (London 1807) p 266.
[3] MCA MSS. Joseph Entwisle to George Marsden, 30 November 1802
[4] MCA MSS. Jabez Bunting to Richard Reece, 15 July 1803 (copy). Cf same to same, 11 June 18[03]: same to George Marsden, 10 June 1803.

ment to Manchester with a serious recession brought about a resounding rupture with the Band Room Methodists there. It was in hard times when the appeal of Methodism flagged that the revivalists were most tempted to go it alone and were most irked by the luxury as well as the formalism of the Methodist upper-crust. The Manchester preachers admitted privately to have been looking for 'the annihilation of the party',[1] and Bunting was not the man to let the opportunity slip.

Revivalism then threatened not merely the peace of congregations but the forms of Wesleyan spirituality and instruction. But what moved Conference ultimately against camp-meetings was not the fissiparousness of revivalism, but its capacity for union. In 1805 the first conference of Independent Methodists was held in Manchester, uniting the revivalists not merely of the Band Room, but of Oldham, Warrington, Stockport and Macclesfield as well. The Primitive Methodist connexion was another unpremeditated union of revivalists,[2] who had begun and remained in close touch with the Independents, but who obtained great expansiveness by a degree of connexionalism and a paid, though poorly paid, ministry which picked up much of that rural ranterism which had been spreading since the mid-1790s. They profited also from that more general unspiky, undenominational evangelicalism propagated at the same time. Baptist Chapels, Independent, New Connexion, even Wesleyan chapels were opened to them, and Union chapels the very cataloguing of which has not yet begun admitted them to their cycle. Though on a small scale, these coalitions created the impression, later more actively canvassed in America than in England, that revivalism rather than denominationalism was the fundamental antidote to the tensions of church and society.

That this was not quite true was one of the lessons of the last great wave of urban revival which the preachers had to face. In 1816 Methodism seemed again on the flood-tide, especially in the towns of the north-west, of Derbyshire, and about Leeds.[3] But before long it was reported from York that while 400 new members 'of the lowest order' had been added, the pews were unlet as the chapel respectability were driven away to the Independents.[4] Social tension had already passed the

---

[1] MCA MSS. W. Jenkins to Jabez Bunting, 29 January 1806.

[2] Clowes, *Journals*, pp 94–5.

[3] MCA MSS. J. Barber to George Marsden, 7 February 1816. J. Braithwaite to B. Slater, 10 September 1816; W. Leach to Jabez Bunting, 20 January 1816; James Nichols to Jabez Bunting, 8 February 1816; R. Wood to Jabez Bunting, 9 March 1816; M. Wilson to Jabez Bunting, 17 March 1816: Hartley Victoria College, Manchester, James Everett's MS, Memoranda Book I, fol 219.

[4] MCA MSS. Miles Martindale to Jabez Bunting, 9 July 1816.

point at which it could be sublimated in religious revival, and as events slid toward Peterloo even Bunting's much-prized unity of the church was put at hazard.

Cornwall, however, was a different story. Here the modest liberty of tinner and fisherman, the cohesiveness of village life, the indifference of the Cornish to the politics of parliament or class, made spontaneous revival possible right into the 1830s, while the unpopularity of the Cornish Church left no obvious alternative to Methodism for the more substantial classes. Revival broke out at Redruth in 1814 in a staggering meeting which would not break up for nine successive days and nights. We read that[1]

hundreds were crying for mercy at once. Some remained in great distress of soul for one hour, some for 2, some 6, some 9, 12, and some for 15 hours before the Lord spoke peace to their souls – then they wd. rise, extend their arms, & proclaim the wonderful works of God, with such energy, that bystanders wd. be struck in a moment, & fall to the ground & roar for the disquietude of their souls.

Events of this kind continued till 1819, and broke out again in the 'thirties.

The Cornish revival was far too explosive for the Methodist machine. The official system of collecting weekly class-monies which worked properly hardly anywhere, was here almost inoperative. Circuits made shift according to their lights, and poverty led them to keep down their ministerial staff to the lowest practicable level.[2] The Cornish local preachers never quite amassed the power of those of the Isle of Man who established themselves as an unofficial Manx Conference,[3] but they seem to have gathered huge classes during the revival and kept them under permanent oversight as class-leaders. The double hold of converting power and pastoral leadership gave them an ascendancy which did not bend easily to preachers' pressure. The hazards were aggravated by poverty, for it was no sacrifice to a Cornish artisan to grasp professional status by taking a class of a hundred into separation, and living humbly as a preacher on their offerings.[4] But poverty also protected Cornwall from much in English Methodism, and in the 'thirties

---

[1] MCA Tyerman MSS III, fol 355. Another account of the same events by the same writer was reprinted in the *Monthly Repository*, 1814, pp 377–8 from a flysheet published at York.

[2] MCA MSS. James Blackett to Jabez Bunting, 12 September 1828; W. Dale to same, 15 July 1842; same to same, 12 July 1839.

[3] MCA MSS. John Mercer to Jabez Bunting, 14 March 1820.

[4] MCA MSS. John Baker to Jabez Bunting, 16 June 1834.

Bunting's streamlined schemes for levies per head of members in districts, seemed impossible even to ministers hottest for standard connexional practices.

Fed by reports from Cornish preachers of irregular ways, and even by demands that the President or Secretary of Conference should annually attend the Cornish District Meeting to keep things in order,[1] Bunting regarded the Cornish as 'the *mob of Methodism*, they have always been rude and refractory'.[2] Yet this judgement was to miss the main point which emerges from a splendid series of preachers' reports. George Russell who had been unbearably irked by my own forbears among the impudent Derbyshire Ranters whose religion, he declared, bore 'a near resemblance to the religion of old Nick',[3] took a cool and not unfavourable view of the Cornish revival at Helston in 1814. He perceived that the Cornish people, under native impulses, were making Methodism a popular establishment, a *Volkskirche*, without parallel in any comparable area in England.[4] Cornish society was free and disorderly, and so was Cornish Methodism. But if it could not yet be overtaken by *episkope* as officially understood, it had the strength arising from popular community observance, and hence a freedom from the quirks to which English revivalists were subject. Too much has been made of the excitements aroused by Dr Warren in 1835 and Wesleyan Reform in 1849. What finally undid Cornish Methodism was not liberty but the erosion of Cornish separateness by more powerful forces from across the Tamar. Of these, Buntingism and its Methodist rivals were only the foretaste.

The Wesleyan preachers' feud with the revivalists was soon overshadowed by the second great challenge, that of convulsive social discontent. In 1810 Daniel Isaac was risking life and limb in desperate opposition to trade unionism on the North Eastern coal-field,[5] and in the following year the Luddite movement in Yorkshire and Lancashire severely tested the cohesion of the body. In the 1790s the Methodist flock had been so much on one side of the social divide as to leave the preachers no real option but to follow them and turn against the propertied trustees who clung to the Church. Now as the preachers wept for the great Methodist Burton family who brought up the cannon to defend their print works at Rhodes, and mowed down the

[1] MCA MSS. W. Dale to Jabez Bunting, 15 July 1842.
[2] T. Shaw, *A history of Cornish Methodism* (Truro 1967) p 81.
[3] MCA Tyerman MSS, I, fols 358–9. [4] *Ibid*, I, fols 362–3.
[5] MCA MS. Copy of a circular sent by Mr Isaac to the Superintendents of circuits. December 1816.

hands to whom they were said to be so kind,[1] it was clear not only that Methodists stood on both sides of the social conflict but that forces within the connexion were differently aligned. There were ecclesiastical as well as political inducements for the conservative stance of the Old Connexion preachers; for it brought back magnates from the New Connexion, frightened, it was reported, by 'the connivance of some of their preachers and other official persons at the Luddite system and practices'. Even the Old Chapel at Huddersfield which the Kilhamites had carried off in 1797 was believed to be ripe for the picking.[2]

In 1812 Bunting was stationed at Halifax in the heart of the West Riding troubles. So firm was he with the Luddites that for months on end he could not go out at night alone. Late in January 1813, 17 Luddites were hanged at York, 6 of them sons of Methodists, and Bunting commented privately:[3]

However solicitous to make the best of this, it is after all an *awful* fact – and it confirms me in my fixed opinion, that the progress of Methodism in the West Riding of Yorkshire has been more swift than solid; more extensive than deep, more in the increase of numbers, than in diffusion of that kind of piety which shines as brightly & operates as visibly *at home* as in the prayer meeting and the crowded love feast. I read of no people, professing serious religion, who have not as a body far outstripped us in that branch of practical godliness, which consists in the moral management & discipline of children.

The Methodist tub, in short, could no longer contain the torrent of anti-establishment sentiment: what was needed was less revival and more denominational drill, and in particular, one of Bunting's current nostrums, the control of Sunday schools.

The post-war crisis was, however, very much worse. A dramatic fall in prices made every social adjustment more painful, and in Methodism as elsewhere the hackles rose unbearably. In 1815 Bunting concluded that Manchester 'must have a firm Superintendent'.[4] At Peterloo they had John Stephens, a former Cornish tin-miner, and a man of 'morbid disposition' but of stern action when roused. His junior preacher, the famous Thomas Jackson, was required to patrol the streets at night keeping order, supported as he recalled by 'a noble band of men', the flower of the Manchester Methodist plutocracy.[5] Stephens painfully enforced discipline in the Leaders' Meeting, in his first year removing

[1] MCA MSS. Joseph Entwisle to T. Stanley, 27 April 1812.
[2] MCA Thomas Allan MSS. J. Stamp to T. Allan, [19 June 1813].
[3] MCA MSS. Jabez Bunting to George Marsden, 28 January 1813.
[4] MCA MSS. Jabez Bunting to George Marsden, 24 June 1815.
[5] T. Jackson, *Recollections of my own life and times*, ed B. Frankland (London 1873) pp 171–9.

400 from the membership roll, and admonished them to go 'either to the New Connexion or the devil'.[1] He followed up the Peterloo clash by a sermon on Mark 14: 7, 'For ye have the poor with you always', explaining to the poor the advantages of this state of affairs, and proclaimed his intention to 'blow the sacred trumpet to call Jehovah's hosts to battle; and manfully unfurl the banners of his country, his Sovereign and his God'.[2] Stephens was genteelly but firmly supported by an address from the connexional Committee of Privileges.

On the other side the radical *Manchester Observer* mercilessly flayed the Wesleyans and their discipline,[3] and all over the north as desperate superintendents sought to cut the canker from the body, rumours mounted ever wilder about the confidential relations of the Methodist leadership with the government. Jacobins at Bolton claimed that Stephens had 'received a check for £10,000 for services done to Government, signed *Sidmouth*'.[4] Yorkshire radicals alleged that the connexion had 'lent the Government half a million of money to buy cannon to shoot them with'.[5] At Marple they made it a million.[6] The truth was more prosaic, but perhaps more discreditable; the upper crust were using the full Halévy doctrine that Methodism was saving society from revolution, to demand legislation making camp-meetings illegal while securing the indoor gatherings of Wesleyans.[7]

Of course, in the smaller textile towns where there were few men of substance for the preachers to call on, they could be desperately isolated. J. B. Holroyd, preacher at Haslingden in Rossendale, reported that two thirds of the population in his circuit were radicals, and there being no magistrate or chief constable, they were manufacturing pikes and drilling nightly.[8] Five 'marked kingsmen' were to be assassinated on the day of revolution, including the Anglican incumbent and himself.

---

[1] *Manchester Observer*, pp 894–5. Cf *A letter to the Rev. John Stephens occasioned by some recent transactions and occurrences in the Methodist Society in Manchester* (Manchester 1820).

[2] J. Stephens, *The mutual relations, claims and duties of the rich and poor* (Manchester 1819).

[3] For a case which has the ring of truth about it see, e.g. *Manchester Observer*, p 1000.

[4] MCA MSS. J. Hanwell to J. Everett, 15 October 1821. Cf J. Hebblewhite to J. Everett, 15 March 1820.   [5] MCA MSS. J. Edmondson to J. Crowther, 16 November 1819.

[6] MCA MSS. H. & S. Kellett to T. Ingham, 24 February 1820.

[7] PRO, H.O. 42.198 (1819) quoted in D. A. Gowland, Methodist secessions and social conflict in South Lancashire, 1830–57 (Manchester PhD thesis 1966) p 14; MCA MSS. J. Hebblewhite to J. Everett. 15 March 1820; Robert F. Wearmouth, *Methodism and the working-class movements of England 1800–1850* (London 1947) pp 145–6; MCA Thomas Allan MSS. Thomas Allan to John Eliot, to Rev. Mr. Collison, and to Lord Liverpool, all on 3 December 1819.

[8] MCA MSS. J. B. Holroyd to Jabez Bunting, 23 December 1819. Cf same to same, 26 January 1820. A similar letter to the first reached the Home Office. Wearmouth, *Methodism and working class movements*, pp 146–7.

One evening a few weeks since just as I came out of my own door to go into the chapel, the procession was just drawing up in front of the house. I did not judge it prudent to go through the crowd but stood inside the garden gate; they gave three of the most horrid groans I ever heard, and with each groan, a young man brandished a pike within a yard of my breast, accompanied with such dreadful oaths, enough to make one's blood run chill...It is with grief I say that our society is not free from the contagion. Some have left us this quarter...They do not think it right to give anything toward the support of those who encourage and pray for a number of tyrants...The above are not the sentiments of our leading friends in Haslingden, quite the reverse, but they can render the preachers no efficient support in opposing the general impetus ...[The previous Sunday he had been attacked by a group of office-holders about Castlereagh's Six Acts] when they told me in plain terms that [the] Methodist preachers were as bad as the Church ministers in supporting Government, but it was asked, Will Lord Castlereagh support you?

So far as camp-meetings went, the answer, fortunately, was that he would not.[1]

Holroyd here set out the basic pattern of the Methodist crises of the next generation, depicted in a thousand private letters; the great social division in the flock, with the poor and the radical on the one side, and the preacher in alliance with 'the leading friends' in the other, with calumny on one side opposed by church discipline on the other. The itinerant ministry which only yesterday had been a device for retrieving the lost from the highways and hedges, and compelling them to come in, was now being used as a social regulator in a way ruinous to the self-respect which had been one of Methodism's greatest gifts to many of her humble sons. The preachers did not need Bunting to tell them that Methodism hated democracy as it hated sin; recession and democracy killed their evangelistic appeal, and set the flock by the ears. Nor could the New Connexion and the sects which championed the radical cause capitalise the opportunity. A generation later the Chartists were to find that they had a hard core of leaders and organizers; a considerable and potentially stable body of the second rank who were prepared to play supporting parts and who enjoyed the fellowship of the movement; and a vast mass who were swept in and out of the movement in response to the trade cycle, and whom it was impossible to organise for long. In effect Bunting and his coadjutors were acknowledging that this was already true of Wesleyanism, and were welding the first two groups into a denomination at the cost, perhaps on a certain level of realism, the

[1] *Ibid*, p 168.

small cost, of writing off the third, that great mass which had poured into the Sunday schools and chapels since the mid-1790s.

For there was no lack of quite explicit *realpolitik* amongst the Methodist preachers.[1] One of their characteristics in the age of Bunting was an uncanny capacity to anticipate the manoeuvres of the big battalions, a shrewdness which in the 'forties proved intolerably irksome to men of strait principles. And already pastoral coarseness set in. By February 1821, John Stephens was monarch of all he surveyed, assured that the trade cycle would raise Manchester Methodism to more than its former glories.[2]

The objects we have kept in view are, 1st. to give the sound part of the society a decided ascendancy. 2. So to put down the opposition, as to disable them from doing mischief. 3. to cure those of them who are worth saving. 4. To take the rest one by one, and crush them when they notoriously commit themselves ...They are completely at our mercy...They are down and we intend to keep them down. That they are not annihilated is rather from want of will than power...Methodism stands high among the respectable people.

Even now there was a loss of 5000 members, 'such a blow', said Adam Clarke, 'as we never had since we were a people'.[3] What the preachers could not foresee was that Peterloo had for ever severed official Methodism from urban revivalism. No doubt Manchester would in time have exhibited the same metropolitan secularism as made London the graveyard of religious enthusiasm, but what actually happened was that the great flood-tide of 1816 and 1817 was suddenly terminated and never returned. As happened more broadly with the Wesleyan reform secessions of the 'fifties, the connexional machine could repair the membership losses, but could never evoke the old expansiveness. The years 1819–20 were the moment of truth for the Wesleyans, as the years 1792–3 had been for the Church; Wesleyanism was never going to be a popular urban religion.

The alliance of the preachers with the men of substance in the denomination was clinched by the third great challenge, the direct impact of the post-war economic difficulties upon the Methodist machine. Methodism now paid cruelly for the euphoria of the previous decade, when normally sober men had believed that it was about to subdue the world,

---

[1] E.g. 'The lower orders of society...unless led on by men of talent, wealth, and fame, can never overthrow any government possessed of even a moderate share of strength': J. Macdonald, *Memoirs of Rev. Joseph Benson* (London 1822) p 311.

[2] MCA MSS. J. Stephens to Jabez Bunting, 1 February 1821. Cf T. Jackson to same, 26 March 1821.

[3] James Everett, *Adam Clarke portrayed* (London 1843–9) III, pp 251–2.

and the hundreds of young preachers were called out on whose shoulders Bunting climbed to power. In these years the connexion came to resemble a modern cut-price motor insurance company tempted or deluded by a large cash flow into prodigal disregard of its future liabilities, and falling into a number of morally venial but financially ruinous mistakes of a basically actuarial kind. The Methodist system of paying not a stipend, but allowances for travelling and the maintenance of a house and family created an open-ended liability. The problem of ministerial allowances was taking shape before the end of the war, but the collapse of prices afterwards made the burden, and especially the continual increase of preachers' families seem intolerable. Seasoned preachers could see no way between bankruptcy and exhausting the patience of the flock.[1] Anxious statisticians throughout the connexion were betting on the fertility of the manse and astonishing proposals were made to dismiss preachers with large families, or to station them according to the ability of circuits to pay.[2] In 1819, the year of Peterloo, the candle seemed consumed at both ends. The intake of new preachers had to be restricted,[3] and the Legalised Fund, a kind of group-insurance scheme by which the preachers provided for their widows, and for the retirement of aged and disabled brethren, a fund which should have been bursting at the seams with the subscriptions of recent young recruits, could not meet its obligations.[4]

Everyone knew that the principal cause for the multiplication of preachers was the multiplication of chapels, and hence of pews to be let and mortgages to be serviced, for whatever the aspirations of Conference to be the living Wesley, it was not behaving as Wesley had behaved. In his lifetime, reported William Myles,[5]

there were never more than one third of the preachers married...And he would not let a chapel be built unless two thirds of the money was subscribed before a stone was laid, and it stated whether it would call for an additional preacher. Now near three fourths of the preachers are married, and chapels are

[1] MCA MSS. Joseph Entwisle to George Marsden, 2 March 1816.

[2] MCA MSS. R. Miller to R. Reece, 11 July 1816; W. Worth to Jabez Bunting, 23 January 1818; R. Miller to T. Blanchard, 13 March 1819; same to Jabez Bunting, 1 April 1819 (2 letters); Jabez Bunting to Samuel Taylor, 10 March 1814; Miles Martindale to Jabez Bunting, 9 July 1816. Eventually Conference fixed the number of children circuits should support in proportion to the membership and arranged for any surplus to be maintained by a connexional Children's Fund. MCA MSS. James Akerman to Jabez Bunting, 31 July 1821.

[3] Bunting, *Life of Bunting*, II, pp 162–3: MCA MSS. J. Edmondson to J. Crowther, 16 November 1819; J. W. Cloake to Jabez Bunting, 29 March 1820.

[4] MCA MSS. J. Sharp to Jabez Bunting, 20 April 1819.

[5] MCA MSS. W. Myles to Joseph Dutton, 3 June 1814.

built or purchased without, in some cases, one fifth of the money subscribed, and immediately a travelling preacher called out.

Every historian knows how the agricultural industry agonised to meet high wartime debts from low peace-time prices, but no industry was more heavily mortgaged than Methodism. What had been a running sore, became suddenly a disease of fatal proportions, and Conference's modest application of central control to future extensions in 1817 and 1818, could not lighten existing commitments.

I have discovered no trace that the preachers could analyse the economic roots of their difficulties; what vexed them was the loss of an impetus which they had fondly ascribed to sound doctrine and polity.

About five or six years ago [wrote Jonathan Crowther in 1817][1] our machine seemed to possess such incalculable force, that almost all things seemed to be possible to us, yea, even in temporal things... We are now arrived at a new crisis of our affairs. The connexion is in danger of being overset by its own weight.

In 1818 Charles Atmore feared that 'the *zenith* of Methodism' was past, and could not imagine how they could get through Conference without driving 'the people mad with our collections'.[2]

It was a matter of remark, moreover, that itinerancy in the old sense was rapidly coming to an end. A market in urban religion had been discovered which could be commercially tapped. The right kind of chapel in the right site could attract a congregation of gratifying number and affluence. But as the preachers made no bones privately, the brethren were only too willing to be anchored by connubial bliss and by the financial and pastoral obligations of the new causes, to the neglect of their rural ministry. From the large Yorkshire towns ministers ventured into the country but returned home nightly.[3] They confessed their dilemma. Country congregations were being neglected, and ground lost to the Ranters; on the other hand without a resident minister the town causes in which the financial stake was so huge could not thrive. The old hands in the ministry were quite bitter.[4] 'Paul taught the people publicly and from house to house', wrote one.[5] 'We have very little of domestic teaching.'

[1] J. Crowther, *Thoughts upon the finances or temporal affairs of the Methodist connexion...* (Leeds 1817) pp 24–5.
[2] MCA MSS. Charles Atmore to George Marsden, 3 April 1818.
[3] Bunting, *Life of Bunting*, II, p 80; MCA MSS. W. Myles to Jabez Bunting, 5 June 1819.
[4] MCA MSS. M. Martindale to Jabez Bunting, 9 July 1816.
[5] MCA MS. Letters of Presidents of Wesleyan Methodist Conference, I, 1744–1838, fol 58; J. Taylor to G. Marsden, 7 February 1811.

This was a cut indeed. For if the rise of Methodism on the macroscale had been an aspect of the rise of the provinces against the centre, on the microscale it had often been an aspect of the rise of the fringes of the parish against the nuclear village, the parish church, and the central apparatus of service and control. For one remote parish in Montgomeryshire, it has been shown how the revival forwarded this process by shifting the centre of worship from the parish church to the hearths of outlying farm kitchens, and that even when domestic prayer and prophecy were institutionalised, the chapel buildings were scattered at remote intersections of routes avoiding the village, a monument to the centrifugal forces which underlay them.[1]

What was true of Llanfihangel was true of many English parishes too, and the steady decay of the old style of itinerancy which involved journeys from home sometimes of weeks on end, sleeping, praying and preaching with the people in their homes and rural meeting places, involved subtle changes thoroughly unpalatable to many who remembered what Methodism was orginally like. No doubt this distaste did play into the hands of the Primitives[2] who harvested a second crop from the Wesleyan mission fields, were always more decentralised and more rural than the Wesleyans, and in some parts of the country maintained an old-style itinerancy into the present century.

There were two symbols of the new era which bore directly on the financial crisis. The first was the steady disappearance of the circuit horse.[3] For circuit stewards had it calculated that 'the expenses attending a horse support a single Preacher'[4] who might be of more service to the central chapels, but who, unlike the horse, would ere long establish a claim to additional allowances for wife, house and children, coals, candles and servant. If when the horse was exchanged for an unmarried preacher the country societies could be disposed of to a new circuit, the local financial advantage could be maximised.[5] This ruinous process, the creation of financially unsound country circuits, was the second symbol of the decline of itinerancy. It was a general abuse, particularly notorious in the old Methodist urban centres of London, Bristol and the North-East, and it aggravated the burdens created by

---

[1] Alwyn D. Rees, *Life in a Welsh countryside* (Cardiff 1968) pp 102–6.
[2] There were independent reports of great losses to the Primitives in the villages because of dissatisfaction with the Wesleyan constitution, and 'the wish for a cheaper religion'. *Monthly Repository*, 1820, p 168.
[3] MCA MSS. W. Worth to Jabez Bunting, 23 January 1818.
[4] Crowther, *Thoughts upon finances*, p 12.
[5] *Ibid*, p 11.

Thomas Coke's domestic missions which gave rise to forty circuits hardly any of which were capable of spiritual or financial independence.[1]

Methodist connexionalism being what it was, these mistakes at the fringes had immediate repercussions at the centre, and the preachers in Conference found themselves struggling to pay what was due to them as individuals in the circuits. The theory of methodist finance was that each society contributed to the support of the preachers stationed in the circuit, while the chapel supported the trust.[2] Thus pew rents serviced or reduced the chapel debts, while the society through its class monies or otherwise met the preachers' allowances. If the pew rents failed to meet the expenses of the trust, and especially the interest upon debt, then the trust also must be supported by the society. Circuits which could not meet their obligations (the chief of which were the preachers' allowances) returned a deficiency to the District Meeting; and District Meetings which could not meet their deficiency returned it to Conference. Conference in turn must meet the accumulated deficiency from the proceeds of the Yearly Collection, a fund apparently first opened for the temporary sustenance of Coke's Home Missions, but soon used as a milch-cow by all the insolvent Districts in the connexion. If Conference could not meet the deficiencies, preachers whose circuits had defaulted on their allowances did not receive them at all. Unscrupulous circuits, discovering that they were not absolutely committed to their financial undertakings, would bid for preachers by offering ample allowances they intended to return as deficiencies for someone else to pay;[3] unscrupulous preachers connived at circuits which cooked the books and avoided returning deficiencies by contracting illicit debts for their successors to discover and pay.[4] Savage deflation had destroyed the connexion's financial control and acutely raised the question of what the proper remuneration of a preacher was. Certainly the preachers compared their lot with that of their dissenting and Anglican brethren and steadily raised their financial and pastoral pretensions. From a Conference viewpoint the interests of the work of God and the professional interests of the ministry were in this crisis inseparable; neither could survive without the money of those who had it to give, without sacrifice on their own part, or without an absolute determination to enforce

[1] *Ibid*, pp 16, 29; MCA MSS. W. Myles to R. Blunt, 1 November 1813; J. Entwisle to Jabez Bunting, n.d. [before 18 December 1812]; T. Lessey Snr. to same, 6 May 1815.
[2] MCA MSS. Jabez Bunting to I. Clayton, 14 July 1815.
[3] MCA MSS. Samuel Taylor to Jabez Bunting, 22 July 1819.
[4] MCA MSS. E. Hare to Jabez Bunting, 12 June 1810; Z. Taft to same, [7] May 1818; John Mercer to Jabez Bunting, 14 March 1820. Cf W. Evans to same, 2 August 1820.

discipline on themselves and their people. In 1818 the preachers could see no way of meeting a deficit of £5,000 except by bearing it themselves, relinquishing claims to unpaid allowances for half the sum, and taking up the unsold publishing stock of the Book Room for the rest;[1] in 1819 they cut back recruiting; in 1820 they elected the first President who had not travelled with John Wesley, and the youngest ever, Thomas Coke excepted. But he was Jabez Bunting, the toughest and most iron-willed of their number.

It was now too that the preachers laid claim to the full dignity of the Pastoral Office which Wesley and some of his immediate successors had been so anxious to deny them,[2] and their ideal was subtly transformed from feeding and guiding to teaching and ruling. In 1818 Conference tacitly defied the Conference rule of 1793, adding the title of Rev. to the names of all the preachers on the Missionary Committee;[3] in 1819 ex-President Jonathan Edmondson announced his intention of writing 'a Treatise on the Pastoral Office, adapted to our circumstances as itinerants';[4] in 1820 Bunting created an uproar in Conference by proposing from the Presidential chair that the young preachers be received by imposition of hands.[5] On this point Bunting could not yet carry his brethren with him, but he gathered up the Conference conversation in the Liverpool Minutes which set forth so compelling a picture of the new ideal Methodist minister that Conference required them to be read annually at District, and later, circuit meetings, and by candidates for the ministry. Thus deeply did the Peterloo crisis and Bunting leave their mark, a mark appropriately engraved at the point where the body of the preachers made their transition from a genuine itinerancy to the sham, church-based itinerancy they have maintained ever since.

In his important study of the Wesleyan doctrine of the ministry Dr Bowmer maintains that the doctrine of the Pastoral Office was not 'devised to defend an otherwise intolerable situation'.[6] I have endeavoured respectfully to suggest the contrary by examining the situation itself. One last point is in order. As the storm broke the connexion was known to be precariously dependent on four districts which paid their way, produced a surplus on their Yearly Collection and gave up the whole of their profits on the book trade to assist other Districts. The

---

[1] George Smith, *History of Wesleyan Methodism* (4 ed London 1866) III, p 5.
[2] *Ibid*, III, p 34.   [3] *Ibid*, III, p 35.
[4] MCA MSS. J. Edmondson to B. Slater, 11 November 1819.
[5] MCA MS. Conference Journal, 1820–1.
[6] John C. Bowmer, 'Church and ministry in Wesleyan Methodism from the death of John Wesley to the death of Jabez Bunting '(Leeds PhD thesis 1967) p 304.

four pillars of financial salvation were Liverpool, Manchester, Leeds and Halifax.[1] It was an unfortunate accident that these were the areas where the class war was hottest; but no accident that the radicals recognised a change in preachers contending not for order but for survival, for resources that disorderly Cornwall could never produce; no accident that Bunting, John Stephens, Richard Reece and the other toughs of the connexion migrated among the town circuits which were the core of those districts; no accident that in every one of those circuits there took place between 1825 and 1835 at least one of those great constitutional conflicts in which the high Wesleyan doctrine of the ministry was hammered out.

It has often been asked whether with greater personal elasticity the age of Bunting might have been spared the damaging separations with which it ended. Upon a broad view this seems a misplaced question. The social stresses which toppled the monarchies of the continent in the 'forties, in Britain divided the churches. The Church of England defeated as a national church in the 1790s lost relatively little, but the Church of Scotland was disrupted, the Old and New Methodist Connexions were broken, there were great losses among the Independents and Baptists. In a community where a weak state had for so long depended on informal networks of influence, it was the informal networks rather than the state which bore the brunt. Lacking both the concentration of authority which underpinned the German establishments, and the continuing role of their American brethren, the English churches suffered terribly. Marx was right in relating their struggles to a wider contest about authority, but betrayed by continental habits of mind into supposing that religion was epiphenomenon, for here it was near the heart of the matter. The highly pitched claims, the screwed-up courage incarnate in a man like Bunting, the deductive theologies designed to bind conscience, the newly-invented ethical scruples, were the characteristic outcome of excess pressure upon the informal networks, of the apparent inseparability of gospel, ministry and public order. Of course the private sector could not bear the weight put upon it, and because it could not, there was no escaping that apple of historians' discord, the revolution in government, the development of those formal methods of central and social adjustment, which implied that England would never be so free or so disorderly again. The *Landeskirche* and the would-be *Volkskirchen* drew their battle, lost many of their functions to the state, and surreptitiously buried the doctrinal and ethical devices for ana-

[1] Crowther, *Thoughts upon finances*, p 18.

thematising out-groups and consolidating in-groups which they had employed against each other. The religion of the people, that undenominational evangelicalism which took root when the structure of authority cracked in the 1790's, survived impervious to the Pastoral Office and the Apostolic Succession alike, and constitutes most of what religion is left in the churches and outside. The victim of the débacle was the empirical frame of mind in which that religion was born. If there is one thing odder than the attempt to unite two bodies of Christian people by reconciling the Pastoral Office with the Apostolic Succession, it is the recent attempt to represent Methodism as a sort of *philosophia perennis* welling up opportunely in a great church metaphysically conceived.[1] But this you may think is the last rant of an old Ranter.

[1] R. E. Davis, *Methodism* (London 1963) p 11.

PAPISTS, PROTESTANTS AND THE
IRISH IN LONDON, 1835–70

by SHERIDAN GILLEY

THE increasing interest in nineteenth-century popular religion must serve as the excuse for this summary of my study of one aspect of two great nineteenth-century religious revivals: the 'second spring' of the Church of Rome in the 1840s, and that older evangelical rediscovery of the Gospel which in the same decade bore such abounding fruit in the parochial ministry of the Church of England. I have sought to chronicle the institutional development of both these movements in their impact upon the proletarian Irish migrants into mid-victorian London: the least infidel portion of that huge, half-heedless multitude of the destitute against which the best religious impulses of the period lashed themselves so devotedly, and too often in vain.

The background is one of conflict on the plane of ideas and institutions, between two religious traditions in the process of becoming more exclusive, and therefore ever more hot in competition for Irish souls. For Catholics, the religious revival in England in the 1840s was a repudiation of the liberal and national strains of cisalpine old Catholicism. The recusant mass had once been called prayers, and invested with all circumspection of dress and decoration, might almost have been so.[1] But that tradition had been in decline from the 1790s under the impact of the French clerical refugees, bishop Milner and the young Ullathorne; it received its *coup-de-grâce* in the 1840s, when the Church threw off the threadbare rags of outlawry and became fully Roman. Thus catholic devotional life aped the religious fashions of France and Italy as a means to reclaim Irishmen, convert England, and as an all-desirable end in itself. Under the renewed papist attack from without, and tractarian betrayal from within, the anglican Evangelicals acquired a new bitterness and narrow strength, sometimes in alliance with resurgent

---

[1] While an evening prayer service, loosely modelled on vespers, was hardly to be distinguished from an anglican Evensong. *Evening Devotion for Sundays performed in the Catholic Chapel of Moorfields* (London 1802) Archives of St Mary Moorfields.

Nonconformity; and nowhere perhaps was this narrowness and strength more apparent than in the evangelical parochial ministry in its lowest social reach, in unrelenting struggle with Roman priests in the London slums.

The mood of regenerate English Catholicism was one of sanguine hope for the conversion of England, and of a boundless faith in the new wisdom of the ultramontanes, and the Irish gave the revival an object in their need for missions, retreats and schools, as poor to be relieved, and as an outlet for a religious zeal yearning for expression in self-sacrifice.[1] The outcome – a renascent Roman Church – could only astound an ardent Evangelical, assailed in his deepest prejudice, and spurred to a new endeavour thereby; and so the Roman Church deployed its re-established hierarchy and lay associations, its wealthy converts and religious orders across the urban wastelands against an evangelical parish even more bountiful and blessed in its improved standards of charitable activity and ministerial efficiency, its cohorts of tracts distributors, Lady and District Visiting Associations, City Missionaries and Biblewomen.

The clash was also one of social theory. Catholics and Evangelicals attributed Irish spiritual and material destitution to violation of respectable standards of religious observance and moral behaviour; while their cures for the condition – a proper fulfilment of class obligation, salvation by self-help – were the same, and were learned from each other. But their rivalry bore fruit in notably dissimilar notions of almsgiving, and a notably dissimilar charitable idea. The literature of evangelical social comment on the Irish could see little in their destitution but the degradation which was the natural consequence of superstition, and from which the Gospel alone could save them, while the Catholic recognised in Our Lady Poverty a prime source of holiness, and though deploring its corruption in the brutish nastiness of St Giles's, was forced by polemic into a pietistic appreciation of the Irishry, which he found reflected in a celtic proletarian sanctity enshrining the virtues of ultramontane hagiography, and the highest idea of an ideal good with which the Church strove to nourish the life of her poor. Commentators from Mayhew to Booth mingled praise and blame in their studies of Irish cockneydom; they supplied catholic social critics with their materials, and told a tale of working-class woe, for use by the priest of the slums to win aid from his wealthy brethren. Moreover, while the English Catholic's response to the Irish was tainted by insular

[1] See Fr William Amherst, S.J., Review of Edward Lucas, *The Life of Frederick Lucas*, *Dublin Review*, New series, XVI (October 1886) pp 403–4.

prejudice and class obtuseness, he inherited that consciousness of the duties of wealth embodied before 1840 in a remarkable range of London catholic charities. Thereafter, his receptivity to contemporary continental social Catholicism gave him a wider perspective than England alone could provide, and continental ultramontanism brought a demand for the recatholicisation of catholic social methods in a better personal witness to that ideal of 'poverty of the spirit', which was reborn in the flowering of monastic and neo-feudal and pseudo-medieval romance, and was also of a piece with loyalty to Rome. The outcome might be seen in the new brother- and sisterhoods, in a higher standard of priestly ministration, in a higher view of the priestly office, and in the foundation of new charitable associations – the first-fruits of revival, dedicated to the service of the Irish poor.

The contest was hardly an equal one. The Evangelicals were better equipped, more numerous and much richer than the Catholics. But if Catholics pursued the will-of-the-wisp of converting England, evangelical interests were even more diffused, and though Evangelicals and Catholics were overwhelmed by the huge population whom they sought to save, Catholics could bring every sort of social pressure, the whole body of inherited Irish loyalties, to bear upon the lost celtic children of Mother Church. The resemblances between the two religious parties were nonetheless as striking as their differences. Both put heavy devotional and pastoral emphasis on redemption from a burning sense of penitence for sin forgiven through Christ's passion, both had recourse to the unrestrained ardour of the popular revival, and both rejoiced in the *élan* of great movements in their infancy, delighting in divine assurance of victory. They could take comfort in souls won, and a more tangible achievement in brick and Kentish rag, and as churches and poor schools multiplied, flexed the limbs of giants reawakened to the conquest of the world.

Indeed the nineteenth-century religious historian must draw out other than insular themes. The London slum priest and cleric were sustained by a wider international perspective that carried them in imagination far beyond their miserable surroundings to the new mission fields overseas. The protestant witness to the Irish in England was less English than Irish and Scottish in its inspiration and personnel, and if it owed little to continental Protestantism, it prayed for the conversion of Spain and China and all the lands in between – even Rome. Rome itself could more reasonably aspire to universality; and every

Latin nation – most notably, France – poured into the Roman Church in London a golden stream of men and women, of money and ideas. These likenesses of outlook in the urban religious missions mirrored a whole or partial repudiation of all religion by the Irish themselves. The Anglican Establishment was only in degree more foreign to the celtic immigrant than the Roman Church in England, which in him confronted a manner of man remote from its own experience. Its priests ministered to a devout gentry; they had now to serve a pious proletariat. The faith in England had survived in the country; the Irish flocked to the towns. English congregations were small, and mostly worshipped in manor chapels; the Irish multitudes would require cathedrals. The English catholic squire resembled his heretical neighbours both in their virtues and their vices; and his exclusion from English public life had preserved in him the insular prejudice of a simpler age. Class, culture, and a uniquely quietist traditional piety shut him off from the Irish poor, and created the distinction which a common creed might alone hope to overcome.

But a significant minority of catholic Englishmen were to transcend the limited sympathies of their class, and, fortified in their faith by the religious revival of the 1840s, lavished funds on the mission to their poor, upon charitable relief for their worst distresses, on self-help societies and soup kitchens, orphanages and almshouses, reformatories, convents, chapels and schools. Such an allocation of meagre resources did not pass unchallenged. Some Englishmen felt that Irish poverty held a special evangelical virtue, affording a challenge which men seeking sanctity must face; other ignored the poor as a distraction from the task of converting England, or worse, deplored their celtic folkways, their brawling, drinking, their rags and revolting smell. Proletarian *mores*, the enforced idleness of the casual labourer, the necessity of Sunday work, required an effort of the imagination, a kind of social understanding which some English gave, and others refused. The rich layman might feel that he owed the Irish nothing, or a little occasional charity, or a life of devoted service, mere sympathy with their admitted grievances in protestant prisons, workhouses, barracks and schools, or a campaign of redress to outrage the timid conservative loyalties of the catholic gentleman. And given these loyalties, the cleric could encourage or inhibit Irish resentment of manifest social injustice, when his approval might incite riot, and his opposition leave his flock leaderless, and perpetuate the misery from which he sought to save them. The priest who espoused the political aspirations of his people divided his

Church; and the priest who denied the popular voice might destroy the respect which the people paid him, and risk the salvation of Irish souls.

The Roman Church in London had its special problems. Catholic historians have too readily assumed that the metropolitan chapels were suddenly overwhelmed by the migration of the 1840s; but they had been outgrown long before the famine. The diocesan statistics submitted to the *Propaganda Fide* give a London catholic population of 25,000 in 1746; of 20,000 in 1773; but of 50,000 in 1814.[1] There had been sporadic Irish movements in the seventeenth and eighteenth centuries into particular areas, like the East End invasions of the 1630s and the 1760s, while Irish settlement in St Giles's began in the reign of Elizabeth.[2] But migration only became continuous from the 1790s, reaching new heights in the 1820s with the coming of cheap sea-travel between England and Ireland, and the labour traffic at harvest time.[3] As early as 1816 the Vicar Apostolic of the London District confessed that his resources were wholly inadequate to his task;[4] but there was little school and chapel building to receive the flood. While Irish migration into London between 1820 and 1830 was described and denounced by the Mendicity Society,[5] the officials of the metropolitan parishes, and a succession of House of Commons Select Committees,[6] the Vicar Apostolic erected only one new church. By 1840, the so-called Irish leakage from the faith – as measured by religious practice – was, through sheer want of chapels, hopelessly beyond control. The problem of numbers had become insoluble before any attempt had

[1] Maziere W. Brady, *Annals of the Catholic Hierarchy in England and Scotland* (London 1877) pp 163, 169. The Bishop of London's estimates – 12,230 (1787) and 13,379 (1780) are probably too low. *Returns of Papists*. Lambeth Archives.

[2] Robert Sinclair, *East London* (London 1956) p 227. Dorothy George, *London Life in the Eighteenth Century* (London 1965) esp pp 118–31, 236–8. Of St Giles-in-the-Fields it has been said that neither Irish poor nor aliens are mentioned by name in the parish books until 1640 – at which date entries appear in the Vestry Minutes suggesting an influx from Ireland, but there were probably Irish migrants in the district before. R. Dobie, *History of St Giles-in-the-Fields and St George, Bloomsbury* (London 1829) p 194.

[3] B. M. Kerr, 'Irish Seasonal Migration to Great Britain, 1800–38', *Irish Historical Studies*, III (London 1942–3) p 365.

[4] Bernard Ward, *The Eve of Catholic Emancipation*, II (London 1912) p 156.

[5] Mendicity Society, Appendices 7 and 8, in [*Report to the*] *Select Committee on Emigration* [*from the United Kingdom*], *Parliamentary Papers*, 1826–7, V, pp 802–13.

[6] *Report from the Select Committees on the Existing Laws Relating to Irish and Scotch Vagrants*, *Parliamentary Papers*, 1833, XVI; on *Irish Vagrants*, 1833, XVI: Appendix *to the Reports of the Commissioners on the Poor Laws Parliamentary Papers*, 1836, XXXIV. Also the *Select Committee on Emigration*, p 7, on Ireland, 'whose population, unless some other outlet be opened to them, must shortly fill up every vacuum created in England or Scotland, and reduce the labouring classes to a uniform state of degradation and misery'.

been made to solve it, and the neglect of the first half of the nineteenth-century was beyond the remedies of the second.

Irish movement into London inspired no sense of crisis in the clergy until the influx of the 1840s, which increased in a decade the city's catholic population from perhaps a hundred to a hundred and fifty thousand, mainly Cockney Irish and Irish-born.[1] But while the catholic revival had then begun at last to increase the number of chapels and schools, the priesthood confronted both newcomers – victims of the famine – and the children of an earlier immigrant generation left unprovided with churches through years of neglect. Ecclesiastics were well aware that not half the faithful went to their duties in 1851; there were fewer than forty thousand attendances at morning mass in London chapels on Census Sunday.[2] For the Irish of the pre-1840 migration, the catholic revival came ten or twenty years too late; and however readily the priest might call upon the recent migrants' traditional piety, he had also to reclaim the Irish Cockneys whose faith had all but died away.

But the Church could profit from the Irish tendency to crowd into enclaves within the courts and squares in the slums to which their poverty consigned them: a species of concentration also apparent in the overall compactness of Irish settlement. Pauper migration into London before 1850 packed the historic core of the old city, living in the heart rather than the perimeter. The Irish and their children born in London oc-cupied only a small area in relation to their numbers, and were else-where concentrated in three broad bands, forming more than a tenth of the population in the census district of St James's, east through the Strand, St Giles and Holborn, and in the two waterfront areas north and south of the river: Poplar, Stepney and St George's-in-the-East; and St Olave's, Southwark, with the adjacent unions of St Saviour's,

[1] The 1841 and 1851 census returns show an Irish-born population of 75,000 to 100,000, representing an estimated influx of 46,000 in the decade. H. A. Shannon, 'Migration and Growth of London 1841–1891', *Economic History Review*, V (London 1935) p 81. The size of the London-born Catholic population can only be guessed; by the Church's own estimates, computed by parochial census, or by multiplying its remarkably high baptismal figures by thirty (the ratio of births to population for the population of England) are given below. Uniformly impressive totals are cited in the eighteenth century, and in the 1820s; they indicate a nominally catholic Cockney population of considerable size. Of the intelligent contemporary estimates, cf F. Engels, 'The Condi-tion of the Working Class in England', in *Karl Marx and Frederick Engels in England* (London 1954) p 124.

[2] Of those churches which submitted returns, 35,584. I estimate at less than 4,000 worship-pers the congregations of those chapels which did not submit complete returns. *Popula-tion Census, Religious Worship, England and Wales: Accounts and Papers*, 1852–53, LXXXIX: on London, pp 3–9; also the *Rambler* articles on the religious census, I, pp 183–90, 257–80, 356–75; *Tablet*, 5 July 1851.

Bermondsey, Lambeth and Rotherhithe.[1] New catholic chapels were opened in most of these slumlands between 1840 and 1860; and if in some, Irish numbers fell during the '50s in migration further afield, to Kensington and Camberwell, chapels were rising to receive them, under the impulse of Irish communal self-help, and of the new dedication in English Catholicism.

Yet despite the intrinsic importance of the subject, my starting point has been the underdeveloped state of nineteenth-century roman catholic studies, as roman catholic religious effort is generally ignored by non-catholic historians,[2] and has been unduly neglected by Catholics themselves. There have been many biographies of varying value of the victorian cardinals and the few important intellectuals, but this species of two volume *Life and Letters* for the most part ignores social questions for ecclesiastical and theological controversy, and even most of the roman catholic bishops have still to receive their biographical due. Converts come a good second, which is why my study leans so heavily upon them; the regular clergy and the Mother Superiors – again, most notably ex-Anglicans – have been the next best served, but more by hagiographers than historians; while the secular priesthood and laity, noblemen and commoners, English and Irish, who were socially important if individually unremarkable and intellectually uninteresting, have for the most part gone unwept, unhonoured and unsung.

This is only to say that the social history of Catholicism in victorian England has still to be written. The Irish communities in England, their political attitudes and activities have only begun to be studied; indeed have been thoroughly described in London alone.[3] But John Bossy's essays[4] and the magnificent biographical indices to the Newman letters aside,[5] there is no equivalent work in progress on the English catholic

---

[1] [Lynn Lees], 'Social Change [and Social Stability among the London Irish'](unpublished PhD thesis Harvard 1969) pp 55–72.

[2] Thus there are only three references to Catholic charity in David Owen, *English Philanthropy 1660–1960* (London 1965): all dealing with the dubious legality of Catholic charitable endowments under English mortmain law (pp 201, 319–20, 576–7). Sectarian ignorance probably explains the exaggerated claim that 'Roman Catholic social work...was almost entirely educational...' Kathleen Heasman, *Evangelicals in Action: an Appraisal of their Social Work in the Victorian Era* (London 1962) p 13.

[3] J. A. Jackson, 'The Irish in London' (unpublished MA thesis London 1958); *The Irish in Britain* (London 1963); *Social Change*.

[4] John Bossy, 'Four Catholic Congregations in Rural Northumberland 1750–1850, *Recusant History*, IX (Oxford April 1967) pp 88–119; 'More Northumberland Congregations', *Recusant History*, X (January 1969) pp 11–29.

[5] Stephen Dessain, *The Letters and Diaries of John Henry Newman 1845–1863*, XI–XX (London 1961–70).

laity. The few good parish histories also lack the social interest; moreover, like the few sacerdotal biographies, they are not available in the
copyright libraries, and have to be obtained from the parish priest. Thus
there is an obvious and equal need for research of an institutional kind,
into diocesan and parochial organisation and finance, beyond the well-
trodden paths of ecclesiastical chronicle; nor is there yet any history
of the devotional and theological impact of the ultramontane revival,
though the materials are plentiful enough in easily accessible sources,
while there has been no proper study of the impact upon English
catholic and protestant charitable activity and attitudes to the poor of
continental social Catholicism. One scholar has essayed the history of
the Guild and Confraternity movements in northern England,[1] but they
have not been described for London; nor has the significant range of
other lay catholic institutions with a social purpose: the Associated
Catholic Charities and its many lesser metropolitan auxiliaries, and the
Society of St Vincent de Paul, the Catholic Institute and the Catholic
Poor School Committee. Also unwritten is the restoration of the great
active religious orders, the rediscovery of the social utility of the convent and monastery and brotherhood and sacerdotal institute, of the
Sisters of Mercy and Society of Jesus.

There has been much more anglican religious history, especially on
the institutional level, but there are still great gaps in the picture of
evangelical parochial organisation, church finance, church extension,
and a better administration of parochial charity. Even the mutations of
protestant forms of devotion and worship are still mostly embedded in
local chronicle, from which general study should rescue them. Again,
many significant missionary societies which ministered to the metropolitan poor still lack adequate histories, though they have left abundant
printed records at least: the London City Mission, the Ranyard Bible
Mission and their local equivalents, while despite the new interest in
victorian anti-Catholicism, historians have yet to chart and compare and
contrast the rise of the Protestant Reformation Society, of the Protestant
Association, of the 'popular Protestantism' of the anti-catholic opera-
tives' movement, and of the Evangelical and Protestant Alliances and
the Protestant Truth Society. They span the century together, in a
continuing witness to the same fixed hatred of the Church of Rome, but
they have yet to find their place in the untracked wastes of nineteenth-
century religious history.

[1] J. H. Treble, 'The Attitude of the Roman Catholic Church towards Irish Participation
in Trade Unionism in the North of England, 1833–40': a paper presented to the Urban
History Conference, Durham, 1969.

THE CHURCHES AND SOCIETY IN
NINETEENTH-CENTURY ENGLAND:
A RURAL PERSPECTIVE[1]

by DAVID M. THOMPSON

I

IN recent years discussion of the relationship between the Churches and society in nineteenth-century England has concentrated on a topic that very much concerned contemporaries: the absence of the working classes from public worship. Much stress has been laid on the parlous position of the Churches in the towns, particularly the large towns where the proportion of the population attending church was lowest and where the working classes, however defined, were most numerous. Because on average church attendance was better in the countryside,[2] and because it is known that the growth of urban population owed more to migration than natural increase before 1851, it has been suggested that the transition made by migrants from a rural to an urban society may explain the difficulties experienced by the urban churches in attracting worshippers.[3] Modern research has shown that church attendance is one of the habits likely to be dropped by migrants;[4] and thus it is suggested that migrants coming from the countryside where church attendance was normal dropped the habit as part of the 'cultural shock' of the move to the very different social life of the town.

Clearly this alienation from the Churches was a gradual process; and because only nonconformists possess long runs of membership figures, these have been examined for clues to the timing of the change. Some historians have noted that the periods of rapid growth in Nonconformity,

---

[1] This paper is a revised version of one given at a meeting of the Cambridge Historical Society on 27 January 1970 where several helpful comments were made.

[2] According to the 1851 Census of Religious Worship, the following percentages of the population attended worship:

	Morning	Afternoon	Evening
Rural areas	28.1	25.5	17.8
Large towns	23.9	10.5	15.3

'Report on the Census of Religious Worship, 1851', *Parliamentary Papers*, H.C. 1852–3, LXXXIX, p clv. [3] E.g. D. Martin, *A Sociology of English Religion* (London 1967) p 29.
[4] E.g. M. Stacey, *Tradition and Change* (London 1960) p 73.

particularly Methodism, coincide with periods of economic or social strain. The implications of this have been variously interpreted, but working-class involvement with Nonconformity is usually taken for granted. Other historians have stressed the middle-class nature of Nonconformity as a social context for political radicalism. Indeed this link between Nonconformity and radicalism may be seen as a clue to the decay of the Liberal Party at the end of the century, because of its concentration on dying issues, such as disestablishment. To resolve the tensions between a supposedly middle-class and a supposedly working-class Nonconformity, the various nonconformist denominations have been given different positions in the social hierarchy: middle-class Congregationalism is contrasted with working-class Primitive Methodism, etc.

Always, however, it is the towns which provide the scenery. The rural working classes, it has been observed, do not appear in Professor Inglis's *Churches and the Working Classes in Victorian England*.[1] The countryside is invoked as the religious society, to be contrasted with the irreligious towns. This reminds us, perhaps to our surprise, how little we still know about the nineteenth-century English countryside and its society. Asked to describe a typical English village, most people will describe a community based on arable farming with a resident squire and parson, and everyone in his place. Agricultural historians have been exposing the naïveté of this picture, and some sociologists have also questioned the traditionally sharp distinction between the intimate and personal rural society and the remote and impersonal urban society.[2] This paper is concerned with the religious diversity of the countryside.

2

Is it true that migrants to the towns came from a countryside where church attendance was normal? Certainly levels of church attendance were higher in the countryside than the towns, according to the Census of Religious Worship of 1851, but the difference is hardly striking. Detailed work on individual villages reveals considerable variations.[3]

---

[1] W. R. Ward, 'The Tithe Question in England in the early nineteenth century', *JEH* XVI (1965) p 67.

[2] E.g. the approach of J. Thirsk, *Agrarian History of England and Wales*, IV (Cambridge 1967) Ch 1; F. Benet, 'Sociology Uncertain: The Ideology of the Rural-Urban Continuum', *Comparative Studies in Society and History*, VI (The Hague 1963-4) pp 1-23.

[3] The Religious Census is the only source which allows comparisons between town and country: for problems in using it, see D. M. Thompson, 'The 1851 Religious Census: Problems and Possibilities', *Victorian Studies*, XI (Bloomington 1967-8) pp 87-97.

The Churches and society

What follows is based on calculations for Leicestershire, a relatively devout county in 1851 with both the Church of England and Non-conformity quite strong by comparison with the rest of the country.[1] Calculation of the percentage of the population attending church in the morning, afternoon and evening for each village shows that the average figures for the county as a whole conceal wide variety.[2] Most places had between 20% and 40% of the population at church at least once on Sunday; but where there was industry or a large population the percentage dropped well below 20% and was below 10% for the Church of England in some places. In very few villages did it approach 100%. In the 1870s only about half a dozen anglican clergymen said in their Visitation Returns that everyone or nearly everyone attended church in their village.

Further analysis leads to three main conclusions. First, church attendance is significantly below average in the registration districts which consist mainly of industrial villages.[3] Secondly, church attendance is significantly below average where population is large (over 600) and significantly above average where population is small (below 200). This is not very surprising, but it is interesting that a population of over 600 is large. Although this category includes 19 places over 1,400 – the largest was Loughborough with 11,000 – it is unlikely that this has distorted the results, because the percentage of attendance in many places between 600 and 1,400 was actually lower than in the larger places. Thirdly, church attendance is significantly above average in villages where most of the land is owned by a resident squire ('closed' or 'squire's' villages) and is significantly below average in villages where most of the land is owned by small freeholders ('open' or 'freehold' villages). Other work on Leicestershire had shown a correlation between freehold villages, large population and early development of industry.[4] The weakness of church attendance in all these conditions is another link between them.

---

[1] These paragraphs are based on my doctoral thesis: D. M. Thompson, 'The Churches and Society in Leicestershire, 1851–1881'(unpublished Cambridge PhD thesis) pp 50–66.
[2] Average percentages are as follows:

	Morning	Afternoon	Evening
Leicestershire (excluding Leicester)	24	34	26
Leicester	18	3	22

[3] This comparison is based on the occupational analysis in the published Census reports, which are unfortunately not available for units smaller than registration districts. For individual villages it would be necessary to consult the original schedules in the Public Record Office.
[4] D. R. Mills, 'Landownership and Rural Population, with special reference to Leicestershire in the mid-nineteenth century' (unpublished Leicester PhD thesis).

Church attendance means here attendance at all the churches in a village, not just the Church of England. The presence of Nonconformity made relatively little difference to the percentage attendance in the villages. This is not because the numbers attending nonconformist chapels were small relative to the Church of England, though this was, of course, sometimes true. It is mainly because nonconformist chapels flourished in those places where the level of church attendance was low in any case – the open, freehold village. Nearly half the villages in Leicestershire with nonconformist chapels in 1851 were of this kind. Only six out of more than a hundred freehold villages had no Nonconformity in 1851; and three of these were the scenes of nonconformist evangelistic activity soon afterwards. The places where church attendance was highest – closed villages dominated by a resident squire – were just those places were Nonconformity found it most difficult to get a foothold, particularly land on which to build a chapel.

It is therefore a mistake to imagine that villages are necessarily places where church attendance is strong. Some are; but others, particularly those with coalmining or domestic industry, have levels of attendance no better than towns the size of Leicester with a population of 60,000. Even if industrial villages are excluded there remain interesting differences between agricultural villages. The influence of a resident squire has long been recognised; but only 10% of Leicestershire villages had a resident squire. It would be interesting to know whether this proportion is typical. Another 30% of the villages were owned by a single absentee landlord (either an individual or a corporate body); but although landlord influence might have been exercised in them, it is more likely that they were like Flintcomb Ash in Thomas Hardy's *Tess of the d'Urbervilles* – a village cared for neither by itself nor its lord.

A rural migrant to a growing town, therefore, might well have come from a place where it was not normal to go to church. Indeed as the larger populations were found in the open villages, it is perhaps more likely that a migrant would come from such a place. Open villages were places where religious diversity was possible, a diversity which included absence from church as well as Nonconformity. Religious indifference does not begin with the move to the town.

3

The 1851 Religious Census also showed the strength of rural Nonconformity. The Reverend John Kennedy, who analysed the Census for the Congregational Union, said in 1854, 'It does not appear so true as we thought, that the strength of Dissent is to be found in our great cities and large towns.'[1] Other denominations were more sharply aware of their rural heritage. Although John Wesley had no interest in the countryside, either in the farmer whom he regarded as dull and un-happy, or in the farm labourer whom he regarded as grossly stupid, Methodism spread widely in the villages, and Jabez Bunting reminded Wesleyans in 1854 that theirs was originally a rural system.[2] The Primi-tive Methodists were from the beginning a rural movement, and their historian comments on the reluctance of some of their early preachers to enter the towns.[3] The first half of the nineteenth century saw a great expansion of rural Nonconformity of all kinds, and the money of ur-ban nonconformists was poured into the support of country ministers, evangelists and struggling churches to a remarkably late date in the century. Sometimes this was at the expense of church extension in the towns, and it provoked the protests of some ministers. Others pointed to the country's contribution to the towns: the Reverend G. W. Humphreys told the Baptist Union in 1881, 'From remote country churches have come some of the ablest of our ministers, and many of the most active and generous of our deacons and church members.'[4] Baptists could name Spurgeon and Clifford as examples.

Changes in the countryside may illuminate some of the puzzling features of the growth patterns of Nonconformity. Membership of the Free Churches grew for most of the century, but unevenly. The periods of most rapid growth were the first forty years and the last twenty-five. In the early 1850s there was standstill and even decline in some. If membership is related to population, then the growth of the first half century stands out even more sharply.

The stagnation of the early 1850s has puzzled historians. Dr Hobs-bawm, linking nonconformist growth and economic and social strain, associates the setback with the decline of Chartism and radicalism. Dr Kitson Clark has reservations about the extent of the setback, but refers to the effects of the Crimean War cited by some contemporaries and to the explanations offered by the Primitive Methodists, including emigra-

---

[1] *Congregational Year Book, 1855* (London 1854) p 37.

[2] R. Davis and E. G. Rupp, *A History of the Methodist Church in Great Britain*, 1 (London 1965) p 58; T. P. Bunting and G. S. Rowe, *The Life of Jabez Bunting* (London 1887) p 733.

[3] H. B. Kendall, *The Origin and History of the Primitive Methodist Church*, (London n.d. – *c* 1905) 1, p 298.

[4] *Baptist Handbook, 1882* (London 1881) p 59.

tion and the wesleyan troubles. Dr Currie believes that the wesleyan rate of growth was already slackening in the late 1840s before the *Fly Sheet* controversy.[1] There is no doubt that this controversy turned a slackening growth rate into an absolute loss of 100,000 members to Wesleyan Methodism between 1850 and 1855. But as the main demand of the wesleyan reformers was for a greater lay voice in church affairs, which *a priori* might be expected to appeal to more radical nonconformists, it is difficult to see why the wesleyan controversy should have adversely affected other denominations. It is even possible that Primitive Methodists may have suffered from the activities of the Mormons, who drew some of their followers away, and reached a maximum membership in England in the early 1850s before they were ruined by the announcement of polygamy in 1853.[2]

The existence of continuous membership figures from the 1830s for all methodist and baptist churches in Leicestershire (nearly 70% of all nonconformists in the county) makes it possible to look at the picture in miniature. In Leicestershire the number of nonconformist churches increased six-fold between 1800 and 1851, most of them being in the agricultural villages. The number of new churches formed after 1851 was very much less. The main period of growth for Wesleyans and General Baptists ended in 1845. After a period of fluctuation membership only passed the 1845 levels in the 1880s. The Particular Baptists also had a period of fluctuation after 1845 but it only lasted ten years. After 1855 they grew steadily and rapidly, indeed the most rapidly of all. The Primitive Methodist growth rate did not slacken until 1854, but thereafter it fluctuated and did not increase steadily again until the 1880s.

These differences are striking and make it difficult to generalise about Nonconformity as a whole. Wesleyans, who declined, were supposed to be a lower-middle-class denomination; but so were Particular Baptists who grew fastest of all. General Baptists who were strong among artisans and labourers declined; but Primitive Methodists, appealing to similar sections of the population, grew. Comparison of General Baptists with Particular Baptists is even more interesting, for the General Baptists, who declined, actually baptised more new converts than the Particulars in many years; but they lost more through separation, death and removal.

[1] E. Hobsbawn, *Primitive Rebels* (Manchester 1959) pp 129–30; G. S. R. Kitson Clark, *The Making of Victorian England* (London 1962) pp 187–8; R. Currie, *Methodism Divided* (London 1968) p 92.
[2] T. B. H. Stenhouse, *An Englishwoman in Utah* (London 1880) pp 20–1, 91; W. O. Chadwick, *The Victorian Church*, I (London 1966) pp 436–9.

The Churches and society

The outstanding feature is that the denominations which grew gained their new members in the towns, and especially in Leicester. Between 1835 and 1890 the membership of Particular Baptist churches outside Leicester rather more than doubled: in Leicester it increased twelvefold. The Leicester Primitive Methodist circuits trebled their membership in those sixty years and probably accounted for most of the increase after the 1870s. (As methodist circuits linked town and country churches it is difficult to be absolutely certain here.) Both denominations built several new chapels in Leicester as the town grew. The Wesleyans, by contrast, were slow to build new chapels in Leicester, and were, of course, affected by the *Fly Sheet* troubles: and the General Baptists failed to build new chapels altogether. In other words, in Leicestershire the nonconformist growth of the first half century, which is the most rapid, is rural, whilst that of the second half, which is less rapid, is predominantly urban.

If this were true of the country as a whole, it would show why the Free Churches were so worried about the difficulties of their country churches in the 1870s and 1880s. Between 1870 and 1896 the Primitive Methodists gave up 516 village causes; even so it was reckoned in 1896 that nearly 75% of their churches were in the villages.[1] Some argued that nonconformists were the people most likely to migrate from the villages: the Reverend John Clifford told the Baptist Union in 1876,

Only villagers who have a soul venture in them, the best brains and most resolute will, are ready to leave the traditions and associations of the old home for the risks of the sea and the hazards of a crowded town; and these are precisely the men and women who have had courage enough to think for themselves, to mark out an independent path, and in fidelity to conscience join the conventicle in the village back street.[2]

Nonconformists did lose many by emigration, and they founded the colonial churches. The *Primitive Methodist Magazine* contained an Emigrants' Corner which provided news about likely places. But more recent work on rural depopulation has cast doubt on any selective theory of migration.[3]

Others argued that concentration of land in the hands of fewer owners led to the elimination of many smallholdings and tenant farmers. The

---

[1] R. F. Wearmouth, *Methodism and the Struggle of the Working Classes, 1850–1900* (Leicester 1954) pp 103–4; *Minutes of the Primitive Methodist Conference, 1896* (London 1896) pp 183–4.
[2] *Baptist Handbook, 1877* (London 1876) p 109.
[3] J. Saville, *Rural Development in England and Wales* (London 1957) pp 125–30.

Baptist Union Council in a special report of 1894 on Village Churches said, 'Those who remember the state of our churches many years ago can recall the fact that the tenant farmers of this country were the backbone of religious Nonconformity. That class of supporters may today be looked for almost in vain among our village churches.'[1] Their solution was the creation of a class of small-holding proprietors, and the Congregational Union Assembly listened to a paper in 1897 on 'How to increase the class of small farmers' with the same end in view.[2] Modern economic historians are not convinced that there was a significant reduction in the number of small farmers in this period: thus, while small farmers may have been lost to Nonconformity, this may not mean that they disappeared altogether. More research is necessary here, and the strength of Baptists and Congregationalists in the counties worst hit by the agricultural depression is probably significant.

4

This raises once again the question of social distinctions between denominations. The rural evidence reminds us that the importance of social class is limited by other factors. Where there was more than one nonconformist church in a place, social distinctions emerged. In one Leicestershire village it was said, 'All the six shopkeepers are Dissenters. Baptists prevail amongst the more educated.'[3] But which social groups went where depended on the choice of denomination available. In one village there might be farmers at the Congregational chapel and labourers at the Wesleyan; in another, farmers at the Wesleyan and labourers at the Primitive Methodist. This makes national generalisations about denominations hazardous, and emphasises the importance of place.

Where there was only one nonconformist chapel in a village, its denomination was almost irrelevant. In another Leicestershire village, the vicar said, 'The chapel is called Wesleyan but all the dissenters without distinction attend.'[4] The identity of Nonconformity in such a place was defined by its difference from the Church of England. The relationships between the two were not necessarily unfriendly, certainly not for ordinary villagers. More than one clergyman might have echoed the Leicestershire parson who said 'In country villages they go to church

[1] *Baptist Handbook, 1894* (London 1893) p 77.
[2] The paper was by the Rev J. G. Paton: *Congregational Year Book, 1898* (London 1897) pp 78–86.
[3] Northamptonshire Records Office: Diocese of Peterborough – Incumbents' Visitation Returns 1881 (Misc L 600): Hose.   [4] *Ibid*, Great Glen.

and chapel also.'[1] Another parson divided his villagers into 'Church', 'Chapel', and 'Church and Chapel'. But towards the end of the century differences did harden. Many parsons suffered reductions in income because of the agricultural depression. There was an increase in ritualism, even if this did only mean a surpliced choir and flowers on the altar. Village nonconformists with dwindling congregations knew that it was in the villages that the education issue hit them most sharply. Anglican insistence in some places that day scholars should attend anglican Sunday schools made the issue politically explosive. It is not surprising that urban nonconformists who poured so much money into the country chapels should feel so strongly on an issue which had a less direct impact in the towns.

Social differences between denominations, however, do not explain why some people went to church while others in the same class did not. This question has not so far received the discussion it deserves, although it is in many way the most important. And evidence from the towns where a greater variety of social distinction was possible has tended to obscure it, whilst the suggestion that absence from church was due to the move from country to town leads the discussion in a completely different direction. Once again the open village poses the problem, because here indifference to worship existed alongside the nonconformist chapels where some at least of the working classes found a sense of identity. Joseph Ashby's Tysoe illustrates this.[2] Every occupation in Leicestershire was cited by some anglican clergyman in the Visitation Returns of the 1870s as an obstacle to church attendance: so it is clear that occupation alone cannot explain anything. The Leicestershire evidence does, however, suggest that where there was no dominating figure, who combined social prestige with economic control over the villagers, religious diversity was possible. This diversity included indifference as well as Nonconformity. Only when diversity is possible can the influence of social class be felt. Even so, very few historians have pointed out that, as the working classes are the largest section of the community, it is perhaps not surprising that they should be a majority of the absentees from church.

It may have been noticed that nowhere so far has it been suggested that belief had anything to do with church attendance. This is not because of any cynical assessment of the importance of religious belief: it is rather because the evidence suggests that more than belief was

---

[1] *Ibid*, Stonesby.
[2] M. K. Ashby, *Joseph Ashby of Tysoe* (Cambridge 1961).

involved and that there were important social influences which gave belief a social context and church attendance or the opposite a social significance. Thus it is only when the social influences have been investigated that the significance of belief can be assessed. Here too the rural perspective may be valuable. The open village is a paradigm of the situation, increasingly common in the nineteenth century, where the Churches had few social advantages: their success depended on the commitment of their members.

The religious diversity of the countryside therefore suggests some new directions which might profitably be explored in the study of the Churches and society. In particular the further study of the open village as a community alongside the closed village and the growing town and combining features of both, will greatly aid our understanding of the nineteenth century as a whole.

PRATIQUE, PIETE ET FOI POPULAIRE DANS LA FRANCE MODERNE AU XIXEME ET XXEME SIECLES

by A. LATREILLE

L A question que je voudrais examiner avec vous est la suivante: peut-on, et par quelles méthodes, avec quels documents, mesurer la vitalité religieuse d'un groupe humain, au sein d'un pays catholique, à une époque déterminée?

I

Depuis longtemps on ne réduit plus l'histoire religieuse à l'histoire des institutions ecclésiales, de leurs structures, de leur personnel et des relations des églises avec les sociétés politiques: mais on s'intéresse au comportement et à la spiritualité du peuple des fidèles ou des moins fidèles, aux croyances, aux dévotions, à la sensibilité religieuse des diverses catégories d'hommes et de femmes, à travers les générations successives. Or la difficulté est grande de rejoindre ceux qui ne se sont pas distingués de la masse par leur héroïsme ou leur sainteté, par leurs écrits ou par leurs œuvres. On a fait des histoires du sentiment religieux en partant des textes des docteurs, des fondateurs de communautés et de mouvements, voire d'écrivains de second ordre: et un Henri Brémond a magistralement démontré tout ce que l'on pouvait tirer même d'auteurs de second ordre, qui ne furent pas forcément les moins influents ou les moins représentatifs. En revanche il paraît malaisé de donner une idée précise de la mentalité, à plus forte raison de la conviction et de la ferveur, d'une société prise dans son ensemble, ou de 'l'homme de la rue' qui ne s'est pas exprimé et n'a pas laissé d'archives ou de postérité spirituelle.

Trop souvent les historiens se tiennent dans des généralités, enregistrant quelques témoignages de contemporains qui sont censés expressifs de 'l'opinion' du temps, sans voir qu'ils sont trop fragmentaires ou trop subjectifs pour permettre de porter un diagnostique valable. Prenons un exemple.

La plupart des ouvrages généraux traitant de l'atmosphère religieuse de la France dans la première moitié du XIXème siècle assurent qu'entre 1830 et 1848 se serait produit un renouveau catholique frappant, une 'splendide renaissance' dit même l'un d'eux.[1] Il est de fait que la Révolution de Juillet 1830 fut suivie d'une crise d'anticléricalisme si brutale que certains témoins crurent pouvoir annoncer la mort de la vieille religion nationale, grièvement blessée par les événements de 1793 et de 1811, achevée par l'effondrement du Trône et de l'Autel. Ensuite il y aurait eu une remontée du sentiment religieux assez vigoureuse pour qu'en février 1848 on relève jusque dans les milieux populaires et chez les révolutionnaires une déférence à peu près générale pour l'Eglise et une sorte de christianisme diffus. Or rien n'est moins assuré que la courbe d'évolution ainsi reconstituée.

Quand on y regarde de près, on s'aperçoit qu'elle a été suggérée par des témoins qui, d'une part, étaient tous parisiens et jugeaient mal des réactions de la province, ou qui, d'autre part, appartenaient au groupe des catholiques libéraux, lesquels s'étaient effectivement employés, non sans succès, à dissiper certains malentendus entre l'Eglise et le siècle, mais dans les sphères gouvernementales et les classes dites dirigeantes. En 1830, le catholicisme n'était pas moribond, loin de là, et le voltairianisme agressif de la bourgeoisie libérale, l'hostilité des émeutiers parisiens ne doivent pas dissimuler son enracinement profond dans la plupart des provinces. Quant au retour qui se serait produit vers lui sous la Monarchie de Juillet, il ne fut ni général ni toujours très profond. A l'époque, l'*Ami du Clergé* mettait en garde les optimistes contre la tentation de confondre la religiosité à la mode dans la littérature avec l'adhésion à l'Eglise. Le socialiste Proudhon déclarait brutalement que le choc de 1830 avait fait ce que la Révolution n'avait pu opérer: le divorce definitif entre la classe ouvrière et l'Eglise. Dans la suite, les historiens qui ont étudié de près les populations paysannes du Centre de la France. Sevrin[2] pour la Beauce, Mme Marcilhacy[3] pour l'Orléanais, ont découvert un 'déclin continu' de la pratique, une indifférence croissante malgré tous les efforts d'évangélisation.

Ce genre d'approximation n'est que trop courant. Et l'historien y est particulièrement exposé dès qu'il généralise sommairement et dès qu'il

---

[1] J. Brugerette, *Le Prêtre français et la société contemporaine*, I, *La Restauration catholique*, 3 vols (Paris 1933–8) p 67.

[2] E. Sevrin, 'La Pratique des sacrements et des observances au diocèse de Chartres sous Mgr Clausel de Montals', *RHEF*, XXIV (July/Sept 1938) p 344.

[3] C. Marcilhacy, *Le Diocèse d'Orléans au milieu du XIXème siècle* (Paris 1964).

s'occupe de ce petit peuple qu'il est si difficile de tirer de l'ombre où il a vécu.

C'est en partant des ces constatations que, au cours des trente années, ceux qui, par curiosité scientifique ou avec des vues pastorales, s'intéressaient au problème des variations de la vitalité religieuse en France ont été amenés à imaginer des méthodes d'analyse nouvelles. Au premier rang de ces novateurs, il faut placer Gabriel Le Bras († 1970), travailleur aussi ingénieux qu'inlassable, qui pendant quarante années devait faire figure de pionnier, de chef d'école, d'animateur, et qui restera comme le fondateur de la sociologie des religions. Juriste et spécialiste de droit canon, le doyen Le Bras possédait une prodigieuse culture d'historien, de géographe, de sociologue, une connaissance merveilleuse des hommes et un sens des choses religieuses, un art incomparable d'ouvrir des pistes à la recherche et d'entraîner des travailleurs à sa suite. J'ai un peu honte d'être réduit a ne retenir d'une œuvre aussi riche que la sienne qu'un aspect, – celui qui nous intéresse le plus ici, mais dont on verra cependant toute la portée: l'élaboration d'une méthode de mesure de la *pratique religieuse*.[1]

Observant que 'toutes les religions proposent agrégations, observances et dévotions', assemblées de prières et gestes cultuels, mais qu'entre toutes les Eglises, l'Eglise romaine présente un code de prescriptions précises et impérieuses, ne réputant fidèles que ceux qui s'y conforment exactement, Le Bras suggère aux spécialistes

– de procéder au dénombrement des actes cultuels accomplis par les baptisés, depuis les plus fondamentaux (assistance à la masse, communion pascale, réception des sacrements) jusqu'aux pratiques surérogatoires de dévotions;
– d'utiliser à cette fin des catégories de documents jusqu'ici negligées et qui apportent des données chiffrées et des éléments de statistique, depuis les visites pastorales de l'Ancien Régime jusqu'aux enquêtes contemporaines d'organismes spécialises;
– de procéder a l'établissement (au besoin par courbes) de comparaisons entre groupes d'age, groupes sociaux-professionnels, ainsi qu'entre époques différentes afin de saisir le mouvement de la ferveur croissante ou décroissante.

Il a toujours beaucoup insisté sur le fait que de pareils dénombrements et calculs ne livreraient que l'*extérieur* de l'état religieux des personnes et des groupes, si bien qu'il faudrait chercher les motivations des attitudes

---

[1] G. Le Bras, 'Statistique et histoire religieuse', *RHEF*, XVII (1931) pp 425–49; *Introduction à l'histoire de la pratique religieuse en France*, 2 vols (Paris 1945); et les innombrables articles et notes prodigués par le même auteur, jusqu'à sa mort. Sur l'œuvre de Doyen Le Bras, vz les hommages rendus à sa mémoire à l'Assemblée Générale de la Société d'histoire ecclésiastique de France, dans *RHEF*, LVI (July/Dec 1970).

enregistrées, comme aussi l'influence de causes historiques et conjoncturelles au plan socio-économique ou au plan intellectuel et politique. Mais il tenait pour un préalable indispensable d'en finir avec ces à peu près dont se contentaient trop facilement jusque-là les catholiques et qui le savaient porté, relevait-il avec humour, au cours du précédent demi-siècle, à soutenir, tantôt qu'ils formaient l'écrasante majorité de la nation, puisque 90% des Français recevaient le baptême à la naissance, tantôt que l'irréligion minoritaire avait par des manœuvres obscures arraché à l'Eglise la totalité de la classe laborieuse et des régions entières, au point transformer la France en 'pays de mission'.

Les méthodes d'investigation suggérées par G. Le Bras ont rencontré un accueil immédiat parmi les historiens et les sociologues.

D'une part elles survenaient à un moment où l'école historique française, sous l'impulsion de Marc Bloch et de Lucien Febvre, s'orientait vers l'étude des 'mentalités populaires'. Ces deux maîtres répétaient que l'histoire des civilisations, des modes de vie et des manières de pensée des populations importent plus que le récit de la succession des événements ou de la geste des grands politiques et conquérants qui passent pour conduire le monde. Que, si l'on veut mesurer la distance qui sépare le passé du présent, il faut surtout restituer avec ses couleurs propres la psychologie des masses, des hommes du commun, avec leurs conceptions du monde, leurs croyances, leurs aspirations et leurs rêves. Si donc les sociétés médiévales ou d'Ancien Régime avaient été des communautés de baptisés, de croyants, orientées par l'enseignement de l'Eglise, il importait au plus haut degré de déterminer dans quelle mesure les hommes du XIIème ou du XVIème siècle avaient assimilé la doctrine catholique, plié leur conduite à ses commandements, obéi ou résisté à la pression sociale et au conformisme religieux…Ainsi ces historiens et les disciples qui ont subi leur influence étaient-ils venus par une autre voie à des analyses de sociologie religieuse dont L. Febvre devait donner un chef d'oeuvre dans sa célèbre étude sur Rabelais ou *Le Problème de l'Incroyance au XVIème siècle.*[1]

D'autre part, aux yeux des clercs et des fidèles préoccupés dans ce temps de pastorale et d'apostolat, les nouvelles directions de recherche apparaissaient comme d'un très grand prix. C'était l'heure des mouvements 'd'action catholique', hantés par le souci de prendre la mesure

---

[1] L. Febvre, *Le Problème de l'incroyance au XVIème siècle: la religion de Rabelais* (Paris 1947). On notera que Lucien Febvre, le chef de l'école des *Annales: Economies, Sociétés, Civilisations,* a trouvé l'essentiel de son analyse dans des documents littéraires, et n'a guère pratiqué 'l'histoire sérielle', plus tard exaltée par ses disciples, comme Pierre Chaunu. On pourrait en dire presque autant du Doyen Le Bras.

Pratique, piété et foi populaire

d'une déchristianisation qu'il s'agissait de combattre pour refaire chrétiens les hommes les plus éloignés de l'Eglise ou ramener les 'déliés' à la pratique et à la religion personnelle. Aussi est-ce très largement parmi les prêtres et les équipes d'action catholique que Le Bras trouva des continuateurs: les animateurs des enquêtes diocésaines généralisées entre 1950 et 1960, (nous en possédons une cinquantaine avec la caution de sociologues patentés); les auteurs d'études locales ou générales qui prirent la forme de thèses soutenues à Lyon par l'abbé Ligier[1] et le Père Pin,[2] à Paris par l'abbé Huot-Pleuroux.[3] Au tout premier plan de ces travaux il faut mettre l'œuvre du chanoine Boulard,[4] la plus approfondie et la plus continue à la fois, depuis les premières esquisses en sociologie religieuse (1947), qui nous ont valu la première carte d'ensemble de la pratique religieuse pour la France rurale, jusqu'au tout récent volume sur *Pratique religieuse et régions culturelles* (1968), qui montre comment une analyse de plus en plus fine des données chiffrées peut permettre de rectifier des idées qu'on tenait pour acquises, notamment sur l'influence villes-campagnes ou sur la continuité de la déchristianisation.

Aujourd'hui des chantiers de recherche, qui font une large part à ces préoccupations, sont ouverts un peu partout, à Paris avec le Centre international de Sociologie des Religions, le Centre Catholique de Sociologie, l'Institut d'Ethnologie et de Sociologie Religieuse des Facultés Catholiques, et en province, notamment à Lyon où notre Centre National de Recherches d'Histoire du Catholicisme a tenu en 1963 un Colloque qui a ouvert trois années de travaux sur le thème de la Déchristianisation.[5]

Une des conséquences les plus heureuses de ce mouvement a été de provoquer un effort à l'échelle nationale pour classer et inventorier les

---

[1] S. Ligier, 'Recherches sociologiques sur la pratique religieuse du Jura' (thèse complémentaire pour le Doctorat ès Lettres, Lyon 1951, non-publiée): un des ouvrages peut-être les plus complets du genre.

[2] E. P. E. Pin, *Pratique religieuse et classes sociales dans un paroisse urbaine, St Pothin à Lyon* (Paris 1956).

[3] [P]. Huot-Pleuroux, 'Le Recrutement sacerdotal dans le diocèse de Besançon de 1801 à 1960'–'La vie chrétienne [dans le Doubs et la Haute Saône de 1860 à 1900]' (thèses lettres, 2 vols, Paris 1966).

[4] F. Boulard, avec A. Achard et H.-J. Emerard, *Problèmes missionnaires de la France rurale*, 2 vols (Paris 1947); *Essor ou déclin du clergé français* (Paris 1950); etc.; et, en collaboration avec J. Remy, *Pratique religieuse urbaine et régions culturelles* (Paris 1968).

[5] Colloque international d'Histoire religieuse de Lyon, 2 vols, *Cahiers d'Histoire* [Lyon, Grenoble], VIII–IX (1963–4); cf [A.] Latreille, ['La Déchristianisation en France à l'époque moderne'], à Colloque de Cambridge 24–8 Septembre 1968, dans *Miscellanea Historiae Ecclesiasticae*, III, ed Derek Baker (Louvain 1970) pp 287–313, et *Cahiers d'Histoire*, XIV, I (1969).

documents qui peuvent subsister, en dresser des catalogues, en préparer éventuellement la publication. C'est ainsi que, sous l'impulsion conjointe de la Société d'Histoire Ecclésiastique de France et du Centre de Lyon, il a été possible de provoquer une remise en ordre des dépôts d'archives ecclésiastiques, qui, souvent mutilées lors de la Séparation, se trouvaient dans plus d'un évêché négligées, faute de personnel et d'une appréciation exacte de leur importance.[1] Parmi les catégories de documents les plus révélateurs pour l'étude de la pratique et de la vitalité religieuse, on a été amené à placer au premier rang les comptes rendus de visites pastorales et les comptes rendus de missions. Nous venons de lancer une enquête destinée à dresser un répertoire de l'ensemble des visites pastorales depuis le Moyen-Age jusqu'à l'époque actuelle. Une grille codée établie par MM. J. Gadille, de Lyon et M. Venard, de Paris, doit permettre de signaler par des chiffres conventionnels les diverses catégories de renseignements qu'on trouvera dans chaque compte rendu, sur le personnel ecclésiastique, sur état matériel des édifices du culte, sur les œuvres paroissiales, sur l'assiduité de la pratique, sur le comportement moral des populations, etc... Ce catalogue permet dès maintenant de réaliser que le nombre des indices entrant en combinaison dans l'appréciation de la vie religieuse est allé sans cesse croissant au cours des trente années de mise au point des méthodes et devrait permettre de serrer plus exactement le problème.

2

Cependant, si féconde qu'elle ait été, la sociologie religieuse à base mathématique et statistique orientée sur la mesure de la pratique risque de trouver assez vite ses limites.

Il est peu probable qu'on puisse dans ce domaine, à l'instar de ce qui se fait dans l'histoire économique, constituer une 'histoire sérielle', faute de séries de chiffres continues et de chiffres comparables entre eux. J'ai souligné ici même l'an dernier[2] – et je n'y reviendrai pas – deux raisons fondamentales qui expliquent que le champ d'application de cette méthode soit limité:

– la discontinuité des séries. Il est trés difficile de s'en servir pour 'L'Ancien Régime', parce que jusque vers la fin du XVIIIème siècle la statistique administrative est à peu près ignorée. D'autre part parce que la pratique religieuse

---

[1] Sur le classement des archives diocésaines, cf les notes de J. Gadille dans *RHEF*, XLIX (1963), LIII (Jan 1967). Sur le dépouillement des visites pastorales cf D. Julia, J. Gadille, M. Venard dans *RHEF*, LV (Jan./Juin 1969).

[2] Latreille, p 297.

étant obligatoire, imposée par les autorités étatiques et par la pression sociale, les chiffres relatifs à la réception des sacrements, aux vocations religieuses, etc... n'ont pas du tout la même signification que ceux que nous obtenons pour la période moderne. On ne commence guère à avoir des enquêtes épiscopales systématiques, détaillées et suivies que vers le milieu du XIXème siècle: M. Henri Gazeau, étudiant 'l'évolution religieuse des pays angevins de 1824 à 1870' ne peut guère utiliser des statistiques de pratique qui manquent pour cette époque; par contre, Mme Marcilhacy a pu faire un tableau du diocèse d'Orléans dès 1849 en s'appuyant sur les enquêtes canoniques que Mgr Dupanloup, un des premiers, a exigées de ses coopérateurs.

– le fait que les chiffres n'expriment pas à eux seuls le tonus religieux d'une époque ou d'un groupe humain. Ils ne disent ni la sincérité ni l'élan des démarches, ni la logique ni les contradictions de la conduite des croyants, ni la ferveur et la puissance créatrice du sentiment religieux. Sur tous ces points rien ne remplace le témoignage, qui seul permet d'aller de l'extérieur, du geste, à l'intérieur aux dispositions intimes surtout lorsque ce témoignàge émane de spirituels ayant une expérience profonde des âmes. Des publications récentes viennent de prouver, tant pour l'Ancien Régime que pour le XIXème siècle, combien peuvent être éclairants les témoignages d'un simple curé de paroisse ou ceux des prêtres prédicateurs de missions à travers tout un diocèse.

Arrêtons-nous sur un exemple particulièrement significatif.[1] Prenons pour guides les missionnaires du diocèse de Besançon qui, pendant un demi-siècle, de 1860 à 1900, ont parcouru deux départements de l'Est de la France, le Doubs et la Haute-Saône, en y donnant des missions, c'est-à-dire des stations de prédication, d'enseignement catéchétique, avec des offices solennels, destinées à ranimer le zèle des fidèles et à ramener à la pratique ceux qui s'en étaient éloignés, – en un mot à provoquer un 'réveil' religieux.

Notons, pour la clarté, que ces prêtres sont des hommes du terroir, ayant la fibre populaire, évoluant dans une 'région culturelle' caractérisées: sans doute le diocèse n'est pas homogène, puisqu'il comprend un pays montagnard et rural, traditionnaliste, fortement attaché à ses traditions religieuses, le Doubs; et une pays de plaines ouvertes aux influences extérieures, en voie d'industrialisation, avec des noyaux

---

[1] Les citations de cette page et des suivantes jusqu'à p 286 sont tirées de Huot-Pleuroux, *La Vie chrétienne*. Ce qui achève de donner leur prix à ces appréciations 'qualitatives', c'est qu'elles se prêtent à des comparaisons à travers les siècles. Or les publications de ce genre ont été nombreuses en France soit pour l'Ancien Régime – cf divers, 'Missionnaires catholiques à l'intérieur', *Bulletin de la Société d'étude du XVIIème siècle*, IV (Paris 1958); M. Venard, 'Les Missions des Oratoriens d'Avignon aux XVIIème et XVIIIème siècles', *RHEF*, XLVIII (1962) pp 5–16 – soit pour le XIXème siècle – cf notamment Y. M. Hilaire, 'Les Missions intérieures dans la region du Nord au XIXème siècle', *Revue du Nord*, CLXXX (Lille 1964) pp 51–68.

protestants importants, tenu pour médiocre, voire pour hostile à 'la religion', la Haute-Saône. Toutefois, dans l'ensemble, il s'agit de populations fortement marquées par l'empreinte d'un long passé catholique, qui a contribué à l'orginalité provinciales: c'est ce qu'atteste le langage des missionaires, jugeant communément une paroisse bien ou mal 'conservée', selon qu'elle a – ou non – gardé les 'traditions de religions', se montrant moins soucieux d'évaluer la majorité fidèle que l'importance de la minorité qui ne fait plus 'ses devoirs'.

On peut distinguer comme trois degrés dans l'approche qu'ils tentent d'effectuer du sentiment religieux dans le public paroissial.

1. D'abord, le degré de pratique. Présence aux offices, aux instructions, réception des sacrements, nos missionnaires font des totaux, visant même à établir des proportions par catégories sociales ainsi à Pont-de-Roide, centre ouvrier important, en 1897, ils estiment que près de 1,900 personnes (dont 850 hommes) ont 'fait leur mission'; 50 à 60 hommes seulement s'y seraient refusés, 'les bourgeois, quelques négociants, quelques fonctionnaires'. On ne croit pas qu'un seul ouvrier ait manqué à l'appel. On a eu 480 hommes à la communion générale. La procession finale a rassemblé 3,000 personnes.

Dans ces supputations, les missionnaires semblent honnêtes, encore que un peu portés, bien sûr, à souligner les retournements heureux produits par leurs efforts; mais ils sont capables d'enregistrer leurs échecs: à Planche-les-Mines (près Lure; 2,638 hab.) 100 à 130 personnes le matin, dont 3 hommes, la 'décadence de cette paroisse' paraît insurmontable.

Or ce qui me semble le plus digne de remarque, c'est que, lorsqu'ils ont compté leurs gens, c'est moins cependant au chiffre qu'ils attachent de l'importance qu'à l'atmosphère de la réunion. Sans doute, ils ne interrogent pas sur ce qu'il y a de formalisme chez les fidèles (ils souhaitent presque que la pression sociale continue à s'exercer en faveur de la religion, comme le prouve l'insistance qu'ils mettent à souligner le poids de l'exemple des notables, du maire, des fonctionnaires, des gendarmes, du directeur d'usine...). Mais en revanche ils sont très attentifs à la qualité de la participation des présents: il leur arrive d'écrire, au sujet d'une paroisse où presque tout le monde a communié: 'la majeure partie de cette population a conservé les pratiques les plus essentielles à la religion, mais *la piété y fait complétement défaut*'. Ou encore: 'C'est un bon peuple, et il a bien conservé les pratiques catholiques...[mais il] est lent et somnolent. Il vient aux instructions, mais toujours en retard, et il y dort.' Remarques qui vont loin: il faut non seulement l'accomplissement du précepte, mais une certaine chaleur d'adhesion de 'l'enthousiasme' et de 'l'entrain'; dans ce cas seulement, on parle d'une bonne mission. Il arrive même à ces observateurs de reconnaître, là où la pratique est tombée très bas, la persistance de qualités chrétiennes: 'Si les pratiques religieuses indiquaient la valeur réelle d'une paroisse, celle-ci mériterait la mauvaise réputation dont elle jouis', mais le peuple, 'gai, vif, sympathique' est capable de répondre a l'appel qui lui est adressé. D'une autre (Mercey, près de Gray, la ville la plus indifférente du département): 'Cette paroisse...est dans un état pitoyable au point de vue religieux...Du reste la population a ceci de particulier qu'elle est excessivement sympathique' et elle a suivi la mission 'avec entrain'.

2. Deuxième degré: le comportement moral des baptisés. Si le réveil religieux recherché est évalué d'abord selon les présences et l'afflux aux sacrements, il doit aboutir à la réforme et l'amélioration de la conduite des fidèles. Les missionnaires prêchent surtout sur la morale – une morale plus individuelle que sociale – sur l'observation des commandements. Pour eux l'abaissement du niveau religieux a pour signe et pour cause l'inobservation de ces commandements, notamment dans leur région du fait de

– l'ivrognerie, commune chez les travailleurs même à la campagne, mais encore plus dans les agglomérations où le cabaret a la pire influence; et la violence, suite de l'intempérance;

– la 'légereté', le goût des jeux et du bal, particulièrement dans les villes ouvrières parmi les jeunes et les femmes;

– le déclin de l'esprit familial (remarquons ici que les prêtres de ce temps s'inquiètent parfois de la dénatalité mais plutôt comme d'une marque d'éloignement des saines traditions que comme d'un manquement intrinsèque à la loi, et ne semblent pas pousser très loin les entretiens sur la morale conjugale).

Manière d'apprécier la moralité chrétienne un peu élémentaire, à nos yeux peut-être un peu négative en ce qu'elle ne semble pas développer les aspects sociaux de la loi de charité. Mais qui n'est pas ignorante des dimensions ni des conditions sociales de la moralité, la décadence religieuse leur paraît s'annoncer dès que 'la famille et le dimanche' ne sont plus l'objet du respect des chrétiens, et un des points qui les préoccupent le plus est l'inobservation du repos dominical dans les manufactures et même aux champs.

3. Troisième élément d'appréciation: la persistance de la foi.

A défaut de la pratique, de la bonne conduite, nos missionnaires savent encore se préoccuper de déceler des restes de foi, susceptibles d'être ranimés chez des baptisés. C'est ce que dit assez joliment ce croquis de la petite ville de Lure, 4,500 habitants, capitale de la libre-pensée en Haute-Saône, pleine de francs-maçons': 'A la vérité, Lure n'est pas un couvent où tous disent leur chapelet, ni même une Thébaïde où l'on se donne la discipline chaque jour, mais la foi chrétienne est restée vivace dans ce peuple'; et les attaques même des adversaires font que 'personne ne reste indifférent' au problème religieux.

L'indifférence semble bien être ce que ces apôtres redoutent le plus, la dernière étape de la déchristianisation. Il est assez difficile de discerner, à travers la suite de ces textes, si au cours d'un demi-siècle d'efforts pour la combattre, ces prêtres croient à un progrès de l'irreligion: certaines notations font penser que, vers 1900, ils relèvent moins d'hostilité militante qu'en 1879-80, mais qu'ils constatent plus de détachement. Evolution qui semble rapportée par eux, comme tout à l'heure un certain matérialisme pratique, à des causes locales plus qu'à des causes générales, au 'malheur des temps', à l'esprit du siècle et de la 'civilisation' évoqués, rarement, comme un fond de tableau. Comme leur ouailles, ces prêtres zélés ont un horizon limité, et ils raisonnent comme si le niveau de la vie spirituelle des petites communautés paroissiales dépendent plutôt de la somme des efforts individuels de fidélité, de docilité à l'égard de l'Eglise, que des conditions de vie faites aux hommes par le régime économique, ou de l'ambiance créée par les grands débats intellectuels et politiques du temps.

Il ne faut pas demander à ces témoins plus qu'ils n'ont prétendu donner. Leurs relations ne s'élèvent jamais à une vue globale du milieu national, même pas du milieu régional où sont insérées les paroisses dont ils ont la responsabilité pour un temps: mais elles ont précisément le mérite de nous mettre en garde contre les généralisations et de faire ressortir la variété des situations locales jusqu'à l'échelon communal. Et, à cette échelle elles nous apportent précisément le commentaire, l'appréciation qualitative indispensables pour interpréter des données chiffrées et quantitatives. La statistique nous livrerait peut-être des chiffres exacts, mais en pareille matière plus que l'*exact*, ce qui importe, c'est le *vrai* que nous livrent les appréciations d'homme d'expérience et de discernement. Ainsi, en distingant comme ils le font trois sortes de critère de la vitalité religieuse: pratique, comportement moral, croyance, – ils nous donnent une clef d'analyse fort intéressante. Ils nous mettent en garde contre le risque de 'définir l'énergie ou la faiblesse de la foi par les manifestations plus visibles de la dévotion... qui, étant plus basse, tombe sous nos calculs' (J. Guitton) et se prête plus facilement aux procédés d'enquête de l'histoire sérielle, de la sociologie mathématique, de la psychologie, voire de la psychiâtrie. Avec des documents de ce genre, que la vogue de la sociologie religieuse a contribué à faire sortir, nous rejoignons bien cette masse commune des hommes que nous voulions atteindre et nous débouchons déjà sur une certaine vue du sentiment religieux.

3

La mise en œuvre des méthodes quantitatives de la sociologie religieuse constitue donc aujourd'hui un préliminaire indispensable à toute tentative d'évaluation de la vitalité religieuse d'une époque ou d'une région donnée. Mais elle doit être complétée par l'étude qualitative et conjoncturelle du sentiment religieux. Pour l'individu comme pour le groupe, le niveau religieux se mesure sans doute aux gestes de participation au culte, aux actes posés, mais aussi dans une très large mesure à l'idéal reconnu comme norme de vie et à la prédominance des préoccupations spirituelles sur les matérielles. De là l'importance de l'étude de la littérature religieuse et de l'art religieux, dont on peut redouter que la vogue de la sociographie ait trop largement détourné les historiens modernes. De là aussi l'importance de l'histoire de la spiritualité,[1] faite à travers les œuvres des docteurs, des maîtres à penser, des saints et des héros, car c'est chez les plus grands, et non à l'échelon inférieur de la médiocrité statistique que doivent être saisies la pensée et les aspirations d'une collectivité.

Un des historiens à qui nous devons le tableau probablement le plus complet et le plus fouillé de la physionomie religieuse d'une région française de la fin du XIXème au milieu du XXème siècle, M. Gérard Cholvy,[2] vient de montrer dans deux vigoureux articles que, si la sociographie a envahi l'histoire et lui a apporté des collections d'observations, des techniques et des orientations précieuses, néanmoins elle ne saurait se substituer à elle. Dès qu'il s'agit d'interpréter les phénomènes enregistrés, il faut chercher le secret de leur explication dans le passé et dans des comparaisons à travers le temps. On ne saurait alors négliger ni l'impact des événements (et des grandes crises qui en brisent le cours), ni

---

[1] Vz la très utile *Histoire spirituelle de la France* (Paris 1964) par E. Labande, A. Rayez etc; extraits du *Dictionnaire de Spiritualité*, v, art. 'France'.

[2] G. Cholvy, *Géographie religieuse de l'Hérault contemporain* (Paris 1968); 'Sociologie religieuse et Histoire', *RHEF*, LV (Jan 1969) pp 5–28; 'L'Apport de la Sociologie à l'histoire religieuse' *Cahiers d'Histoire*, XV, 2 (1970) pp 97–111.

l'influence des hommes qui parfois les dominent et les infléchissent. J'ajouterais, en utilisant précisément une remarque du doyen Le Bras, qu'il faut tenir grand compte des mutations de civilisation et du bouleversement des mœurs communes par l'évolution des techniques: car une 'civilisation profane qui substitue aux distractions religieuses les distractions mondaines, à la tranquillité des soumissions une fièvre d'indépendance, à la préparation de l'éternel l'exploitation du viager', enlève à l'Eglise un plus grand nombre de fidèles que les arguments de la philosophie ou les préjuges de classe.

Il se pourrait précisément que nous assistions en ce moment à une rupture du cours de l'histoire capable de remettre en question les résultats obtenus par les efforts concertés de la sociologie et de l'histoire en ces trente dernières années. Et ceci sous l'effet soit de mutations intérieures à l'Eglise romaine depuis Vatican II, soit de transformations dans les moeurs et les manières de pensée du public.

Nous avions érigé en règle de comptabiliser les actes religieux et voilà que la crainte du formalisme et le discrédit du juridisme dans l'Eglise vont renlever toute signification à des critères tenus jusqu'ici pour particulièrement expressifs. Ainsi pour la réception des sacrements. Le baptême des petits enfants, prescrit naguère aux parents dans les plus brefs délais, est aujourd'hui systématiquement retardé par les prêtres soucieux de s'assurer du sérieux de la démarche des parents qui le demandent, parfois même refusé lorsque manque la garantie d'une véritable éducation religieuse pour l'enfant. De même, il est au moins conseillé aux prêtres de s'abstenir de célébrer une cérémonie religieuse de mariage, s'ils ont lieu de croire que le passage par l'Eglise n'est souhaité que pour des motifs de convenance mondaine par les fiancés ou leurs proches. Par conséquent, dans un avenir proche, il n'y aura plus rien à tirer pour la mesure du sentiment religieux des statistiques sur les délais du baptême, et bien peu à deduire de la chute du pourcentage des cérémonies religieuses par rapport au nombre des mariages.

Quant aux deux démarches tenues, depuis toujours pourrait-on dire, commes les signes propres d'appartenance à l'Eglise romaine: l'assistance à la messe dominicale et le communion pascale, elles risquent de ne plus pouvoir faire l'objet d'aucune évaluation certaine dans le cadre de la paroisse, voire de l'agglomération, avec les déplacements des citadins en fin de semaine vers les résidences secondaires ou les centres touristiques, comme avec le décalage de la messe dominicale reportée au samedi.

Que dire enfin de certains étalons de mesure qu'on utilisait à titre complémentaire, – comme le nombre d'édifices cultuels bâtis dans une aire géographique déterminée? Hier preuve de vitalité et d'élan religieux au point que le langage usuel confondait 'l'âge des cathédrales' avec 'les siècles de foi', l'empressement à construire des églises aura-t-il un sens lorsqu'on ne souhaitera plus la célébration de la Parole que dans de petits cénacles d'amis ou dans des edifices sans affectation sacrée?

D'une manière générale, il devient évident que, dans le public des baptisés catholiques, le sentiment du caractère obligatoire ou simplement de l'importance des pratiques prescrites par l'Eglise est allé s'effaçant rapidement. Nous manquons de données pour mesurer le changement. Cependant une enquête de l'Institut Français d'Opinion Publique en 1969 auprès des jeunes de 15 à 30 ans peut en donner une idée: elle enregistre que 23% seulement des jeunes catholiques disent aller régulièrement à l'église, alors qu'il y a neuf ans (en 1958) la proportion s'élevait à 37%. Ce qui appelle deux remarques:

1. La brutalité de la chute est frappante. Jusqu'ici les statisticiens constataient la relative stabilité de la pratique, qui accusait une 'erosion lente', mais se maintenait pour une même région ou une même catégorie autour des mêmes chiffres globaux. M. Cholvy notait pour l'Hérault que la pratique pascale s'était maintenue de 1911 à 1931 autour de 32.5%, et n'avait fléchi qu'à 28% de 31 à 62. Maintenant on a un effondrement de plus du tiers en neuf ans seulement. Il faudrait donc supposer que, dans la période précédente, un nombre de pratiquants important aurait obéi à la tradition ou au conformisme plutôt qu'à une ferveur active, et que leur fidélité relative aurait été emportée, depuis 1960, dans le courant de changement qui secoue familles, sociétés et églises.

2. On assiste à une dissociation de plus en plus fréquente entre la pratique, dont on se détache, et la foi, qui persiste à s'affirmer. Les observateurs constatent le maintien, et peut-être un accroissement, du nombre des catholiques soucieux d'une religion personnelle et d'une ferveur authentique, même s'ils ne sont pas toujours très dociles à l'Eglise. Et d'autre part, parmi les gens détachés de l'Eglise, ils sont surpris par le nombre de ceux qui se disent croyants, qui croient en Dieu, qui entretiennent des relations de confiance avec le Christ, fils de Dieu.

Donc on assisterait en ce moment à un changement saisissant non seulement dans les chiffres et les proportions fournis par les statistiques, mais dans un changement de signification des notions de pratiques, de devotion, de foi. Notions naguère bien distinctes, et fondamentales, et significatives, aujourd'hui confuses comme le langage même employé pour les exprimer. Quand les missionnaires du siècle dernier notaient chez certains indifférents la persistance de 'la foi', ils entendaient sous ce mot la foi de l'Eglise catholique romaine, avec son catalogue précis de croyances contenues dans des formales rigoureusement immuables. Aujourd'hui ceux qui scrutent l'évolution de la pensée contemporaine à travers la production littéraire,[1] s'ils notent la persistance de la foi dans des esprits détachés de l'Eglise, n'entendent par là qu'un sentiment religieux vague, la soif de Dieu, la nostalgie du Christ homme-Dieu, le refus d'admettre l'athéisme d'une civilisation qui, sans Lui, serait privée de tout idéal. Il y a loin de cette seconde acception à la première. La crise de la pensée s'exprime dans la crise même du langage, qui fait que les mots sont pris comme ayant, non pas un sens, mais une fonction pour le moment présent.

Cette situation présente met en cause, non pas seulement des procédés d'évaluation quantitative, dont l'historien a toujours su et affirmé qu'ils demandaient à être interprétés et complétés mais bien l'ensemble des méthodes d'approche du fait religieux, mises au point dans une période de stabilité des institutions, des mœurs, du langage. Le chanoine Boulard nous avait avertis: 'Toutes les fois qu'il y a mutation brusque de la civilisation humaine, le problème chrétien est entièrement reposé à neuf'. Nous voici aujourd'hui en pleine crise de civilisation: il devient de plus en plus malaisé d'acquérir une idée de ce phénomène complexe qu'est le niveau religieux d'une génération ou d'une communauté d'hommes. Il nous faut reviser nos méthodes d'investigation, sans sacrifier aucune de celles qui nous ont permis des progrès dans le passé, mais en prenant toujours mieux conscience de leur insuffisance pour introduire l'histoire jusque dans secret des consciences individuelles et des mentalités collectives.

[1] J. Duquesne, *Dieu pour l'homme aujourd'hui* (Paris 1970); Anonyme, *Pour vous, qui est Jésus-Christ?* (Paris 1970).

THE WELSH REVIVAL OF 1904-5:
A CRITIQUE

by BASIL HALL

IN the *Lancet* for 26 November 1904, there was a brief and caustic account of 'curious psychological phenomena...in connexion with the religious upheaval in progress' in Wales, in which 'the chief instigator of this tumult' [that is, Evan Roberts] is quoted as saying to a journalist who interviewed him for the *Western Mail*: 'When I go out to the garden I see the devil grinning at me but I am not afraid of him. I go into the house, and when I go out again to the back I see Jesus Christ smiling at me.' The *Lancet* also cited a description of the young revivalist by the same journalist: 'His restlessness is marvellous, he is walking about all day with the springiness of a man treading on wires, his arms swaying unceasingly'; and referred to accounts of the revivalist lying on the floor at meetings for long intervals 'weeping and writhing in agony'. The *Lancet* commented that if among the friends of the preacher there were any medical practitioners it would be a kindness on their part to point out to him 'the peril which menaces his intellectual equilibrium'.[1] This judgement was shrewd for towards the end of 1906 Evan Roberts had broken down, and he never sufficiently recovered from the intense and prolonged nervous excitement of the revival period, but lived in retirement as a near recluse in England from 1906 to 1925, and thereafter in South Wales until his death in 1951.[2] It is a sad story of a young former miner and blacksmith from the background of deep piety in the Welsh calvinist methodist chapel at the village of Loughor in Glamorgan, who was preparing himself for the ministry at a denominational preparatory school prior to theological college training – a man sincere, sensitive and deeply religious, earnestly praying for a revival of religion in Wales – who was caught up by the

---

[1] The *Lancet*, 1 (London 1904) p 1514.
[2] The most recent account of Evan Roberts and the Revival is [Eifion] Evans, [*The Welsh Revival of 1904*] (Port Talbot 1969). This does not raise the issues which are the purpose of this paper, since its aim is more edification than historical analysis, but it contains many useful references in the notes, and provides in chapter 11, pp 178–82, a useful summary of the secluded life of Roberts after the end of the Revival.

wave of intense religious emotion which the revival released and who found himself shining before the world in excited newspaper reports throughout Britain and Europe in a blaze of glory, fanned by journalists and religious publicists, as brief as it was excessive.

There are inevitably some difficulties in the way of studying this revival: there is no collective archive, there are no organisational records, and there is the problem posed for non-Welsh speakers by many reminiscences of the period appearing in Welsh.[1] Nevertheless, it is remarkable that while revivalism from the Great Awakening under Jonathan Edwards in New England to the activities of Moody and Sankey, Torrey and Alexander and the late Billy Sunday, had received scholarly research and discussion nothing of real historical value has appeared on the Welsh revival of 1904–5 to compare with the writings of W. G. McLoughlin or T. L. Smith, on American revivalism.[2] A major difficulty is that almost all that has been written on the Welsh revival, whether in Welsh or English, is based on well-intentioned piety which weakens or ignores the principles of historical criticism. Only one book known to me written by a Welshman attempted a critical appraisal of the revival and although some useful points were made it was as rhetorical as it was verbose.[3] It is strange that the two most reliable, scholarly and objectively written accounts of the revival and of Evan Roberts's activities, are to be found in the books written by two Frenchmen from first-hand experience in Wales at the time.[4] The two worked independently of each other and unknown to each other, and they came from different backgrounds, though both were thorough professionals in their respective careers in philosophy of religion and

[1] The National Library of Wales, Aberystwyth, possesses a few items of secondary importance relating to Evan Roberts including a few letters, and has files of the *Western Mail* and the Calvinist Methodist weekly paper, *Y Goleuad*, relating to the Revival period. The Library also possesses pamphlets made up of extracts from the *Western Mail's* reports of Revival meetings. There is a bibliography in the memorial volume for the Revival, *Cyfrol Goffa Diwygiad 1904–1905*, ed Sidney Evans and Gomer M. Roberts (Caernarfon 1954): this bibliography, together with the references in *The Welsh Revival* by Eifion Evans, forms the most complete bibliography yet available.

[2] Calvin Colton, *The History and Character of American Revivals* (2 ed London 1832); W. Warren Sweet, *Revivalism in America: its Origin, Growth and Decline* (New York 1944); T. L. Smith, *Revivalism and Social Reform in mid-nineteenth century America* (New York 1957); *Lectures on Revivals of Religion by Charles Grandison Finney*, ed W. G. McLoughlin (Harvard University Press 1960); [W. G.] McLoughlin, *Modern Revivalism* (New York 1959); W. G. McLoughlin, *Billy Sunday* (New York 1961).

[3] [J. Vyrnwy] Morgan, [*The Welsh Religious Revival, 1904–5, A Retrospect and a Criticism*] (London 1909).

[4] [Henri] Bois, [*Le Réveil en Pays de Galles*] (Toulouse 1907); [J.] Rogues de Fursac, [*Un Mouvement mystique contemporain, le réveil religieux du Pays de Galles*] (Paris 1907).

psychology. Henri Bois was a professor at the faculty of theology at Montauban and later dean of the faculty of protestant theology at Montpellier. He wrote a book entitled *De la connaissance religieuse* which showed how far he had turned away from the traditional calvinist orthodoxy of his Church and also from much in the theology of protestant evangelicalism, and sought through religious experience an essential source for Christian belief. J. Rogues de Fursac was different: he was a professional psychiatrist, to use the modern word, and the author of standard works in the period on psychology and on nervous diseases. Moreover his book on the revival in Wales appeared in a series containing titles by E. Durkheim, M. Nordau and H. Spencer, names which point to a very different world from that of Henri Bois. Rogues de Fursac stated in his Introduction: 'Ces notes ont été prises au cours d'une mission dont j'ai été chargé par le Ministère de l'Intérieur, au printemps 1906, dans le but d'étudier l'influence du mysticisme sur le développement des maladies mentales.' It is worth remembering that in 1905 in France Church and State had been formally separated, and there was a fair degree of religious excitement there. In spite of their holding respectively different views from those prevailing in Welsh religion at that time both Frenchmen were very fair-minded and objective in their work.

It is now time that Welsh historians should undertake studies of that revival, its setting, and its impact on Welsh social life, but in the meanwhile I, an Englishman who once taught church history in Wales and acquired a sympathy for that land and its people, offer this brief critique to serve until someone writes a thorough historical analysis.

Whatever else it was, the Welsh revival was a remarkable example of popular religion: it came from the people, from ordinary folk of the mining valleys and the villages of the countryside; their emotions and their religious aspirations shaped it, and they consciously repudiated professional ministerial guidance or other attempts to guide and control it along lines traditional to revivals of the past. It gloried in what for the *Lancet* were examples of acute hysteria, these manifestations seemed to the participants to form both the goal and the driving force of the revival: these physical effects to those who underwent them demonstrated divine power and provided a focal point and a catharsis for a state of latent malaise and excitement in Welsh national consciousness. Both the French writers referred to above drew attention though very briefly to those latent causes of pressure in Wales on the eve of the revival. Henri Bois pointed to the strong feeling in Welsh Nonconformity against the status and privileges of the established Church in Wales. The mounting pressure for disestablishment found in 1903 a target in the privileges of Church schools reinforced by the terms of the new Education Act of 1902: freedom of education and disestablishment were two strong causes of religious feeling in Wales at that time – and the church schools and the established Church represented for Welsh Nonconformists an English and therefore potentially alien influence in Wales. Rogues de Fursac noticed the emotional commitment to political aspirations in Wales, whether of Socialism in the Rhondda Valley, or of Liberalism there and elsewhere. The Liberal party in Wales was built upon Nonconformity. Dr Vyrnwy Morgan writing in 1909 of the situation in the first years of the century wrote bitterly: 'Nonconformity in general, and Welsh Nonconformity in particular, has become the annexe of the Liberal party', and pointed also to the fact that the most sacred hymns in the Welsh language had been prostituted into being 'war-cries for the Radical hosts'.[1] It will not be overlooked that 1906 brought the Liberal landslide victory: the latent association in the Welsh popular religious mind between Liberalism and what it stood for (Welsh disestablishment among other things) and religion can be seen most clearly in the collapse of a Liberal political gathering into a revival service in the presence of which even Lloyd George had to abdicate. In the last weeks of his career as a revivalist Evan Roberts was urgently requested by Lloyd George not to be present at a large Liberal meeting in Caernarvon during the election campaign of 1906: they compromised by being photographed together – the two were the numinous representatives of Welsh national feeling at the time.[2]

Again, a factor difficult to define, but which was part of other changes from Victorian certainties in the Edwardian period was the unease and search for new ways in religious experience produced by the growth of liberal theological views. R. J. Campbell had been preaching at the City Temple in London on lines he was to develop in his *The New Theology* of 1907 in which vague moralistic and immanentist religion replaced the old theological certitudes of Nonconformity. Another popular pulpit figure of the time was the Presbyterian, Dr John Watson of Sefton Park Church, Liverpool, who under his pen-name of Ian Maclaren wrote 'kailyard' novels popularising, as did his sermons, von Harnack's

---

[1] Morgan, pp 211, 221.
[2] Bois, pp 554–6. 'Le Réveil a eu une indiscutable influence sur la campagne électorale: l'agitation politique et l'émotion religieuse s'y fondues et soudées d'une admirable et originale façon.' Lloyd George's majority jumped from 296 to 1244.

views of the fatherhood of God and the brotherhood of man. On an altogether different level of exposition were the writings of L. A. Sabatier, not least his *Les religions d'autorité et la religion de l'Esprit*, and those of William James, especially his *Varieties of Religious Experience*. Sabatier reflected the strong tendency of the time to oppose dogmatic, authoritarian and institutional Christianity by the concept of a spiritual and partly mystical Christianity: his brother's *Life of St Francis* also reflected this mood.[1] James's work opened for many people new possibilities in the way of experiencing and understanding religion. Further, it was the period in literature of such manifestations, in a descending scale, as the Celtic Twilight, *Peter Pan*, Madam Blavatsky's theosophical disciple Annie Besant, Spiritualism and the beginnings of Psychical Research, and the appalling popularity of the religious novels of Hall Caine and Marie Corelli. The briefest leafing through of the popular literary magazines of the period demonstrates the vague, diffuse religiosity which accompanied and sought to challenge the coarser aspects of Edwardian life. There is, of course, no direct line from, for example, Marie Corelli to the band of ardent young men and women who accompanied Evan Roberts at the revival meetings in Wales. But popular literary culture reflects the aspirations of its time. A vaguely conceived Christian mysticism, anti-dogmatic and anti-clerical in mood, seemed to many, when it took the form of emotional response to the Holy Spirit coming among singing and praying groups, a satisfying substitute for the drier orthodoxies of traditional evangelical Nonconformity.

It was this aspect of the revival, its unordered spontaneity, so frequently commented on by observers, which makes it unique in the history of revivals: it is this unique quality which should have occasioned critical inquiry before now. Those who felt the impact of the Welsh revival ('bent like corn before the wind') were addressed by no great preachers like Jonathan Edwards, Charles Finney or Howell Harris. It was not prepared for, and carefully organised by professional revivalists on the lines of Torrey and Alexander, working at that very time in London, nor on the more sophisticated methods associated recently with Billy Graham.[2] It is true that there had been for some time numbers of prayer meetings across the Principality, and there was

[1] It is interesting that in his book, which gives an edifying account of the Revival in South Wales, H. Elvet Lewis, a London Welsh minister, cites the example of St Francis: *With Christ among the Miners* (London 1906) p 151.

[2] For an analysis of these various methods see the full and admirable account in Mc-Loughlin, *Modern Revivalism*.

a deep longing in evangelical circles – dismayed at the falling off in attendances at Sunday services and Sunday schools as well as by the advances of theological liberalism – for a religious revival. But all those preparations and methods so thoroughly analysed, for example, in Finney's famous *Lectures on Revival* were either ignored or used only occasionally and haphazardly before January 1905 by Roberts and his helpers. We must remember here the powerful influence in Welsh Nonconformity of the doctrine of sovereign grace which had come to be called Calvinism. That strong theological preoccupation opposed attempts to set a revival in motion along the lines of American revivalism, and preferred to wait upon God's initiative in sending 'showers of blessing'. The revival in this view must not be initiated by man for it depends on God. This theological commitment when combined with the popular wish to experience the coming of the Spirit untrammelled by the exhortations of the professional preachers of repentance and judgement on sin, and with the wish to be free from guidance and organisation by ministers and denominational committees, led to the characteristic emphasis of the Welsh revival on youth, even on children, on spontaneity and on the emotion of joyful acceptance of the power of the Spirit. This was further emphasised by the feeling of solidarity and togetherness which Welsh people experienced in the emotive power of hymns and ecstatic prayer in their own language.

It was in this context of singing and praying with little time for preaching, or for formal guidance of meetings which began in the early evening and were prolonged well into the early hours of the morning, that Evan Roberts and his young associates, men and women, found their opportunity. It should be remembered, however, that the revival along more traditional evangelical lines had begun in Cardiganshire and had appeared in other places in South Wales before Roberts had yet attended a meeting. But he soon became a catalyst for the occurrence of intense waves of emotion leading to contortions, prostrations, and outcries which to cool observers like Rogues de Fursac were collective hysteria but to the devout were signs of the Spirit's presence.[1] Roberts profoundly believed that these crises were the work of the Spirit: he prepared nothing beforehand but waited for the Spirit to guide what he would say, or to forbid him to speak but to pray, silently or publicly, or to call for singing. He did not remain in the pulpit or on the platform,

[1] Cf [William] James, [*The Varieties of Religious Experience*] (London 1902) p 251 : 'On the whole, unconsciousness, convulsions, visions, involuntary vocal utterances, and suffocation, must be simply ascribed to the subject's having a large subliminal region, involving nervous instability.'

but moved also about the aisles and into the galleries, exhorting and praying.[1] Singing went on at the same time as several people were praying aloud in different parts of a building. The effects were powerful and intense and even the cautious W. R. Matthews describes the strong influence on himself of the testimonies of Welsh students at a meeting in London.[2] Henri Bois, long accustomed to the dignified and stern worship of the French Huguenot tradition was embarrassed and astonished at the extravagances which occurred in meetings he attended, though he concluded that in spite of the eccentricities there was divine power behind the revival for he was himself a committed Christian.[3] But there were critics: not only Rogues de Fursac, who was neither unkind nor contemptuous, like the writer in the *Lancet*, disapproved of this nervous excitement. For him one simple test would suffice: put a French working man among the Welsh miners at a typical meeting and there would be no hope of converting him since, he argued, these conversions took place because of the 'milieu' in which a Welshman grew up in an environment of Bible, of Sunday school and of hymns, utterly alien to that of the wholly secular 'milieu' of a French working man.[4]

After the first months of innocent glory for Roberts difficulties began which he willingly assigned to the influence of Satan. He repeatedly refused to go to Cardiff though ministers pleaded with him to do so: he replied steadfastly that the Spirit would not allow him to go there – he cited the words used by the voice of the Spirit in Welsh – and no doubt one reason why he did not go to Cardiff was his unreadiness in English for an almost monoglot English-speaking city.[5] But a severe challenge to the validity of his claim to be guided by the Spirit was made by a congregationalist minister at Dowlais who wrote a letter to the *Western Mail* on 31 January 1905, stating that Evan Roberts 'talked glibly of the Holy Spirit as a child speaks of its toy, but somewhat more off-handedly'. For the writer, Peter Price, there were two revivals at work in Wales: a genuine revival which was of God and

a sham revival, a mockery, a blasphemous travesty of the real thing...My honest conviction is this: that the best thing that could happen to the cause of the true religious Revival amongst us would be for Evan Roberts and his girl companions to withdraw into their respective homes and there to examine them-

---

[1] The basis of his exhortations he himself summed up in four articles: a confession to God of all sins of the past hitherto unconfessed; the giving up of everything doubtful; open confession of Christ; ready and immediate obedience to every impulse of the Spirit.

[2] W. R. Matthews, *Memories and Meanings* (London 1969) p 59.

[3] Bois, pp 315ff.   [4] Rogues de Fursac, pp 70ff.

[5] *Ibid*, p 36.

selves and learn a little more of the meaning of Christianity, if they have the capacity for this. It is this mock revival – this exhibition – this froth – this vain trumpery – which visitors see and which newspapers report; and it is harmful to the true Revival, very harmful.

Not unexpectedly Price received a large mail ranging from a postcard asking if he were a shareholder in a brewery, to the comment on the newspaper's description of Price as an Honours graduate in Moral Sciences of Queens' College, Cambridge, that though he was a BA with 'honours in morality' he 'cannot be forgiven for this blasphemy against the Holy Ghost'.[1] Evan Roberts made no reply to this violent attack but that it affected his balance can be seen in the fact that at a meeting at Cwmafon a month later he cried out sobbing on his knees that he had a terrible message to give: 'There is a lost soul present: lost because he disobeys the Holy Spirit.' When people cried 'pray for him', he said 'too late! too late! it is forbidden to pray for the lost soul'. Rogues de Fursac commented on this – 'delirium'.[2]

The day after this incident (21 February 1905) Roberts went into retreat in a room in a private house in Neath, refusing to speak (like Ezekiel), and saw no one save one of the team of young women who had helped him, who took him meals. He had been invited to lead meetings in the Welsh chapels in Liverpool and Birkenhead – towns where more Welsh was spoken than in Cardiff – and he had come to believe this might be the beginning of a great extension of the revival beyond Wales itself. He part-filled a note book with accounts of visions he received in the 'Room of Silence', and claimed that the Spirit taught him many mysteries including how to hold a hand in a handshake to test whether a person was receptive to the Spirit. These visions were both visual and auditory.[3] He went to Liverpool later in 1905 where he refused to speak in English, and became more eccentric in his behaviour, at one time remaining silent for an hour and a half in a pulpit. He would interrupt attempts to guide the meetings in Liverpool and claimed that ministers of the Gospel present were refusing to submit to the Spirit, and in Birkenhead cried out that someone was trying to hypnotise him. A large meeting in a Welsh chapel at Liverpool, near Watson's Sefton Park Church, closed in claims and counterclaims of

[1] Morgan, pp 143 ff.

[2] Rogues de Fursac, p 87. Bois also comments on this incident (pp 435–6) with the understatement: 'ce récit met mal à l'aise'.

[3] Bois gives full extracts from this curious notebook (its whereabouts are apparently now not known) in his French version made from the materials published from it in the *Western Mail* (Bois, pp 437–62).

lack of genuine power and faith.[1] After a brief period in Caernarvon and Anglesey, Roberts then left Wales in 1906 for nearly twenty years.

Rogues de Fursac, a trained psychiatrist, met briefly with Roberts who held his hand throughout the interview, and commented on Roberts afterwards that he was a pleasant person with great mobility of the features, extremely emotional and with a hyperactive imagination. He described him as in a state of intense automatism, at the extreme limit of the normal, suffering from 'psychic asthenia' which, combined with exaltation of the ego, produced a 'hyperactivity of mental automatism' – according to Rogues de Fursac a 'well-established law of psycho-pathology'.[2]

Among other leaders of the revival besides Evan Roberts there were his brother Dan, and his own friend and fellow student Sidney Evans, together with Annie Davies and others from the group about him, who helped in the meetings in South Wales, all of whom were young and new to this type of work: but there were also evangelists who worked on more traditional lines like Rosina Davies, as well as those ministers like Keri Evans and R. B. Jones who sought to guide and lead evangelistic services during the revival,[3] the people whom Peter Price probably had in mind as guides of what he called the true revival. However, in North Wales a farmer's wife was remarkable for taking meetings at which she claimed she had visions of lights on trees, hillsides and village roofs, and also heard the voice of the Spirit. Both Bois and Rogues de Fursac dismissed her as a subject of hallucinations.[4]

But there were also dissentients. For example, Bois reported that the Reverend Daniel Jones, minister of the calvinist methodist chapel at Loughor where Roberts had begun his career as a revivalist, resigned because he disapproved of the nature of the meetings conducted by Roberts, and because of £60 worth of damage to chapel property during the excitement of the meetings.[5] But the chapel members preferred the excitement of revival to Mr Jones – Roberts made a generous gift later to cover the expenses concerned.[6] (There is no evidence that Roberts made personal financial gains from his work as a revivalist; on the contrary he spent his own savings, made for his training for the ministry, to maintain himself during the revival.)

---

[1] Bois, pp 470ff.   [2] Rogues de Fursac, pp 162, 101.   [3] Evans, pp 28, 31.
[4] Bois, pp 346–94; Rogues de Fursac, pp 145ff. Again William James provided in advance a description of this psychological phenomenon: 'There is one form of sensory automation which possibly deserves special notice on account of its frequency. I refer to hallucinatory or pseudo-hallucinatory luminous phenomena, *photisms*, to use the term of the psychologists' (James, p 251).   [5] Bois, p 52, n 1.   [6] *Ibid*, p 466.

What conclusions may be drawn about the effect of the revival in Wales? It is argued by its defenders that it revitalised the religious life of Wales, as may be seen from the statistics of church membership.[1] It is claimed that nearly 100,000 converts were made (though these were in many instances already connected with the churches), and certainly membership figures for the denominations increased. On the other hand it can be claimed on statistical evidence that the Anglican Church in Wales showed a steady increase of members during and after the revival although its congregations, in contrast to the other Welsh denominations, had been least affected by the revival. It is also plain that a large number of the converts fell away during the years before 1914. Dr Eifion Evans points out that many dissatisfied converts turned to Pentecostalism and other sectarian activity – and it is significant that the Pentecostalist movement in this country was associated in time with the beginnings of the revival.[2] A further line of defence for the revival was that it had a strong ethical impact making for greater stability of social life in Wales, for example, in reducing drunkenness and petty crime.[3] But how can one interpret over-simplified or selectively made statistics? One could reasonably expect help on this and other sociological aspects of the revival from an article on it in the *British Journal of Sociology*, 1952, but no effective statistical research was provided by its author who was content with raising some questions and providing vaguely grounded generalisations.[4] His claim that drunkenness ceased to be a problem is too sweeping and is unsupported by adequate evidence.[5] Both Bois and Rogues de Fursac considered this question and gave evidence from the Chief Constables' returns in South Wales (but what of Central and North Wales?). The point was well made by one chief constable, that the decline in drunkenness related to small towns and rural districts: the impact of the revival in this respect for Cardiff and Swansea was minimal. The author of the article on the revival in the *British Journal of Sociology* claimed that there appeared 'many politically

[1] Evans, p 146.
[2] *Ibid*, pp 192–7: the founder of the Elim Pentecostal Movement, George Jeffreys, was converted during the revival at Nantyffyllon.
[3] Rogues de Fursac, p 122; Bois, p 582.
[4] [C. A.] Williams, ['The Welsh Religious Revival, 1904–5', *The British Journal of Sociology*, III (London 1952) pp 242ff. Among other matters, for example, he confuses 'the new theology' of the theological colleges with that of R. J. Campbell, whereas it was derived from the impact of Higher Criticism and the writings of von Harnack, Herrman, Troeltsch and others acting as a solvent on the evangelical tradition. Theological college teachers would have found Campbell's writings too unscholarly to be particularly disturbing.   [5] Williams, p 259.

progressive ministers after 1904...' and that this was 'too much of a coincidence if it had no connection with the revival'.[1] But this was a universal trend in the Churches as a whole, as one example among many there was the movement among Anglo-Catholics in England to political involvement which occurred at the same period, and a similar trend is observable in France in the years before 1914. In any event no-one connected with the Welsh revival meetings had shown interest in, or knowledge of, politically progressive ideologies or activities (other than support for the Liberal Party) – most if not all of the revival's leaders were politically analphabetic. One other point about the effect of the revival leads back to the sour comments in the *Lancet*: the superintendent of the asylum at Bridgend in South Wales claimed an increase of 4% in religious psychoses in 1905, and Bois reported from a Liverpool newspaper a discussion at a committee meeting of the North Western Counties Lunatic Asylum, Denbigh, where a physician argued that nine out of seventeen (this seventeen represented 25% of patients) admitted at the height of the revival showed that the primary cause of mental alienation was religious fervour.[2] But little that is useful emerges from such figures.

Turning from these matters to a judgement based on sincere religious conviction Evan Roberts himself may be quoted considerably: 'The mistake at the time of the Revival in Wales in 1904 was to become occupied with the *effects* of the Revival, and not to watch and pray in protecting and guarding the cause of the Revival.'[3]

One last word: there is an unfortunate tendency for some readers to identify the personal interests of an historian with his subject-matter, therefore, I should add that I share the distaste of the late Father Ronald Knox for 'Enthusiasm' in religion from Montanism onwards, although I hope I have given more considerate attention to the needs and situation in which the Welsh revival arose than he was willing to give to all the targets of his criticism.

[1] Williams, p 257.
[2] Rogues de Fursac, p 122; Bois, pp 576–81: he adds references to French studies of religious mania.
[3] Evans, p 138, citing *War on the Saints* (London 1912) by Mrs J. Penn Lewis and Evan Roberts.

PURITANICALISM, SPORT, AND RACE: A SYMBOLIC CRUSADE OF 1911

by STUART MEWS

RACE and recreation are two contemporary social problems which historically have had a close connection with religion. Religion has both sanctioned racial discrimination and provided the inspiration to overcome it. It has both opposed and encouraged particular forms of popular recreation. Sociologists and social historians are increasingly investigating the various combinations of these 3 Rs – religion, race, recreation. A great deal of work has been done on the relations between religion and race,[1] quite a lot on race and recreation, especially in the form of sport,[2] and a beginning has been made on religion and recreation.[3] To my knowledge, no attempt has yet been made to bring these three elements together.

One recent occasion on which these three items were juxtaposed occurred in the controversy in the early summer of 1970 on the question of race and sport in which two very well-known bishops, David Sheppard and Trevor Huddleston, played a significant role. The campaign to 'Stop the Seventy Tour' went through a number of stages beginning with a protest against the reception of a racially selected

---

[1] Especially in the USA, e.g. Joseph R. Washington, Jr, *Black Religion. The Negro and Christianity in the United States* (Boston 1964); Donald G. Mathews, *Slavery and Methodism: A Chapter in American Morality* (Princeton 1965); Robert M. Miller, 'The Attitudes of American Protestantism Towards the Negro, 1919–39', *J[ournal of] N[egro] H[istory]*, XLII (April 1957) pp 118–31; Robert T. Handy, 'Negro Christianity and American Church Historiography', in [Jerald C.] Brauer [(ed), *Reinterpretation in American Church History*] (Chicago 1968) pp 91–112.

[2] Harry Edwards, *The Revolt of the Black Athlete* (New York 1969); E. B. Henderson, *The Negro in Sports* (Washington 1969); R. Thompson, *Race and Sport* (London, 1964).

[3] Brian Harrison, 'Religion and Recreation in Nineteenth Century England', *Papers Presented to the Past and Present Conference on Popular Religion, 7 July 1966* (mimeo), and published in a shorter version in *PP*, XXXVIII (1967) pp 98–125; William Pickering, 'Religion – A Leisure-time Pursuit?' in David Martin (ed), *A Sociological Yearbook of Religion in Britain* (London 1968), pp 77–93; Patrick Scott, 'Cricket and the Religious World in the Victorian Period', *Church Quarterly* (London) III, 2, October, 1970, pp 134–44; M. Hörrmann, *Religion der Athletum* (Stuttgart, 1968); Siegfried von Kortzfleisch, 'Religious Olympianism', *Social Research* (New York) XXXVII, 2, Summer 1970, pp 231–6.

cricket team from South Africa, and ending with a growing public concern about the effects of the feelings and resentments aroused by the controversy on race relations in this country; a concern which eventually led to the intervention of the then Home Secretary, Mr James Callaghan.

This paper seeks to draw attention to another controversy about another sporting fixture which took place sixty years ago, and which reveals a growing sensitivity to racial problems on the part of some British religious leaders, as well as shedding light on their attitudes to the use of leisure. It also provides evidence for a comparative examination of the motivations and strategies of two puritanical protest movements[1] which were provoked by similar events in both Britain and the United States of America.[2] This particular protest also went through two stages. It was launched at first for reasons very different from those of the 'Stop the Seventy Tour' committee, but it also ended with increasing concern for the damage which might be done to race relations in Britain, and her Empire, and it also closed with the intervention of the Home Secretary of the day, Mr Winston Churchill.

The leading part in this earlier campaign was taken by the secretary of the National Free Church Council, the Reverend F. B. Meyer, a prominent baptist minister, and the object of his attack was a boxing match announced for October, 1911, at Earl's Court, London, between Jack Johnson, an American Negro who was heavyweight champion of the world, and his British challenger, Bombardier Matt Wells. Although Wells was to sink into obscurity, Johnson's name lives on, not only for his boxing prowess, but also for his significance in the struggle of the American Negro.

Jack Johnson's life was a mixture of tragedy and triumph. As the first Negro to take a world title, he could be justly proud of his achievement. But his triumph was marred by the tragic times in which he lived. It was Jack Johnson's misfortune that he reached the peak of his boxing career at a crucial moment in the history of two American protest movements: that of the Negroes, and that of the native, rural, protestant middle class. Both these groups were experiencing the steady erosion of their hard-won rights and statuses by the turn of the century. White supremacy, theoretically smashed in the Civil War, had been

---

[1] By 'puritanicalism' is meant the narrow and negative aspect of nineteenth century Puritanism.

[2] This aspect of the paper is offered in response to, and in agreement with, the call by Winthrop S. Hudson for a more comparative treatment of church history: 'How American Is Religion in America?' in Brauer, pp 155ff.

effectively restored by 1900, and the oppression and resentment of the Negro was, if anything, on the increase.[1] Two strategies were possible. The accommodators led by Booker T. Washington[2] held that in a desperate situation the only realistic policy was temporarily to abandon the open fight for social and political equality, to request tolerance, and for every Negro to work hard, save, and prosper, in the pursuit of 'property, economy, education, and Christian character'.[3] The accommodators were opposed by the agitators – a much smaller group of northern intellectuals known as the Niagara Movement and led by W. E. B. Du Bois[4] – who demanded full civil rights, immediate assimilation, and complete identification with white culture. 'One not familiar with this phase of Negro life in the twelve- or fourteen-year period following 1903,' wrote one Negro leader, 'cannot imagine the bitterness of antagonism between the two wings.'[5] In such a situation, the name of Jack Johnson, the Negro who had made it to the top, was bound to be tossed about like a shuttlecock in the propaganda of these two rival groups.

Another social group concerned with the defence of its status and influence also threatened the boxer. The cultural struggle of the traditional rural protestant society against the alien morality of the urban immigrants was dramatically embodied in various public morality campaigns, the most sustained and temporarily successful of which was to culminate in Prohibition.[6] The Anti-Saloon League of America, which claimed to be 'the churches organised to fight the saloon', though in reality supported mainly by Methodists and Baptists, entered its most militant phase of activity under the leadership of W. B. Wheeler in the period from 1903 to 1916.[7] It is easy to see why the sort of people who made up the League hated Johnson. He was not only a friend of publicans and sinners, but made no secret of the fact. He com-

---

[1] [August] Meier, [*Negro Thought in America, 1880–1915. Racial Ideologies in the Age of Booker T. Washington*] (Ann Arbor 1963) pp 161–5; [Gunnar] Myrdal, [*An American Dilemma. The Negro Problem and Modern Democracy*] (New York, 20th Anniversary Edition, 1962) p 452.

[2] For Washington, see Samuel Spencer, Jr, *Booker T. Washington and the Negro's Place in American Life* (Boston 1955); Donald J. Caliston, 'Booker T. Washington: Another Look', *JNH*, XLIX (Oct. 1964) pp 240–55.

[3] Booker T. Washington, *The Future of the American Negro* (Boston 1902) p 132.

[4] For Du Bois, see Francis L. Broderick, *W. E. B. Du Bois, Negro Leader in a Time of Crisis* (Stanford 1959).

[5] James Weldon Johnson, *Along This Way* (New York 1934) p 313.

[6] [J. R.] Gusfield, [*Symbolic Crusade. Status Politics and the American Temperance Movement*] (Illinois 1963).

[7] [Clifton E.] Olmstead, [*History of Religion in the United States*] (New Jersey 1960) p 464.

bined the shameless extravagance of an Adam Clayton Powell with the quickness, skill, loud mouth, and taunting gesture of a Cassius Clay. His ostentation aroused disapproval amongst both white and coloured moralists. The London *Times* described his American reputation as that of 'a "flash nigger"', a type not to be encouraged by those who have to keep millions of black men in subjection to the dominant race'. It went on to describe 'his golden teeth and the multitude of diamonds which cause him to resemble a starry night'.[1] His open patronage of those establishments on the seamy side of Chicago which provided liquor, gambling, and prostitution, together with his often expressed preference for white women, were a major affront to the Law and Order Leagues, Committees of Public Decency, and Protective Societies, which were springing up throughout America as expressions of middle-class indignation in the first decade of this century.[2]

The moral reformers began to direct their fire at Johnson in 1910 when arrangements were being made for him to fight Jim Jeffries, the former champion, who came out of retirement especially for the purpose of defeating this upstart Negro, whose ability to beat every white man he fought was presented in many quarters as a serious threat to the supremacy of the white race.[3] As soon as it was announced that the match was to be held in San Francisco, the reformers got to work. J. R. Gusfield has argued that another wing of the American moral reform movement, the temperance campaign, at different periods adopted two diverse attitudes to reform which he calls 'assimilative' and 'coercive'.[4] Up to the last decade of the nineteenth century, most attitudes to temperance reform were of the assimilative type. The assimilative reformer was confident that his norms were dominant in society, and looked in sympathy and pity on those too weak to help themselves. The emphasis in this period was on persuasion; the persuasion of the drinker to abandon alcohol if he wished to be accepted by respectable society. In the 1890s, however, the assimilative attitude was being replaced by the coercive. The immigration explosion, the expansion of the cities, and the new wealth created by industrialism, all contributed to the undermining of the traditional puritanical morality which was increasingly being replaced by the new ideology of what Thorstein Veblen, himself the personification of rural protestant virtues,

[1] *The Times*, 4 July 1911, p 4.
[2] [Finis] Farr, [*Black Champion. The Life and Times of Jack Johnson*] (London 1964) pp 72, 53.
[3] James Weldon Johnson, *Black Manhattan* (New York 1969) p 66.
[4] Gusfield.

called 'the leisure class'.[1] In a society in which styles of leisure and consumption increasingly became the outward and visible signs of one's place in the social hierarchy, the distinguishing characteristics of puritanism – sobriety, temperance, industriousness – came to seem provincial and outmoded. The attitude of the reformer was now no longer one of sympathy but hostility. He recognised that the object of his attention was not simply a moral weakling but a hostile exponent of an alternative way of life. When puritanism ceased to set the standard for polite society, and over-all social agreement was lost as to how respectable people should behave, the moral reformer had to fight with all the weapons available against the rival moralities which made their own claim to universal validity.[2] The main thrust of the campaign was switched from the drinker to the men who made and supplied the drink. Such men did not recognise the validity of the social and moral norms of puritanism. Discussion and persuasion were impossible. Coercion, as a result of agitation for legislation and government action, was the only effective way of meeting the enemy.

By the turn of the century, both assimilative and coercive attitudes were to be found in the reform movement, but the latter were clearly in the ascendancy. The agitation against the Jeffries–Johnson fight in 1910 was conducted almost entirely on coercive lines. It was directed not against the boxers or their promoter – no attempt was made to persuade them to call the match off – but appeal was made to the only man who could take effective coercive action, the governor of California. Most of the opposition was organised from Ohio, a rural state which was a stronghold of Prohibition and Populism. From Cincinnati, Ohio, a million postcards were distributed for signing and posting with the message 'STOP THE FIGHT. THIS IS THE 20TH CENTURY.'[3] Complicated telephone relays were set up so that reformers in the middle west could make their protests directly to the governor in California. Fifty ministers held a prayer meeting in front of the state capitol to beseech the Almighty to change the governor's mind.

But it seems that the power of prayer was not quite as effective as the power of the dollar. The governor's mind seemed to change after the president of the San Francisco Board of Trade had received a telegram from Congressman William S. Bennett of New York City, a

---

[1] [Thorstein] Veblen, [*The Theory of the Leisure Class*] (New York, The Modern Library, 1961; first edition 1899).

[2] A similar conflict in an English context is worked out by Alasdair MacIntyre in *Secularization and Moral Change* (Oxford 1967) ch 2.

[3] *N[ew] Y[ork] T[imes]*, 6 June 1910, p 9; Farr, pp 86–7.

member of the House Committee on Foreign Affairs. Bennett warned
that the prospective fight could put obstacles in the path of their efforts
to secure the Panama–Pacific Exposition of 1913, an attraction which
was expected to draw large crowds to San Francisco throughout the
summer.[1] Congressman Bennett, it seems, had recently been a delegate
to the General Assembly of the Presbyterian Church which had resolved
to call upon all citizens and legislators to consider the evils of prizefighting and do all in their power to stamp them out.[2] The governor,
of course, claimed that he had simply been convinced that the proposed
fight was illegal, and that he had in no way been influenced by Bennett's threat. Not everyone believed him, but there were reformers who
preferred to think that the power of prayer and the light of reason had
triumphed. The Reverend H. R. Jamison of Cincinnati declared:

Within the last few days there has gone to the Governor of California such a
deluge of letters from all parts of the country that I believe he has come to a
rightful appreciation of the fight question, and that he has seen through all this
betting and 'fixing' business only a way to the pocketbooks of the people.

I believe he has seen the light of a good life, and that it has called to him so
earnestly by day and by night that he has decided that the Jeffries–Johnson
fight must not come off.[3]

Jamison's words reflect the two attitudes represented in the reform
movement at that time. In one breath he upheld the view of the assimilative reformer that prayer and persuasion were still effective. In the
next he expressed a deeply-felt belief of the coercive reformer that
prizefights, like the drink trade, were part of a conspiracy formed by
evil men from the cities of the east to cheat and rob the people.[4] The
real villains were not the principal performers, but the men who have
been called the 'secondary producers',[5] of whom the most culpable
were the promoters, members of a new occupation which had arisen as
boxing became more lucrative. The promoters and the bookmakers
were the chief enemies of righteousness in the eyes of the reformers.

[1] *NYT*, 16 June 1910, p 2.
[2] *Ibid*, Farr, pp 87–8. Three weeks later Bennett was announced as a candidate for the
Republican nomination for Governor of New York. The *NYT* (7 July 1910, p 5)
explained that his supporters in the Progressive wing of the party had high hopes of
success, partly because as a result of his 'zeal in having the Jeffries–Johnson fight banned
from California, he will have behind him the church people and the moral sentiment
vote'. [3] *NYT*, 16 June 1910, p 2.
[4] Gusfield, p 97; Richard Hofstadter, *The Age of Reform* (New York 1955) pp 70–86.
[5] John W. Loy, Jr, 'The Nature of Sport: A Definitional Effort', in [John W.] Loy, [Jr]
and [Gerald S.] Kenyon, [*Sport, Culture, and Society: A Reader on the Sociology of Sport*]
(London 1969) p 69.

Puritanicalism, sport and race

Undeterred by the setback in California, the resourceful promoter switched the fight to Reno in Nevada, the state which had fewer laws than anywhere else – the Divorce Colony – which had only a negligible number of ministers and of the type of middle-class lady who was elsewhere so prominent in the reform movement. The fulminations of the reformers were intense. The Reverend M. P. Boynton, a Chicago baptist minister, protested that:

Prizefighting has been driven into the nation's backyard, that portion of the country that seems to have to promote and protect the sins of the nation that have been outlawed everywhere else. There should be some way by which our nation could recall the charter of a state that has become a desert and a moral menace. Nevada has no right to remain a part of our nation, with the powers of a state.[1]

In Nevada, the churches were mobilised in opposition to the fight. On the day of the contest 'there was scarcely a church in the State to-day that didn't send its plea up that some thing will happen to prevent this so-called blot on the fair name of Nevada'.[2]

But it was not just the moral decadence of the prize-ring which was so disturbing. It was the fact that Johnson was now pitted against the best that the white race could put up against him. Some Negro leaders tried to dispel the idea that the Reno fight symbolised a struggle between the races. The Reverend Reverdy C. Ransom, of Bethel African Methodist Church, New York, the most prominent ministerial supporter of the Niagara Movement,[3] naturally tried to minimise the racial aspect. In a letter to the *New York Times*, he claimed that 'No respectable colored minister in the United States is interested in the pugilistic contest between Johnson and Jeffries from the standpoint of race. We do not think that Jack Johnson thinks or has ever thought of holding the championship for the "black race".'[4] But that was precisely what some of Johnson's supporters did think.[5] On the morning of the fight, the minister of St Mark's African Methodist Episcopal Church, Chicago, held a prayer meeting which continued as long as the fight lasted.[6] 'In Kansas the negoes have been praying for his triumph.'[7]

[1] Farr, p 106.   [2] *NYT*, 4 July 1910, p 14.
[3] For Ransom, see Meier, pp 159, 180, 185, 220–1, 229, 233; Reverdy C. Ransom, *The Spirit of Freedom and Justice* (Nashville 1926).
[4] *NYT*, 6 June 1910, p 6.
[5] Farr, p 83. The notion that Johnson was the symbolic champion of the Negro race was repeatedly stressed by the *Chicago Defender*, the first highly successful crusading newspaper founded by and for Negroes. On the role of the Negro 'glamour personality', see Myrdal, pp 734–5.   [6] Farr, p 108.   [7] *NYT*, 5 July 1910, p 12.

STUART MEWS

This was to be the match of the century. To add to its attractions,
H. G. Wells was suggested as referee, and an actual invitation sent to Sir
Arthur Conan Doyle, which he regretfully had to decline.[1] The result
of the match and its repercussions were sensational. As the writer Jack
London commented, 'Once again has Johnson sent down to defeat the
chosen representative of the white race, and this time the greatest of
them'.[2] Throughout America, Negroes were euphoric, and in some
cities took to the streets. Elsewhere, gangs of white youths incensed by
the result roamed the streets looking for Negroes on whom they could
wreak their revenge. By the following morning, reports of death and injury had come from cities and towns in Pennsylvania, Maryland, Ohio,
Mississippi, Virginia, Missouri, Georgia, Arkansas, and Colorado.[3]

The ferocity of the fight and its aftermath scandalised reform elements throughout the nation. That it had taken place at all was bad
enough, that it should have happened on the Fourth of July was in ex-
District Commissioner MacFarland's words 'a desecration'. 'Such
patriotic anniversaries', he said, 'are intended to mark the ascent of our
Nation from barbarism to civilisation, instead of celebrating the power
of brute force.'[4] But there were even worse horrors in store. William
Shaw, general secretary of the United Society of Christian Endeavor,
declared that 'Independence Day had been dishonored and disgraced
by a brutal prizefight; that the moral sense of the nation had been outraged, but that this evil was as nothing to the harm which will be done
by allowing children and women to view the production of the Jeffries–
Johnson fight by moving pictures.'[5]

What has been called 'the first flickering, commercial motion picture' was a four-minute film of a prizefight in 1895.[6] As the popularity
and technical competence of the new medium increased, it became

[1] Farr, pp 77–8.
[2] [John P.] Davis, ['The Negro in American Sport'], in John P. Davis, *The American
Negro Reference Book* (New Jersey 1966) p 783.
[3] *Ibid*, and NYT, 6 July 1910, p 3.
[4] NYT, 5 July 1910, p 18. For the place of the Fourth of July in the ritual calendar of what
has been called the American civil religion, see Robert N. Bellah, 'Civil Religion in
America', *Daedalus* (Winter 1967) pp 1–21.
[5] NYT, 6 July 1910, p 3. The London *Times* had also expressed disgust at the number of
women at the ringside in Reno (5 July 1910, p 11). R. H. Gretton claimed that one of
the reasons for the opposition to the Johnson–Wells fight in London was that English
public opinion was revolted by 'the invasion of such spectacles by women, who...were
being accused, with their sports and their cigarette-smoking and slang and "ragging",
of aping men to a deplorable extent'. *A Modern History of the English People 1910–1922*
(London 1929) p 55.
[6] John Rickards Betts, 'The Technological Revolution and the Rise of Sport, 1850–1900'
in Loy and Kenyon, p 161.

Puritanicalism, sport and race

possible to film entire fights, and by selling copies throughout the world to increase the profits very substantially. Having failed to stop the fight, the reformers could now get to work in opposition to the films. The lead in this campaign came from the Christian Endeavorers, who unlike the Ohio reformers could not be accused of opposition to manly sport.[1] Apart from their shock at the thought of women and children watching the spectacle, they seemed to be as much opposed to the medium as the message, and more specifically to the passive role of the spectator. Games, with all their spiritual and moral benefits, were to be played, not watched.[2]

The racial tensions created by the unexpected victory of the Negro gave additional weight to this campaign. W. E. B. Du Bois, the leader of the Niagara Movement, protested that 'when Jack Johnson beat a white man at a white man's game before an audience of a hundred millions, with what mingled motive did those millions, from the United Society of Christian Endeavor to the hoodlums of the nation, join hands to shout "Shame!"'[3] The films of the fight were banned in most of the southern states, and after an appeal to the President for a federal ban, Shaw announced that the fight was to be carried overseas by three branches of the Christian Endeavor society in Europe and Australia.[4]

Ripples of protest soon spread across the oceans. The first overseas reaction came from South Africa, where Press opinion was firmly against the films.[5] The clergy of New South Wales, Australia, asked their Prime Minister to prevent them being shown, and similar protests were made in New Zealand and India.[6] In England, opposition initially

---

[1] For the link which Veblen saw in the YMCA and YPCE between the sporting temperament and religious zeal whereby 'sporting activities come to do duty as a novitiate or a means of induction into that fuller unfolding of the life of spiritual status which is the privilege of the full communicant alone', see Veblen, pp. 222–3.

[2] The possibility of rivalry between the minister and the promoter – two professional organisers of leisure-time activities – should also be noted. Parallels can be drawn between the mass, professionally organised sports of the late nineteenth and early twentieth centuries, such as football and boxing, and the new mass, professionally organised religious revival campaigns of the same period, such as those associated with Charles Finney, Dwight Moody, and Billy Sunday. Although this type of revivalism was a 'performance' before 'spectators' (Olmstead, p 456), there was always room for audience participation at the end. For American academic concern with the spectator at this time, see George Elliot Howard, 'Social Psychology of the Spectator', *American Journal of Sociology*, XVIII (Chicago 1912) pp 35–50. For English concern, see W. T. Stead's denunciation of professional sport: 'Our young men do not play themselves, they look on while professionals play.' *The Revival in the West* (London 1905) p 14.

[3] 'The Souls of White Folk', *Independent*, 18 August 1910 – extract in [Meyer] Weinberg [(ed), *W. E. B. Du Bois. A Reader*] (New York 1970) p 303.

[4] *NYT*, 6 July 1910, p 3.   [5] *The Times*, 7 July 1910, p 4.

[6] *Ibid*, 8 July 1910, p 5.

came from the Reverend F. Luke Wiseman of Birmingham Wesleyan
Central Mission, who was to be president of the Wesleyan Conference
in 1912. He urged the chairman of his local Watch Committee to ban
the film: 'It has no redeeming artistic, scenic, educative, or social
value. It is wholly brutal, disgusting, and demoralising.'[1] In the House
of Commons, the Home Secretary told Sir Howell Davies that he had
no powers to suppress the film, at which point Will Thorne, the Labour
MP, interjected, 'Does the right hon. gentleman think that if Jeffries
had knocked out Johnson there would have been so much "slobby"
talk about this subject as prevails at the present time? (Laughter and
cheers)'.[2] The only effect of the very mild opposition in England seems
to have been in London where Silvester Horne's congregation at
Whitefield's Central Mission had requested the County Council to take
action.[3] On 12 July, 1910, the Council somewhat lamely resolved that
'the public exhibition at places of entertainment in London of pictures
representing the recent prize fight in the United States is undesirable'.[4]

One person who significantly does not seem to have been involved in
any way in this agitation was F. B .Meyer, the man who was to lead the
opposition in the following year. But then, Meyer in July 1910 was
engaged in another campaign. On 15 July 1910, he was to be found with
Beatrice Webb, Bramwell Booth, and W. T. Stead on the platform at
a conference on Public Morals organised by the National Social Purity
Crusade. Following a discussion on 'noxious literature' (which included according to publisher John Murray, the writings of Karl Marx
and Henry George) Meyer advocated the sending of a deputation to the
Home Office in support of 'strengthening and simplifying the law
against all that may be opposed to public decency', a proposal which
W. T. Stead believed would 'make the conference the laughing stock
of the world'.[5] Clearly Meyer was ready to fight sin wherever he
thought he saw it, a characteristic which might make anyone wary of
him. But this apart, Jack Johnson's promoter had no special reason for
being apprehensive about Meyer when he arranged a match in London
with Bombardier Wells.

The announcement of the Johnson–Wells match was made a year
after the Reno contest, and at first drew no response. The first hint of
trouble came on 13 September 1911 when the chairman of the London
County Council informed the licencee of Earl's Court that he had received a resolution from the Synod of the Second London District of the

[1] *Ibid*, 12 July 1910, p 11.   [2] *Ibid*.   [3] *Ibid*.
[4] *Ibid*, 14 September 1911, p 4.   [5] *Ibid*, 15 July 1910, p 4, and 16 July 1910, p 4.

Wesleyan Methodist Church emphatically protesting against the fight. He reminded him of the resolution passed by the council in the previous year deploring the exhibition of the films of the Reno match, and warned that 'I feel bound to add my personal view that if the proposed contest takes place at Earl's Court Exhibition it may very seriously imperil the renewal of the license by the Council in November next.'[1]

However, this was only a personal view, and did not sound too serious. Nor is it likely that the promoter was over-worried by the news that the Reverend F. B. Meyer intended to raise the matter before the General Committee of the National Free Church Council. After all, there had been many boxing matches before in Britain. There had been matches between members of different races in Britain before. *The Times* unearthed an account of one in 1811. Why should the Free Church Council object now?

That was a question which was often asked after the Council had decided to support Meyer's protest. One answer would be a conviction that championship contests with the enormous sums of money involved were morally worse, and offered a greater threat to moral integrity than ordinary boxing matches. At another level, an answer might be found in the psychological necessity of a victory for the Free Church Council movement. By 1911, the confidence of the Free Church Council movement had been severely shaken.[2] The glorious possibilities of 1906 when more Nonconformists had been returned to Parliament than at any time since Cromwell's day had raised high hopes. The Reverend Thomas Phillips of Bloomsbury Central Baptist Church was expressing hopes which had been much more widely entertained nine years earlier when he wrote to David Lloyd George in 1915: 'You know I have always wanted to see you at the head of a great Christian democracy.'[3] These hopes lingered long as the subsequent machinations of Robertson Nicoll and J. H. Shakespeare on Lloyd George's behalf in 1916 were to show.[4] But in 1911, it looked as if something had gone wrong with the plan.

[1] *Ibid*, 14 September 1911, p 4.
[2] John F. Glaser, 'English Nonconformity and the Decline of Liberalism', *American Historical Review*, LXII, 2 (Jan. 1958) p 362. As early as 1908, John Clifford was writing to Asquith: 'It seems that one foremost need of the Liberal Party is the maintenance and increase of the enthusiasm of Free Churchmen...I fear that many of our Free Churchmen are losing heart.' John Clifford to H. H. Asquith, 23 September 1908 (Oxford, Bodleian Library MS Asquith 20/27).
[3] T. Phillips to D. Lloyd George, 18 September 1915 (Beaverbrook Library: Lloyd George Papers. D/20/2/21).
[4] See [Stuart] Mews, [*Religion and English Society in the First World War*] (Cambridge: forthcoming).

The Free Churches felt betrayed on the key symbolic issues of education and licensing. After the General Election of 1910, the Liberal Government had been compelled to rely on the Irish Nationalists for a majority, and they were unsympathetic to undenominational teaching and restrictions on the sale of alcohol. The decline in the influence of the Free Church movement had been symbolically foreshadowed by the action of Thomas Law, their organising genius, in committing suicide in April 1910.[1] Law had been handpicked for the post of first organising secretary by Hugh Price Hughes in 1896. He had first attracted attention by persuading the Free Churches of Bradford to divide their town into Nonconformist parishes, an arrangement which he commended to the first meeting of the National Council, and which was subsequently taken up in various parts of the country, most notably in Birmingham. He was a brilliant organiser, and supervised the setting up of local councils throughout England and Wales. In preparation for the Election of 1906, he wrote to leading nonconformist laymen urging them to stand for Parliament, published a booklet *Organising for Elections*, and set the Council's machinery to work on behalf of the Liberal Party. Some Nonconformists regarded him as little more than a party hack. Dr J. C. Carlile, later to be chairman of the Baptist Union, has written openly that he did not trust him. It was Law who was often held responsible for giving the impression that 'the Council was merely an organisation of a political party though masquerading as an ecclesiastical body'.[2] But the inner circle who dominated the Council, and led opinion within the movement: Clifford, Horne, Jowett, J. D. Jones, and Campbell Morgan, had golden opinions of his worth. It came as a tremendous shock, therefore, when the news came that Thomas Law, tired, strained, cruelly maligned, depressed, and disillusioned, had taken his own life in 1910.

In the autumn of that year, F. B. Meyer, minister of Regent's Park Baptist Church, took over the secretaryship on a temporary basis, which later became permanent. He took over, as his biographer, W. Y. Fullerton, says, at a time 'when disaster seemed to threaten that organisation after the tragic death of the Rev. Thomas Law'.[3] Meyer was therefore in his first year of office when the Johnson–Wells match was announced. Though well-known in Free Church circles, he was not at

[1] For Law, see E. K. H. Jordan, *Free Church Unity. History of the Free Church Council Movement 1896–1941* (London 1956) pp 136–8.
[2] [J. C.] Carlile, [*My Life's Little Day*] (London 1935), p 178; J. Ernest Rattenbury, *Evangelism and Pagan England* (London 1954) p 34.
[3] [W. Y.] Fullerton, [*F. B. Meyer. A Biography*] (London n.d.) p 97.

this time well-known to the general public. He had yet to acquire the status of a national spokesman for the Free Church interest, and this he achieved in the controversy he was about to launch. But it was not just Meyer in need of a campaign in which to win his spurs which explains the agitation. In 1911, the Free Church movement needed some national issue on which it could unite and fight. The great dilemma which always confronted the movement was how to keep its organisation in running order throughout the country. The best way of keeping up attendance at local councils was to have something always on the boil. After Meyer's death, the *Daily Telegraph* (30 March 1929) noted that 'It was Meyer's lot to toil through a half a century, when to be a Non-conformist was to be militant or nothing, and to launch a maximum of eloquence for a minimum of effect.' But if the eloquence did not have much effect on social and political life, it did help to keep the machinery of the Free Church movement in running repair. Fullerton quotes 'a leading journal' as saying 'during the midst of Dr Meyer's Secretariat' – a period which lasted from 1910 to 1920:

We are glad to know that the genius, hard work, and magnetic personality of Dr F. B. Meyer have stimulated into new life many local Councils that had become nearly moribund. But we know too, that many still remain lifeless, and that most are in danger, upon the removal of one or two persons from their locality, of lapsing into a living death. What would happen did Dr Meyer cease to distribute driving power from the Memorial Hall we shudder to think.[1]

Periodic campaigns seem to have been necessary to sustain the morale of local representatives, but when those campaigns had political implications they tended to alienate those Free Churchmen who objected to being what J. C. Carlile called 'a department of the Liberal Party'.[2] The social and political unrest of the early decades of the twentieth century made this dilemma even more acute and accentuated tension within the movement. Confronted by a national labour stoppage, the Free Churches could only issue statements which contributed nothing to the settlement of the dispute in question and only succeeded in alienating some of their own supporters – usually the more prosperous middle class. Three weeks before the Johnson–Wells controversy, Meyer had been interviewed about the Free Church attitude to the national railway strike. The newspapers had been asking what the

---

[1] *Ibid.*

[2] Carlile, p. 178. Even some Free Churchmen who were staunch Liberals objected to this identification: A. G. Gardiner, *Life of George Cadbury* (London 1923) pp 184–5.

churches were doing about it. 'I may tell you,' said Dr Meyer, 'that we have been watching events most closely, and on Saturday a notice appeared in the Press that if the strike lasted over Sunday we should call together the General Committee to draw up an appeal for a settlement by arbitration, or in the dry light of reason.'[1] At a time when the political structure was being reconstituted on class lines, the impotence of the Free Churches on the great issues of the day was plainly obvious.

Taking into account all these factors, Meyer had probably made the right decision in seeking to persuade the Council to oppose the Johnson–Wells match. Here was a safe, non-political issue which was almost certain to secure the unanimous support of Free Churchmen throughout the land. Indeed in the early stages of the campaign, Meyer went out of his way to state repeatedly that he did not want the Home Secretary's help. This was a fight which could be waged without the help of the Liberal Party, and, indeed, it was only when the protest had spread beyond the Free Churches, and had become a national concern that Meyer agreed to send a memorial to Winston Churchill.

Moreover, unlike the American opposition to the San Francisco fight, this campaign was waged on assimilative, not coercive lines. Meyer's refusal to take coercive action carried with it an assumption that in responsible middle-class circles there were still certain generally agreed criteria as to what came within the bounds of good taste. He gave the impression of being convinced that James White, the promoter, like the Prodigal Son, would come to himself, and abandon the match. Meyer recognised that a great deal of money was at stake, and to make it easier for White, he offered to raise a fund to cover the costs of cancellation.[2] Throughout the controversy, Meyer regarded White as a delinquent who could yet be saved, rather than as an enemy to be defeated. He was determined to fight in a clean and sporting manner, and announced that 'he would shake hands at the close of the contest with Mr White whatever happened'.[3]

It is difficult to say whether or not Meyer expected to succeed when he first took up the issue. His strategy in the campaign involved the as-

---

[1] *British Weekly*, 24 August 1911, p 507. The Labour unrest of 1911 gave rise to many discussions about the attitude of the churches. Charles Brown, the Free Church president, believed that 'the Church should openly ally itself' with those demanding higher wages – a vew which met strong resistance: *Spectator*, 7 October 1911, pp 538–9.

[2] *The Times*, 19 September 1911, p 5. This act puzzled other Free Churchmen; Robertson Nicoll felt that the promoter should pay for his own mistakes: B[ritish] W[eekly], 21 September 1911, p 595.

[3] M[anchester] G[uardian,] 20 September 1911, p 4.

sumption that middle-class puritanical values still set the standard of respectability. Yet it is difficult to believe that Meyer really held such a view. His biographer quotes a personality sketch drawn in 1904 by a journalist who detected pessimism beneath Meyer's cheerfulness and serenity – a 'very gentle pessimism, a pessimism undemonstrative and unaggressive, but still pessimism decided, well thought out, scientifically reasoned and accounted for'.

Mr Meyer is one who has the courage of his convictions and he reads the signs of the times as they appear to him actually to portend. With the almost inevitable result that he takes a somewhat sad and pessimistic view of the present and future of the body politic generally.

He does not consider that the present day makes for the righteousness of the community as a whole or that humanity in the mass is on the upward path.

Whilst fully conscious of the increased earnestness of the age in many respects, he recognises more keenly still that the hostile influences are more vigorously vibrant and vital than ever they were before. Scepticism, immorality to an appalling extent, absolute and entire indifference to all religious teaching, the total absence of ideals, the growing materialism of the day, the utter disregard of the things of the spirit world; all these things he regards as massed as a hostile army, against the striving after a higher and a better life which is still characteristic of a noble-hearted minority. But still it is a minority and this is where his sadness and his pessimism comes in.[1]

This social and cultural pessimism, which Meyer shared with other eminent Edwardians (of whom the most prominent was probably J. N. Figgis, the Mirfield monk and political theorist[2]) was to some extent lightened by his adventist beliefs. 'He came to hold with the belief that the world was growing worse and that the day was becoming darkened. He thought that shortly Christ would come to crown the Church with triumph.'[3] So strong did this conviction grow that when the Balfour Declaration of 1917 seemed to be the fulfilment of prophecy, Meyer became president of the Advent Testimony and Preparation Movement and issued a manifesto declaring that 'the signs of the times pointed towards the close of "the times of the Gentiles"'.[4]

---

[1] Raymond Blathwayt in *Great Thoughts*, January 1904, quoted in Fullerton, p 173.
[2] David Newsome, 'The Assault on Mammon: Charles Gore and John Neville Figgis', *JEH*, xvii, 2 (1966) pp 227–41. Figgis detected the growth of a 'leisure class' in Britain; he associated 'paganisation' with 'the increase of riches and the Americanisation of society (by which I mean a world living apart from the sources of the money which the owners have nothing to do but spend).' *Religion and English Society* (London 1910) p 31.
[3] A. Chester Mann, *F. B. Meyer, Preacher, Teacher, Man of God* (London 1929) p 81.
[4] *Ibid*, p 82; for adventism in the First World War, see Mews.

At the beginning of 1911, Meyer seems to have believed that the new year would be a moment of destiny – a *kairos* – in the life of British society. 'The time is ripe for our testimony,' he told the London Federation of P.S.A. Brotherhoods in January. 'The year 1911 – the first year of the second decade of this century – is likely to be the most fateful year of a new era – one in which democracy shall be able to take its untrammelled course. The old conditions will no longer predominate.'[1] This apocalyptic theme was still running through Meyer's mind during the boxing match controversy. On 18 September, he told the National Brotherhood convention that 'we were at one of the crises of our national life. Two ages were meeting like sundown and sunrise in the Arctic sky. The rule of the few was being superseded by the rule of the many.'[2] Yet it is clear that Meyer did not believe that the rule of the many would promote and reinforce the moral beliefs for which the Free Churches stood. Hence the need for greater vigilance and more resolute witness. Success in a campaign of assimilative reform at such a time was tantamount to an assertion that the puritanical principles previously associated with the middle class were still setting the moral standard for society. The old order might be passing away, the nonconformist middle class might be losing its political power, but it could still make its bid for moral power in the new order.[3]

But why select the Johnson–Wells match for such a trial of strength? Perhaps because the legal status of boxing was still unclear, and it might have seemed an easy target. It has always been illegal in Britain to fight with naked fists for money, though this did little to stop the enormous popularity of prizefights in the late eighteenth century and the Regency period. Indeed, their popularity was such that magistrates rarely dared to interfere. In the more sober mid-Victorian era, when Evangelicalism was at the height of its social influence, boxing went underground and was carried on with great brutality at a secret rendez-vous. It only began to re-emerge when manliness and muscularity again came into vogue. Thomas Hughes' graphic description in *Tom Brown's Schooldays* of the fight with Slogger Williams became one of the best-known scenes in Victorian literature, and contributed to the growing conviction that 'Fighting with fists is the natural and English way for English boys to

---

[1] *BW*, 26 January 1911, p 501.   [2] *MG*, 18 September 1911, p 8.

[3] These hopes were symbolically invested in Arthur Henderson, who described himself in *Who's Who in Methodism* (London 1933) p 330, as a 'Life-long abstainer and Temperance Reformer'. Three years later he was to be one of Meyers' successors in the Presidency of the National Brotherhood movement. Will Thorne, with his dismissal of 'slobby talk', represented another moral tradition in the Labour Movement.

settle their quarrels'.[1] Partisans of the sport believed that the introduction of the Queensberry Rules in 1866, which compelled the wearing
of gloves, put them within the law, but this had yet to be tested before
the courts. A number of prosecutions were brought against boxers in
the years between 1890 and 1901, which seems to have been a crucial
period in the re-emergence of the sport. The case in 1890 attracted the
attention of the young fifth Earl of Lonsdale, who put up the money for
the defence at this and subsequent trials.[2] In none of these cases was
boxing declared illegal, but at the same time no court was prepared to
say that it was legal. Lonsdale believed that social recognition would
come when the game succeeded in shaking off that disreputable side
which was particularly associated with gambling. This was the purpose
of the National Sporting Club of which Lonsdale was President. It is
perhaps worth noting that despite the fact that the Marquis of Queensberry and the Earl of Lonsdale played such a prominent part in securing
social acceptance for boxing, they were both regarded as mavericks by
their peers. And as the latter's biographer points out, 'The National
Sporting Club was not made up of the glittering galaxy of the aristocracy. It was a middle class club run by a group of extremely astute
businessmen who realised that boxing cleanly run and free from scandals
was good business.'[3] The significance of this is that when the Free
Church Council went into battle, it was not against the aristocracy
which Hugh Price Hughes used to blame for the low moral tone of
society, but against the same sort of self-made businessman who was with
lessening frequency to be found in nonconformist congregations, and
who once would have given lip-service at least to the general moral
attitudes which the Free Churches commended.

After the court case of 1901, opposition to boxing gradually died
away, partly because of the keen interest taken in the sport by the new
king. As the fear of prosecution receded, the umbrella of respectability
provided by Lonsdale and the National Sporting Club was no longer
needed. Rival establishments began to spring up, and the new profession of boxing promoter came into existence.[4] Bouts were regularly

[1] *Tom Brown's Schooldays* (London 1921 ed) pp 307–8, quoted in David Newsome,
Godliness and Good Learning (London 1961) p 213. The whole of Part IV of this book on
'Godliness and Manliness' provides an excellent exposition of the growth of the cult of
manliness in late Victorian England.

[2] Lionel Dawson, *Lonsdale. The Authorised Life of Hugh Lowther, 5th Earl of Lonsdale,
K.G., G.C.V.O.* (London 1946) p 88.

[3] Douglas Sutherland, *The Yellow Earl. The life of Hugh Lowther, 5th Earl of Lonsdale,
K.G., G.C.V.O. 1857–1944* (London 1965) p 173.   [4] *Ibid*, p 176.

held at the White City Stadium, and it looked as if public opinion was reconciled to the continuance of the sport in its revised form. Dr Meyer and the Free Church Council, were therefore rather late in the day in the action which they took against the Johnson–Wells match of 1911, and James White, the promoter, was evidently not over-worried.

On 15 September 1911 a letter was issued by the Free Church Council signed by the President, Charles Brown, and Meyer as secretary. It began by pointing out that they were *not* against 'the art of self-defence, or whatever makes for the true manhood of our people'. They contended that this contest did not come under that category.

It is the direct outcome of the fight last year at Reno of which the correspondent of a leading Chicago paper writes: 'The struggle was one of great fierceness and attracted a horde of profligate people. There was much gambling. The pictures were banned from a large number of leading American cities, and where shown at all it was in music-halls of low character.'

The idea of the circulation by cinematograph of the details of the proposed fight is unthinkable. The manager of a leading topical film department says: 'The cold-blooded repetition of a boxing contest is more brutal than the actual contest because it gives the brutal side but lacks the human interest.'[1]

On these and other grounds we venture to ask all ministers of religion to refer to the matter on the coming Sunday with the view of arousing the conscience of the nation against a spectacle in which two men do their utmost to batter one another, not in self-defence nor to protect the weak, but for high stakes, and...to gratify that craving for the sensational and the brutal which is inconsistent with the manhood that makes a great nation.[2]

The original protest made no mention of race, and can perhaps be summed up as an expression of horror at the exposure of the masses to the diversions of blood and cinemas.

Meyer's move provoked the usual reactions from the usual quarters. On Meyer's side, Prebendary Carlile telegraphed the Chairman of the LCC:

Church Army implores you to stop brutal and demoralising Wells–Johnson encounter and degradation by cinematograph. Surely worse then bull and cock fight.[3]

On the other hand, the Reverend Howard Legge, head of the Trinity College, Oxford Mission at Stratford, himself an ex-public school

---

[1] On the Church's attitude to the cinema, see R. G. Burnett and E. D. Martell, *The Devil's Camera* (London 1932); R. G. Burnett, *The Cinema for Christ* (London 1934); *The Cinema: its Present Position and Future Possibilities* (Report of the National Council of Public Morals: London 1917).

[2] *The Times*, 16 September 1911, p 8.   [3] *Ibid*, 15 September 1911, p 6.

champion and exponent of Muscular Christianity, complained in *The Times*:

I have nothing to do with the private opinions of Mr Meyer and his friends, except that I consider them to be as much entitled to respect as my own. Therefore I protest against the action of the Chairman of the London County Council as a tyrannical and unjust proceeding, likely to make me intolerant of the opinions of Mr Meyer, contemptuous of local self-government and seriously concerned for the welfare of a great and noble form of sport. For of course the match will not be stopped by any action of this kind any more than was the Johnson–Jeffries match. On the other hand, such action will tend to degrade the professional practice of the art of boxing to undesirable surroundings and irresponsible patronage, a result as unjust to the many decent fellows who make a living by it as it would be disastrous to the maintenance of the ideals of stern endurance and manly self-defence which tend nowadays too easily to be obscured.[1]

The following day, Legge was answered by the vicar of Chiswick, a parish not far from Earl's Court. The vicar claimed that shopwindows in the streets of his parish were being filled 'with repulsive and brutalized pictures of prize fights and kindred subjects: I see boys and girls gloating over such pictures; and I know something of the debased and degrading effects of it all. I know, further, of the almost brutalized instincts and tastes of no small section of the population of our great cities and towns, and I say, what everyone of your readers knows perfectly well, that this exhibition, if allowed to proceed, will pander to all that is basest and most brutalized in this class of men.' He concluded with praise for 'Mr Meyer and his friends' and a hope that 'the official Church of this country will not fail to raise its voice with no uncertain sound in the strongest possible protest'.[2]

From the other side, the Press Officer at Earl's Court said he could not understand why this contest was considered objectionable by the Chairman of the LCC, particularly as they had previously permitted a championship fight elsewhere in London. Unfortunately he went on to weaken what seemed to be a strong position by arguing that the only difference between the Johnson–Wells fight and others 'was that this one might conceivably be complicated by the colour question. It might be urged that Imperial considerations rendered it undesirable that such a contest should take place at all. If that were so the matter was for the

---

[1] *Ibid.*

[2] *Ibid*, 16 September 1911, p 8. One of the *Manchester Guardian's* columnists received a letter expressing the hope that the Church of England would be involved in the controversy so that the Free Churches could not claim all the credit: *MG*, 21 September 1911, p 14.

Home Secretary and not the LCC.'[1] The racial aspect was, therefore, first introduced by the men who wanted to stage the match.

Lord Lonsdale weighed in at this point to express his belief that 'these large affairs where money was the chief factor' were not good for the sport. 'Boxing contests should be essentially and primarily a matter of science. The profit element was always most undesirable. In the case of the Johnson–Wells match it was like a three-year-old being pitted against a two-year-old, who was considerably lacking in ripe experience'.[2] Again, words which would probably be regretted later. Lonsdale was probably just annoyed because Johnson had previously refused to box at the National Sporting Club on account of their miserliness. They offered £500 for the winner as against the £8,000 at stake at Earl's Court.

Over the weekend, Meyer and his friends were busy. On Saturday, Meyer addressed the National Brotherhood Conference at the Albert Hall. He said that:

God had led him, so he profoundly believed, to endeavour to put down the proposed fight. They had an opportunity to raise the conception of sport and to uphold the true ideal of Christian manhood untainted by brutality. He would not say one unkind thing of those who differed from many of them in their ideals of sport. He simply said that they had an unenlightened conscience. They belonged to a past age. They belonged to the age of the gladiator and the martyr.[3]

The following day a small crowd gathered outside Regent's Park Baptist Church having heard a rumour that Johnson and Wells intended to be present. They were however disappointed. 'A coloured man was closely scrutinised as he entered the church, but he assured the questioner he was not Mr Johnson and that he never fought.'[4] Inside Meyer preached on 'The Temple of the Body',[5] and during the inter-

---

[1] *The Times*, 16 September 1911, p 8. [2] *Ibid.*
[3] *Ibid*, 18 September 1911, p 5. [4] *MG*, 18 September 1911, p 8.
[5] This was one of Meyer's favourite themes. Throughout his ministry he placed great emphasis on manliness in its widest sense, and admired strong men who were in complete control of their passions. To encourage the true masculine virtues, he frequently lectured to young men on 'Personal Purity' when 'his topics were brutally frank; his maxims, warnings, and appeals deliberately crude to the point almost of coarseness' (Fullerton, p 151). His biographer has remarked on the femininity of his character (Fullerton, p 76) and of his apparently successful attempts to be a 'man's man' which gave the impression of a dual personality (p 111). Perhaps like John Morley, his contemporary in the political sphere, in whom the feminine virtues were also conspicuous, he was attracted by qualities opposite to his own: D. A. Hamer, *John Morley. Liberal Intellectual in Politics* (Oxford 1968) p 57.

cessions prayed for the true conversion of both boxers.[1] In their respective pulpits Charles Brown, the Free Church president, and Prebendary Carlile also denounced the contest.[2] Over the weekend, the General Committee of the Primitive Methodist Church had met, and so had the National Council of the Sunday School Union. Both passed resolutions against the contest and its reproduction in cinematograph pictures. Meanwhile James White, the promoter, announced that all the 10,000 seats were booked, including 38 by clergymen.[3] Letters and resolutions were now pouring into Meyer's office. 'Here is work for the Free Church Councils all over the land', proclaimed the *Manchester Guardian*.[4] Local Councils were enthusiastically following Meyer's lead, and several of them were already putting pressure on their Watch Committees to prevent the showing of films of the fight.

At this point the question of colour began to be raised in the debate, though it was not to be taken up for several days by Meyer. A London County Councillor. George Swinton, explained that he had raised the matter of the films after the Reno match because he had evidence from the West Indies that a previous match involving Johnson in Australia had 'increased the difficulties of the white policeman even thousands of miles away'. 'Today,' he continued, 'it is a question of a fight between a white soldier and a black champion.' He would not have objected if the match had been held behind closed doors at the National Sporting Club, but 'are we not thereby making quite unnecessary trouble wherever the black and white races are side by side?' In his view the Home Secretary should stop it.[5]

Now that the colour question had been raised, the more skilful tacticians on Meyer's side realised that it could be exploited with great effect, though Meyer himself seems to have been reluctant to use it. The secretary of the Baptist Union, J. H. Shakespeare, made out a powerful case:

[1] To some extent his prayers were answered after the First World War when Johnson professed conversion. He appeared in the pulpit on several occasions, addressed methodist bishops on the virtues of self-control and the avoidance of liquor, and in 1924 addressed a Klavern of the Ku Klux Klan on sportsmanship, fair play, and the Golden Rule! (Farr, p 228).
[2] *The Times*, 18 September 1911, p 5.
[3] *Ibid*, and Fullerton, p 121. Very probably one was booked by the only English clergyman who is known to have made friends with Johnson, Harold Davidson, who as Rector of Stiffkey was to be defrocked in a blaze of publicity for his devotion to young ladies in teashops. A photograph of Johnson and Davidson taking tea in 1911 is to be found in Denzil Batchelor, *Jack Johnson and His Times* (London 1956) p 128.
[4] *MG*, 21 September 1911, p 14.   [5] *The Times*, 19 September 1911, p 5.

It is not a question of whether we like or approve of such exhibitions, but rather whether in a country in which glove contests are legal there are special reasons why this fight should be prevented from taking place. I think that these are:

(1) All the considerations which led to the prohibition of the prize-fight apply here. This is not a mere trial of skill, to be decided on points, but it has continued to gather into itself every motive of race, publicity, and occasion which will convert it into a violent, gory, determined pounding of two men into a mass of blood and wounds.

(2) It cannot be separated from the racial animosities which are so perilous in the world to-day. The fight at San Reno cost scores of lives in subsequent riots. Whatever the issue might be, again white and black will be pitted against each other in anger, revenge and murder, especially in those lands like America in which the negro is the gravest of all problems. It is a dangerous responsibility to fan in any degree these smouldering fires.

(3) There can be no greater disservice to the negro race than to encourage it to see a glory in physical force and in beating the white man. Booker Washington is incessant in the cry to his people, 'Educate, educate'. Slowly they are climbing the steep path, but every voice which exalts animal passion in them is that of an enemy. It matters not to us if an Englishman is beaten, for we have proved our place in the realms of courage, endurance, service, art and learning. But to a race which has not yet achieved glory it is a crime to turn its ambitions to such glory as can be found in the Prize Ring.[1]

Shakespeare also hoped for action from the Home Secretary.

The comparison which Shakespeare made between Jack Johnson, the first Negro heavyweight champion of the world, and Booker Washington, the first Negro to get an honorary degree from Harvard, was an apt one. They represented the two alternative ways forward for their race. Washington's message to Negroes was to learn a trade and get on in the world by modest and industrious living. Johnson believed in taking the kingdom by force, and beating the white man at his own game. An attempt to reconcile the two was made in 1910,[2] but when Johnson was put on a vice charge in 1912, Washington joined the chorus of criticism. He told the Detroit YMCA that 'Jack Johnson has harmed rather than helped the race. I wish to say emphatically that his actions do not meet my approval, and I am sure they do not meet with the approval of the colored race.'[3]

It is not surprising that British Free Churchmen preferred the Wash-

[1] Ibid.   [2] Davis, p 783.

[3] Farr, p 153. On the other hand, Washington's rival for influence amongst negroes, W. E. B. Du Bois, supported Johnson at that time, see his article: 'The Prize Fight' Crisis (August 1914) included in Weinberg, pp 428–9.

ington approach, and he was held in high regard by them. They knew that they themselves had once been a despised and peculiar people, and that through loyalty and diligence they had gradually overcome most of their legal disabilities. The struggle of the Negro, as presented by Booker T. Washington, called up an instinctive response from the collective memory of the dissenting denominations, a response which was most dramatically expressed in October 1910 when Washington toured England. At a reception organised for him in London by the Anti-Slavery Society, Dr Robert F. Horton, the Congregationalist leader, 'to the surprise of all' compared the position of the Negro race in America to that of Nonconformists at home. 'Free Churchmen', he said, 'feel a warm sympathy with the coloured people of the United States because we stand in a very similar position at home. We are treated here much as you are treated there. We are admitted to be members of the human race, but in private we are not recognised as brothers and friends. If we have survived, so will the negro'. The *British Weekly* added, 'These sentences give only a faint idea of an impassioned speech which must have been astonishing indeed to the Anglican dignitaries in the room'. 'I can never see the slightest difference', concluded Horton, 'between the coloured races and our own. I have never felt the slightest condescension when the white race reaches out its hands to the negroes. Rather it is the other way.'[1]

Ever since the unfortunate episode in his Oxford days when he was voted down for an examinership by the country clergy,[2] Horton had been especially sensitive on the question of the inferior status of Nonconformists. However, his comparison was not quite as absurd as it may sound. Washington had been presenting a rosy picture of race relations in America, giving the impression that the Negro was gradually gaining ground. Horton may have magnified the iniquities suffered by Nonconformists, but Washington also magnified the progress of the Negro, and it is not surprising that they both found the same level. Washington's Negro rivals were so incensed that a group headed by W. E. B. Du Bois circulated a statement contradicting the false picture which

[1] *BW*, 13 October 1910, p 42. Horton's interest in the colour question was first aroused by conversations with negro students at Yale. Even thirty years later he could recall receiving 'a shock on my first visit to America in 1893 from which I have never recovered'. *The Mystical Quest of Christ* (London 1923) p 145. For another comparison of the problems of religious and social integration, see Talcott Parson's essay, 'Full Citizenship for the Negro American?', reprinted as chapter 13 in his book, *Sociological Theory and Modern Society* (New York 1967).

[2] Albert Peel and Sir John Marriott, *Robert Forman Horton* (London 1937) ch 6.

Washington was disseminating in England.[1] A year later, Free Churchmen had a better opportunity of hearing an alternative interpretation of
the Negro situation when Du Bois visited London for the First Universal Races Conference in July 1911. The Conference was a curious affair
attended according to *The Times* by a mixture of anthropologists and
idealists.[2] Free Churchmen were well represented on the honorary
General Committee and the names of Horton, Scott Lidgett, J. D.
Jones, and at least a dozen more are to be found in a list which also
contained the names of such luminaries of the sociological world as
Emile Durkheim, Georg Simmel, Werner Sombart, and Alfred Vierkandt.[3] F. B. Meyer was one of the vice-presidents of the Conference,
and it is surprising that having officiated in such a capacity in July, he
was not more sensitive to the racial aspects of the Johnson–Wells controversy in September. Du Bois was one of the secretaries, and delivered a
paper which included a vigorous attack on Washington's policy.[4]

On 19 September *The Times* devoted its leader column to the
Johnson–Wells match, pointing out that opinion about the contest cut
across the usual division on such matters. It quoted Lonsdale's view
that the two were unevenly matched, and went on to discuss the colour
issue.

> To those who understand the conditions of the British Empire as a whole
> no consideration can exceed in gravity that of preventing the aggravation
> of 'colour feeling' where it already exists and discouraging its growth where
> at present it is absent. Exhibitions of the kind proposed for Monday week at
> Earl's Court can only have the opposite effect. 'Colour feeling' it is true is
> still largely unknown in the British Isles, but it has already shown signs of
> unexpected growth.
> ...Can anyone who considers these things and the special position of trustee-
> ship for coloured subject peoples which the British Empire holds persuade
> himself that 'scientific' sport is worth the least possible exacerbation of the
> relations between black and white?

The Times was not the only one of the world's leading national
newspapers to take this point of view. The *South African News*, the
Ministerial organ, was also leading an agitation against the fight, and

---

[1] Meier, p 183. However, not all Free Churchmen were as uncritical of Washington as
Horton: Arthur Porritt, *The Best I Remember* (London 1922) pp 194ff.

[2] *The Times*, 28 July 1911, p 8.

[3] For Durkheim, see *Essays on Sociology and Philosophy by Émile Durkheim et al. with ap-
praisals of his life and thought*, edited by Kurt H. Wolff (New York 1960). For Simmel,
Sombart, and Vierkandt, see Raymond Aron, *German Sociology* (New York 1964).

[4] Gustav Spiller (ed), *Papers on Inter-Racial Problems Communicated to the First Universal
Races Congress* (London 1911) p 364.

appealed to the Union Government to prohibit the importation of the films into the province. It feared the effects on the natives and warned that the country could not afford any expansion of the black peril. This view was warmly approved by the moderator of the Dutch Reformed Church.[1]

Back in London, Meyer continued to receive hundreds of letters, some denouncing him in violent language, and the wish was even expressed that he might be physically punished by the Negro pugilist. But by now Meyer had also caught something of the fighting spirit. 'We shall fight to a finish,' he announced, 'the education of public opinion will go on. The opposition is growing stronger every hour. I hope the matter will still be settled without the necessity of intervention by the Home Secretary: but I am afraid we shall ultimately have to appeal to him.'[2] In fact, Meyer must have realised that the enemy was now on the defensive, and that his own side was getting stronger. When he made that statement, he had just received a letter from the archbishop of Canterbury who was resting on the Italian lakes. Dr Davidson not only pledged his support, but also wrote to Churchill.[3] By now it was clear that the conscience of middle-class England was still sound, and could still be roused. Although White still refused to call off the match, it had now been demonstrated that he was the deviant, not the Free Churches. The protest was now sufficiently broadly-based for an appeal to the Home Secretary which would not give the impression that the Free Churches were simply asking a favour from a political ally, and attempting to enforce a minority moral code. As Churchill was waiting on the king at Balmoral, it was decided to get up a memorial, which even at this stage protested only against the brutality of prizefights, and still made no mention of the race question.

James White, the unlucky promoter, by this time regarded himself as a persecuted man, and considered the racial argument as 'mere buncombe'. Nevertheless the agitation was having its effect. An emergency meeting of the Executive of the Boxers' Union appealed to their fellow trades-unionists throughout the United Kingdom to support them against this attack on their livelihood. They pointed out that:

No class in the community lead better lives than the boxers. They are compelled to eschew vices, intemperance, and many worldly luxuries if they have the ambition to ascend in their profession, and the police records prove that the boxer is above the average as a law-abiding citizen.

[1] *The Times*, 20 September 1911, p 4.
[2] *Ibid.*   [3] *Ibid.*

Boxing, they claimed, was less brutal and had fewer casualties than many other sports:

During the past few years that have seen the advance of aviation alone there have been more deaths (and deaths of a most horrible character) than in the whole history of the ring from the beginning to the present day, and if these self-appointed agitators are stirred by a desire to preserve human life they would show a more honest purpose if they directed their attacks upon those more deadly pastimes.[1]

On 22 September, F. B. Meyer referred for the first time to the racial aspect. He put it in a curious way in a letter to the unhappy Mr White:

Whatever safeguards you may adopt in the way of referees, you must admit that the present contest is not wholly one of skill, because on the one side is added the instinctive passion of the negro race, which is so differently constituted from our own, and in the present instance will be aroused to do the utmost that immense animal development can do to retain the championship.[2]

The following day he called on all Free Church ministers to refer to the memorial on Sunday, making it clear that they were not against manly and legitimate sport, but pointing out that amongst vast numbers of the black and subject races the outcome would be looked on as a decisive test of racial superiority. Wherever possible a meeting should be held after the service and a resolution sent to the Prime Minister and Home Secretary.

By this time support for Meyer was coming thick and fast. Almost daily *The Times* reported the name of some notable who had signed the memorial: bishops, the presidents and chairmen of the Free Church denominations, members of Parliament, and headmasters, were well represented on the list. Most of the anglican opposition originally came from Evangelicals for the sort of puritanical reasons which moved Meyer to start the protest. One of the first signs of the widening of the movement came when Dr Edward S. Talbot, bishop of Winchester, and a leader of the High Church wing came out in support of Meyer and indicated his concern about the racial issue:

There is no problem more anxious for the present and the future than that of colour; none about which there are more sinister features; none on which instinct, passion, and prejudice are more inflamed; none, therefore, on which it is more imperative that nothing should be done to inflame or excite.[3]

[1] *Ibid*, 21 September 1911, p 5.   [2] *Ibid*, 22 September 1911, p 6.
[3] *Ibid*, 25 September 1911, p 6.

Puritanicalism, sport and race

Over the next few days, *The Times* published a letter from Lord Stanhope testifying to the difficulties caused in the Fiji Islands by a previous victory of Johnson's, and a special report from their West African correspondent who felt that 'a physical struggle between a white man and a black man, attended by thousands of spectators... waged in the capital of the Empire, would have a thoroughly mischievous effect – especially if the black man won'.[1]

On 26 September, *Sporting Life* reported: 'The Home Secretary, after full enquiry, and having taken the best advice, has arrived at the conclusion that what is contemplated is illegal, and unless the promoters voluntarily abandon the contest, steps will be taken at once to prevent any such illegality taking place.' Next day, the Director of Public Prosecutions took out a summons against Johnson and Wells for contemplating a breach of the peace. Jack Johnson arrived at the court to the accompaniment of loud cheers from a vast crowd, and the case began with a long verbal tussle between him and Sir John Simon, the Solicitor-General. To everyone's surprise Johnson scored heavily in this first round, but the contest was stopped before a verdict could be delivered. The Metropolitan District Railway Company which owned the freehold of Earl's Court sought an injunction restraining the Earl's Court Company from allowing the match to be held on their premises. The injunction was granted, the fight was off, and the Director of Public Prosecutions had to abandon his action.[2] It is perhaps worth mentioning that the judge who granted the injunction, Mr Justice Lush, was himself, by an extraordinary coincidence, a member of Regent's Park Baptist Church, and his brother was the church secretary.[3]

Meanwhile a very gloomy meeting of sportsmen was called by White at the Hotel Cecil. The chairman, Count Hollander, said that 'if things went on as they were, clergymen would soon be stopping boxing at schools, and Englishmen might as well sit down and start darning – there was little else left for them to do'. The Reverend Everard Digby said he did 'not believe the rank and file of the Church was with the present anti-boxing agitation...The attack came from a Puritan party which would kill all sport in English life'. An Irish delegate, Mr Bryan O'Donnell, maintained that 'if boxing was done away with in this country a premium would be put upon the purchase of sword and revolvers'.[4]

[1] *Ibid*, 23 September 1911, p 5; and 24 September 1911, p 6.
[2] *Ibid*, 28 September 1911, p 7.
[3] This fact does not seem to have been noticed at the time, but see the welcome given to his appointment in *BW*, 6 October 1910, p 10.   [4] *The Times*, 27 September 1911, p 6.

But the sportsmen did not need to be so distressed. Although later in the year there was to be another action – this time successful – against another boxing match, 'Mr Meyer and his friends' had secured a rather special victory in special circumstances. After 1911, the legality of boxing was never to be tested again.

Meyer had reason to be pleased with the results of his efforts. For the first time for very many years, a public morality campaign initiated by the Free Churches had succeeded. Even so the *New York Times* commented rather sourly that 'if Johnson had been a white man, there can be little doubt that the British conscience would not have been so tender'.[1] Almost overnight Meyer had become world-famous. *The Times* ever afterwards gave him large type when he wrote to the paper. A Scottish newspaper published a cartoon showing him knocking out both contestants over a caption from the Book of Job: 'And I broke the jaws of the wicked, and plucked the spoil out of his teeth.' A leading American journal claimed: 'Jack Johnson's tribute to the power of the "preachers" marks a step forward in militant Christianity. "They have put the front-rank fighters out of business", he says.' Perhaps the most extravagant praise came in *Joyful News*, the Cliff College Wesleyan paper, where Samuel Chadwick described Meyer as 'A Modern Telemachus'.[2]

But it was not all roses. Both the pagans and the puritanicalists had grounds for grumbling. One paper described the Free Church secretary as 'Meddling, Maudlin Meyer'.[3] On the other extreme the North Glamorgan Welsh Congregationalists meeting at Merthyr were severely critical of Meyer's attitude to boxing. While the conference thanked him for his successful stand, a resolution 'embodying disapproval of his later action in giving his seal of approval of prize-fights and describing them as good sport was unanimously adopted'.[4]

What the North Glamorgan Welsh Congregationalists did not seem to realise was that Meyer would never have won his campaign if he had fought in general opposition to boxing. He would never have been supported by the archbishop of Canterbury, the headmaster of Rugby,

---

[1] *NYT*, 29 September 1911, p 8.
[2] Fullerton, p 121.   [3] *Ibid.*
[4] *The Times*, 20 October 1911, p 10. I have found no evidence to support this charge. Meyer's view was: 'To the present generation of young Englishmen I certainly would never say a word to diminish any incentive to virile manhood. As far as I am concerned I say to all young men – By all means box, gentlemen, box; only 1) do your own boxing and not by proxy; 2) box for points and health and not for cash; 3) box the Devil and all his works' (*The Times*, 22 September 1911, p 6).

Lord Roberts, Sir Robert Baden Powell, and the very many other prominent names which put such weight behind his efforts. As John Kent has written of the Nonconformist Conscience: 'It is broadly true that it was only when most of the religious societies, Anglican and non-Anglican, could agree to fight together on a moral issue that British society was much impressed; by themselves both Anglicans and non-conformists were more vocal than victorious.'[1]

Finally, it is perhaps worth stating that this paper was begun whilst the controversy was raging over the proposed 1970 South African cricket tour. Such circumstances made Winston Churchill's 1911 decision to intervene of more than historical interest. If it had been on the grounds of the damage to race relations, he would surely have set some sort of precedent for his successors at the Home Office. Alas, it was *not* Winston Churchill the resolute defender of the peace and integrity of the British Empire who intervened, but Churchill the sportsman. He wrote from Balmoral to his wife: 'I have made up my mind to try to stop the Wells–Johnson contest. The terms are utterly unsporting & unfair.'[2]

[1] 'Hugh Price Hughes and the Nonconformist Conscience', in G. V. Bennett and J. D. Walsh (eds), *Essays in Modern English Church History* (London 1966) p 182.

[2] W. S. C. to C. S. C., 24 September 1911, quoted in Randolph S. Churchill, *Winston S. Churchill*, Companion Vol II, Pt 2: 1907–11 (London 1969) p 1128.